DISPOSED OF FROM
CWM TAF LIBRARY
SERVICES 2024
NEWER INFORMATION
MAYBE AVAILABLE

A Colour Atlas of

Geriatric Medicine

SECOND EDITION

Asif Kamal FRCP (Lond.)

Consultant Physician in Geriatric Medicine
St George's Hospital, Lincoln

J. C. Brocklehurst MD, MSc, FRCP (Glasgow & Edin.)

Professor of Geriatric Medicine
University of Manchester

Wolfe Publishing Ltd

Published by Wolfe Publishing Ltd, 1992
Printed by Royal Smeets Offset b.v.,
Weert, Netherlands
ISBN 0 7234 1714 8

A CIP catalogue record for this book is available from the British Library.

For full details of all Wolfe titles please write to
Wolfe Publishing Ltd, Brook House, 2–16 Torrington Place,
London WC1E 7LT, England.

Contents

Preface to Second Edition

Since this atlas was first published in 1983 there have been further advances in the medical and nursing treatment and care of the elderly. Hospital geriatric medical departments are now providing most of the acute medical care for the elderly sick while long-stay and continuing care are increasingly based in the community.

Advances have occurred in many different areas, especially in stroke rehabilitation, drugs in the elderly, orthogeriatrics and parkinsonism. There is greater awareness of the problem of abuse of the elderly. Psychogeriatrics has developed into a major speciality to cope with the increasing number of elderly patients with dementia.

In this edition we have made considerable alterations to reflect the various changes in geriatric medicine. The text has been augmented in many places and there are 131 new illustrations. As before, the emphasis is on illustrations and we hope that this edition will be of interest to physicians, junior doctors and trainees, and to nurse practitioners and student nurses.

Preface to First Edition

Clinical presentation of disease in old age is often different from that in younger patients. This and the fact that old people also show the changes of ageing and of multiple pathology, makes clinical assessment, treatment, and rehabilitation all the more challenging.

Interpretation of these subtleties of disease in older patients demands a knowledge of the normal and abnormal phenomena associated with ageing. This atlas shows some of the more important and interesting clinical features of geriatric medicine. The range of illustrations is as broad as possible; inevitably there is overlap with other specialities of medicine. This reflects the breadth of clinical practice in old age and bears out the often-heard statement that geriatrics is the last remaining generalist area among the medical specialists.

This atlas is a comprehensive introduction to geriatric medicine and complements standard reference textbooks on the subject. The emphasis throughout is on clinical features and presentation. Details of treatment, management and rehabilitation are not included because of their complex and extensive nature.

The atlas begins with **three** introductory chapters:

1 **Geriatric medicine**
2 **Special features of illness in old age**
3 **Assessment of an elderly patient**

These are followed by illustrated sections divided on an anatomical basis (i.e. head, face and neck, upper limbs, and so on).

Where relevant, some pictures or groups of pictures are supported by a somewhat longer textual description of the condition illustrated – its aetiology and importance in the elderly. In some cases differential diagnosis is also considered in table form.

We hope that this atlas will be a valuable aid for all who care for ill and frail old people, especially doctors, nurses, physiotherapists, occupational therapists and medical students. It should also be of considerable use to postgraduate students who are preparing for higher professional examinations.

Acknowledgements

We wish to express our most grateful thanks to all those who helped us in the preparation of this atlas, especially our numerous sources and colleagues listed below who loaned us illustrations. Dr D. Prangell (**7–9, 13, 58, 262, 263**), Dr Ian Burton (**10**), Dr C. D. G. Beardwell (**22, 23**), Mr E. N. Gleve (**25**), Dr J. P. Miller (**34, 316**), Dr P. J. August (**36, 68–70**), Dr Allen (**42, 43**), Professor Stanley L. Robins and W. B. Saunders (**57, 116, 117, 122, 124, 127**), Dr Tony Clark (**167, 168**), Dept. of Pathology, County Hospital, Lincoln (**61, 62**), Churchill Livingstone and Dr D. A. Leighton (**88**), Janssen Pharmaceutical Ltd (**99**), Churchill Livingstone and Professor M. S. Pathy (**103, 160–162**), Saskatoon University (**106, 107**), Dr Pauline Sambrook (**113, 114, 118, 259**), Update Publications (**108, 110, 111, 381**), Update Publications and Dr Michael Maisey (**119**), Churchill Livingstone and Dr A. D. Dayan (**146, 149, 152**), Churchill Livingstone and Dr D. M. Bowen & Dr A. M. Davidson (**150**), Churchill Livingstone and Dr H. M. Wisniewski (**151, 153–155**), Dr J. V. Occleshaw (**156a–f**), Dr John Carty (**165, 311, 341**), Dr B. Ottridge (**176**), Dr A. Pomerance (**208**), Dr Ian Paterson (**213, 214**), Dr Brian Scott (**223, 225, 266–269, 271**), University Hospital of South Manchester, X-ray Dept. (**239, 276, 277, 339, 340**), Dr Derek Martin (**247**), Duphur Laboratories (**275, 280, 281**), Dr P. S. Haselton (**277**), Churchill Livingstone (**290**), Churchill Livingstone and Dr R. Grahame (**355**), Churchill Livingstone and Professor A. N. Exton-Smith (**373**), Professor Douglas Gardner (**375, 376, 378**), London Foot Hospital and *Geriatric Medicine* (**411, 428**), Professor Stanley L. Robins and W. B. Saunders (**419**), Professor R. Marks and *Geriatric Medicine* (**442, 449**), Dr J. T. Leeming (**457**), Dr I. H. Taylor (**463**), Dr S. Mejzner (**469**), Dr R. H. MacDonald (**472, 476, 477, 479**), British Geriatrics Society for *Abuse of Elderly People*.

Our sincere thanks are also due to Dr Michael Lye for his helpful advice on the manuscript, to Gus de Cozar and Peter Wilson of the Medical Illustrations Department of St. George's Hospital, Lincoln, to the Medical Illustration Department of University Hospital of South Manchester and to our secretaries. Our special thanks to Maureen Coffey for helping to collect the transparencies and for typing the manuscript.

A. Kamal
J. C. Brocklehurst

1 Geriatric Medicine

Industrialised countries have experienced dramatic population changes in the 20th century. There has, for example, been a considerable increase in the proportion of the population that is elderly. At the beginning of this century, 4.7% of the population of Britain was 65 years of age and over. By 1980 the figure had risen to 15.7%. It seems that this steep rise in the over-65 population is now coming to an end and by 2011 the proportion of people of that age will be 16%. However, the projection from 2011–2025 is a further 3% increase and, if this is the case, the proportion of the population aged 65 and over in 2025 will be 19%. This figure will be exceeded in a number of countries by 2025. Japan and Finland will both have an over-65 population in excess of 20%; Germany, Sweden, the Netherlands and Denmark greater than 22% and Switzerland almost 24% of the population. Another striking figure is that for the population of the United Kingdom aged 85 and over, there will be a 33% increase between 1991 and 2011 and by 2025 this increase will have risen to 42%.

These changes are the result of radical improvements in public health – nutrition, environment, elimination of infectious disease by inoculations and vaccinations, and the spectacular reduction in infant mortality. Almost everyone may now expect to live to be old. While this marks a stage of great success in human development, it also brings its own problems.

As long as ageing is associated with frailty and an increasing likelihood of disabling illness, so the demands on health and welfare services by an ageing population will increase. These include demands on personal social services, on special housing and residential homes as well as on the hospital and community medical services.

By the year 2001, on current trends, elderly males could occupy 75% of all acute male hospital beds and elderly females 90% of all acute female hospital beds.

Definition of geriatric medicine

Geriatric medicine is a branch of general medicine concerned with the clinical, preventative, remedial and social aspects of health and disease in the elderly.

Modern geriatrics and new patterns of care

A well-organised geriatric medicine service has a major role to play in dealing with the consequences of these demographic trends. Most people over 65 years of age live independently in the community. It is the prime function of the geriatric services to help to maintain this independence. The services should be able to prevent breakdown or to deal with it quickly enough to enable the elderly to continue caring for themselves and to help them to enjoy life.

The role of the newly retired

Retirement used to be the gateway to old age. This is no longer true. Today, people live longer but retire earlier. Retirement has become the 'third age' – a time of great opportunity but, to some, a time of bewilderment and boredom. The way in which a person copes with retirement may have a profound effect on his health in old age.

The role of the young

The young also have a considerable contribution to make towards the welfare of the elderly. Grandchildren and grandparents often have a special relationship which benefits both. Young people, through youth and voluntary groups, school and university schemes, and on an individual basis, can help old people in many ways. This can range from giving old people help with their shopping, house cleaning, gardening, laundry and painting. Young people could also be a source of companionship.

Attitudes towards the aged

Society has ambivalent attitudes towards the aged. There is a sizeable gap between the expressed concern for the needs of older people and the action taken to meet such needs. Often people feel hostile towards the aged, but at the same time they enjoy good relationships with the elderly within their own circle. Resentment and antagonism may arise from the lack of a clearly defined role for old people in modern industrialised society and also as a result of their economic dependency. Such negative attitudes are gradually being eroded by education and the development of geriatric medical units, as well as by special organisations that pinpoint the numerous problems.

Families generally care for their aged – a fact that is not always acknowledged publicly. However, today many people who are 75 years of age and over have no surviving children and caring neighbours as well as back-up services are very important.

Inevitably some negative attitudes rub off on medical workers. Hostility or indifference towards the development of geriatric services has been a common phenomenon in many parts of the world. Fortunately, this changes as the geriatric service is able to demonstrate its achievements, and as medical and other students learn about the complexities of medicine and old age and how the service copes.

Deprivation of the aged

The most deprived members of the community are often old people. More than any other social group they live in low-standard housing – badly insulated, damp, draughty, and difficult to heat and sometimes with outside lavatories. Complications of such deprivation include accidental hypothermia, accidents, impairment of mobility, susceptibility to illness, depression, impaired nutrition and, in some cases, a resistance to discharge from hospital.

The complexity of financial benefits available to the old is such that many old people have no idea of their rights and entitlements. The key role of social workers and special organisations is thus apparent.

Breakdown in old age

Ageing is distinguished from disease by the fact that it is universal. From a practical point of view, however, its major quality is that it decreases function of cells, organs and so of the organism. Ageing thus predisposes to breakdown although ageing itself does not produce breakdown. Few old people escape the accumulation of chronic pathologies as they grow older, and the cumulative effect of this is another ingredient in the breakdown.

Multiple pathologies leading to multiple symptoms are often matched by the prescription of many drugs. Unfortunately these in themselves not infrequently predispose to breakdown in independent living, because either singly or in combination they may lead to significant loss of independence. Problems include mistakes in compliance caused by poor memory or poor vision; the changes in pharmacodynamics and pharmacokinetics that occur in ageing people and which many prescribers are still unaware of; and the tendency of some physicians to use drugs with profound side-effects in old age (such as the benzodiazepines) almost as placebos.

All these factors tend to cause breakdown in independent living in the elderly unless counterbalanced by such social and neighbourhood support systems as are available, and by the extent of physical and mental health which the old person maintains, and above all by the desire to retain independence. However, this uneasy equilibrium is easily destroyed by the addition of acute medical illness on the one side and the loss of social or other support on the other.

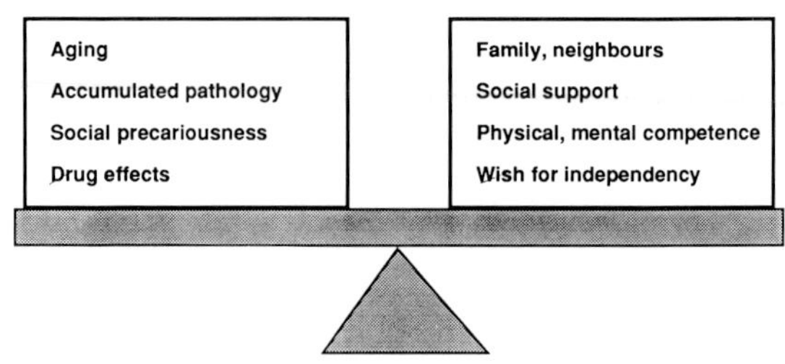

It is in responding to this breakdown, either that which occurs suddenly and acutely as an emergency or gradually over days or weeks, that the geriatric service has its most unique and important role.

Who is a geriatric patient?

Most patients under the care of geriatricians are in their late seventies and eighties and, apart from acute medical illness, they also have multiple chronic disabilities and/or complex social problems. Most geriatricians in the United Kingdom would see their work in the following terms:

- Immediate admission from the community of elderly patients presenting with problems of extreme medical urgency.
- Assessment of patients with similar but less urgent problems, either in their own homes, or at the hospital outpatient clinic.
- The continuing management of physically disabling disease in old age through stages of rehabilitation, both in hospital and in the day hospital, and perhaps indefinite support in the community after that.
- The long-term care of old people who are so physically disabled as to be unable to maintain independence in the community.
- The short-term admission of elderly patients for holiday purposes, which is basically for the relief of relatives and family.
- The transfer of patients from other hospital departments, either for rehabilitation or long-term care.
- Participation in co-operative medical care with one or more of the following departments: psychiatry, orthopaedics, young disabled, stroke rehabilitation, and rheumatology and physical medicine.

The aims of health care of the elderly

- Maintenance of health in old age by continuing social engagement and avoidance of disease.
- Early detection and appropriate treatment of disease.
- Maintenance of maximum independence consistent with irreversible disease and disability.
- Sympathetic care and support during terminal illness.

Geriatric medicine is a dynamic process in which the patient's needs are assessed in detail by a multidisciplinary team. An appropriate plan of medical treatment, rehabilitation and social work is drawn up so as to restore the elderly patient to as normal a life as possible.

Structure of geriatric services

Geriatric medicine is a relatively young speciality and practice varies a great deal. In many parts of the world it is still at an early stage of development. While much of the success of a geriatric service depends on the resources and facilities available, the most important factor is the personality, drive and ability of the clinical team.

Most geriatric services in the UK are based on the principle of progressive patient care and consist of an acute admissions/assessment ward; a rehabilitation ward; a long-term care ward; a minimal care ward; a day hospital; and facilities such as outpatient department, domiciliary assessment visiting, combined clinics with orthopaedic surgeons and psychogeriatricians. Back-up hospital services include laboratory facilities, x-rays and other imaging techniques, physiotherapy, occupational therapy, speech therapy, chiropody and a social services department.

Acute assessment ward
Most admissions to a geriatric department are to an acute assessment ward. The basic function and management on this ward is similar to that of general medical wards. Elderly patients are admitted as emergencies or planned admissions for medical diagnosis, functional and social assessment and for treatment.

The ward must be properly equipped for the elderly with low beds and beds of variable height. There should be easy access to lavatories and the ward should be easily accessible to all other hospital services. Special attention should be paid to aids and equipment on the ward; for example, baths, showers, hoists, lifts, wheelchairs and non-slip surfaces. The nurses should have special understanding and training in care of the elderly, and the medical staff should include young doctors undergoing general medical training.

All discharges need careful planning with the involvement of the therapists, social workers and community support groups. Rehabilitation of the geriatric patient starts right from the beginning, but if this is likely to continue for several weeks after the initial assessment and treatment, then the patient is generally transferred to the rehabilitation ward.

Rehabilitation ward
It is in the rehabilitation ward that geriatric teamwork is most to the fore. The underlying physical problems are varied and include conditions such as cerebrovascular disease, cardiovascular disease, fracture of the femur, amputation, Parkinson's disease and musculoskeletal disorders. The restoration of optimal function may require treatment over several weeks or months. The patients may be transferred here from the acute geriatric ward or medical, orthopaedic and surgical wards. Management is usually through case conferences and once again discharge needs to be meticulously planned.

Long-term care ward
If rehabilitation does not restore sufficient independence for discharge into the community, then long-term hospital care will be required. Wards providing this service have a very different function to those involved in assessment and rehabilitation. They become the patient's home and the most important person in the patient's life is the nurse.

In the past 10 years, however, there has been a major change in the provision of long-term care for elderly people needing nursing, with a decline in the number of National Health Service geriatric beds providing this care and a striking increase in the number of nursing home places in both private and voluntary homes.

Medical investigations and intensive remedial therapy play a small part. It is the quality of life which matters most, and this should stem from an appropriate blend of maximum privacy and maximum safety. Single bedrooms are optimal if they can be provided. Areas for activities should include a quiet room where patients may escape from the noise and distractions which are so inseparably bound to most hospitals. Staff should include activities organisers, and volunteers, relatives and visitors should be encouraged at all times of the day.

In some geriatric departments the three types of ward described above are combined in one. This has some advantages inasmuch as the staff deal with patients with all kinds of problems. On the other hand, the homely atmosphere appropriate to the

A minor illness in an elderly person leading to serious complications

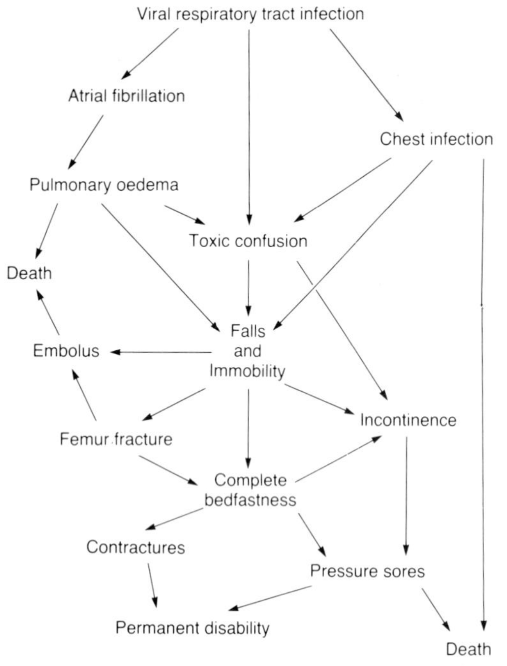

Viral respiratory tract infection
Atrial fibrillation
Chest infection
Pulmonary oedema
Toxic confusion
Death
Falls and Immobility
Embolus
Incontinence
Femur fracture
Complete bedfastness
Contractures
Pressure sores
Permanent disability
Death

quality of life in a long-term care ward is inappropriate in the management of acutely ill patients, so that this compromise is more likely to be of benefit to the staff than to the patients.

Minimal care ward

If there is a shortage of residential accommodation and special housing, it may be convenient to develop a minimal care ward or convalescent ward, where patients may be transferred until suitable accommodation is found. Such wards usually have a lower ratio of nursing staff. Most patients on these wards tend to be fully ambulant and independent in self-care.

Specialist services

Geriatric services are dependent on a number of other hospital departments with which there are close working relationships. These include:

- The psychogeriatric service – this is usually headed by a consultant psychiatrist with a special interest in psychiatry of old age. It provides an assessment and management service for elderly patients with senile dementia and associated disorders. Psychogeriatrics is a rapidly expanding medical speciality in Great Britain.
- The orthogeriatric ward – this is an in-patient facility run jointly by orthopaedic surgeons and physicians specialising in diseases of old age. The staff on orthogeriatric wards are trained to look after and rehabilitate elderly patients with fractures, especially frail elderly females with fractures of the neck of the femur.
- The stroke rehabilitation ward – this is usually under the care of a geriatrician or a neurologist and provides comprehensive rehabilitation services for patients of all ages who are disabled with strokes. The staff include specially trained nurses, physiotherapists, occupational therapists, speech therapists and clinical psychologists.

In some areas geriatric services have formed strong links with hospices for terminal care and wards for the younger disabled patients.

Geriatric day hospital

Geriatric day hospitals have shown considerable development over the last 20 years. They aim to provide some hospital facilities without the patients having to stay overnight and over the weekend. Patients may attend after in-patient assessment and rehabilitation, but about 50% of the patients attending the day hospital come straight from the community, and so in-patient admission is avoided. The day hospital has four main objectives:

- Rehabilitation.
- Maintenance of treatment – to ensure that levels of independence achieved as a result of rehabilitation are kept at an optimal level.
- Social care of the physically disabled – to provide social companionship for those who are housebound and isolated and so to prevent depression, or else relieve relatives and help them to cope for a longer period.
- For medical and nursing assessment, investigations and treatment.

Facilities in the community

Most people agree that the elderly should be kept in the community for as long as possible and permanent residential care should be used only as a last option. A wide range of facilities for the elderly are available in the community.

- Day centres and luncheon clubs – provided by social services or voluntary organisations.
- Warden controlled flats – usually for frail elderly people who are independent in self-care.
- Part III residential homes – these are run by social services for the frail and usually single elderly people who require supervision and assistance with various activities of daily life, but are generally mobile and independent in self-care. Social workers for the elderly have a major input in the running of these homes.
- Private nursing homes – these belong to the private sector and are for elderly patients who have severe long-term disabilities and require constant nursing care. Nursing homes are inspected and registered by the local district health authority.
- Private residential homes – these are similar to Part III residential homes, but are generally smaller and residents tend to be less disabled.
- Other facilities in the community (this list is not exhaustive) include:

  Meals on wheels for the housebound.
  Home helps to assist with daily chores around the house.
  Health visitors for the elderly.
  Social workers for the elderly.
  Bath nurses.
  District nurses.
  Community psychiatric nurses.
  Community physiotherapists.
  Occupational therapists.
  Continence nurse advisers.
  Stoma care nurses.
  Community speech therapists.
  Chiropodists.
  Terminal care nurses.
  GP screening clinics for the elderly.

2 Special Features of Illness in Old Age

Presenting symptoms

Some of the features distinguishing medicine in old age from medicine in younger age groups are the four cardinal presenting symptoms of illness in old age. These are *mental confusion, incontinence, instability* and *immobility*. Each is a symptom and the common underlying factor is the effect of ageing on the central nervous system. Because of the diminished reserve of cortical neurones many acute illnesses producing anoxaemia and toxaemia overcome the limited reserve of cerebral function and present as confusion. Similarly, the cerebral control of micturition is precarious because of ageing and thus many pathologies, both systemic and local, may precipitate incontinence. Similarly, balance is less certain and postural instability or falling is the third common presenting symptom. Finally, there is a tendency towards immobility, not only as a result of ageing in the central nervous system but also its effects on muscles and joints, together with chronic pathological changes such as osteoarthrosis and foot disorders. Therefore, much illness in old people presents with one of these four symptoms – each requires as careful a differential diagnosis as other symptoms such as pain, fever, vomiting and dyspnea.

Acute illness in the elderly

Acute brain failure or acute confusional disorders are thus compounded of underlying age changes within brain cells and an acute pathology which may further impair blood or oxygen supply to the brain, affect it by toxins or by direct involvement by vascular disorder.

Thus:

- Acute anoxic brain failure may result from bronchopneumonia, congestive cardiac failure, acute bronchitis, pulmonary collapse or an acute impairment of cardiac output, associated with sudden onset of a rapid dysrhythmia or a myocardial infarct.
- Acute infections such as pyelitis, pneumonia, sub-acute bacterial endocarditis and influenza may all present with toxic acute brain failure. Metabolic toxaemia such as hepatic failure, uraemia and hyperglycaemia may all present with a toxic confusional state.
- Acute poisoning with drugs and alcohol and hypoglycaemia may all present similarly.

Sometimes the confusion masks other common presenting symptoms such as pain in myocardial infarction and in acute appendicitis. An elderly person may of course present acutely with any of the wide range of medical illnesses found in other age groups; for example, acute abdomen, subarachnoid haemorrhage, urinary retention, acute pulmonary oedema, pulmonary embolism, etc.

Chronic illness in the elderly

The longer people live the more likely they are to contract chronic disabilities. Chronic obstructive airways disease (COAD) probably affects about 20% of elderly people today. Congestive cardiac failure may be insidious in its onset as may diabetes.

In the central nervous system Alzheimer's dementia is the most common ailment, followed by cerebrovascular disease causing strokes and multi-infarct dementia.

In the musculoskeletal system a major cause of disability is osteoarthrosis, particularly in the hip, knee and spine.

Peripheral vascular disease leading to intermittent claudication, leg ulceration and amputation is another common cause of disability.

Multiple pathologies

Having these aspects of acute and chronic illness in mind it is clear that the range of clinical presentation in old people is tremendous. For instance, a myocardial infarct presenting with mental confusion may precipitate incontinence, and the outcome may be affected also by underlying COAD and diabetes.

A small acute stroke may present with urinary incontinence, to which partial immobility due to osteoarthrosis of the hip may also contribute.

Anaemia, perhaps a symptom of chronic blood loss from hiatus hernia, may present as a series of falls and a developing chairfast state.

Atherosclerosis

Probably the single most important pathological process underlying disability in old age is atherosclerosis. Unhappily, the cause of atherosclerosis still eludes us, although there is now a good deal of evidence about related factors. The most important association is with high levels of total low-density lipoproteins. This occurs both in geographical areas where atherosclerosis is common and in a series of pathological conditions associated with atherosclerosis; for example, the nephrotic syndrome, hyperthyroidism, uncontrolled diabetes mellitus and chronic biliary cirrhosis. Other important factors are hypertension, obesity, smoking, diet and stress.

While atherosclerosis may appear anywhere throughout the vascular tree, its consequences in old age are particularly important in the brain (cerebrovascular disease and multi-infarct dementia), the myocardium (ischaemia and infarction) and the peripheral arteries (leg ulcer and gangrene).

Stroke

While little progress has been made in treating the acute phase of a stroke, in recent years there have been considerable advances in its prevention on the one hand and in rehabilitation on the other. The increasingly widespread control of hypertension in the middle-aged and the treatment of carotid transient ischaemic attacks by aspirin, other antiplatelet drugs and anticoagulants have both contributed to the decline in the incidence of stroke. At the same time an increasing interest in rehabilitation has led to a realisation of the importance of perceptual disorders and disorders of body image, particularly in non-dominant hemisphere strokes.

The development of stroke rehabilitation units has led to a renewed interest among medical and paramedical staff in the management of stroke patients. Future trends are likely to see more domiciliary treatment with better advice to the patient and his relatives at home, so that they may have a clearer understanding of its very complex problems.

Musculoskeletal disease

Myopathies and arthropathies may all present as postural instability or as increasing immobility. The eminently treatable proximal myopathy of osteomalacia is being recognised in the elderly with much greater frequency. The operative treatment of osteoarthrosis has opened new horizons for many painfully disabled old people. The development of combined orthopaedic geriatric units is improving the outcome for the more difficult fractures of the femur.

Instability and falls

Recognition of the many possible causes of falls in old people is leading to a more rational approach in treatment, although some of the most common causes (drop-attacks) still defy explanation and prevention.

Incontinence

It is only in recent years that the widespread prevalence of incontinence among people of all age groups has become realised. Urodynamic assessment units have provided much information but drug therapy of the unstable bladder is still unsatisfactory. On the other hand, the management of stress incontinence and the realisation of the frequency of iatrogenic causes (chronic retention and overflow incontinence as a side-effect of antidepressant and anticholenergic drugs) is far more clearly understood. A better assessment of the place of indwelling catheters and of different types of body-worn protection is developing. Bladder retraining and timed voiding programmes are also becoming more common. Much of this stems from the widespread development in the UK of specialist continence nurse advisers.

Constipation

This remains the great scourge of immobile old people, particularly those in long-term care, and faecal incontinence is its symptom. The management of such a simple and unpleasant condition requires a great deal of straightforward clinical investigation, but of equal importance is a positive attitude on the part of doctors and nurses that faecal incontinence is a treatable and preventable condition.

Hypothermia

One of the greatest successes in health education, in relation to old age, has been in spreading knowledge about hypothermia. As a result it is far more commonly recognised now than 10 years ago. Nevertheless, sub-optimal housing conditions and a need (or perceived need) to save fuel still affect thousands of old people during the winter, resulting in increased morbidity and mortality. This is more of a problem in the United Kingdom than in the United States or Scandinavian countries.

Disorders of the senses

Many people over 70 years of age suffer from hearing disorders which, if diagnosed by an audiologist, would certainly lead to the prescription of a hearing aid. There is a significant correlation between depression and hearing impairment in old age. Amplification is not the whole answer to this problem although a small, behind-the-ear hearing aid has become acceptable. The complexity of presbyacusis is now being recognised and the need for counselling, not just of the patient but also of those who come in contact, as how to speak to elderly deaf people is now being understood.

Visual disorders are usually well dealt with by ophthalmologists, although in many cases underlying senile macular degeneration limits the outcome of treatment.

Psychogeriatric problems

The pathological process which stands alongside atheroma, being the other most common cause of disability in old age, is Alzheimer's senile dementia. The pathological changes are similar to those occurring in Alzheimer's presenile dementia and some of these (for example, the senile plaque and neurofibrillary tangles) are found, although to an extremely limited degree, in the brains of very old normal people. The cause of this pathology is at present unknown, although theories include a slow virus infection, disorder of aluminium metabolism and an inherited defect. Alzheimer's senile dementia and multi-infarct dementia are possibly the two most feared illnesses in the latter part of life. It is estimated that 6% of over-65s and 20% of over-80s have these diseases in moderate or severe form. The problems these conditions generate for families and for the community are well known.

The speciality of psychogeriatrics has developed to provide a special expertise among psychiatrists in the total management of mental illness in the aged. This includes depression, paraphrenia and other disorders as well as the dementias. In the diagnosis of dementia a close collaboration between psychiatrist and geriatrician is important, and is found in most of the developing psychogeriatric units. The role of the specialist nurse in managing brain failure in patients is vitally important. Perhaps one of the most important aspects of the diagnosis of dementia is to discover potentially treatable causes like vitamin B_{12} deficiency, subdural haematoma, normal-pressure hydrocephalus and meningioma.

Malignant disease

Malignant disease is the second most common cause of death in old age (the first being heart disease), and the most common site in both sexes is the gastrointestinal system, particularly the colon and rectum. In some ways it is the most important site because the outcome of the surgical management of colorectal malignancy, if diagnosed at an early stage, is very good. Overall, carcinoma of the prostate is the most common malignancy in aged males. Carcinoma of the breast is runner-up in aged females. Both of these diseases are compatible with many years of life in old age.

Special hospices providing expert terminal care have developed in most of the cities in the United Kingdom and are being developed throughout the world. However, these are more likely to be centres of excellence and trendsetters than the place for the management of all terminal stages of cancer. They have been particularly successful in developing a rational policy of analgesia (ensuring a pain-free death), and in teaching doctors and nurses the importance of the psychological as well as the somatic approach to malignant disease.

Infection

An increasing realisation of the pleomorphic presentation of infection in old age is occurring. The need for blood cultures in patients presenting with acute brain failure for which other causes are not apparent – and particularly if they have a disease of the heart valves or infection of the bladder – is now well established.

Other common disorders

There are certain other diseases which have an inherent predilection for the elderly. Many of these disorders may present in a less dramatic way and in a considerable number of cases the mode of presentation may be altered too; for example, painless myocardial infarction presenting with acute brain failure, chronic constipation as a manifestation of depression, etc. Conditions seen frequently in geriatric medical practice include Parkinsonism, motor-neuron disease, herpes zoster, polymyalgia rheumatica, giant-cell arteritis, pernicious anaemia, folate deficiency, leukaemias, hypothyroidism, tuberculosis, osteomalacia, osteoporosis, hyperosmolar non-ketotic diabetic crisis, scurvy, ischaemic colitis, hiatus hernia and diverticular disease of the colon. This list is of course incomplete, but serves to indicate the range and diversity of medicine in later life.

3 Assessment of an Elderly Patient

The general approach to history and clinical examination in old people is along the same lines as in younger patients. However, numbers of additional procedures should be undertaken in the elderly – this chapter is concerned with these procedures.

History

History is all important and with elderly patients more time is required because of deafness, poor memory, confusion, suspicion and slow responses. Always ask simple, straightforward questions. If it cannot be reliably obtained from the patient then every effort must be made to interview someone who knows what has been the march of events; for example, neighbours, relatives, district nurse, home nurses, etc. The first thing to determine is when the patient was last perfectly normal. In the confused old person the history may be crucial in distinguishing between acute and chronic forms of brain failure and other conditions. If there is reason to suspect that the history being obtained is unreliable, then some form of mental assessment must be carried out during the examination. Allowance must be made for the benign memory loss of normal ageing, in which recall of dates and names may be difficult but the story will be coherent and logical. On the other hand, the patient with mild to moderate dementia who is confabulating may present so plausible a story that it has every appearance of normality, until checked against that of the relatives or neighbours.

In the case of falls a good description is needed. It is usually best to get the patient to concentrate on one fall, probably the most recent, and describe it in detail.

Always ask about micturition habits – how often the patient has to get up at night to pass urine and whether there is any urgency by day. Ask specifically about bed-wetting and wetting the clothes.

Dizziness is a difficult symptom to elucidate. It is very seldom that a history of rotational vertigo emerges and dizziness in most cases is probably a light-headedness, which most elderly people experience in a transitory manner occasionally. It is not a symptom that requires treatment per se.

The social history is particularly relevant in old people: bereavement, family contact, dietary habits and the nature of housing and services that are used. It is also important to find out whether the patient's house is centrally heated, whether the toilet is situated a distance away from the main dwelling, the pattern of daily living and the degree of independence within the house.

Mental testing may be introduced during or at the end of the history. It is useful to use a simple 10-question questionnaire, such as that shown in Table 1. This will not only give an indication of normal cognitive function or moderate or severe abnormality, it will also record baseline data that may be used as points of reference on subsequent occasions. If the patient is sensible it is best to introduce the questionnaire as a test of memory, and it is usually accepted uncomplainingly as such.

Examination

There are certain points that must be remembered while examining an elderly patient. One must remember the prevalence of multiple pathology and also the normal age-related changes. The examination should be gentle at all times and one should try and avoid complicated manoeuvres.

First, get the patient to stand up and, if possible, assess postural stability with the eyes open and closed, and the gait.

The general and systemic examination proceeds in the normal standard way. Common signs of ageing will be seen in the face – the wasting of orbital fat and of the muscles of the face, the arcus senilus, wrinkling of the skin, hair changes, and sometimes scars on the bridge of the nose indicating falls in the past. Other signs to look for are pigmentation, scratch marks, intertrigo, senile keratosis, bruises and state of pressure areas. Breasts should be examined in every case. In the root of the neck, beware pulsations from a kinked carotid artery. Senile purpura is occasionally seen in the neck and very commonly seen on the extensor aspect of the hands and forearms. Its only significance is that it is associated with transparent skin. In younger patients of course, it is associated with steroid medication and rheumatoid arthritis. Look out for Heberden's and Bouchard's nodes and the usual nail changes. In the legs and feet pay particular attention to foot deformities such as overgrown toenails, hallux valgus and corns. Distinguish between pitting oedema and lymphoedema. See if erythema ab igne suggests hypothyroidism.

Cardiovascular system

Systolic murmurs often present problems in old people. Ejection systolic murmurs, best heard at the base of the heart with or without radiation into the neck, may be caused by aortic sclerosis and not stenosis. The former is an increasing rigidity of the aortic ring and the aortic cusps, occasionally causing obstruction to flow. A lower pitched pan-systolic murmur is also commonly present, indicating mitral incompetence by its irradiation around the axilla and possibly into the back. This may be associated with mitral stenosis, secondary to enlargement of the left ventricle or caused by prolapsing leaflet of the mitral valve as a result of necrosis of the valve or of a papillary muscle.

Always listen for murmurs in the carotid artery.

Triple rhythms (third sound, fourth sound summation gallops) are a common harbinger of ventricular failure.

Always measure blood pressure with the patient supine and then repeat after the patient has stood erect for two minutes. This manoeuvre reveals the presence of postural hypotension. Palpation of the peripheral arteries in the lower limbs will probably have been carried out during the general examination.

Respiratory system

In the respiratory system the procedure is a little different from that in younger people. First, deviation of trachea is common as a result of dorsal scoliosis and chest expansion tends to be limited. Hypostatic basal crepitations are common in the elderly and will disappear after a few maximal respirations.

Central nervous system (CNS)

Examination of the central nervous system will depend in part upon the assumed diagnosis. If brain failure is thought to be present, a record of the primitive reflexes should be included (grasp and groping reflex, snout and sucking reflex, and the palmomental and patellar tap reflexes). Their presence indicates widespread involvement of the frontal lobes.

Tremor has to be diagnosed carefully. A familial and a senile tremor are similar. They persist during activity or indeed may get worse, and they may or may not go away at rest. Choreoathetotic tremor is usually characteristic but Parkinsonian tremor is overdiagnosed. Its quality is very characteristic and it diminishes on activity. Orofacial movements, such as tics, grimacing, tongue rolling, chewing and lip smacking, and other dyskinesias should alert one to the toxic effect of phenothiazines or L-dopa. Some facial tics and plucking at the bedclothes are late signs of dementia but also occur in acute toxic confusion. Age-related changes in neurotransmission in the long spinal tracts are thought to account for the diminution or absence of vibration sense of many old people in whom sensation is retained in the upper limbs. For the same reason ankle jerks are quite often absent.

Gastrointestinal tract (GIT)

Always look at the tongue and examine the teeth or dentures. Monilial infections are not uncommon and in their absence a white, sodden tongue may be a non-specific sign of illness, particularly in the gastro-intestinal tract, or it may be one of the signs of vitamin B deficiency. In constipated patients faeces can be felt not only in the left iliac fossa but often in the transverse colon; the caecum, distended and doughy, is often palpable. Beware of tortuosity or aneurysm of the abdominal aorta – it is often misdiagnosed as a malignant abdominal mass. Note also whether or not the bladder is distended. All women with urinary incontinence should have the perineum inspected, looking for leakage on coughing or for atrophy or redness of the genital epithelium, with or without superadded infection, indicating atrophic vaginitis. Vaginal examination is not always necessary, but it sometimes reveals a long-forgotten pessary, which is best removed.

In faecal incontinence and in any alimentary tract disorder, rectal examination is mandatory.

Tests

On any suspicion of hypothermia the temperature should be measured with a low-reading thermometer. If an ordinary clinical thermometer is the only one available it should be shaken right down. One should suspect the presence of hypothermia if there is no measurable rise. If the consultation and examination is the first that has been carried out for a year or more, then haematology and routine biochemistry should be performed (including thyroid function tests), and a chest x-ray and an ECG carried out. These procedures will sometimes provide unexpected clues and in any case will provide baseline data for the future. The 48-hour Holter cardiac monitoring is now fairly generally available and may help to elucidate intermittent confusional episodes. However, remember that published series show as high an incidence of dysrhythmias in elderly control subjects as in symptomatic patients. Therefore, no causal relationship can be imputed unless the timing of the confusional episode is recorded at the same time: 48-hour monitoring will sometimes indicate ventricular arrhythmias or episodes of fast fibrillation which will respond to treatment.

The use of ultrasound or other imaging techniques and computerised axial tomography (CAT) are now generally available and in many situations are as useful in the very old as in the young. However, the

CAT scan is not yet regarded as an essential test in the differential diagnosis of dementia. Its place is where a focal lesion is strongly suspected – and particularly one that is remediable.

Indications for CAT scanning in strokes

- A stroke presenting with atypical features.
- If there is doubt about whether the patient had a stroke.
- To distinguish between a stroke and a tumour.
- To exclude intracranial haemorrhage in patients being considered for carotid endarteriectomy.
- Spontaneous subarachnoid haemorrhage.
- In strokes that may be surgically treatable; for example, supratentorial haematomas, cerebellar haematomas, arteriovenous malformations or aneurysms.
- In TIAs before angiography is considered.
- Other indications for CAT scanning include raised intracranial pressure, cerebral abscess, head injury, encephalitis, coma of unknown cause, unexplained dementia and late-onset epilepsy.

Further tests and investigations will of course be required, depending on the suspected diagnosis and for the monitoring of clinical progress.

The benefits of the investigations should be weighed carefully against the possible therapeutic benefits. However, it is absolutely wrong to deny elderly patients any investigative manoeuvre just because they are old.

Table 1. Short mental status questionnaire for assessing the mental status in chronic brain failure (dementia) (From Hodgkinson, *Age and Ageing*, **1**, 233–8, 1972.)

(Score 1 for each correct response)

1 What is your name?
2 What is the name of this place? or Where are we now?
3 What year is this?
4 What month (or season) is this?
5 What day of the week is it today?
6 How old are you?
7 What is the name of the Prime Minister/the President of this country?
8 When did World War I start?
***Remember these three items. I will ask you to recall them in a few minutes. ***Standard items, bed, chair, window – have patient repeat before proceeding.
9 Count backwards from 20 to 1 (any uncorrected error – score 0).
10 Repeat the three items I asked you to remember. (Score ½ for any item remembered, or 1 for all three.)

Normal: 8 or above
Mild to moderate: 4–7
Moderate to severe: less than 4

4 Disorders of the Head, Face and Neck

1

1 Healthy elderly face. This lady is over 100 years of age, but has a healthy, relatively young looking face, with only a few signs of extreme old age.

2 Ageing face. This lady is also 100 years of age; the face shows signs of old age, with loss of periorbital fat and onset of baldness. Note the ectropion and evidence of a recent fall.

3 Wasted face. A 60-year-old man, looking older than his age. He has cachexia, secondary to carcinoma of the stomach.

2 3

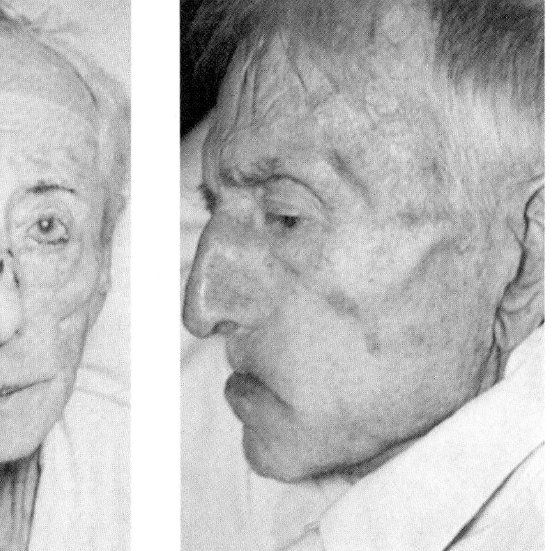

Anaemia in old age

Anaemia is said to be present when the total body haemoglobin is less than 13 g in men and 12 g in women.

Anaemia occurs in 5–20% of the elderly population. There are six main types:

- Iron-deficiency anaemia
- Megaloblastic anaemia
- Anaemia of chronic disease
- Sideroblastic anaemia
- Hypoplastic anaemia
- Haemolytic anaemia

Iron-deficiency anaemia

Causes:

Poor nutrition, poverty, immobility, isolation.
Defective absorption – gastritis, post-gastrectomy malabsorption.
Excessive blood loss – peptic ulcer, hiatus hernia and oesophagitis, gastric carcinoma, carcinoma of the large bowel, haemorrhoids, vaginal bleeding, haematuria.
Drugs – salicylates and other NSAIDs steroids.

Clinical features:

Tend to be non-specific in early stages.
Pallor, weakness, glossitis, confusion, falls, CCF, dysphagia (Plummer–Vinson syndrome), koilonychia and features of the condition causing the anaemia.
Hypochromic microcytic RBCs.

4 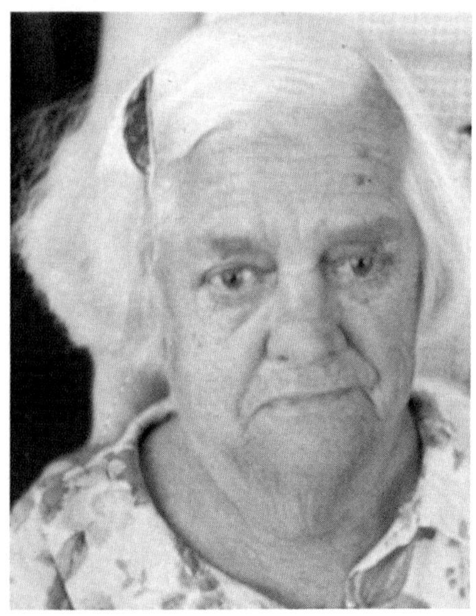

4 Facial pallor. Severe hypochromic anaemia (4.5 g haemoglobin), secondary to chronic salicylate ingestion.

Megaloblastic anaemia

Vitamin B_{12} deficiency:

Poor diet, pernicious anaemia, atrophic gastritis, gastrectomy, carcinoma of the stomach, malabsorption, ileal resection.

Folate deficiency:

Poor diet and malabsorption, chronic diseases, neoplasm, liver disease, drugs, e.g. phenytoin.

Clinical features:

Non-specific signs of anaemia, yellow tinge to skin in pernicious anaemia, anorexia, glossitis, peripheral neuropathy, subacute combined degeneration, mild confusion, depression, dementia. Megaloblasts and macrocytes are typical haematological findings.

Anaemia of chronic disease

Normochromic normocytic anaemia occurring in association with chronic diseases, e.g. TB, diverticulitis, rheumatoid arthritis, pressure sores, malignancy, hypothyroidism, renal failure.

Sideroblastic anaemia

A type of hypochromic anaemia with ring sideroblasts in the bone marrow. Erythroblasts are loaded with iron (sideroblasts), but hypochromic anaemia results.

The primary aetiological factor is defective iron utilisation. There are two main types:

Primary – acquired
Secondary – myeloproliferative disorders
Myeloma, carcinoma, collagen diseases, myxoedema, drugs, e.g. anti-TB, phenacetin, chloramphenicol.

Hypoplastic anaemia

Hypoplastic anaemia results from the failure of bone marrow and is not very common in old age. It may be seen in association with myeloma, carcinomas, myeloproliferative disorders and various drugs.

Haemolytic anaemia

Haemolytic anaemias are frequently seen in old age and some common causes are idiopathic autoimmune haemolytic anaemia, reticulosis, leukaemias, paroxysmal nocturnal haemoglobinuria and drugs such as methyldopa and quinine.

5 Hypochromic anaemia. Facial pallor in an elderly lady due to hypochromic anaemia of long-standing, caused by blood loss from hiatus hernia.

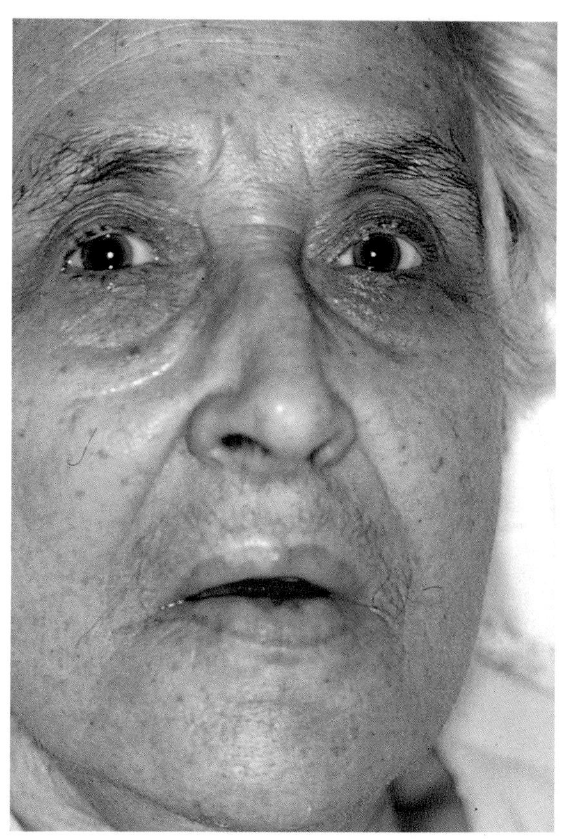
5

6 Pernicious anaemia. Pale face of a patient with pernicious anaemia. There is no significant weight loss.

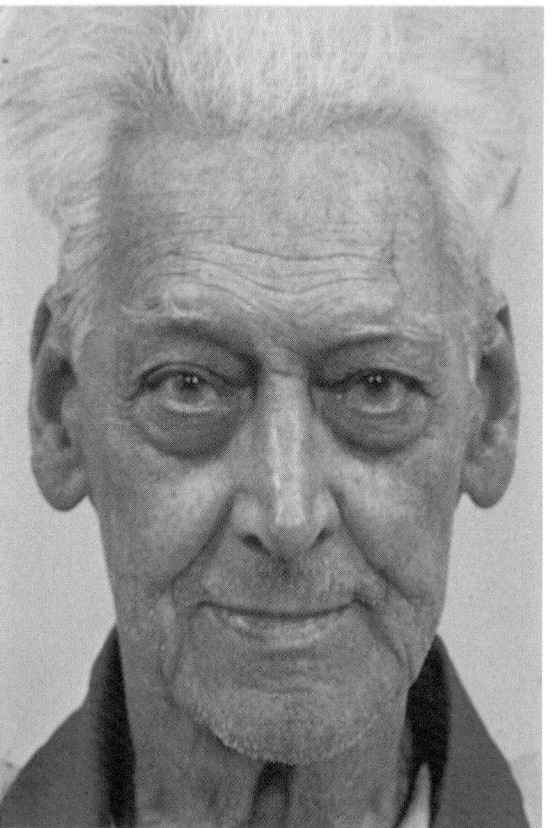
6

7 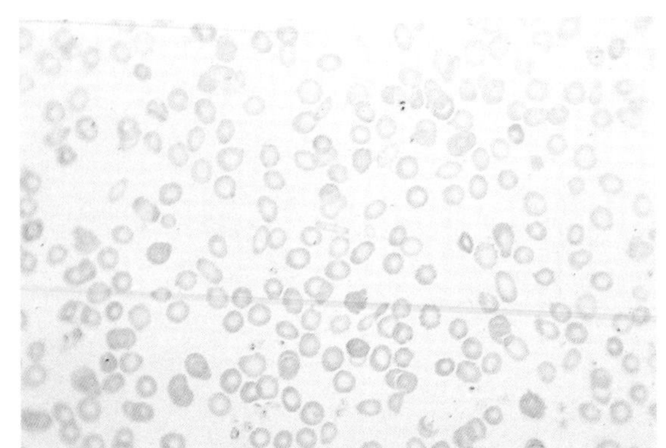

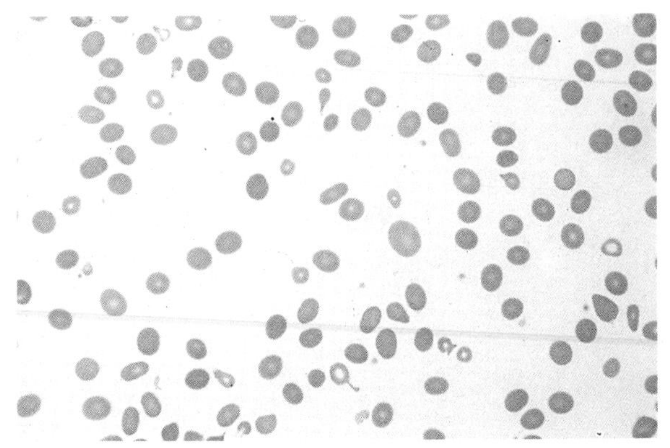 8

9 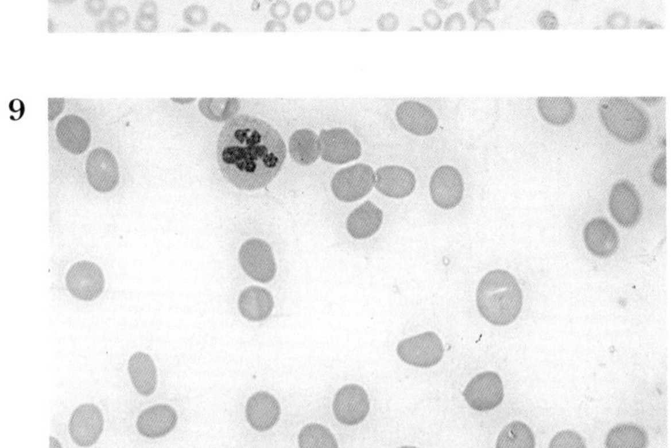

10 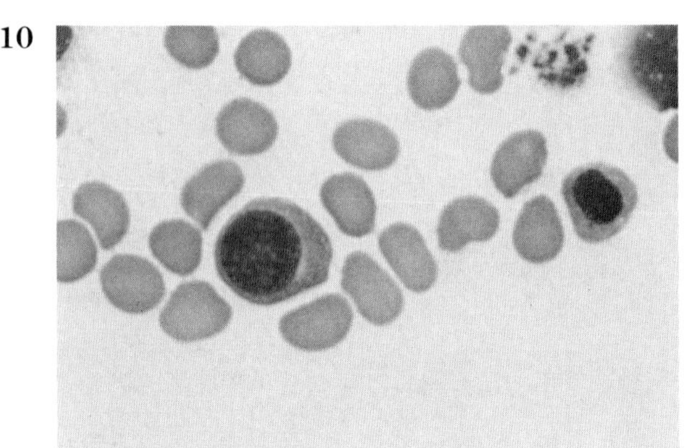

11 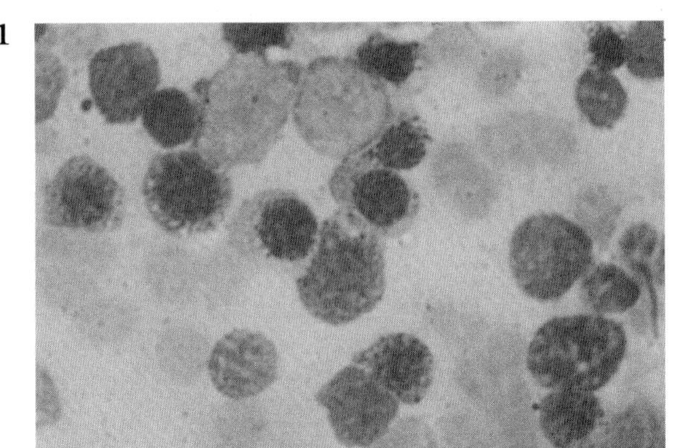

7 Hypochromic RBCs. Blood film from a case of iron-deficiency anaemia. Note hypochromic red cells, microcytosis and pencil cells.

8 Megaloblastic anaemia. Blood film from a case of megaloblastic anaemia showing oval macrocytes, tear drop poikilocytes and moderate anisocytosis (Wright's stain).

9 Megaloblastic anaemia. Blood film in megaloblastic anaemia showing hypersegmented neutrophils and oval macrocytes.

10 Megaloblastic anaemia. Bone marrow showing late (left) and intermediate (right) megaloblasts. (×*1000*)

11 Sideroblastic anaemia. Ring sideroblasts in bone marrow from a case of primary acquired sideroblastic anaemia.

12

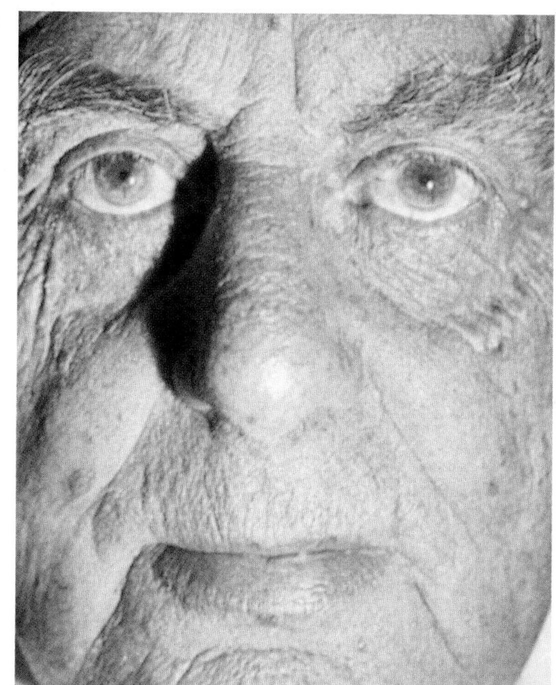

14

14 Polycythaemia rubra vera. Fragment of bone marrow in a smear from a case of polycythaemia rubra vera. Note extreme hypercellularity, absence of fat spaces and great excess of megakaryocytes. (×*100*)

13

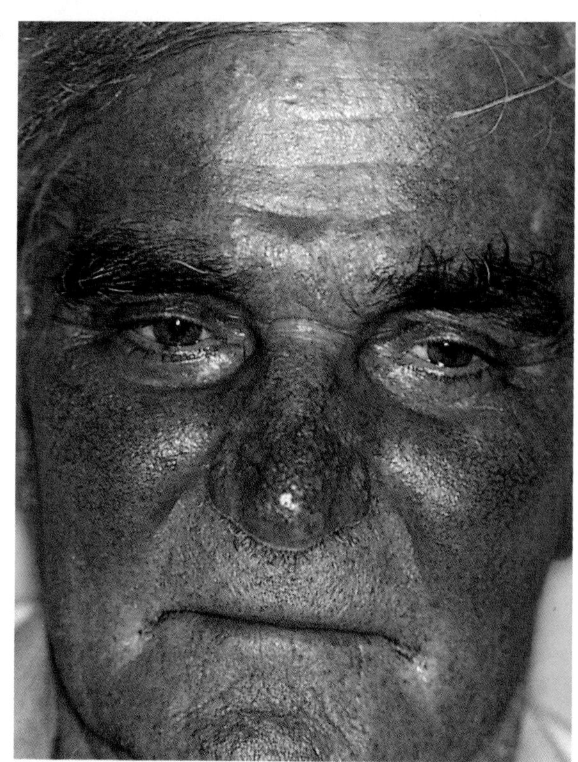

12 Polycythaemia. Plethoric face of an elderly man with polycythaemia rubra vera. The patient presented with features of cardiac failure.

13 Polycythaemia. Facial discoloration due to chronic obstructive airways disease.

Polycythaemia in the elderly

Causes
Idiopathic:
Polycythaemia rubra vera

Secondary:
Chronic cardiac disease
Chronic pulmonary disease
High altitudes
Obesity
Meth. and sulphaemoglobinaemia
Carcinoma of the liver
Kidney disease
Uterine myomata
Phaeochromocytoma

Relative:
Dehydration
'Stress' polycythaemia

Complications
Venous thrombosis
Ecchymosis and bleeding
Hypertension
Coronary thrombosis and CHF
Cerebral thrombosis
Peptic ulcer
Gout
Chronic myelocytic leukaemia in polycythaemia rubra vera

15

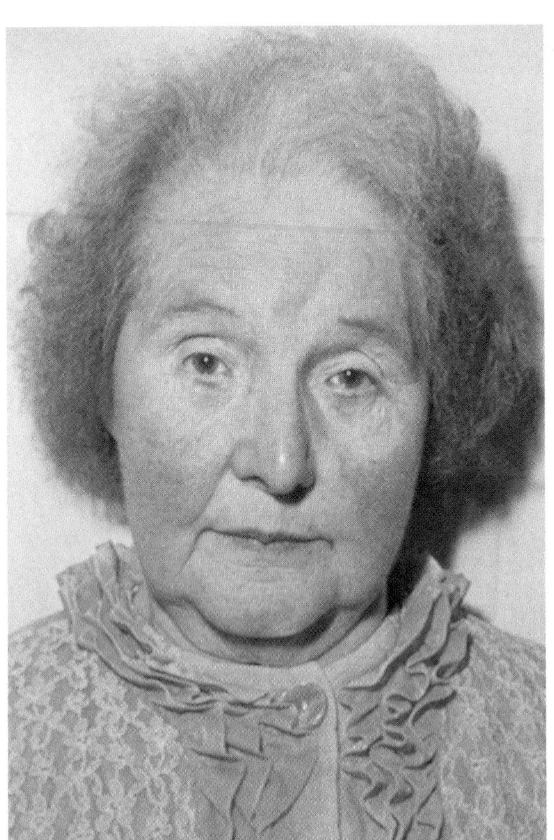

15 Myxoedema. Facial appearance of a case of mild hypothyroidism, whose main presenting complaint was long-standing depression.

16

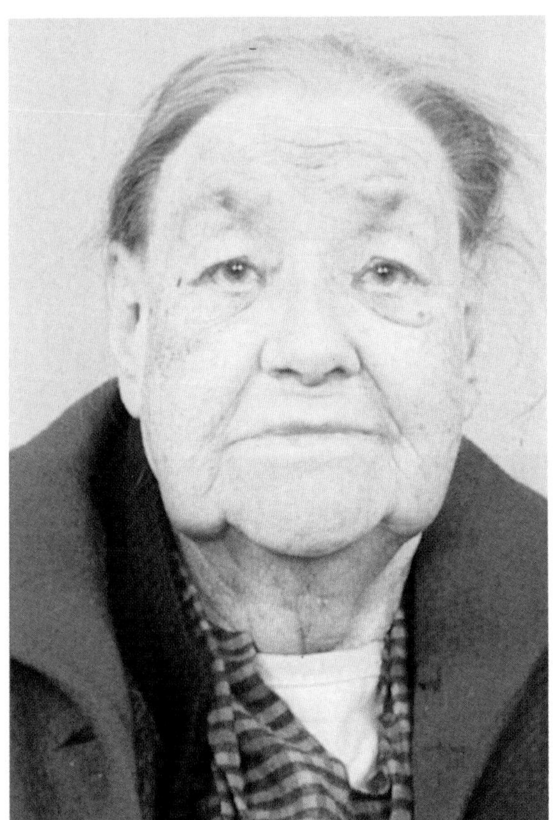

16 Hypothyroidism. Facial appearance of a case of moderate hypothyroidism. The features are puffy and there is some coarsening of the skin.

17 Myxoedema. This elderly lady was admitted suffering from hypothermia, with a rectal temperature of 31°C. Note the dry, puffy facial appearance with coarse hair. The skin was cold to touch and there was mental apathy. She was treated with gradual rewarming, antibiotics, intravenous fluids and triiodothyronine.

17

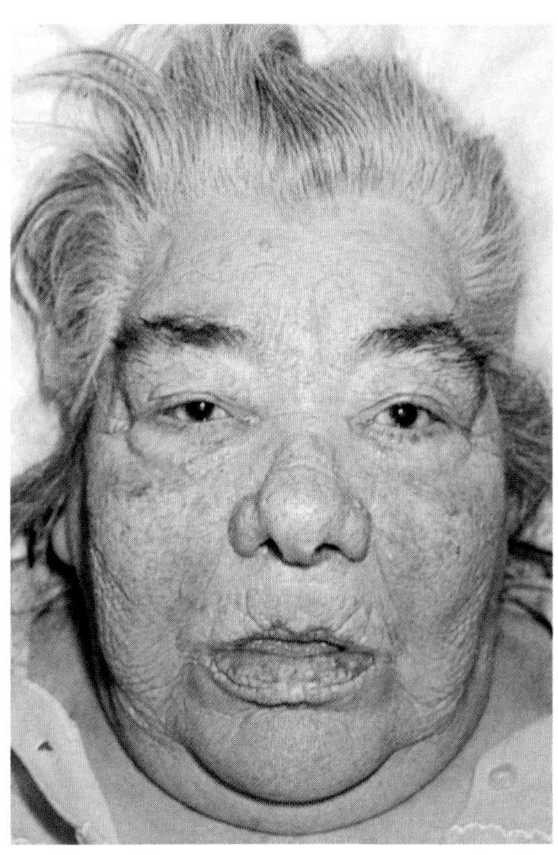

Hypothyroidism – myxoedema

Clinical features

More common in elderly females. About 3–5% of admissions to geriatric units are found to be hypothyroid
Insidious onset
Physical and mental deterioration
Depression
Constipation
Impaired mobility and falls
Increased sensitivity to cold
Loss of hair
Hoarseness of voice
Dry, coarse skin
Confusion leading to dementia
Slow relaxation of tendon jerks

Complications

Neuropathy
Hypothermia
Myxoedema coma
Carpal tunnel syndrome
Pericardial effusion
Ascites
Cerebellar ataxia

18

18 Myxoedema. This elderly lady was admitted to hospital with severe myxoedema. After five weeks treatment with thyroxine, she improved considerably. Her depression and lethargy disappeared. She is now active and more cheerful.

19

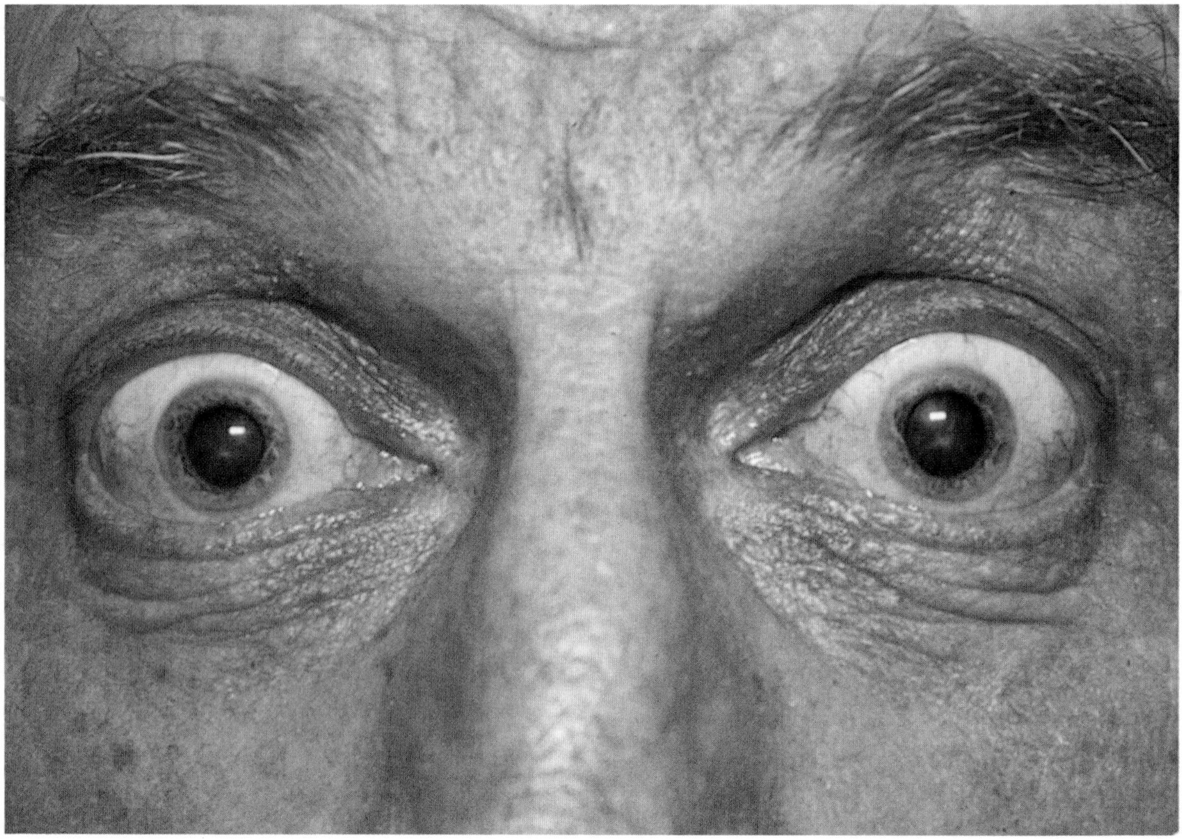

19 Thyrotoxicosis. Note the obvious exophthalmos with lid retraction. The patient also had atrial fibrillation.

20

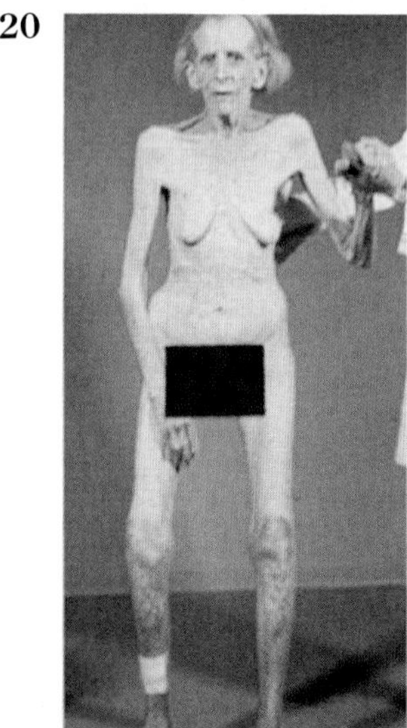

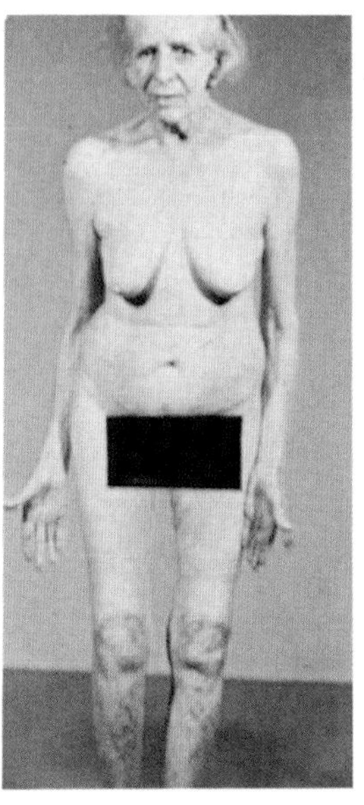

21

Thyrotoxicosis in the elderly

Clinical features

The classic features of thyrotoxicosis in younger age groups may be absent
Muscle weakness with cramps
Depression (apathetic thyrotoxicosis) and confusion
Weight loss
Diarrhoea
Atrial fibrillation which does not respond to Digoxin and CCF
Osteoporosis is fairly common

Signs that are usually absent in the elderly

Exophthalmos and ophthalmoplegia
Warm, sweaty hands
Hyperkinesis
Thyroid bruit
Goitre

20 Thyrotoxicosis. Elderly lady showing features of thyrotoxicosis. She is frail with considerable weight loss.

21 Treated thyrotoxicosis. Same patient as in **20**. The overactive thyroid has been treated. She has gained weight and feels well.

22

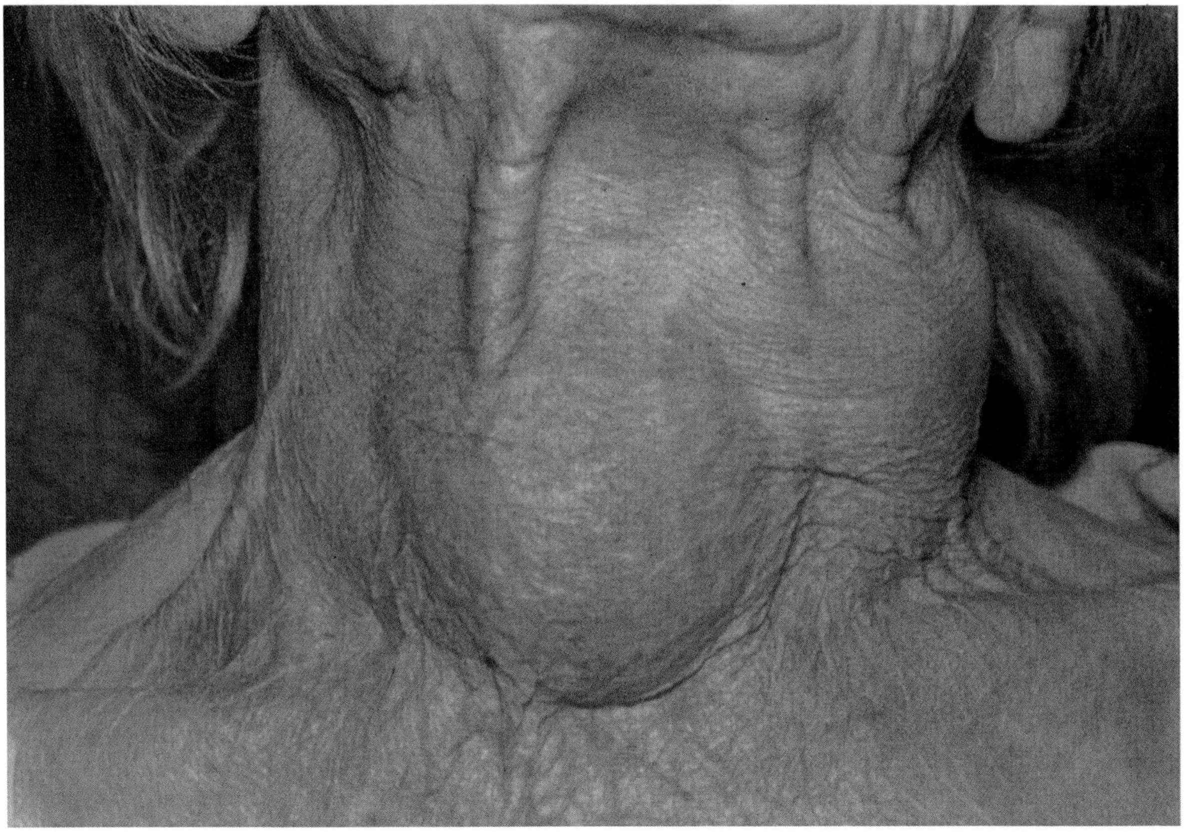

22 Goitre. Long-standing benign thyroid enlargement – a case of Derbyshire neck. (At one time benign goitre was common in the county of Derbyshire (England), because the drinking water supply lacked iodine.)

23 A non-toxic goitre. A lateral x-ray of the neck showing areas of calcification in a chronic non-toxic goitre.

23

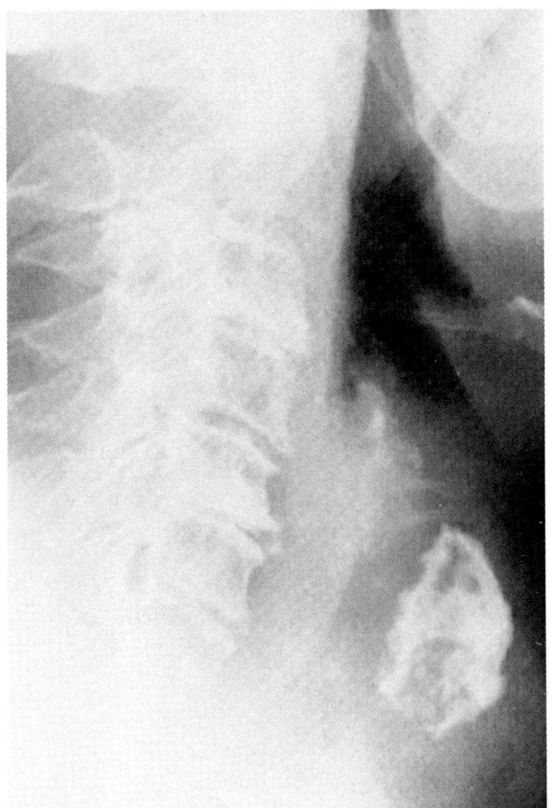

24

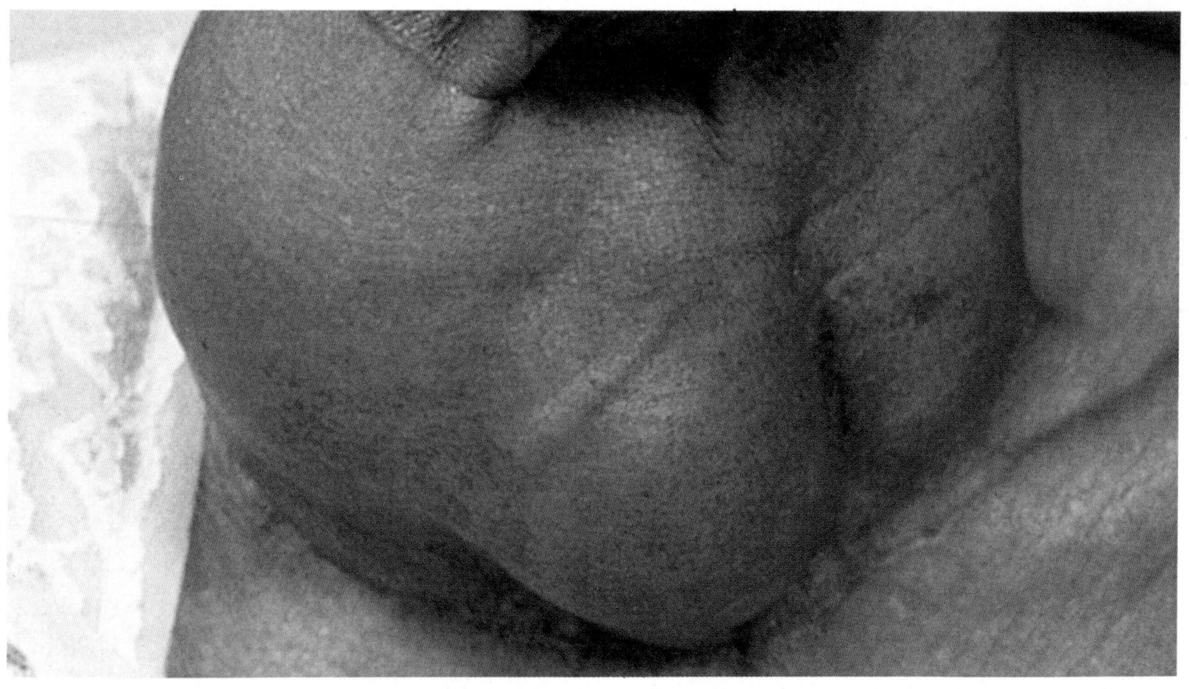

24 Non-toxic goitre. An elderly lady with a large non-toxic goitre. It caused her only mild discomfort.

25

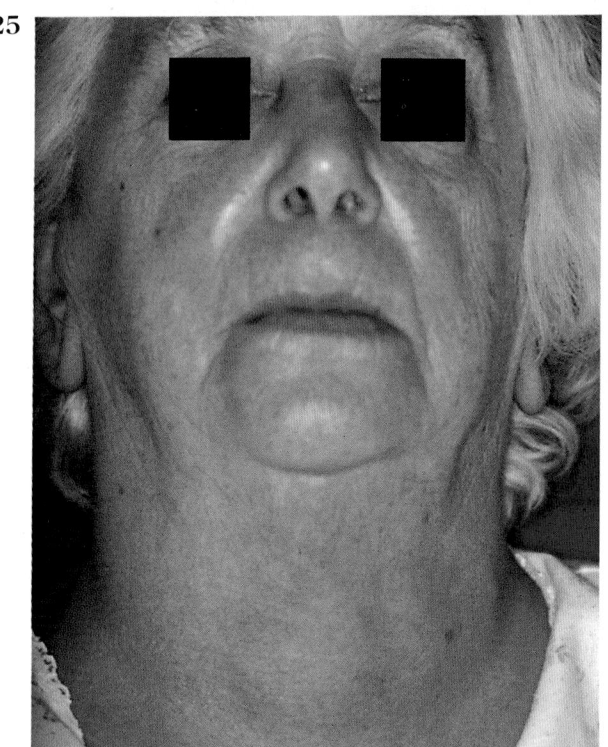

26

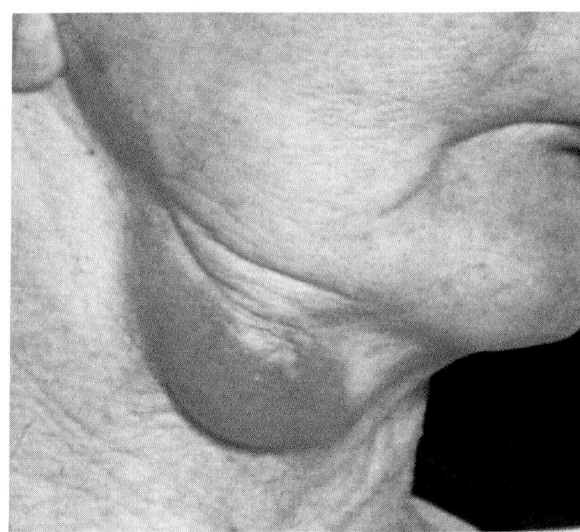

25 Non-toxic goitre. A case of long-standing goitre presenting as hypothyroidism.

26 Thyroid carcinoma. This is an uncommon tumour in old age, but when it does occur it should be differentiated from simple goitre. The incidence is about 2.5 cases per 100,0000 population per year. Hyperthyroidism or myxoedema is very rarely associated with this cancer.

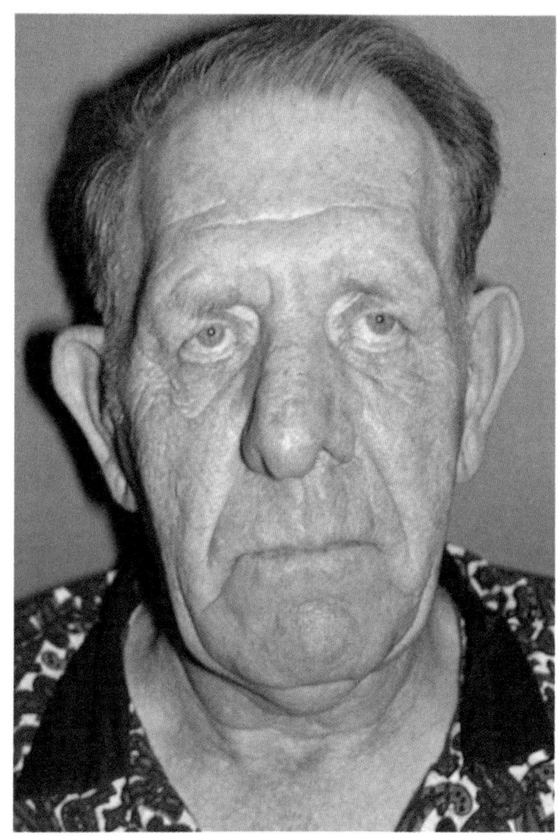

27

27 Acromegaly. The patient presented with lethargy, increased sweating and mild hypertension. X-ray of the skull revealed an enlarged pituitary fossa.

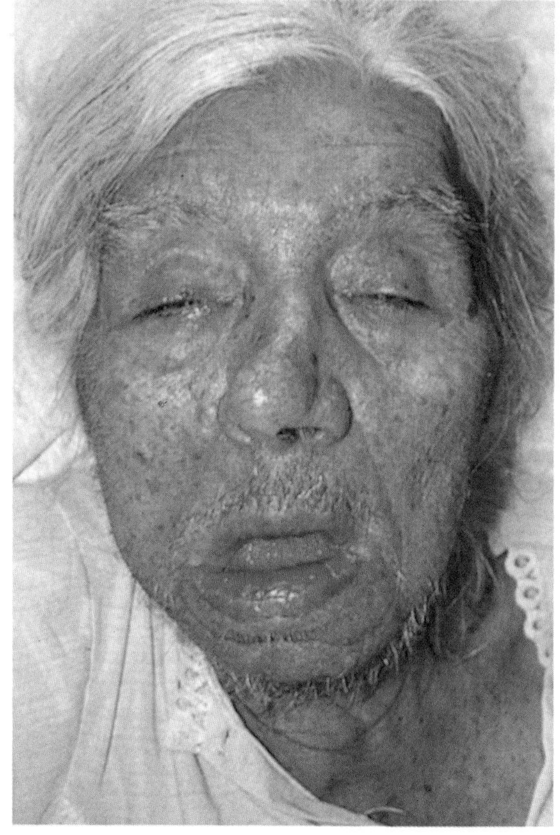

28

28 Acromegaly. This acromegalic female presented with extreme drowsiness. The facial features are enlarged and there is macroglossia. She also had visual disturbances, enlargement of the hands and feet, arthritic changes, mild cardiac failure and glycosuria.

29

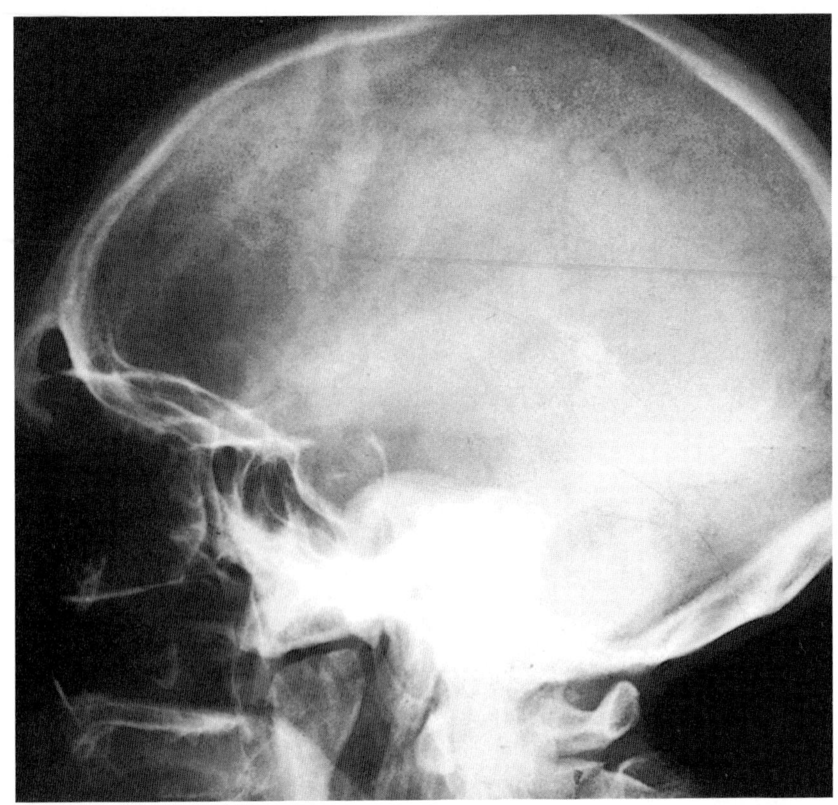

29 Pituitary tumour. Skull x-ray showing an enlarged pituitary fossa caused by a tumour. The patient, who was 80 years of age, had the classic features of acromegaly.

30

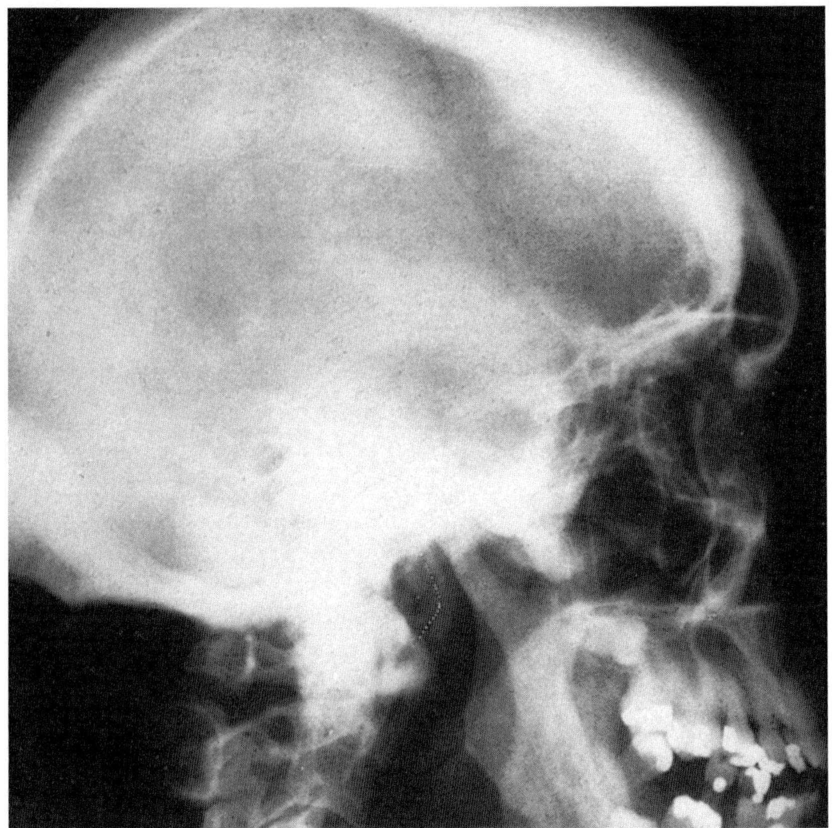

30 Acromegaly. Skull x-ray of another patient, showing enlargement of pituitary fossa and also generalised bone thickening.

Complications of systemic glucocorticosteroid therapy

Weight gain with water and sodium retention
Hypokalaemia
Hyperglycaemia
Cushingoid facies
Adrenal suppression and rebound of disease on stopping the drug
Hypertension
Hyperlipidaemia
Osteoporosis, aseptic bone necrosis
GIT – dyspepsia, peptic ulceration, pancreatitis
CNS – euphoria, psychosis, increased intracranial pressure
Skin – Thinning of skin and easy bruising. Poor wound healing, acne, hypertrichosis
Myopathy
Cataracts
Hypothermia
Withdrawal phenomenon
Infections – viral, TB, fungal

31

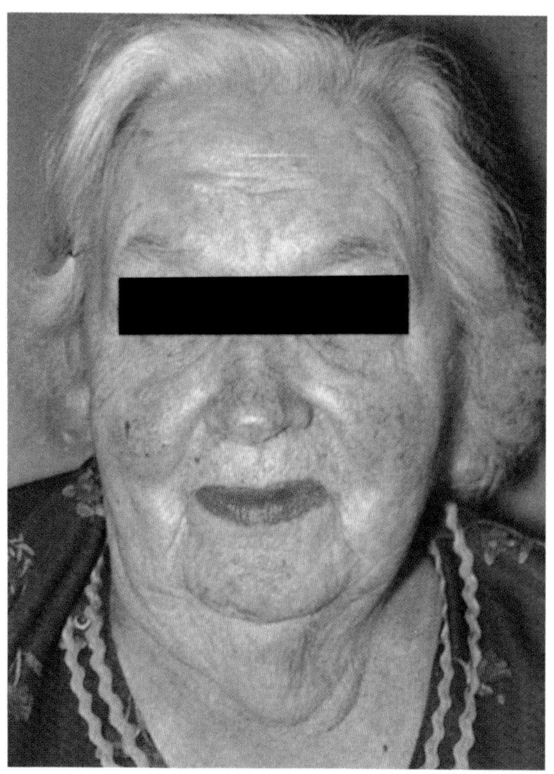

31 Cushingoid face. Flushed, puffy face of an elderly lady who was prescribed corticosteroids for rheumatoid arthritis.

32

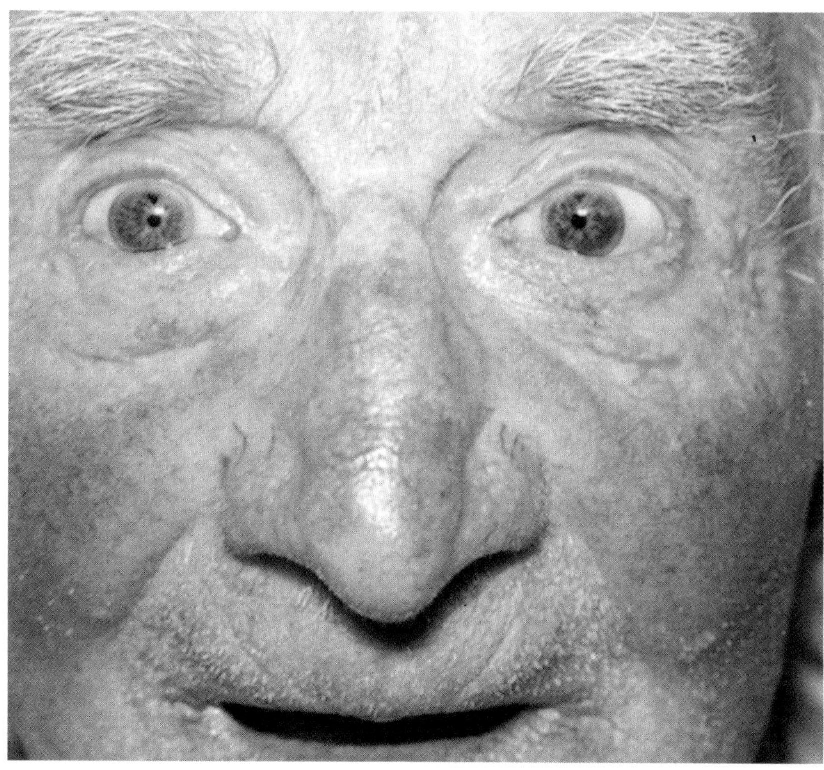

32 Cushingoid face. Another case showing cushingoid features caused by chronic steroid ingestion for asthmatic bronchitis.

33

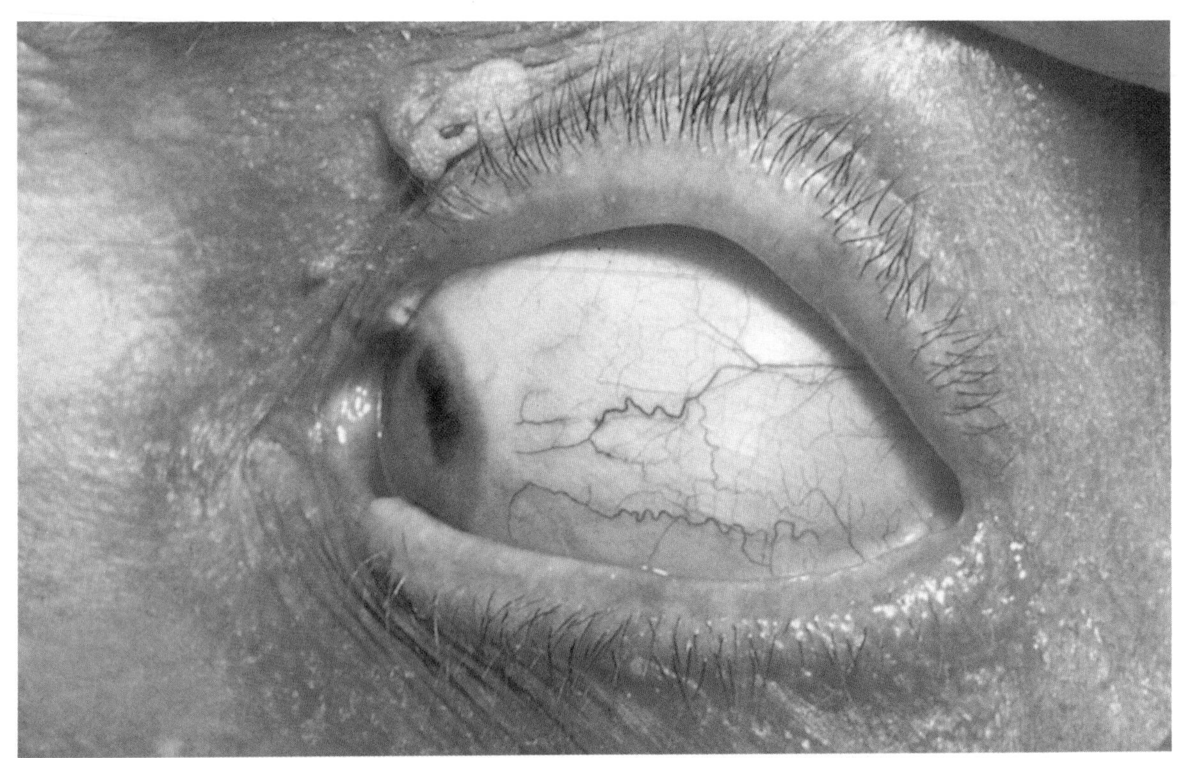

33 Jaundice. Icteric sclera in a case of obstructive jaundice caused by carcinoma in the porta hepatis.

34

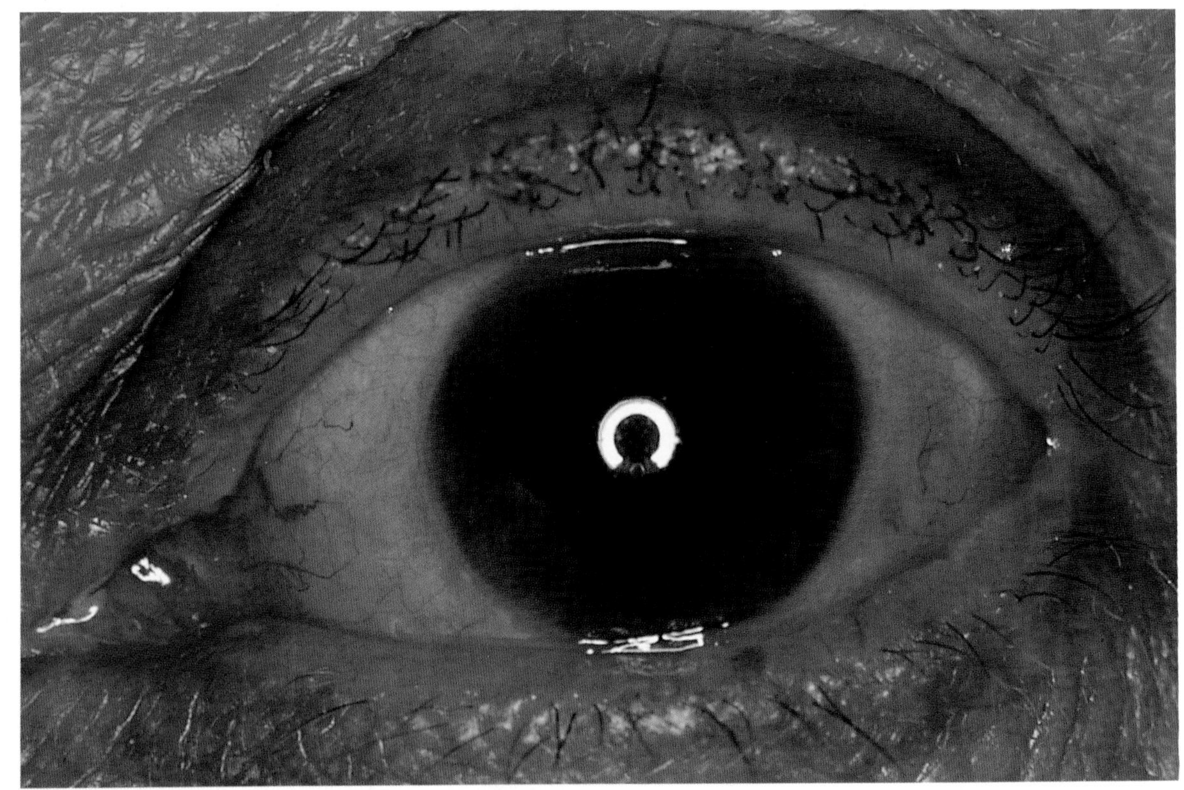

34 Jaundice. This patient presented with jaundice, secondary to chronic phenothiazine ingestion.

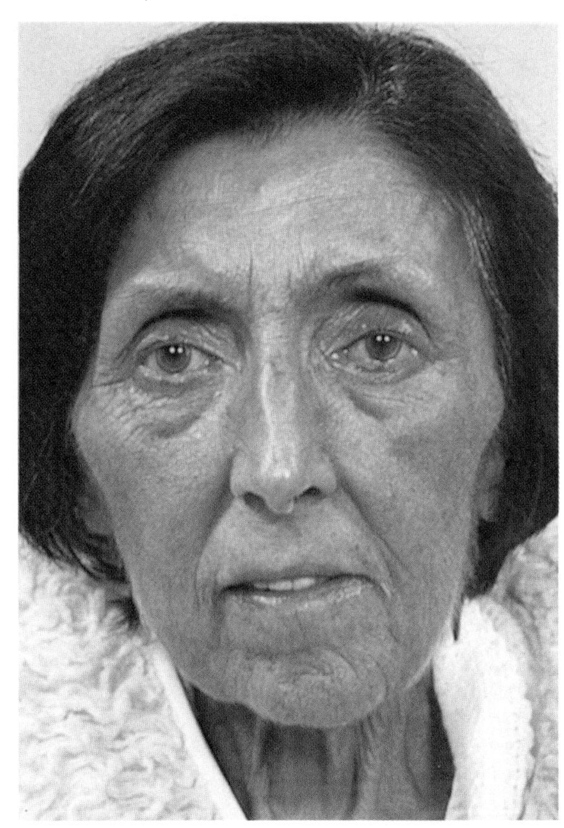

35

35 **Primary biliary cirrhosis.** Note the deep jaundice and marked pigmentation.

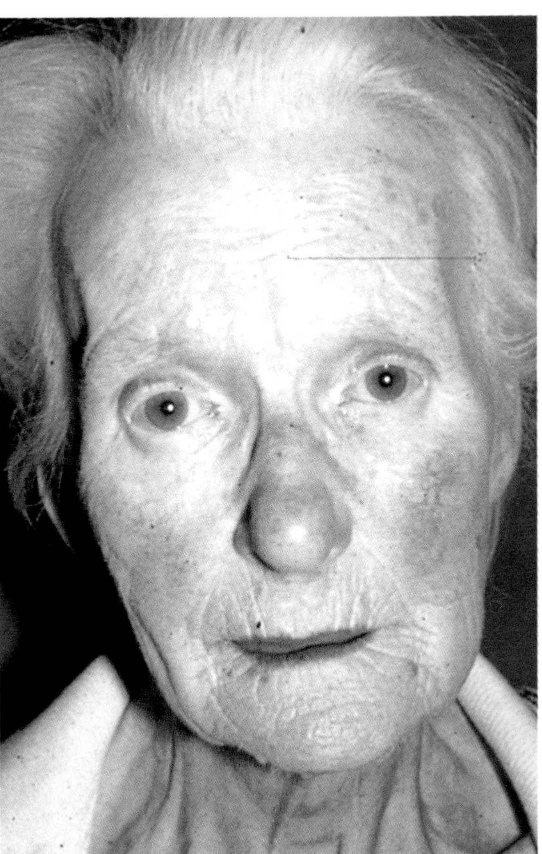

36

Jaundice

Some common causes of jaundice in old age are:
- Biliary stone
- Hepatic cancer, usually secondary
- Carcinoma of head of the pancreas or ampulla
- Liver cirrhosis
- Porta hepatis lymph node enlargement
- Viral hepatitis
- Congestive heart failure
- Pulmonary infarction
- Drugs

36 **Mitral facies.** An old lady with mitral stenosis, showing the typical malar flush and cynotic lips.

37

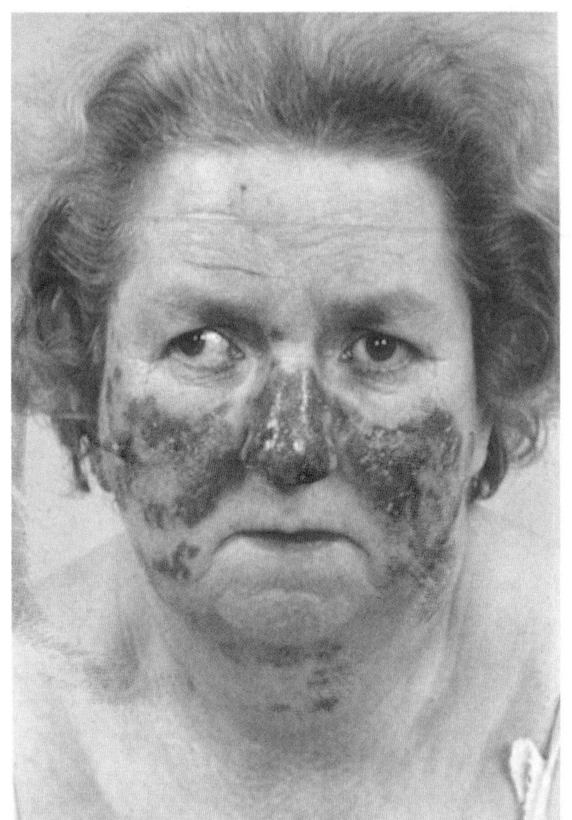

38

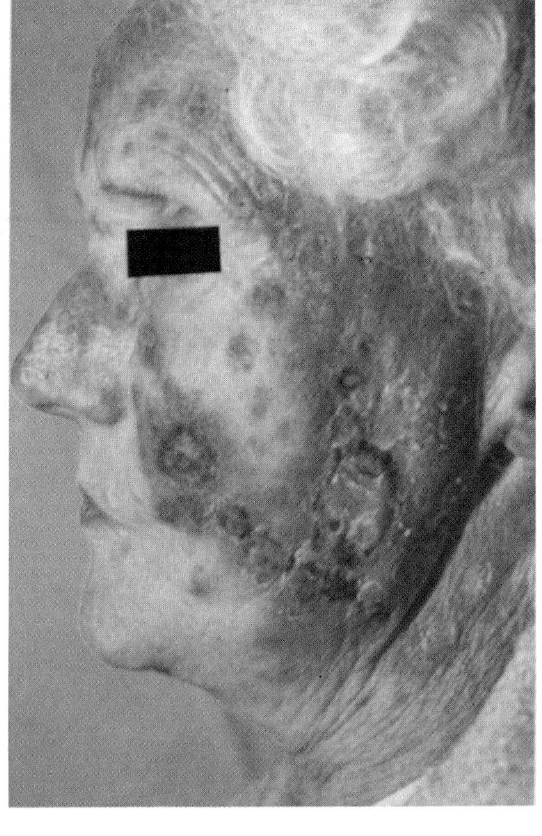

39

37 Lupus erythematosus. Showing typical 'butterfly'-shaped facial rash. (This condition is more common in middle age than in old age.)

38 Lupus erythematosus. A more advanced case showing widespread rash with some necrotic lesions which are painless. This patient also had renal and pulmonary damage.

39 Paget's disease of the skull. Note the large skull and prominence of frontal bones. This patient was also deaf. In the elderly, Paget's disease is usually symptomless but can present with bone pain, deformities, cardiac failure, deafness, optic nerve involvement and fractures. Osteogenic sarcoma is a complication in about 1% of patients.

40

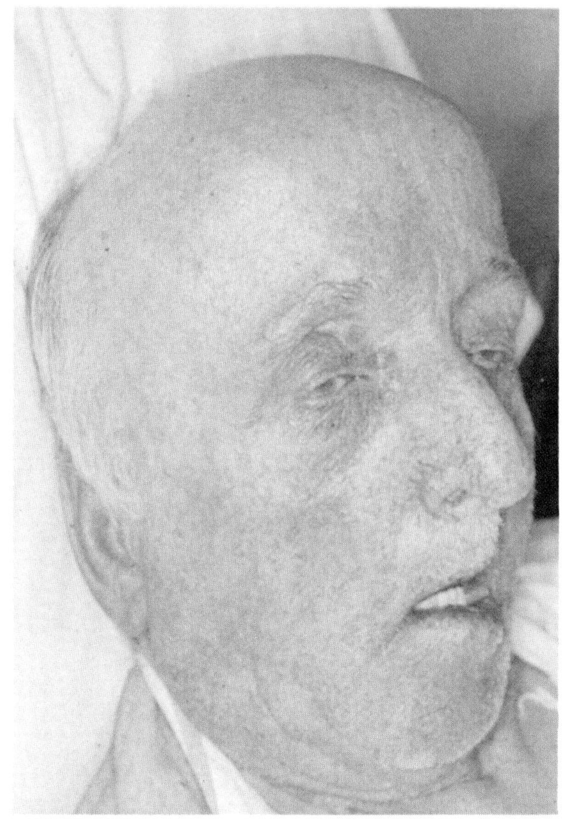

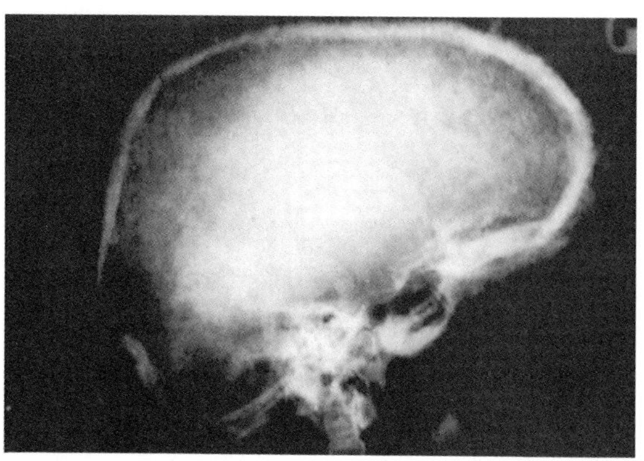

41

40 Paget's disease of the skull. This elderly man has advanced Paget's disease and there is involvement of some cranial nerves. Note the right-sided facial palsy.

41 Paget's disease. X-ray showing thickening of calvarium and the typical disorganised bony architecture.

42 Osteoporosis circumscripta. This condition occurs in association with Paget's disease. Note the rounded translucency in the skull.

42

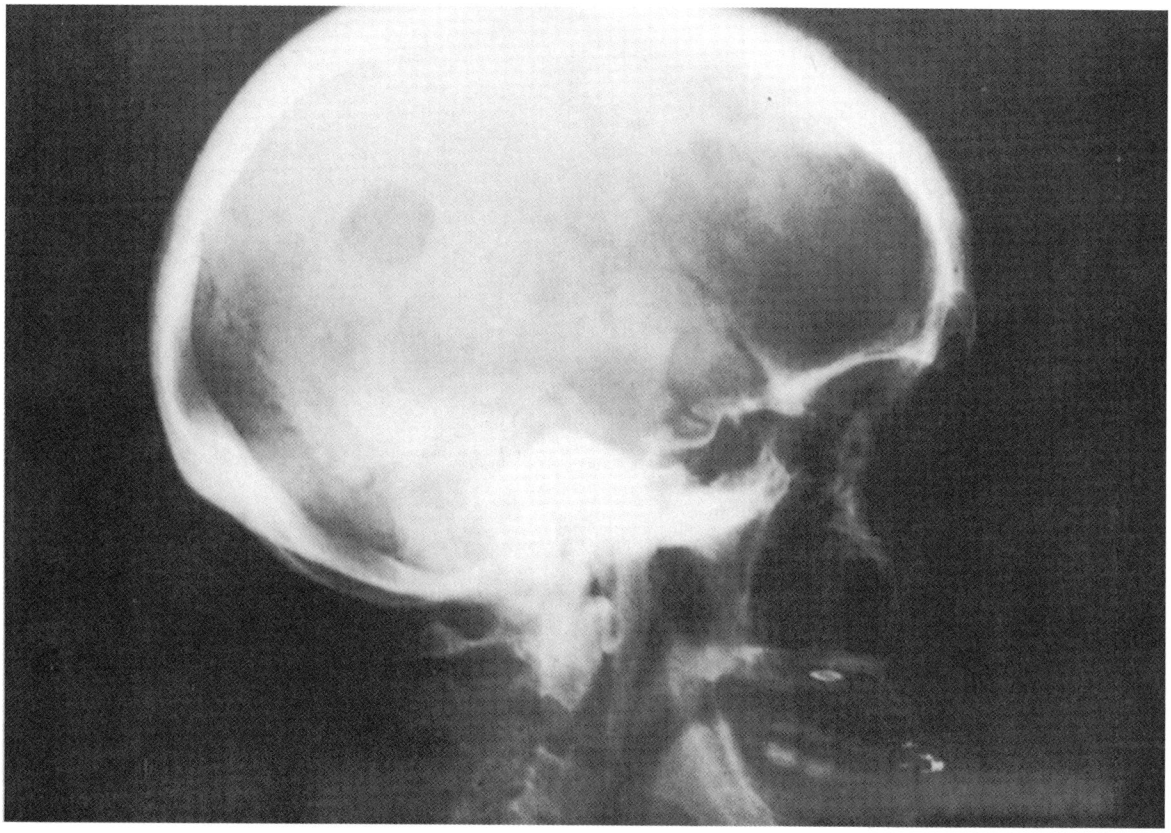

43

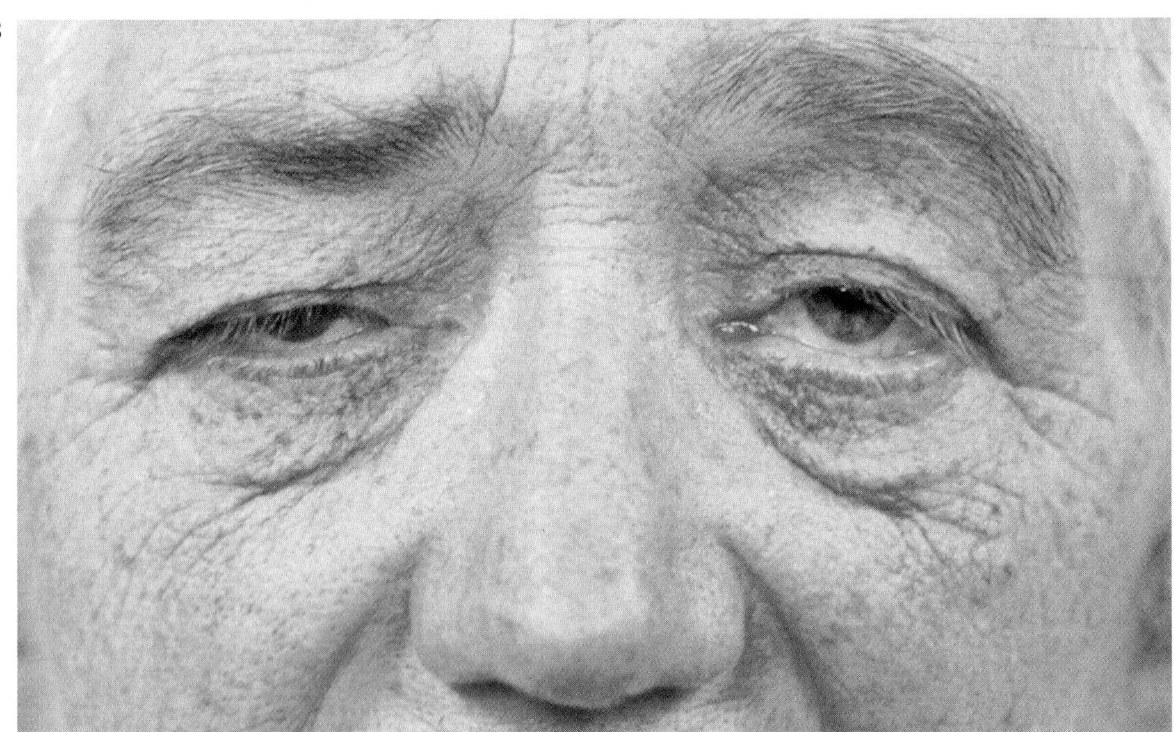

43 Myasthenia gravis. Face of an elderly lady showing bilateral ptosis and arching of the eyebrows. Older patients with myasthenia must be investigated for an occult tumour such as carcinoma of the lung.

44

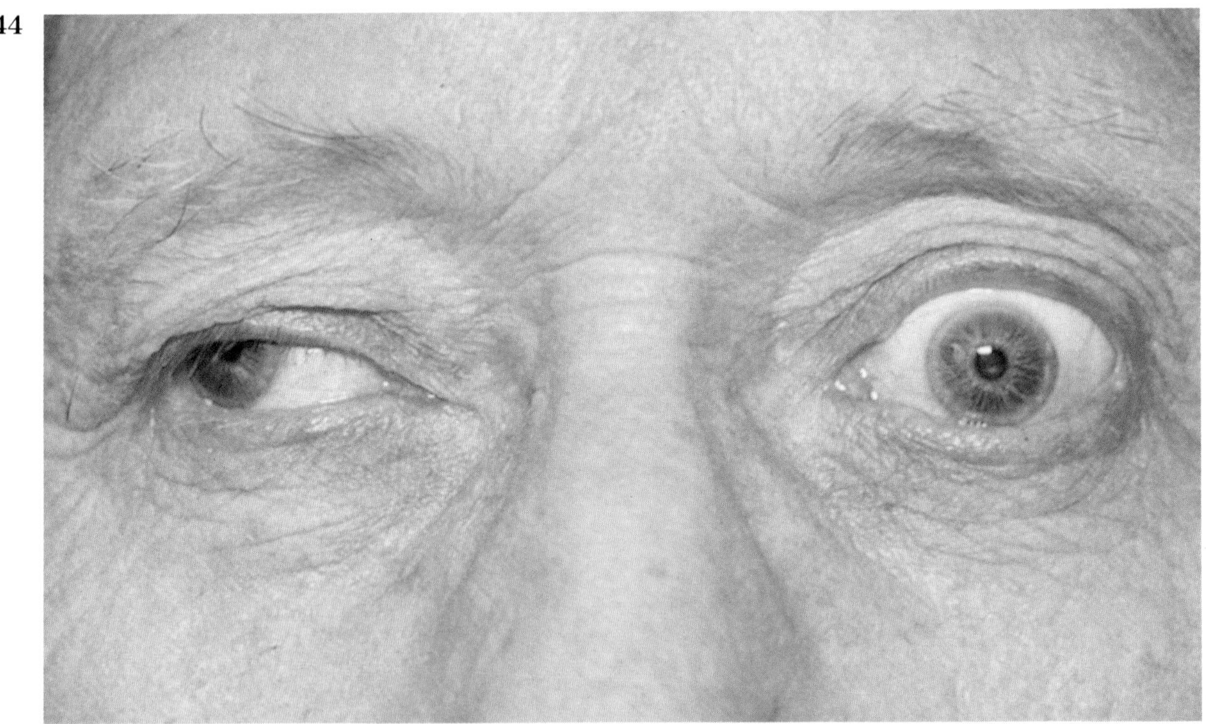

44 Ophthalmoplegia. A case of third-nerve palsy showing right-sided ptosis and divergent strabismus. In the elderly the common causes are cerebrovascular disease, tumours, diabetes mellitus and cranial arteritis.

45 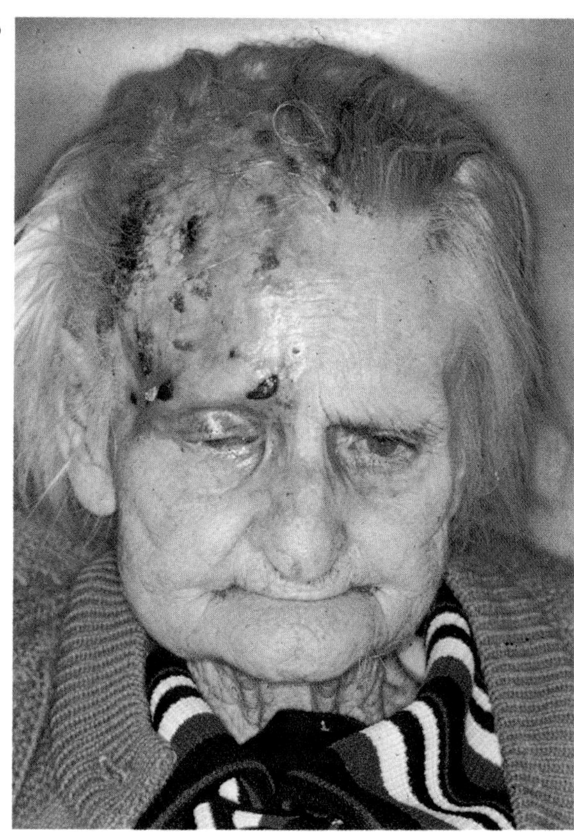

45 Ophthalmic herpes zoster. In this case there is involvement of the ophthalmic divisions of the fifth nerve; the main danger is permanent corneal scarring.

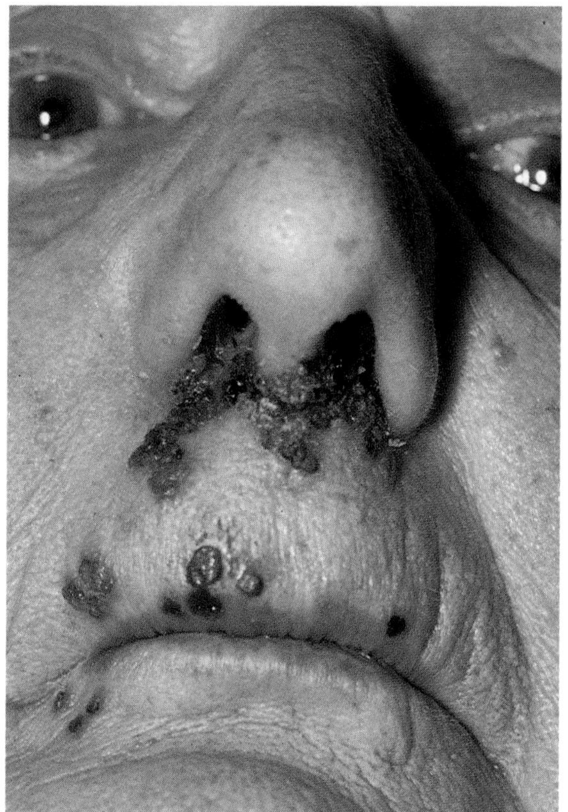 46

46 Herpes simplex. Painful eruption around the mouth and nostrils in a patient who had chest infection and toxic confusional state.

Herpes labialis results from activation of the herpes simplex virus by rise in temperature. It is common in bacterial infections of the respiratory system.

Complications of herpes zoster

Post-herpetic neuralgia and depression
Secondary bacterial infection
Ophthalmic herpes zoster
Ramsay Hunt syndrome – herpes of geniculate ganglion resulting in severe facial palsy and vesicular eruption in external auditory canal
Encephalitis
Generalised herpes zoster

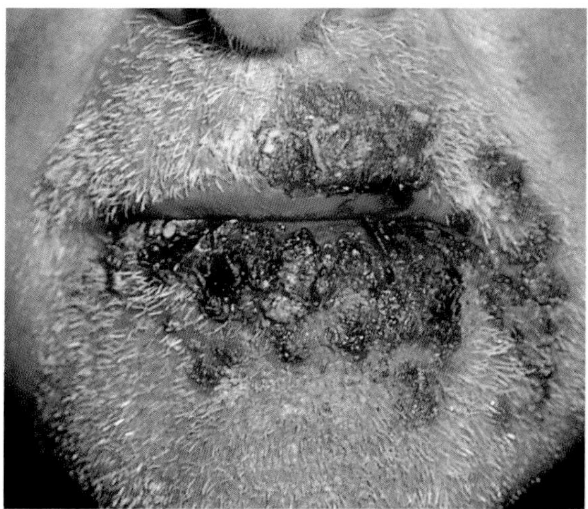 47

47 Herpes simplex. A more extensive case of herpes simplex in a patient with respiratory tract infection.

48

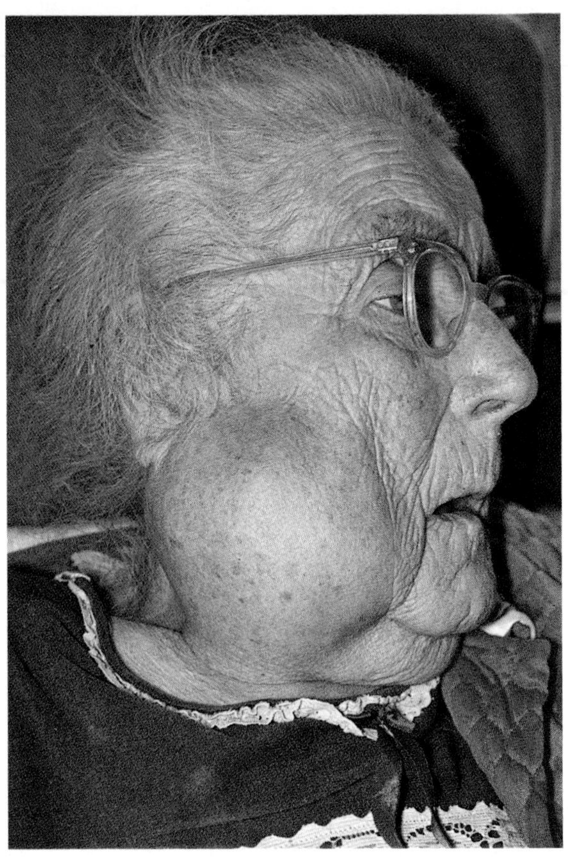

48 Parotid tumour. A large, mixed parotid tumour, apparently causing no symptoms. The patient refused surgical intervention.

49

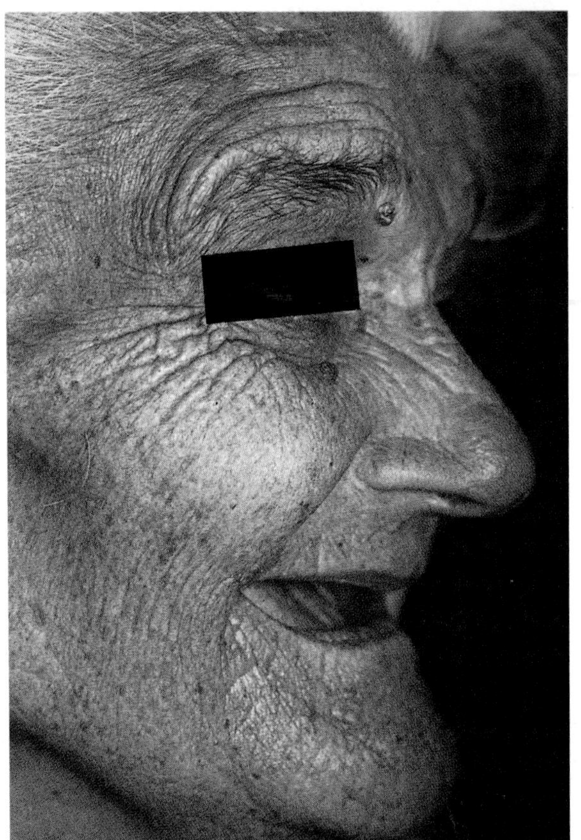

49 Hyperpigmentation. Generalised facial hyperpigmentation in a Caucasian lady. She complained of weight loss and was found to have bronchogenic carcinoma. Further investigations revealed evidence of ectopic ACTH syndrome and cerebral metastasis. Her symptoms were minimal and her general condition remained satisfactory for several months. She eventually developed a dementia-like picture.

Common causes of hyperpigmentation

Racial or genetic
Radiation, e.g. ultraviolet radiation
'Vagabond's itch' – chronic scratching
Hypoadrenalism
Ectopic ACTH from carcinomas
Cachexia caused by malignancy
Chronic infection; for example, endocarditis
Malabsorption
Pellagra
Chronic hepatic disease
Chronic renal failure
Collagen diseases; for example, dermatomyositis
Drugs; for example, busulphan, ACTH, oestrogens, chlorpromazine, chloroquine
Haemochromatosis

50

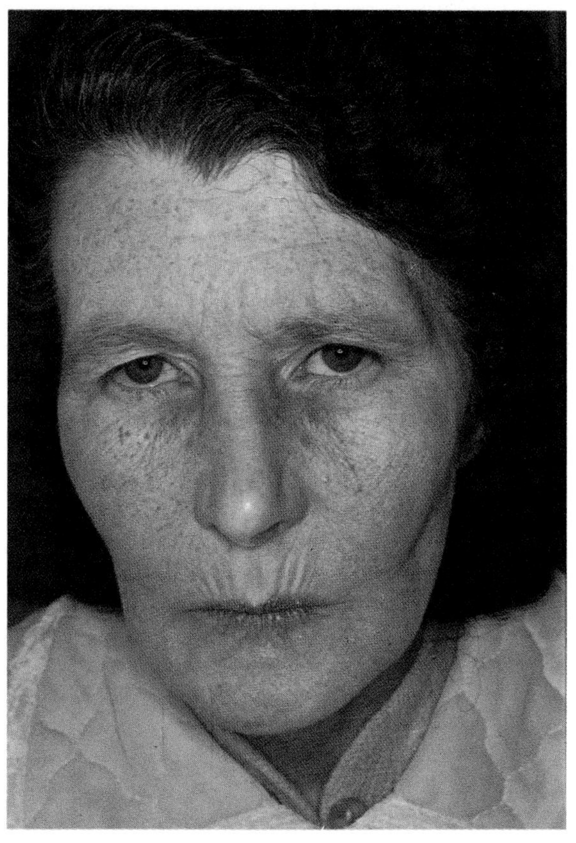

51

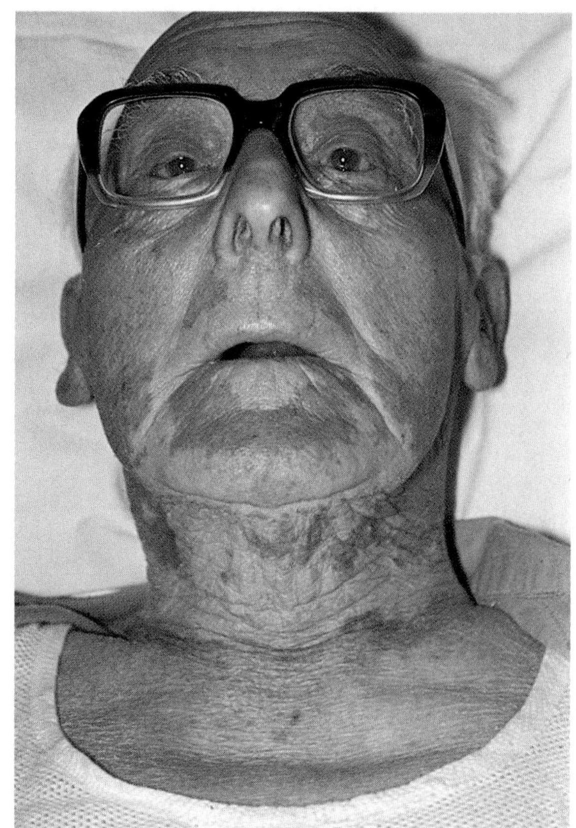

50 Scleroderma. Face of an elderly lady showing the tight drawn skin and pinched lips, giving her a youthful appearance.

51 Vitiligo. Typical patches of hypopigmentation in a patient with hypothyroidism.

52 Torticollis. This occurred in an elderly schizophrenic who had been on long-term phenothiazine therapy. She also had orofacial dyskinesia.

52

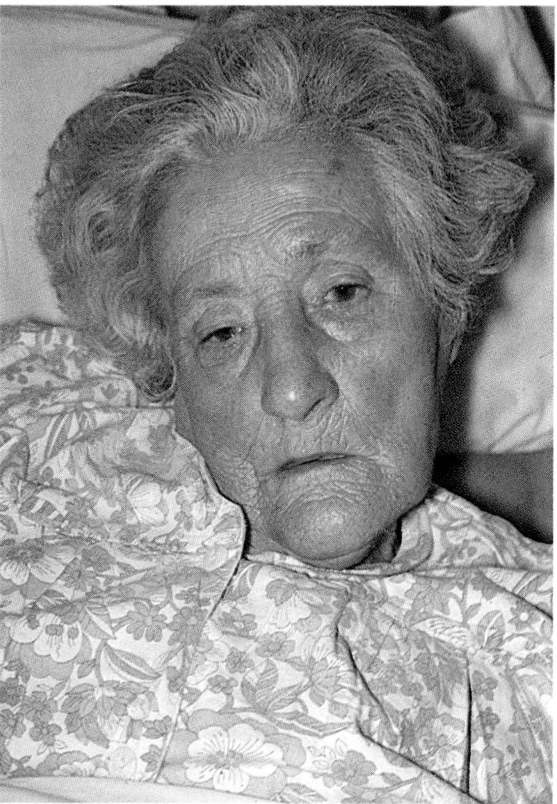

Conditions associated with vitiligo

Autoimmune diseases
- Myxoedema
- Addison's disease
- Pernicious anaemia
- Diabetes mellitus

Alopecia areata
Malignant melanoma

53

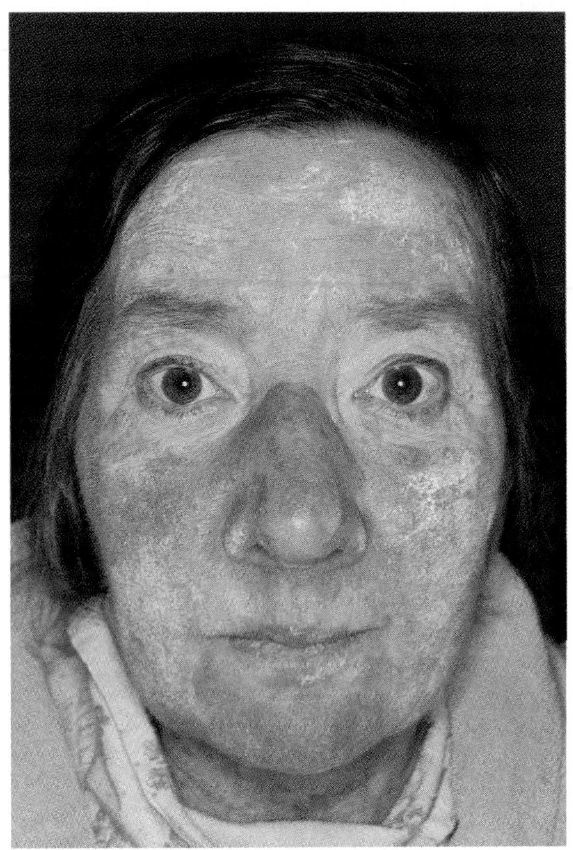

54

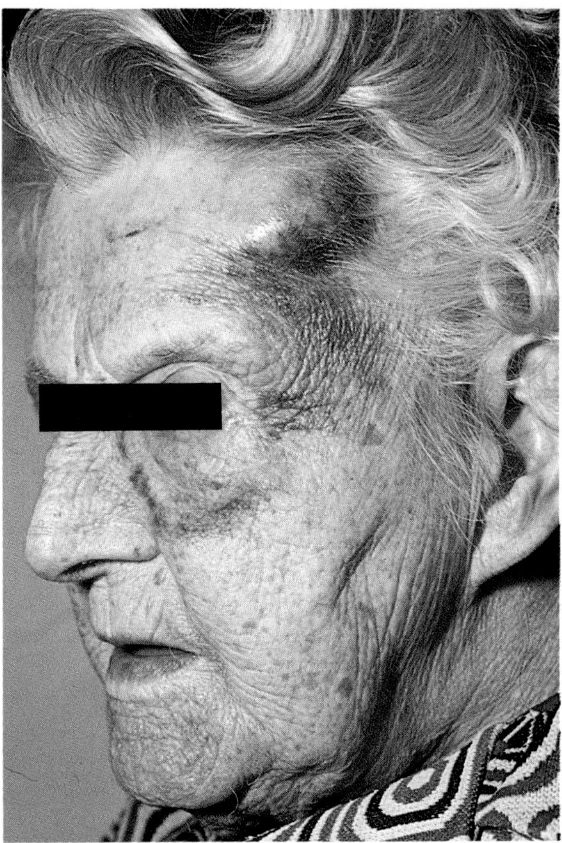

55

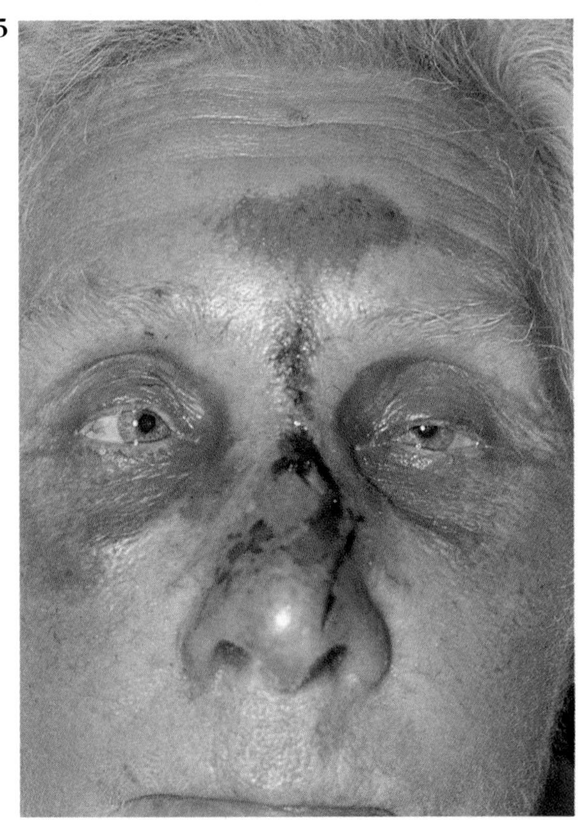

53 Drug-induced rash. Erythematous skin rash; side-effect of an antibiotic. The whitish patches are caused by calamine application.

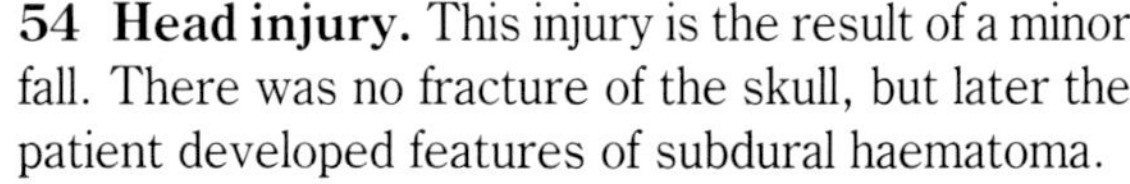

54 Head injury. This injury is the result of a minor fall. There was no fracture of the skull, but later the patient developed features of subdural haematoma.

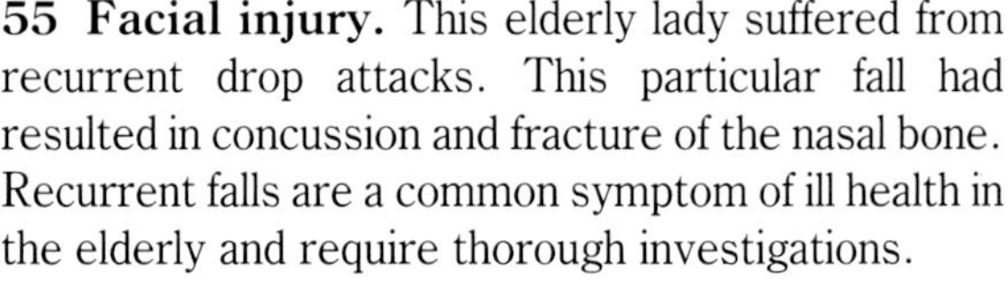

55 Facial injury. This elderly lady suffered from recurrent drop attacks. This particular fall had resulted in concussion and fracture of the nasal bone. Recurrent falls are a common symptom of ill health in the elderly and require thorough investigations.

Falls in the elderly

Occur in 4% of elderly women and 24% of elderly men.

General features
Incidence increases linearly with age
More common in women
Most frequently indoors
Often happen when moving from bed, wheelchair or lavatory
Frequent in elderly people who are socially isolated, depressed or demented

Causes

- Environmental causes – accidental falls
  - Tripping over objects, slips
  - Old, ill-fitting footwear
  - Slippery surfaces
  - Narrow, steep stairs
  - Poor lighting
  - Pets, electrical flexes, etc.
- Musculoskeletal
  - Onychogryphosis (overgrown toenails)
  - Osteoarthritic feet, knees and hips
  - Corns, bunions, hammer toes
  - Hallux valgus
  - Oedema of the feet
  - Muscle weakness
- Nervous system
  - Transient ischaemic attacks
  - CVAs in evolution
  - Epilepsy
  - Parkinsonism and other extrapyramidal disorders
  - Cerebellar disorders
  - Labyrinthine disorders
  - Visual impairment
  - Peripheral neuropathy
- Cardiovascular
  - Silent myocardial infarction
  - Arrhythmias, heart block
  - Postural hypotension
  - Subclavian-steel
  - Anaemia
- Drop attacks
  - Vertebrobasilar insufficiency with cervical spondylosis
  - Transient ischaemia of spinal cord
  - Myxoedema
- Miscellaneous
  - Defaecation syncope
  - Micturation syncope
  - Hypoglycaemia
  - Vagovagal attacks
  - Carotid sinus hypersensitivity

56

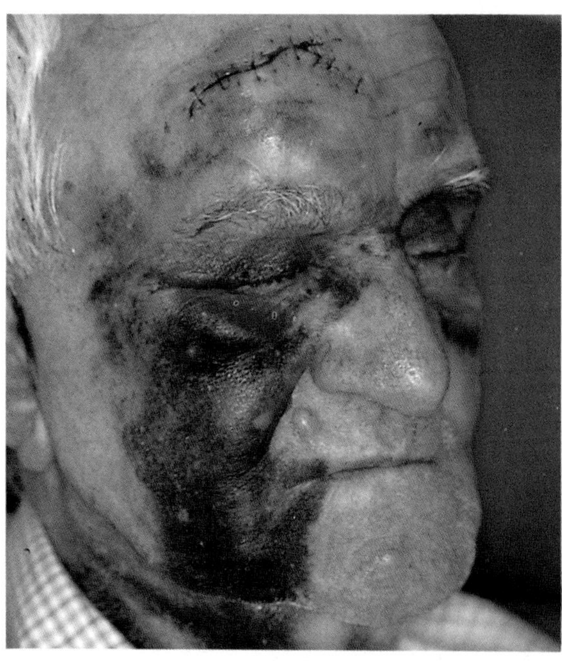

56 Falls. Extensive facial bruising in a case of recurrent falls due to postural instability and hypotension.

57

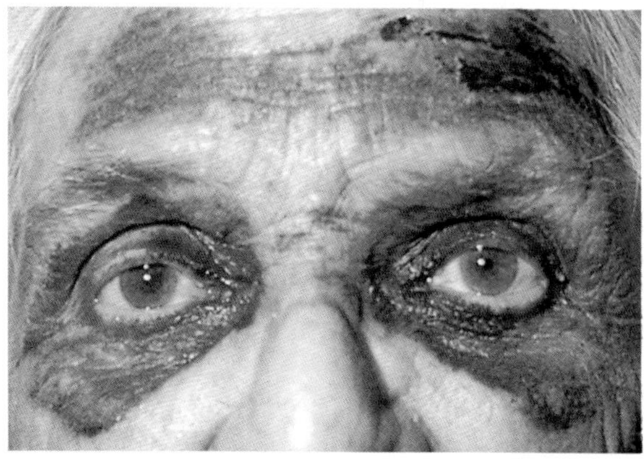

57 Falls. Bilateral periorbital bruising due to falls and facial injury in a case of generalised osteoarthritis.

Complications of falls in the elderly

Fractures, especially of long bones; e.g. fractured neck of the femur
Hypothermia
Burns
Dehydration
Bronchopneumonia
Loss of confidence – immobility
Subdural haematoma

58

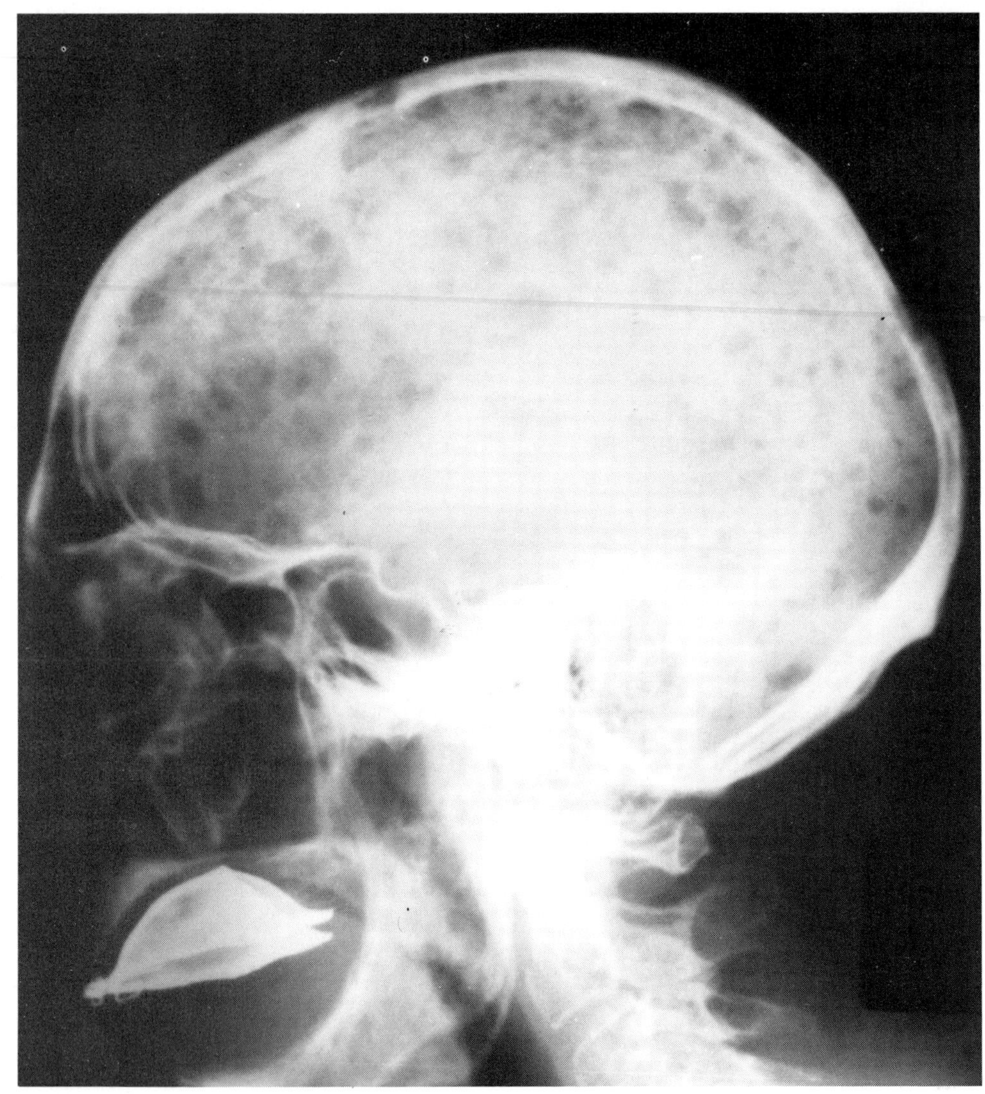

58 Plasma-cell myeloma. X-ray of skull showing classical appearance of multiple myeloma. Note the numerous 'punched out' translucencies.

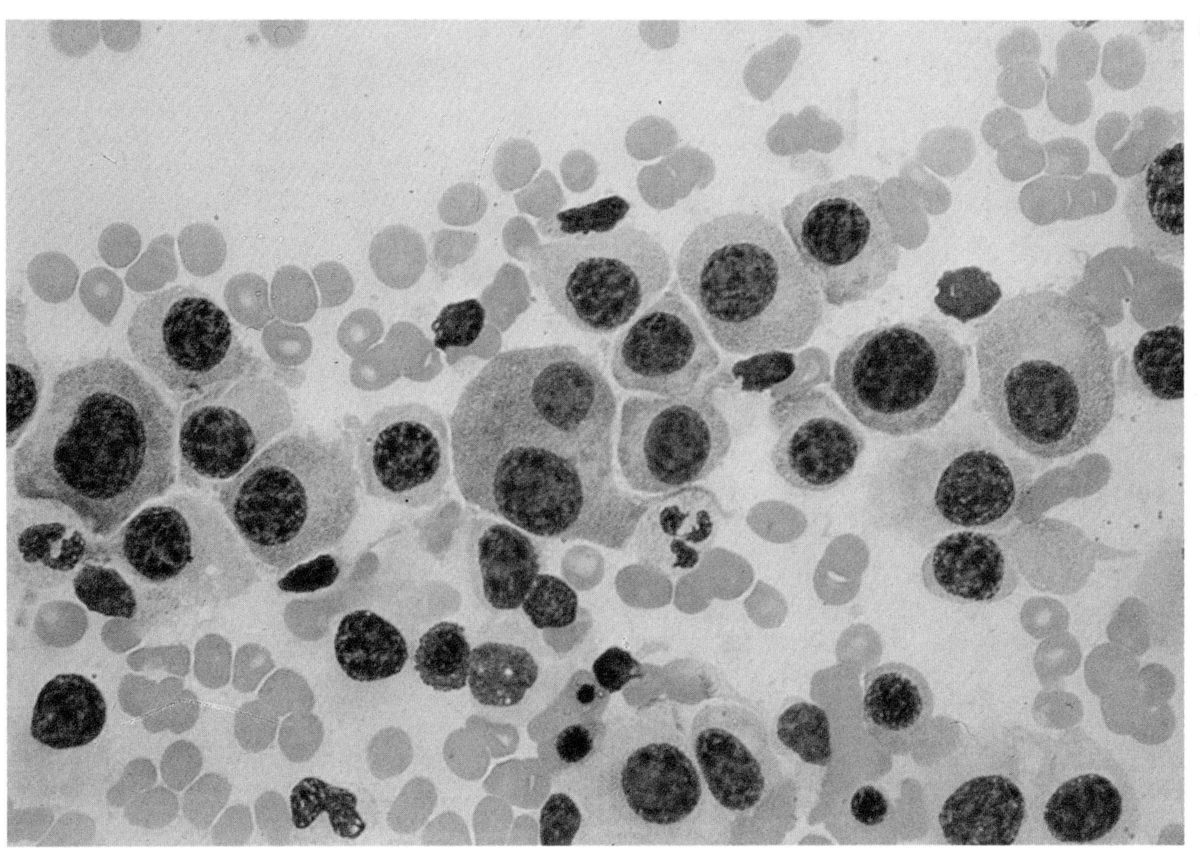 59

59 Multiple myeloma. Bone marrow showing excess of plasma cells. (×*500*)

Multiple myeloma

Malignant proliferation of plasma cells.

Clinical features
General ill health and anorexia
Anaemias
Bone pains and pathological fractures
Hypercalcaemia and renal failure
Peripheral neuropathy
Amyloidosis
Reduced resistance to infection
Hyperviscosity syndrome
Vertebral collapse and cord compression

Investigations
Anaemia is common
ESR very high
Abnormal monoclonal band on plasma protein electrophoresis
Bence-Jones protein positive in 50%
Increased number of abnormal plasma cells in the bone marrow
X-ray may show osteolytic lesions in the skull

60

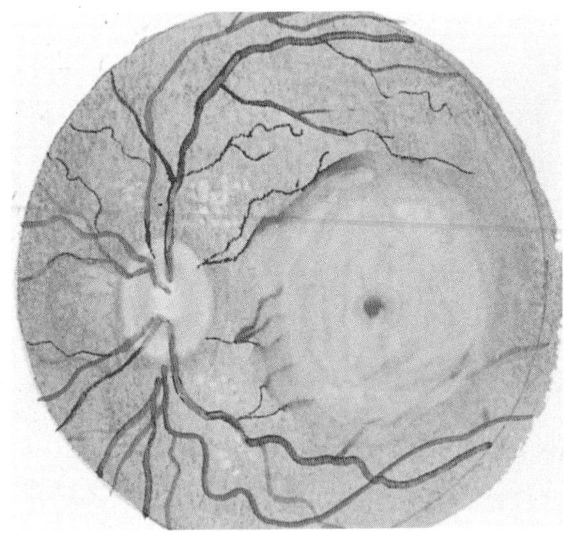

60 Central retinal artery thrombosis (artist's impression). Note the pallor resulting from ischaemia and the 'cherry-red spot'. In temporal arteritis, this can cause sudden blindness.

61

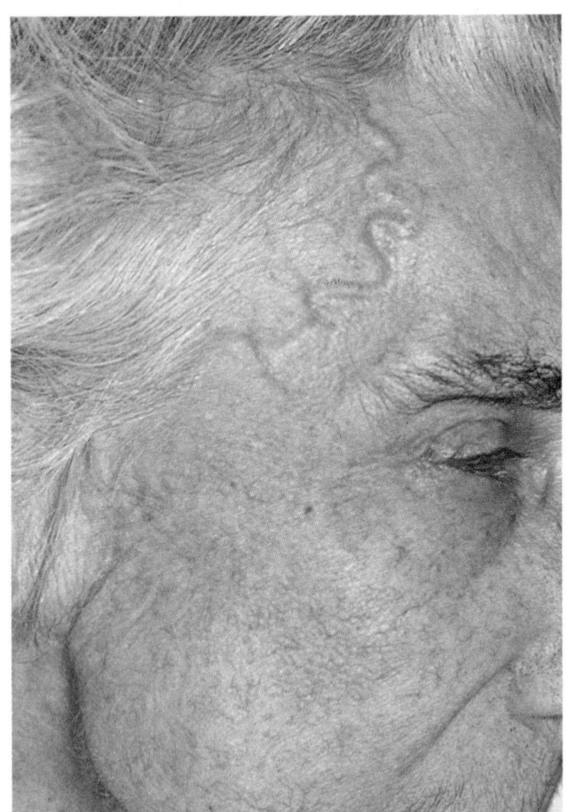

61 Temporal arteritis. An elderly lady presenting with severe unilateral headaches. She had tenderness over temporal artery and the erythrocyte sedimentation rate (ESR) was significantly raised.

Temporal arteritis

This condition is a true panarteritis and affects vessels of all sizes. Once suspected, it should be treated as a medical emergency.

The arterial wall is thickened by granulomatous tissue containing epitheloid and multinucleate giant cells, chronic inflammatory cell infiltration, necrotic foci and areas of fibrinoid change. Aneurysms may develop and sometimes there is segmental occlusion of affected vessels by thrombosis and intimal proliferation, leading to infarction of the tissues supplied by that blood vessel.

Most patients are over 70 years of age and the female to male ratio is 3:1.

Clinical features

Anorexia and weight loss, headaches and hyperalgesia of scalp. The temporal artery may be thickened, non-pulsating and tender
Pain on chewing
Neck stiffness
Blurred vision, sudden loss of vision
Fundi may show ischaemic papillopathy or central retinal artery occlusion. There may be coexistent polymyalgia rheumatica
Stroke

Polymyalgia rheumatica

A collagen disease related to temporal arteritis and occurring in old age.

Clinical features

General ill health and malaise
Anorexia
Aches and pains in the shoulders ('rheumatism')
Stiffness of arms and legs – difficulty in combing hair
Low-grade pyrexia
Headache and scalp tenderness
Normochromic normocytic anaemia
High ESR, usually over 50 mm/h
Increased serum immunoglobulins
Arterial biopsy will show giant-cell granulomata

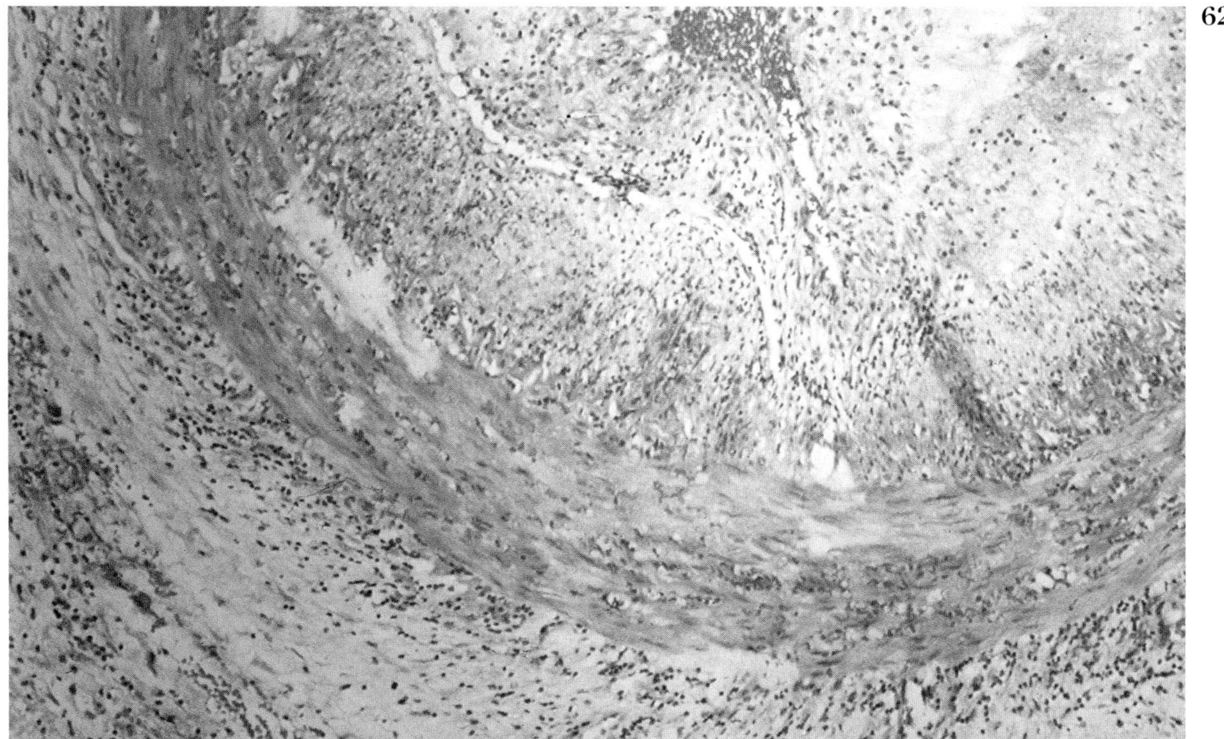

62 Temporal arteritis. Temporal artery biopsy showing inflammatory cell infiltration.

63

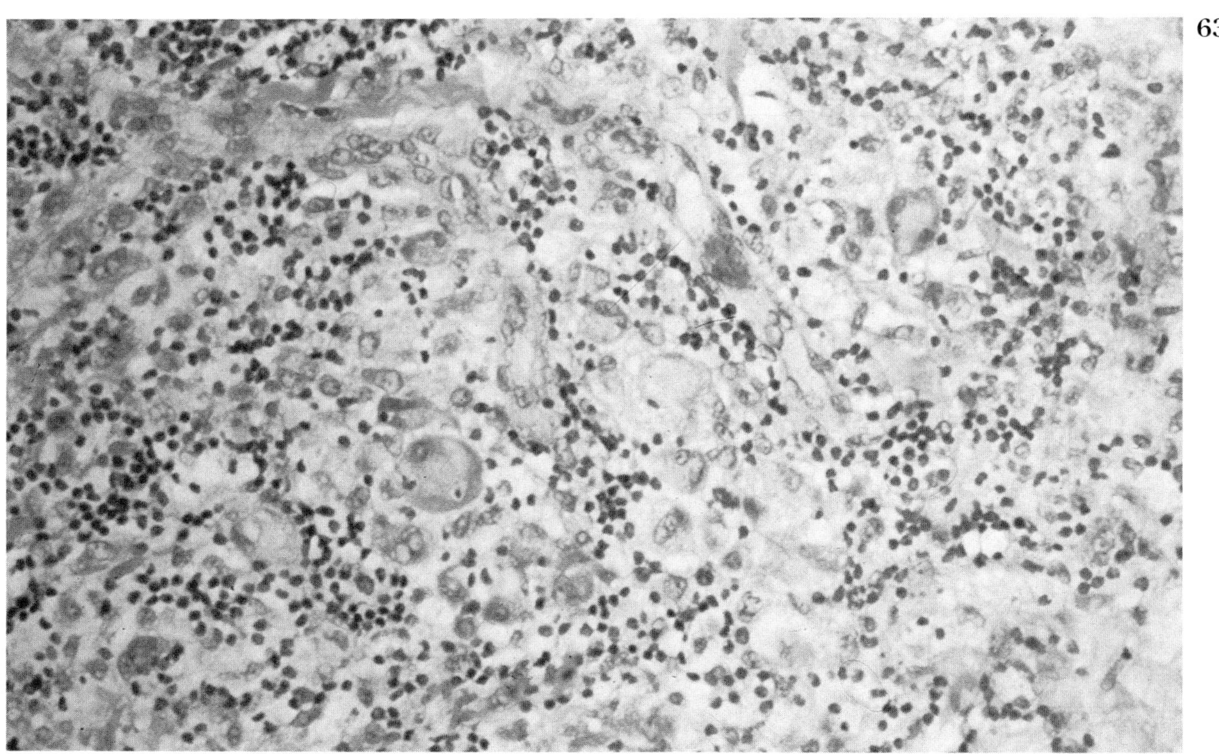

63 Temporal arteritis. Giant cells are visible among the inflammatory cell infiltration in the arterial wall.

64

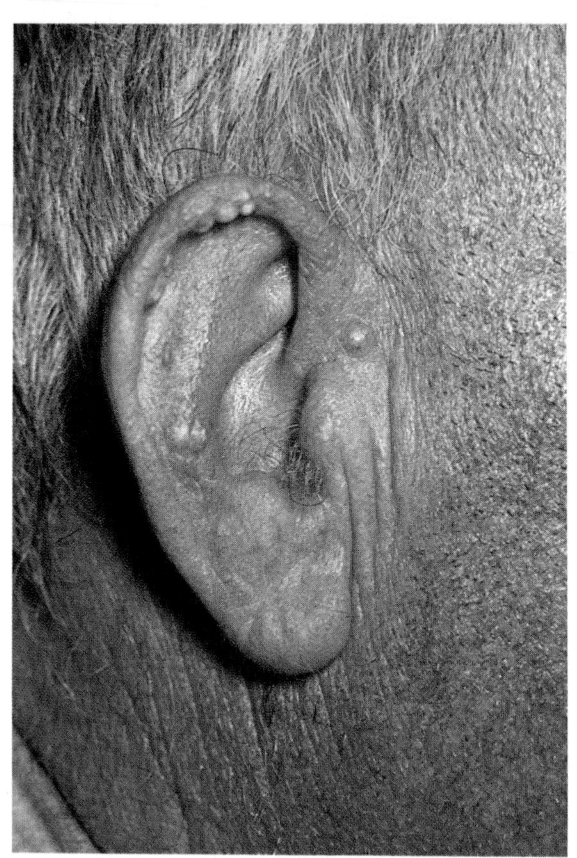

64 Gout. The pinna of the ear shows tophaceous gouty deposits. The patient had chronic gout, but the serum uric acid level was normal.

Common causes of hyperuricaemia in the elderly

Primary gout
Lymphomas
Multiproliferative disease
Chronic haemolytic disorders
Chronic renal failure
Starvation, vomiting
Diabetic ketoacidosis
Diuretics

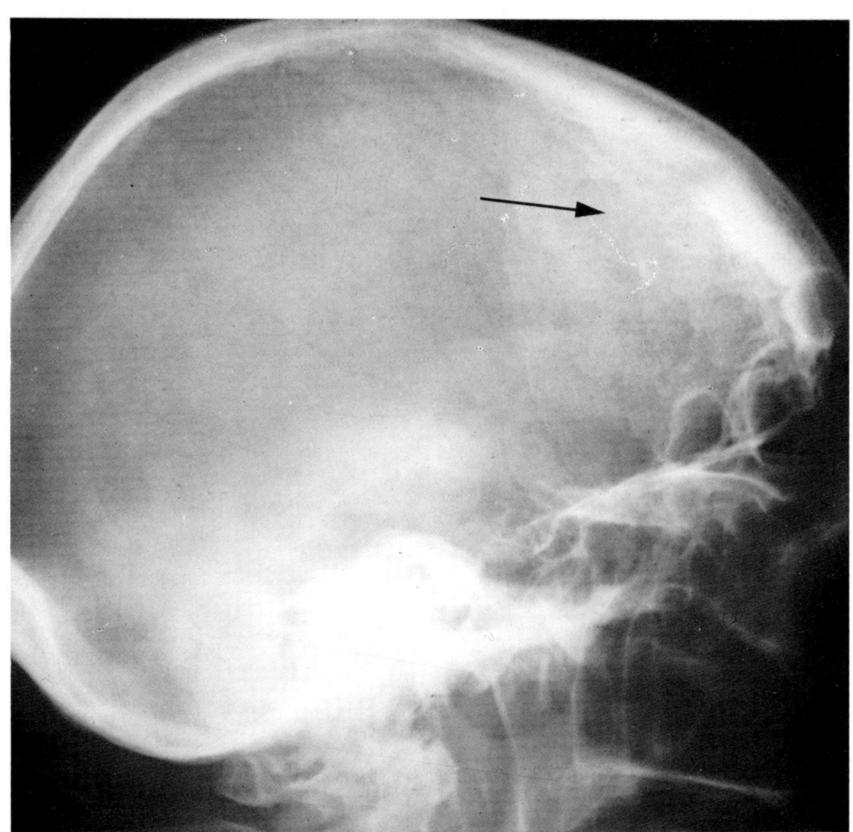

65

65 Hyperostosis frontalis interna (arrowed). A benign radiological appearance seen in the elderly. It used to be thought that this was associated with cerebral atrophy, but the evidence does not bear this out.

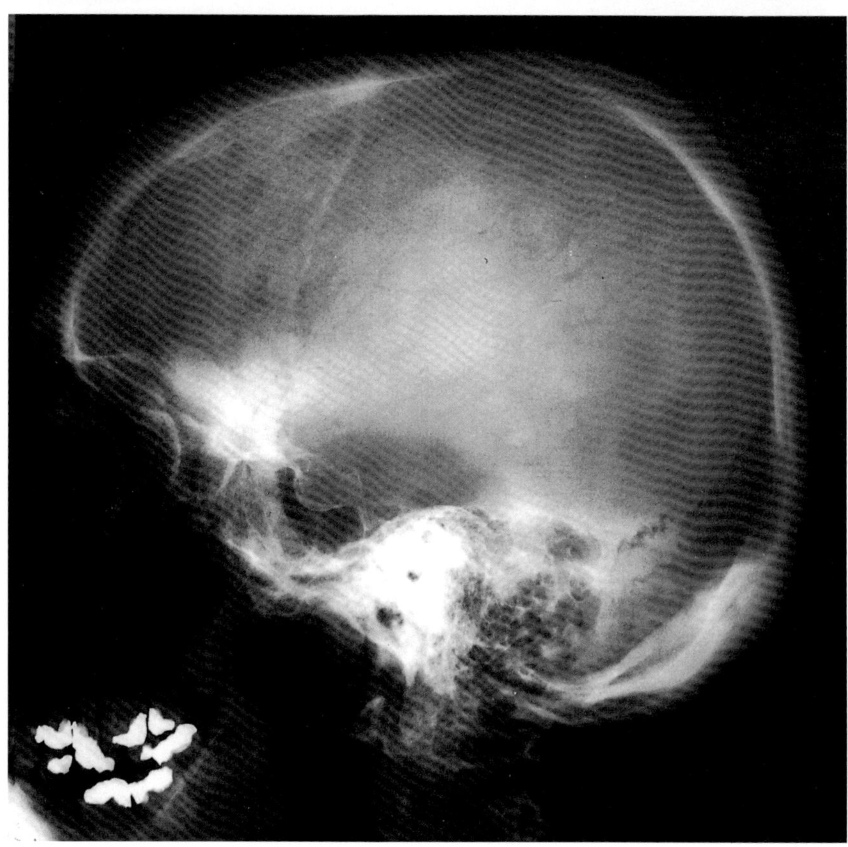

66

66 Sphenoid wing meningioma. Plain x-ray of skull showing hyperostosis, secondary to sphenoid wing meningioma. This appearance may be confused with benign hyperostosis and Paget's disease of the skull.

67

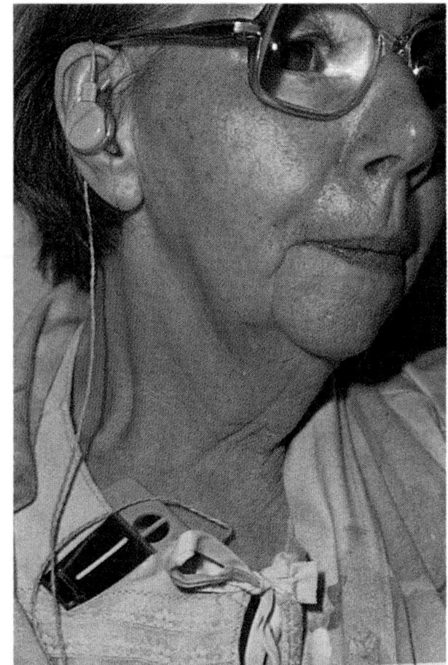

68

67 and 68 Hearing aids. Traditional hearing aids are basically electronic amplifiers. These instruments have limitations and require good maintenance and advisory facilities. Many elderly patients do not use hearing aids properly.

69

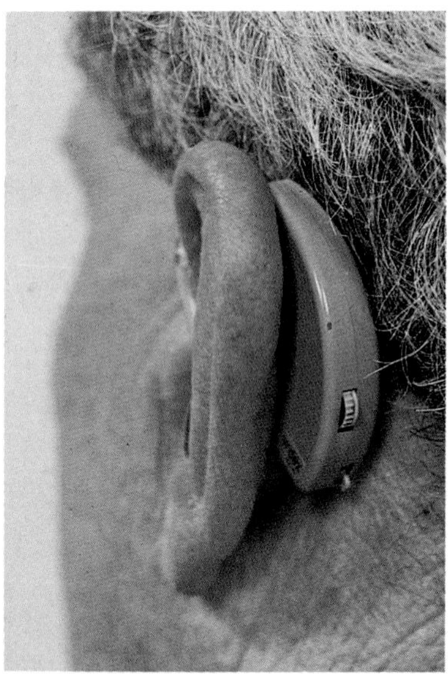

70

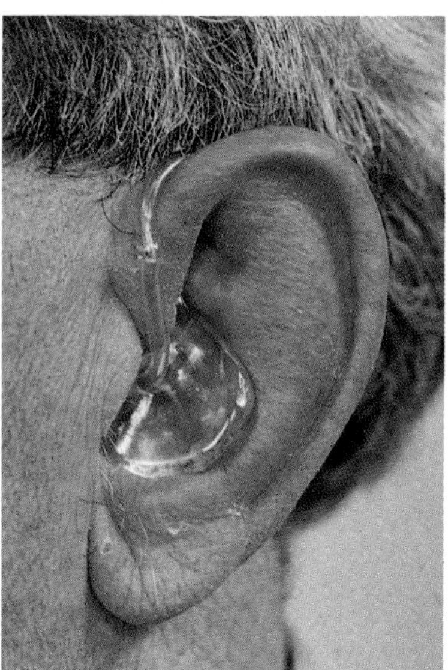

69 and 70 Hearing aid. A more modern form of hearing aid that has some advantages because of its small size and compactness.

71

71 Deaf-aid telephone. Note the additional ear-piece which improves the stereophonic hearing.

Deafness

Associated problems
Sensory deprivation
Social deprivation
Withdrawal
Depression
Slow responses
Agitation

Common causes in the elderly
Presbyacusis – sensory neural hearing loss of between 10 and 60 dB
Wax in external auditory canal
Perforation of tympanic membrane
Otosclerosis
Meniere's disease
Herpes zoster infection
Acoustic neuroma
High-dosage or long-lasting drugs:
- Quinine (for cramps)
- Kanomycin
- Neomycin
- Ethacrynic acid
- Frusemide

72

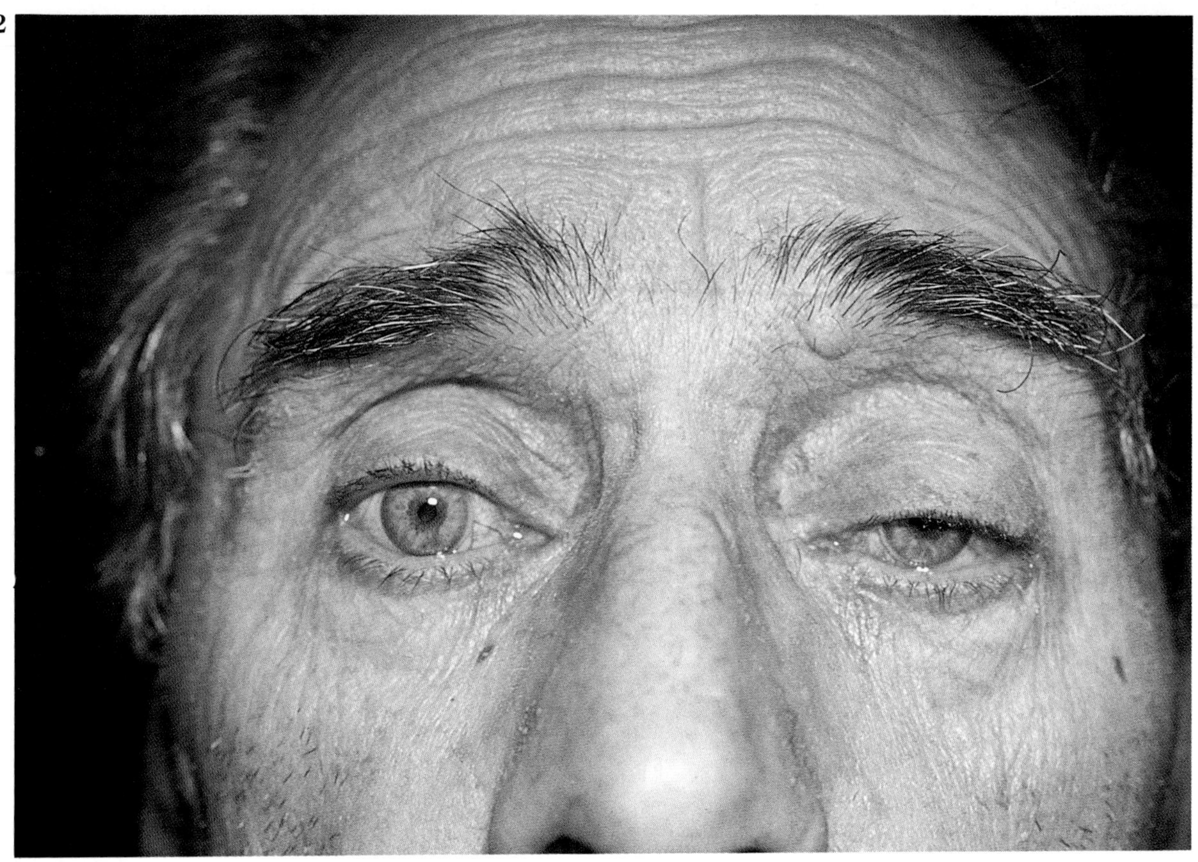

72 Ptosis. Left-sided ptosis caused by a lesion involving the cervical sympathetic chain.

Causes of ptosis

Congenital
Simple ptosis

Acquired
Neurogenic:
Traumatic ophthalmoplegia
Congenital third nerve palsy
Vascular lesions
Tumours
Ophthalmoplegic migraine
Horner's syndrome
Multiple sclerosis

Myogenic:
Senile ptosis
Myasthenia gravis
Late acquired hereditary ptosis
Corticosteroid-induced ptosis

Traumatic:
Surgical and accidental

73

73 Horner's syndrome. An elderly man with Horner's syndrome showing ptosis on the left side.

74

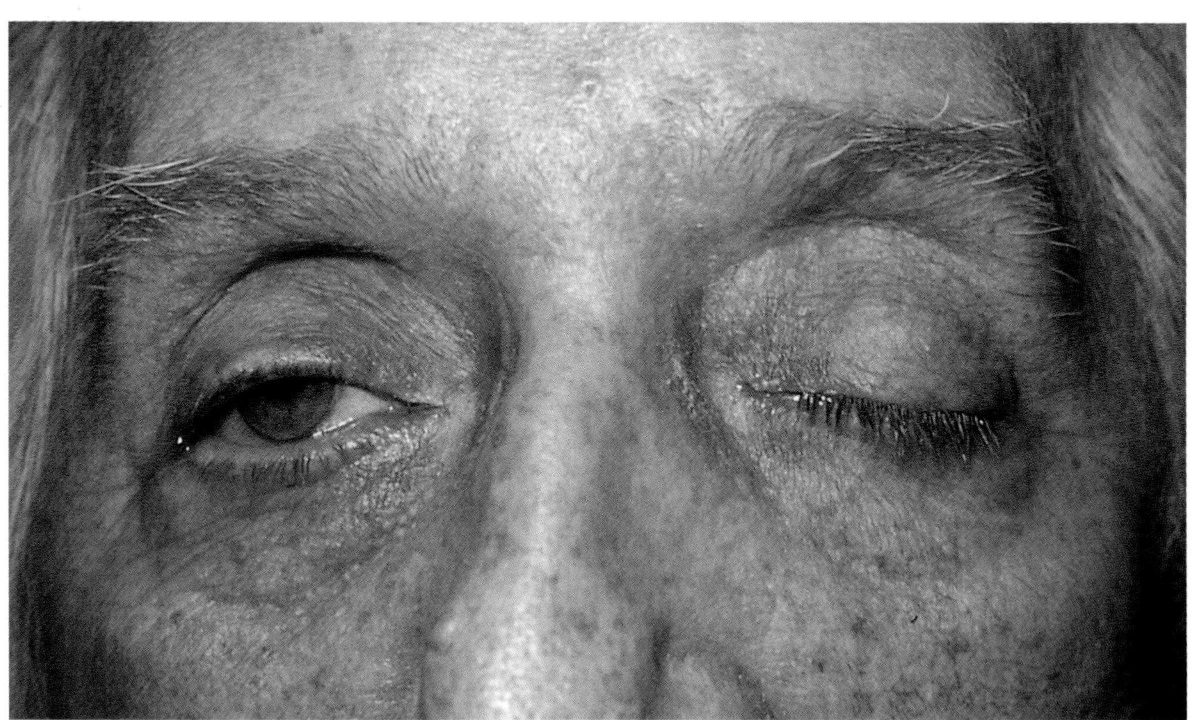

74 Horner's syndrome. Another case, showing complete left-sided ptosis.

75

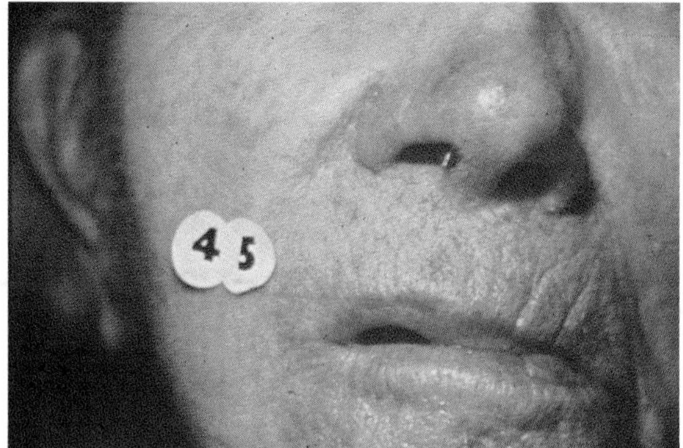

7

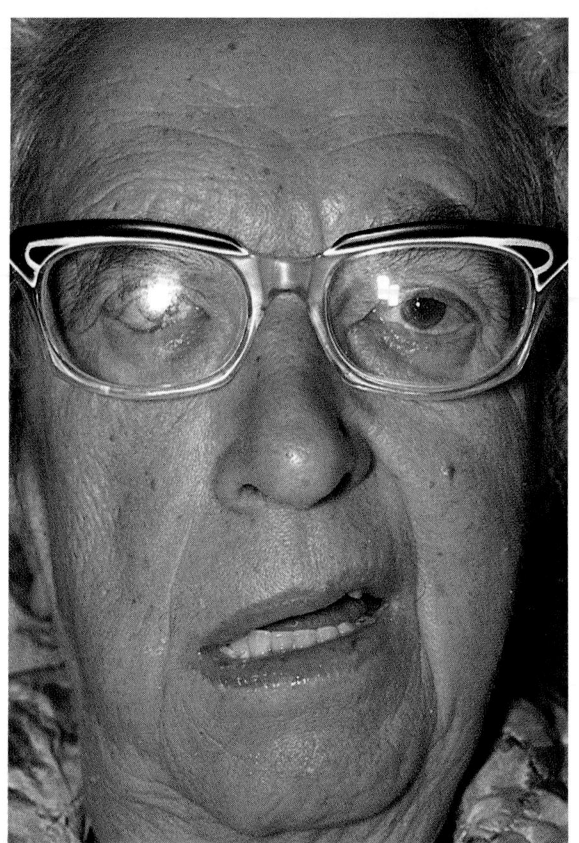

75 Nasolabial seborrhoea in facial palsy. This condition is sometimes associated with vitamin B complex deficiency (in association with cheilosis and angular stomatitis).

76 Facial palsy. Right-sided facial palsy which gradually improved over a period of months. It was associated with a cerebrovascular accident (CVA) causing hemiplegia.

77 Xanthelasmas. The patient had a family history of ischaemic heart disease and presented with myocardial infarction. The blood lipids were only marginally raised.

77

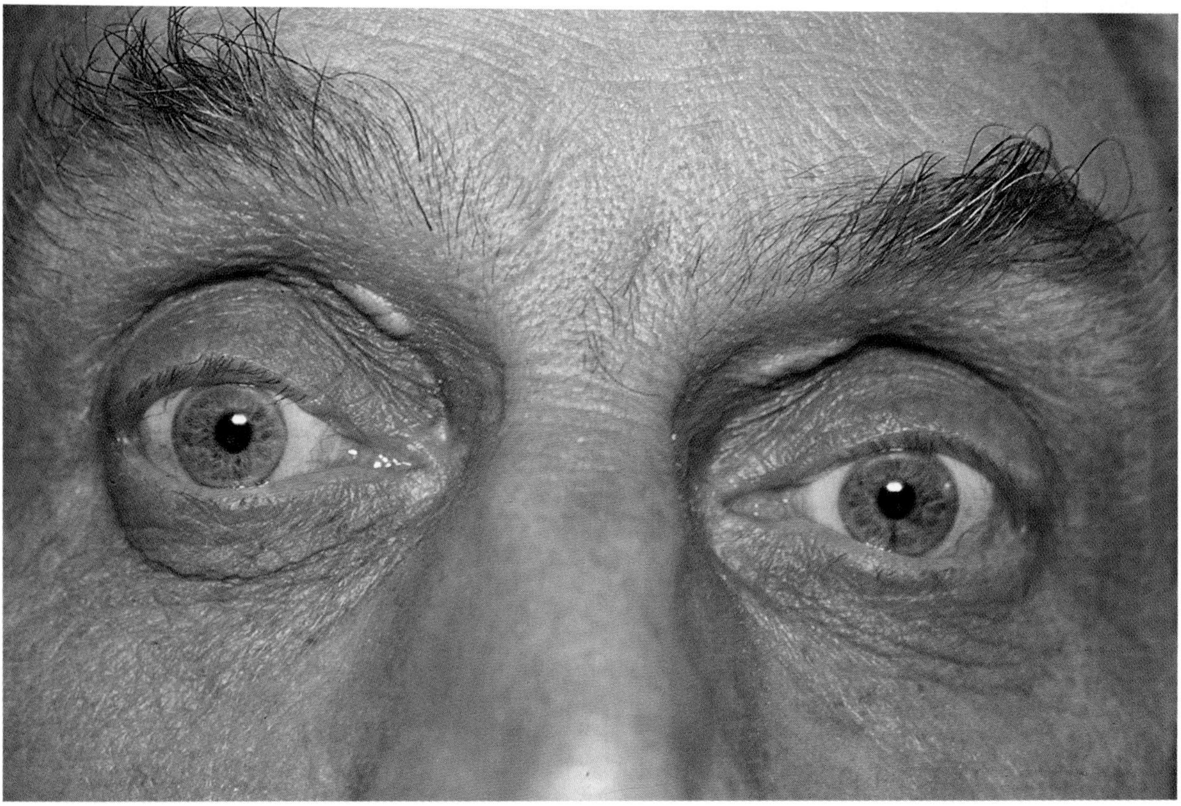

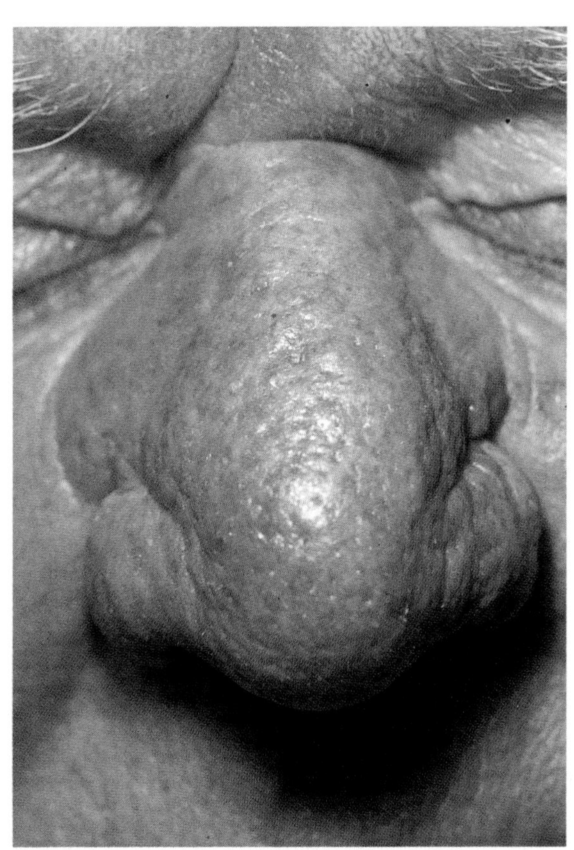
78

78 Rhinophyma. Increase in soft tissue, sebaceous gland hypertrophy and secondary acne may result from increased vascularity in the centre of the face. Rhinophyma is a variant of rosacea.

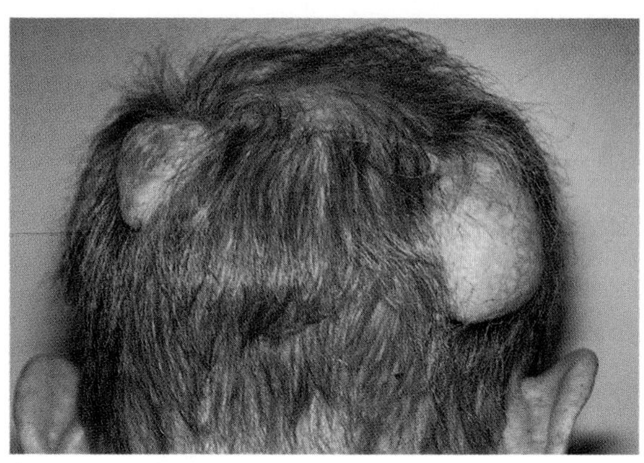
79

79 Sebaceous cysts. Giant sebaceous cysts on the scalp of an elderly man. Most of these are retention cysts caused by plugging of the orifice with sebaceous material. Suppuration is a frequent complication.

80

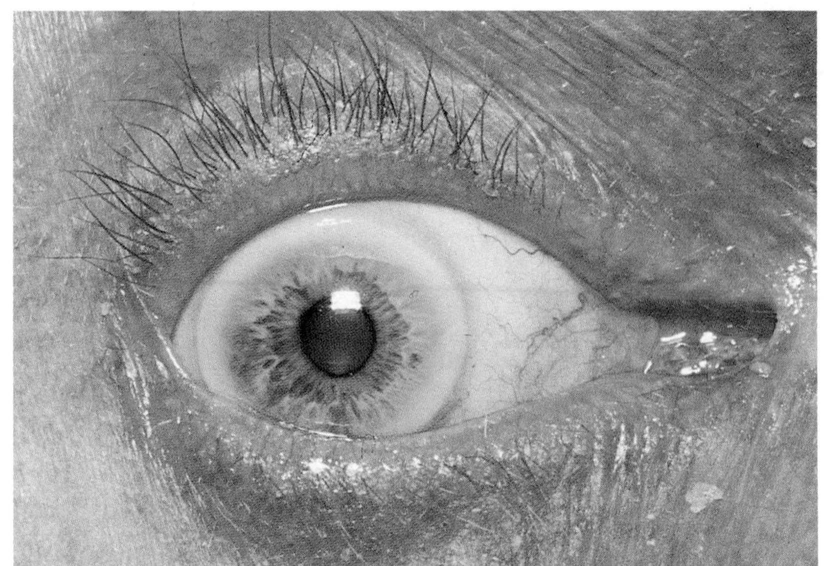

80 Arcus senilis (Gerontoxon). A common finding in the elderly but of no pathological significance. It is formed by lipid deposition at the periphery of the cornea. This condition is also found in familial hypercholesterolaemias.

81

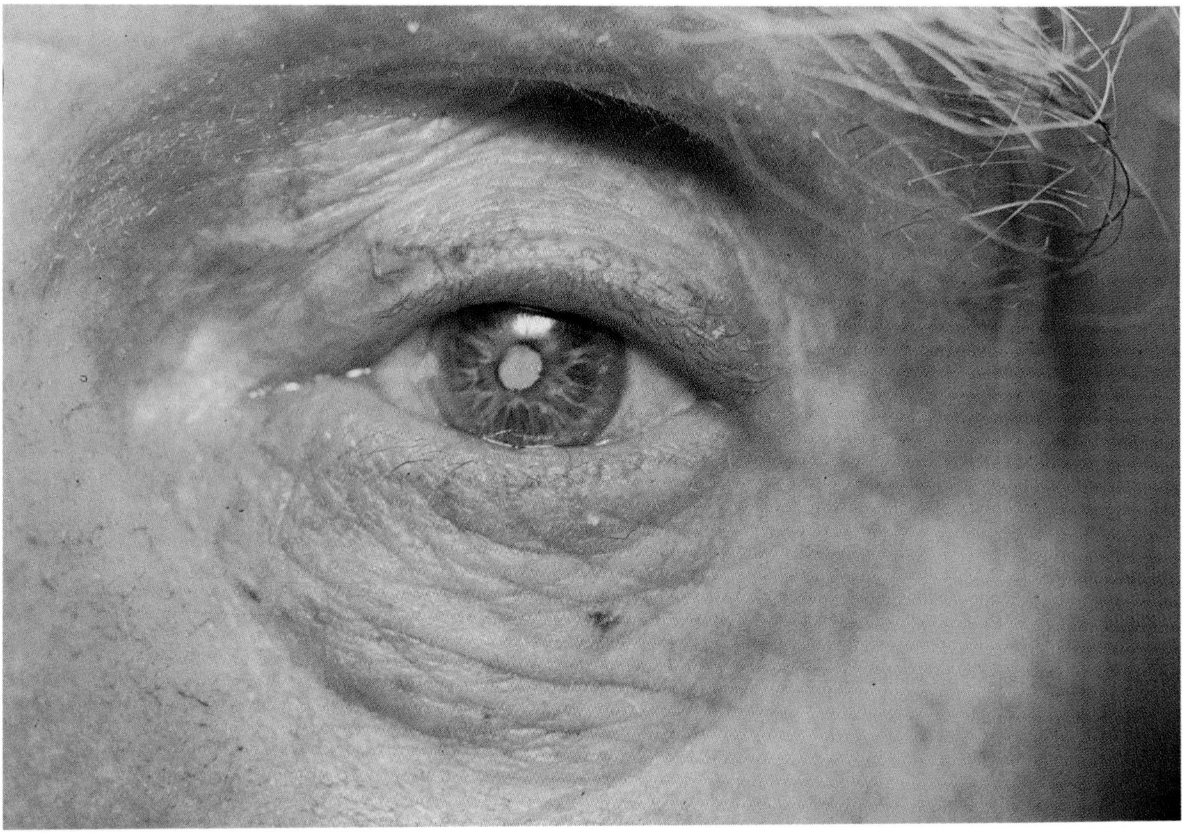

81 Cataract. A mature, senile cataract contributing to the patient's disability and lack of independence.

82

82 Conjunctivitis. A common eye complaint in the elderly, especially residents of long-stay wards. It is usually a keratoconjunctivitis and the aetiologic agent in most cases is an adenovirus.

83

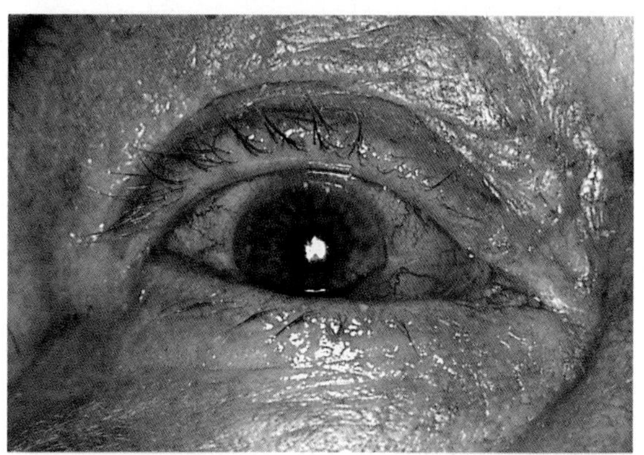

83 Glaucoma. A case of acute glaucoma in an elderly patient presenting with painful red eye and rapid deterioration of vision. The pupil is unresponsive to light and there is oedema of the cornea. This is a medical emergency and urgent treatment is required to preserve the eyesight.

84

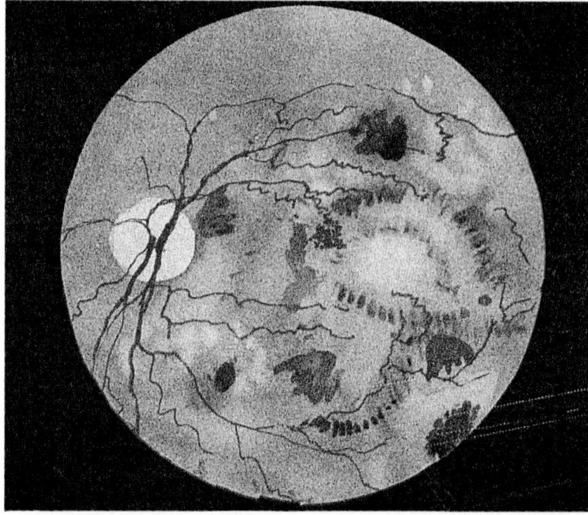

84 Macular degeneration (artist's impression). A common cause of failing eyesight with advancing age. Note the coarse, dark mottling around the macula.

Some important causes of visual impairment in older patients

Cataracts
Glaucoma
Senile macular degeneration
Outdated spectacles
Temporal arteritis
Cerebrovascular accident
Retinal vein thrombosis
Retinal artery thrombosis
Retinal detachment
Old keratitis or uveitis
Paget's disease
Optic nerve atrophy

85

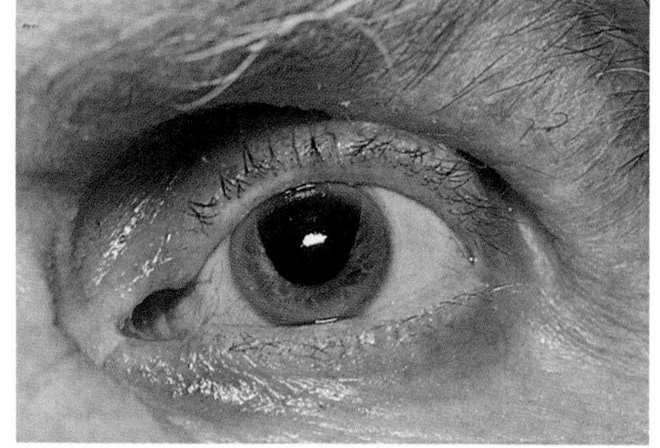

85 Iridectomy. Irregular pupil after an iridectomy for cataract. This irregularity must be differentiated from other causes of pupillary abnormalities.

86

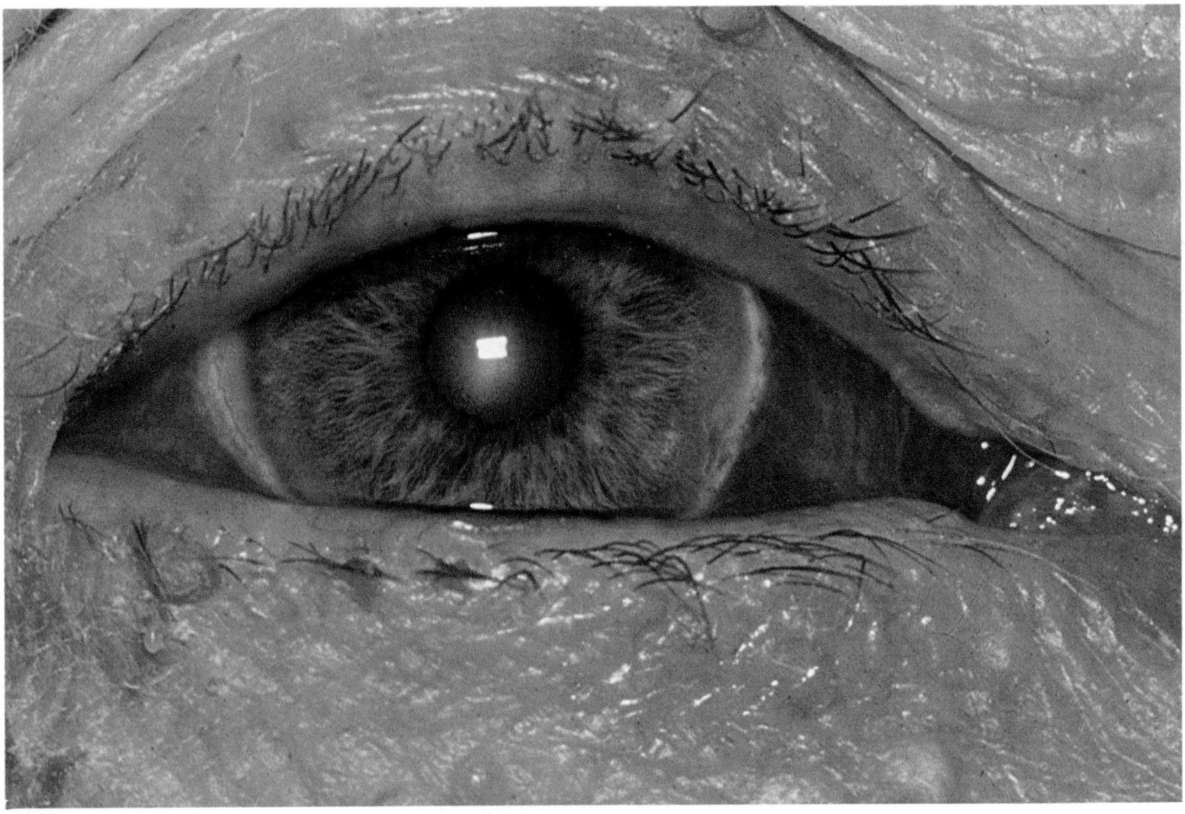

87

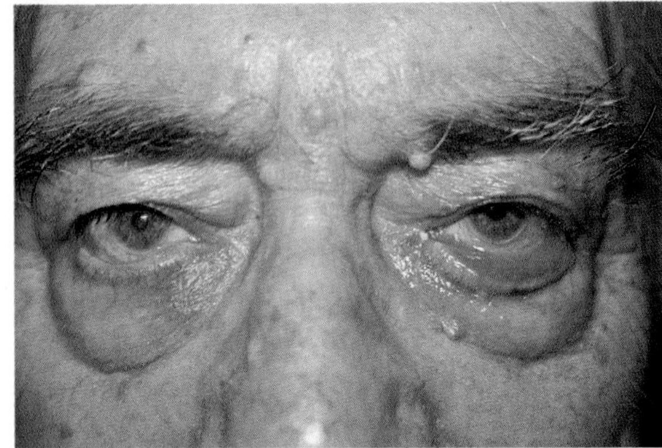

88

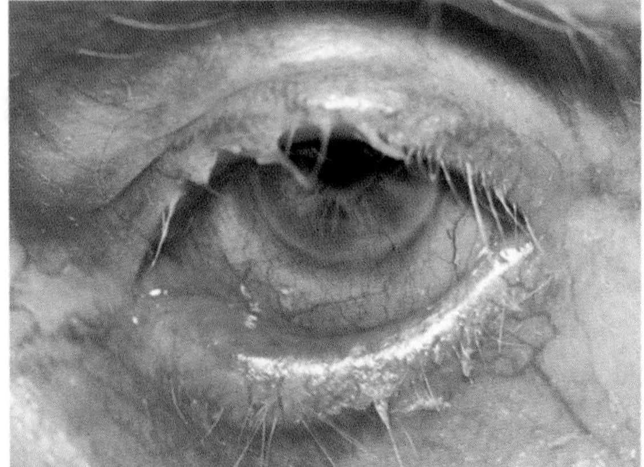

86 Subconjunctival haemorrhage. Alarming in appearance but harmless and self-resolving. In this case it was induced by straining at stools.

87 Ectropion. Chronic ectropion of left lower eyelid resulting in epiphora.

Painful red eye

Stye
Foreign body
Conjunctivitis
Corneal ulcer (e.g. herpetic)
Keratitis
Acute glaucoma
Uveitis

88 Ectropion. Laxity of eyelids is an important mechanism in ectropion of lower eyelid. Wedge resection of lower eyelid with application of skin graft is the method of treatment. This patient also had chronic conjunctivitis.

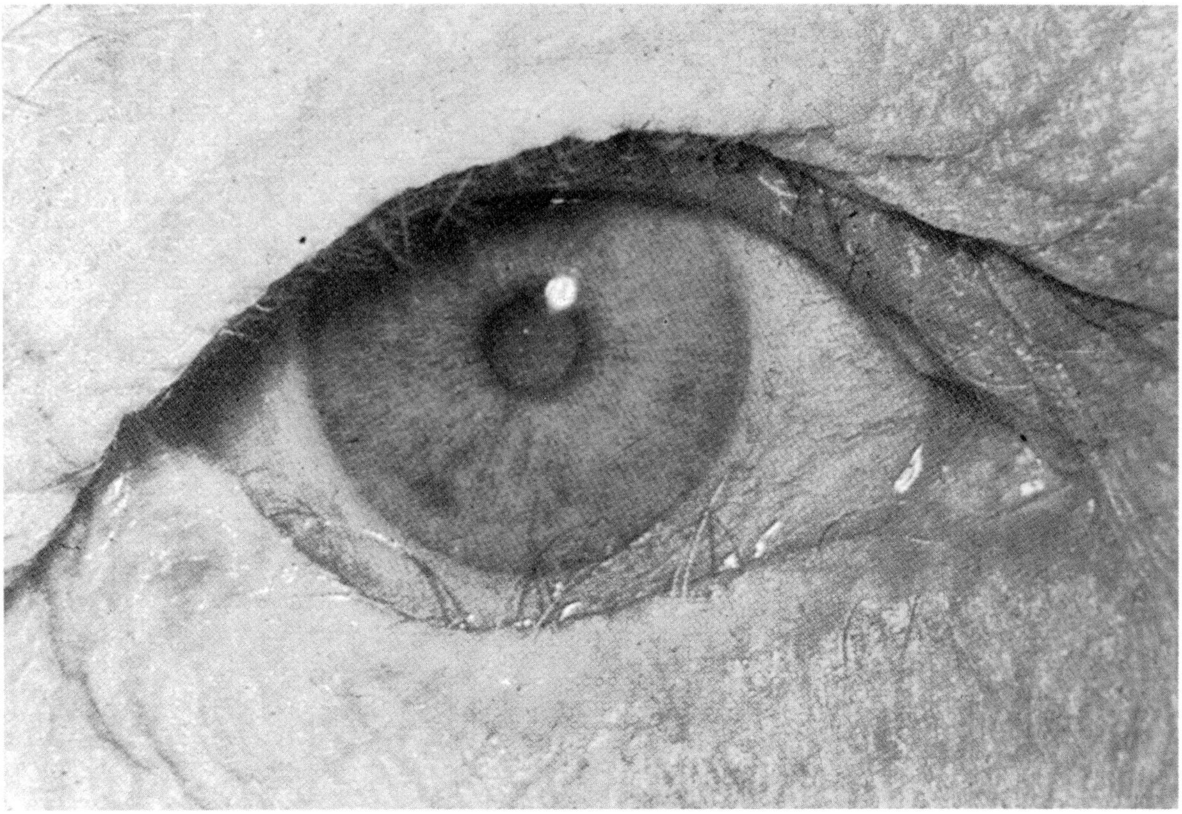

89

89 Senile entropion. The margin of the lower eyelid has rolled backwards and the eyelashes are brushing against the conjunctiva and cornea.

90

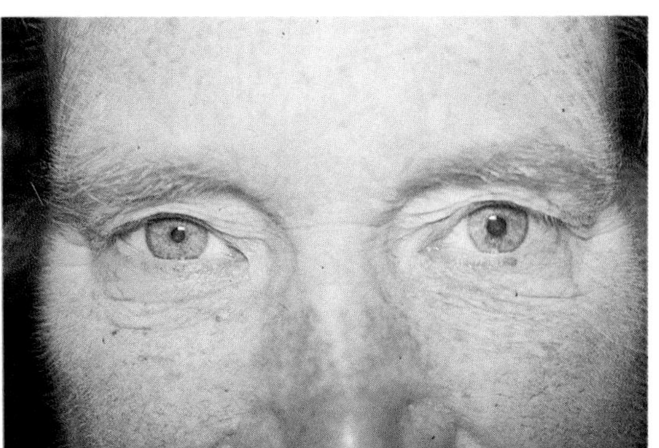

90 Unequal pupils. The right pupil is dilated in a patient with intracerebral haemorrhage. This pupillary dilatation is less than what might be expected in a younger person.

Conditions in which pupillary abnormalities occur

Lesions of sympathetic fibres
Midbrain lesions
Pontine haemorrhage
Subdural haematoma
Tabes dorsalis
Multiple sclerosis
Diabetes mellitus
Holmes–Adie's pupil
Drugs, e.g. atropine, morphine
Local eye disorders

91

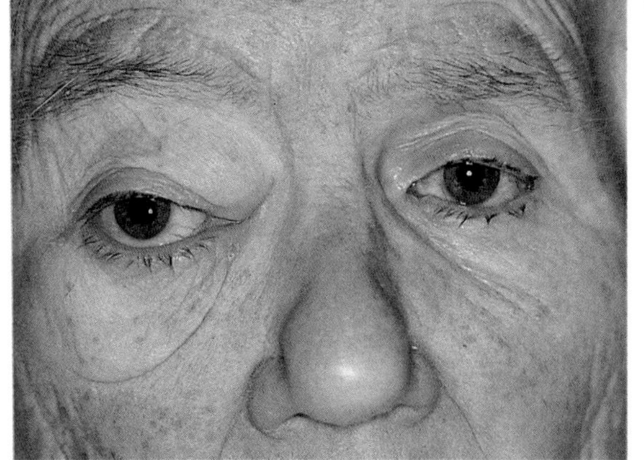

91 Proptosis. The left eye is protruding and also pushed downwards. This patient had a retro-orbital glioma presenting with headaches, unsteadiness, falls and confusion.

92

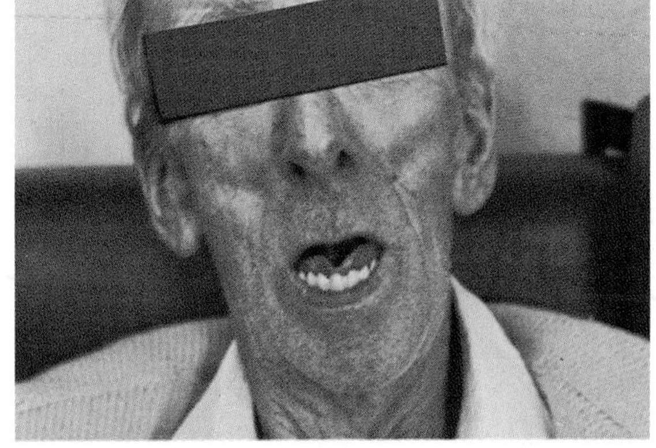

92 Ill-fitting dentures. Caused by shrinkage of the gums and jaw with advancing age. May also occur after a stroke with facial paralysis. Ill-fitting dentures can lead to poor nutrition in the elderly. One-third to two-thirds of patients complain of looseness or soreness.

93

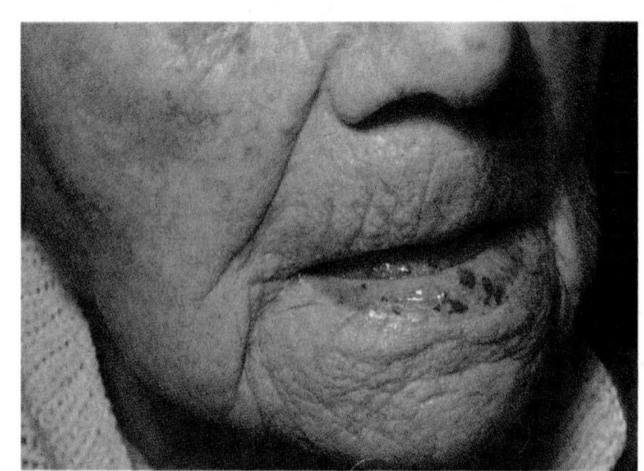

93 Telangiectasia. A case of hereditary haemorrhagic telangiectasia in an elderly man. The telangiectasia are visible in the mucous membrane of lips and increase in number in cases of anaemia, gastrointestinal haemorrhage and as age advances. Epistaxis is a common complaint.

94

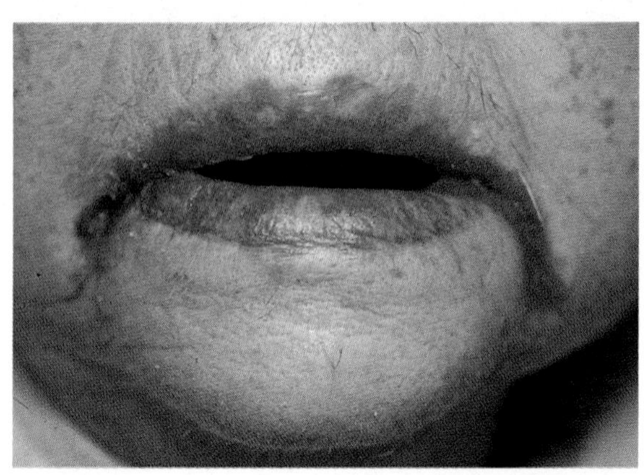

94 Angular stomatitis. This elderly patient, a spinster, was undernourished and had multi-vitamin deficiency.

95

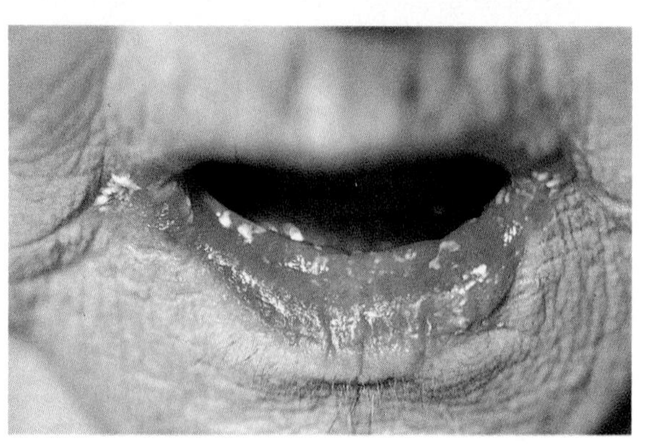

95 Angular stomatitis. Note the associated cheilosis. The patient had iron-deficiency anaemia. This change is often found as a result of nutrient deficiency.

96 Dry-coated tongue. This patient was dehydrated, with high blood urea and low urinary output. Dry tongue may also occur in mouth breathers and is a non-specific finding.

Causes of stomatitis

- Aphthous ulcers
- Debility
- Smoking
- Alcoholism
- Herpes simplex, candidosis
- Pyorrhoea and alveolar abscess
- Stevens–Johnson syndrome
- Neutropenia and leukaemia
- Iron deficiency, vitamin B complex (including vitamin B_{12} and folate) deficiency
- Pemphigus vulgaris and benign pemphigus of mucous membranes
- Lichen planus
- Cytotoxic drugs, antibiotics, emepronium bromide and potassium supplements
- Leukoplakia, neoplasm
- Ill-fitting dentures.

96

97

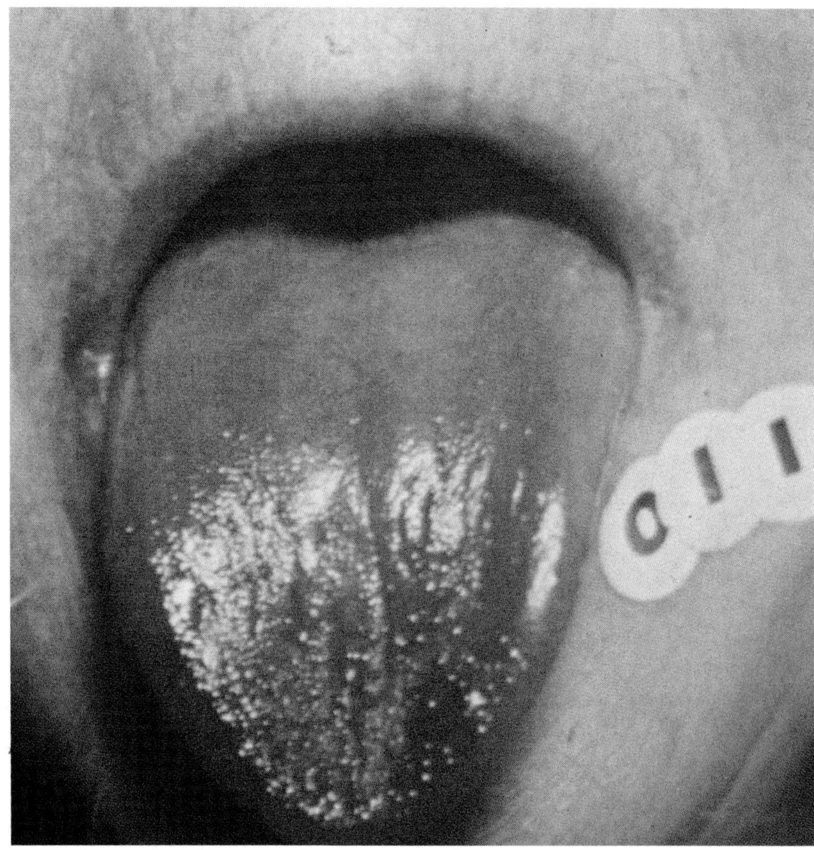

97 Glossitis. Sore, inflamed tongue in a case of Vitamin B_{12} deficiency anaemia. Glossitis can also occur as a result of poor oral hygiene, pipe smoking, etc.

98

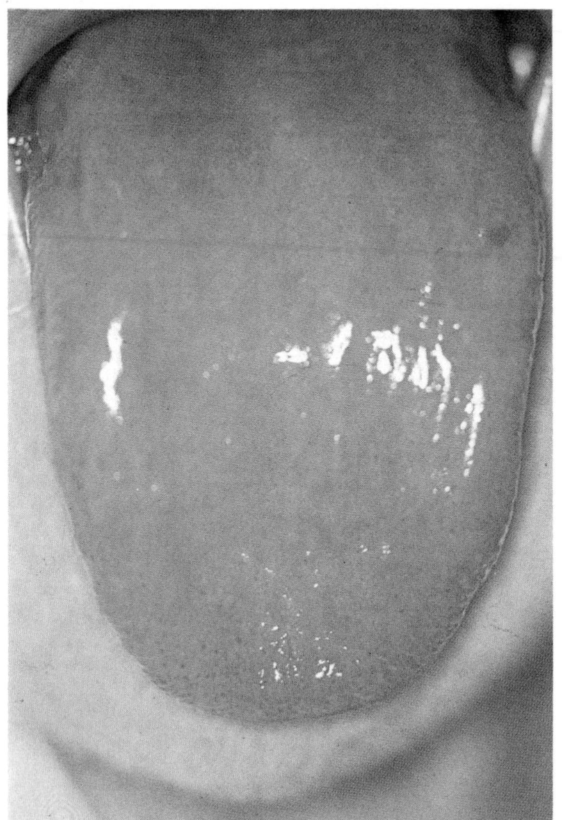

9

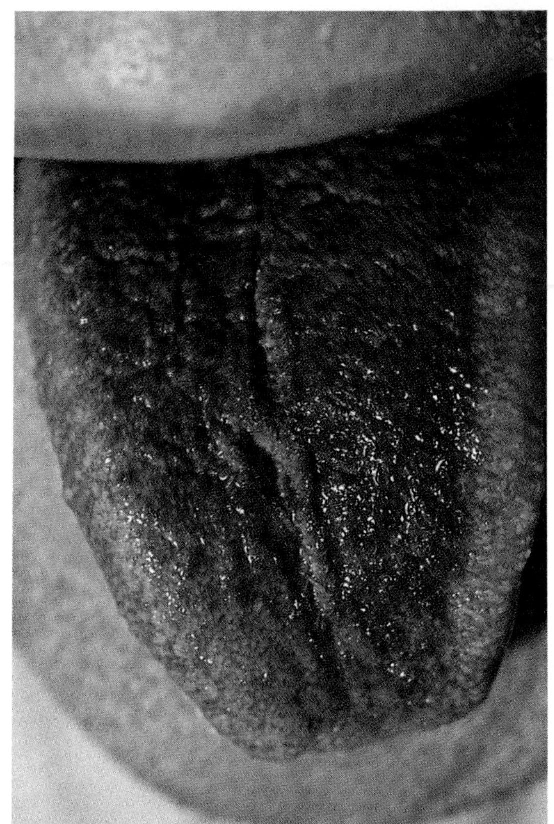

100

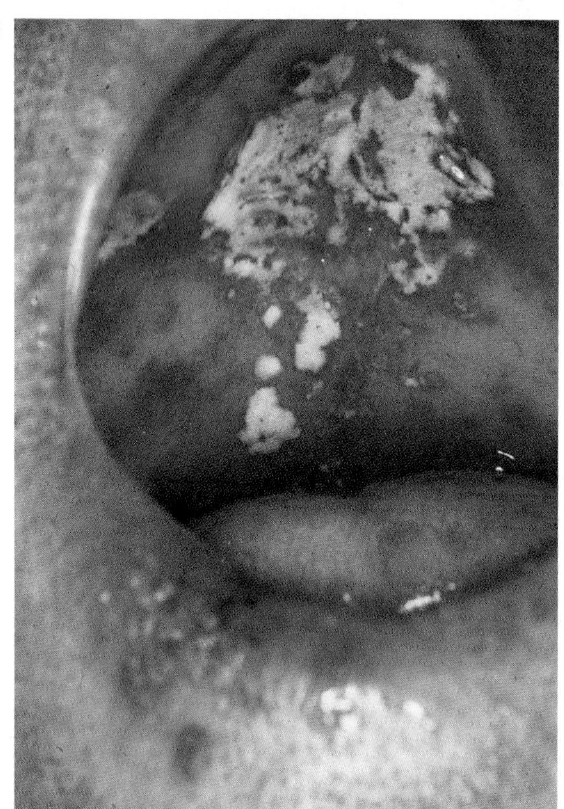

98 Smooth, glazed tongue. Atrophic glossitis in an elderly lady with chronic iron-deficiency anaemia.

99 Hairy (black) tongue. Elongation of filiform papillae of the medial dorsal surface area caused by failure of keratin layer of the papillae to desquamate normally; brownish, black coloration may be caused by tobacco staining, food or chromogenic organisms.

100 Leukaemia. Thrush and petechiae in the oral cavity in a case of leukaemia.

101

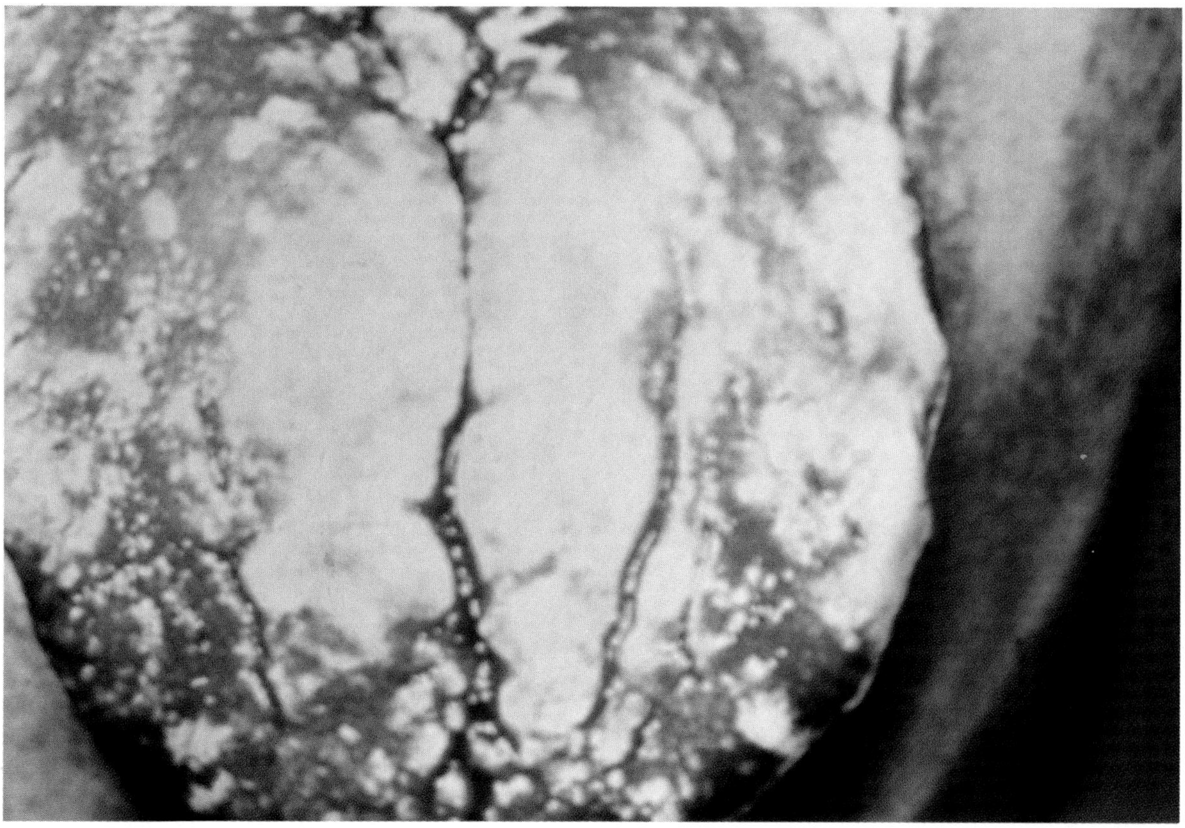

101 Candidiasis (thrush). Involving the oral cavity and mainly the tongue, in this case. The adherent and painful white patches are typical of the condition.

102

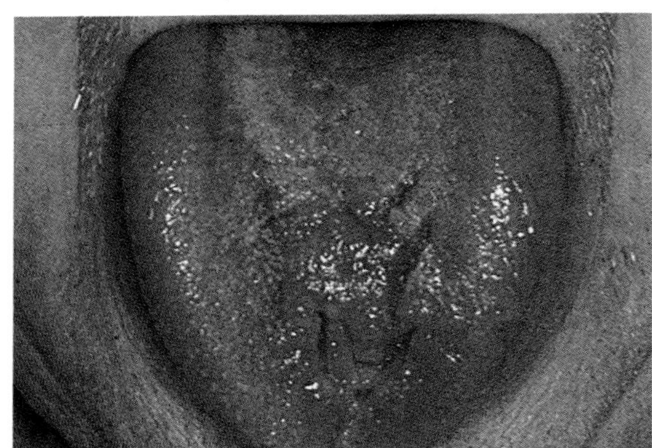

103

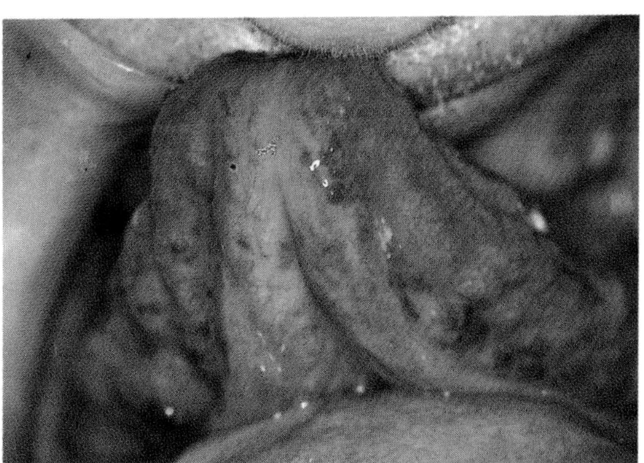

102 Carcinoma of the tongue. A small, painless ulcer on the tongue which failed to heal within a few weeks. Squamous-cell carcinoma is the most common malignant oral tumour; half of these involve the tongue.

103 Sublingual varicosities. A common finding in the elderly that used to be linked to vitamin C deficiency but now known to be of no particular significance.

104

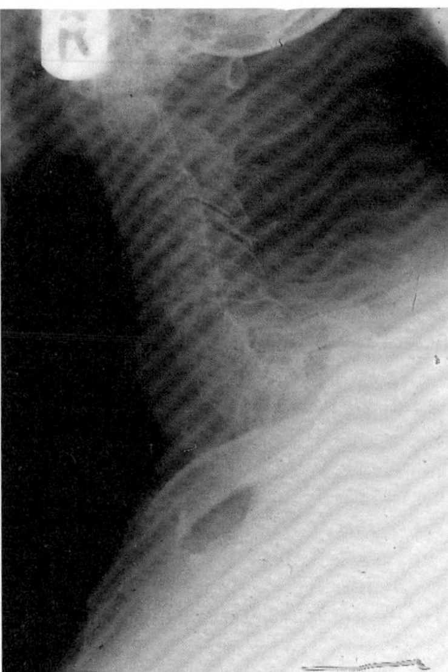

105

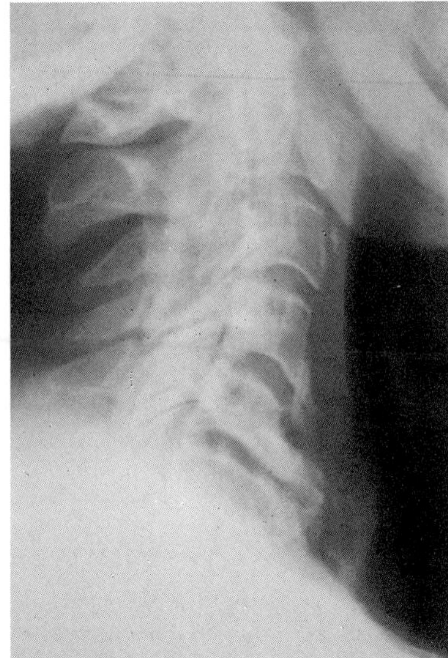

106

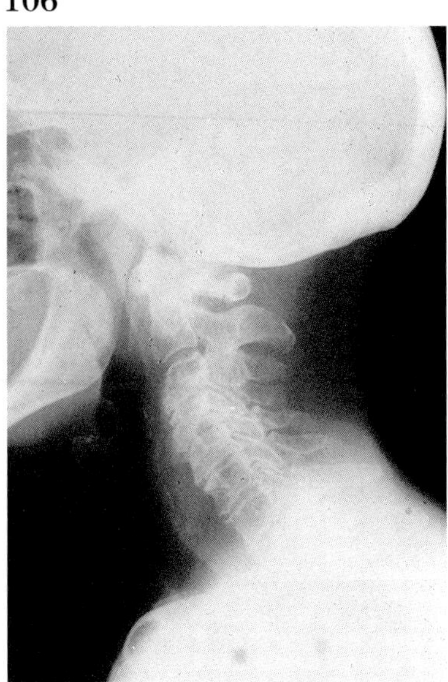

Cervical spondylosis

Radiological changes of cervical spine degenerative disease are almost universal after 70 years of age. The relation between symptoms and x-ray changes is very poor.

There is an association between cervical spondylosis and postural imbalance caused by disturbance of cervical articular mechanoreceptor function.

Cervical spondylosis frequently coexists with vertebrobasilar insufficiency.

Clinical features

Brachial radiculitis – pain and paraesthaesia
Headache, giddiness and faints
Drop attacks
Diplopia
Facial sensory disturbances
Dysarthria
Weakness of legs and unsteadiness
Paraplegia or quadriplegia in severe cases

104 Cervical spondylosis. Degenerative changes are present, with particular narrowing of the disc faces between C6 and C7. There is associated osteophyte formation with encroachment on the intervertebral foramina.

105 Cervical spondylosis. There are advanced degenerative changes affecting most joints. The normal curvature is lost and the patient may present with neckache, paraesthesia in upper limbs, dizziness and drop attacks.

106 Cervical spondylosis. Note that the atlas has shifted forward on the axis (C2). This is an emergency. Urgent orthopaedic attention is required because there is danger of the patient developing quadriplegia.

5 Disorders of the Brain

Clinical manifestations of cerebrovascular disease

- Transient cerebral ischaemic attacks (TIAs)
- Stroke – completed or in evolution
- Multi-infarct dementia
- Pseudobulbar palsy
- Epilepsy

Transient cerebral ischaemic attacks (TIAs)

Disorder of cerebral function resulting from vascular causes in which full recovery occurs within 24 hours. If neurological disability lasts for more than 24 hours it is classified as a stroke-in-evolution or a completed stroke. TIAs are important to recognise because they presage a full-blown cerebrovascular accident.

In cases of suspected TIAs the precise history should be established. The following symptoms tend to occur frequently in the elderly and may be confused with TIAs:

- Chronic unsteadiness and dizziness
- Simple faints or syncope
- Blurring of vision alone
- Confusion alone

They are usually due to conditions other than TIAs. Many of the conditions contributing to development of TIAs can be treated. Treatable causes of TIAs and minor strokes are:

- Giant cell arteritis
- Polycythaemia rubra vera
- Hyperviscosity
- Cardiac lesions causing cerebral embolism
- Atrial fibrillation with rheumatic heart disease
- Acute myocardial infarction
- Artificial valve prosthesis
- Infective endocarditis
- Non-penetrating trauma to carotid artery

Aetiology

Main pathological abnormalities are atheroma and hypertension. Precipitating factors are:

Microemboli from platelet aggregates on artheromatous ulcer.

Hypotension – myocardial infarction, congestive heart failure, dysrhythmias, postural hypotension, 'steal' syndrome.

Miscellaneous – anaemia, polycythaemia, giant cell arteritis, cervical spondylosis, drugs (e.g. sedatives).

Assessment of patients with TIAs

History

Family history, contraceptive pill, smoker, syphilis.

Examination

Especially blood pressure, unequal pupils, neck bruits, retinal changes, heart murmurs, CNS signs.

Investigations

Blood – haemoglobin, PCV, hyperlipidaemia, VDRL.

Chest x-ray – aneurysm, cardiomegaly.

Ultrasound of neck – flow disturbances at carotid bifunction.

Ultrasound of heart – atrial myxoma, abnormal parachute valves.

Angiography – only if surgery is a serious consideration.

24-hour ECG – cardiac arrhythmias.

Clinical features of carotid TIAs

Hemiparesis, paraesthesia, hemianopia, blindness (amaurosis fugax), dysphasia, dysphagia, confusion, carotid artery bruit.

Clinical features of vertebrobasilar TIAs

Vertigo, nystagmus, drop attacks, diplopia, dysarthria, dysphagia, amnesia, sudden weakness.

Completed stroke

In completed stroke the neurological damage reaches its peak in 6 to 24 hours and results in prolonged disability.

Aetiology
Major cause is cerebral infarction due to a combination of thrombosis and inadequate perfusion of brain tissue. Hypertension and other factors that contribute to the development of atheroma are aetiologically important, in both TIAs and strokes. Cerebral damage may also result from embolus from heart or great vessels, cerebral haemorrhage and subarachnoid haemorrhage.

Clinical features
Symptoms and signs depend on extent and site of brain damage. The carotid territory is most often involved.

The onset is usually sudden or rapid:
- Impairment of consciousness
- Hemiparesis with extensor plantar reflex
- Ipsilateral sensory loss
- Hemianopia
- Dysphagia
- Cortical sensory loss when there is damage to parietal lobe
- Disturbance of attention
- Loss of recognition of body image

In left-sided lesions – dyslexia, agraphia, acalculia.
Lesions involving thalamus may produce persistent pain, hypersensitivity and involuntary movements.
Lesions involving dominant hemisphere may produce loss of postural control and gait disorders.
Ischaemia in vertebrobasilar territory may produce a tendency to lean and fall backwards.

Complications following a stroke

Major complications
- Pressure sores
- Respiratory tract infections
- Urinary incontinence
- Constipation
- Deep vein thrombosis
- Spasticity and contractures
- Pain in the shoulder (frozen shoulder)
- Psychiatric problems

Miscellaneous complications
- Oedema of the paralysed limb
- Reversal of sleeping habits
- Malnutrition secondary to pseudobulbar palsy
- Postural hypotension
- Long thoracic nerve palsy – wing scapula
- Ulna nerve palsy – drop wrist
- Median nerve palsy
- Reflex dystrophy of the hand
- Foot drop
- Sciatic neuropathy – caused by prolonged pressure over the sciatic notch in an immobile patient
- Hyperextension of the knee
- Perceptual problems
- Epilepsy in up to 15% of patients
- Osteoporosis in the paralysed limb
- Torticollis
- Complete loss of posture and balance
- Fractured neck of femur, especially in the elderly, because of falls

Prevention of strokes

- *Preventing atherosclerosis*
  Important aetiological factors include hypertension, stress, diabetes mellitus, diet rich in fats, smoking and lack of exercise.

- *Early treatment of hypertension*
  In the elderly, one should balance the advantages of treatment against adverse effects of anti-hypertensive drugs and the cost of treatment. Consideration should be given to such important factors as quality of life, mental state of the patient, coexisting disabilities and the problems of drug compliance.

- *Treatment of transient ischaemic attacks*
  Correct diagnosis should be followed by a thorough assessment to elucidate any aetiology that might be amenable to medical or surgical treatment.

- *Treating known aetiological factors*
  These include diabetes mellitus, temporal arteritis, mitral stenosis, sickle-cell anaemia, thrombocythaemia, bacterial endocarditis and left atrial myxoma.

Multiple cerebral infarcts

This is the second most important cause of dementia in old age – the first being Alzheimer's disease. The underlying pathology consists of multiple small lacunar infarcts.

Clinical features
Stepwise course of both physical and mental deterioration, usually associated with acute recurrent cerebrovascular episodes. Dementia develops slowly with unpleasant changes in personal habits and behaviour. Patient becomes agitated, restless, cantankerous and paranoid. General picture resembles parkinsonism. There is increased rigidity, especially of the legs, resulting in shuffling gait and recurrent falls. Eventually the patient becomes completely immobile and bedfast.

Pseudobulbar palsy
Occurs during the course of diffuse cerebrovascular disease. The clinical picture is the result of bilateral upper motor neurone lesions:

Nasal dysarthria, increased jaw jerk, no wasting of tongue, gross emotional lability, dysphagia, and eventually aspiration pneumonia.

Brain failure classification and aetiology

Acute
Anoxic – pneumonia, heart failure, myocardial infarction
Toxic – infections, drugs, alcohol
Vascular – stroke, subdural haematoma
Discomfort – impaction, urinary retention
Sudden environmental change

Chronic dementias
Senile dementia – Alzheimer's disease
Multi-infarct dementia
Huntington's chorea
Dementia with parkinsonism
Jakob–Creutzfeldt disease
Pick's disease
Kuru
Multiple sclerosis

Organic brain disease
Myxoedema, Vitamin B_{12} and folate deficiencies, drugs like barbiturates, head injury, tumours, alcoholism, neurosyphilis, chronic renal failure, normal pressure hydrocephalus, non-metastatic complication of carcinomas, pellagra, hypercalcaemia, prolonged hypoglycaemia

Dementia

Diffuse impairment of the intellect and personality, of insidious onset and usually progressive.

Conditions mistaken for dementia
Eccentricity
Exaggeration of symptoms by patient, relatives or staff
Social and cultural barriers
Pseudodementia or depression
Diogenes syndrome

Clinical features of senile dementia
Almost normal behaviour in early stages
Forgetfulness, nocturnal restlessness
Habits deteriorate, difficulty in handling memory
Patient faulted on current events and time
Confusional episodes, disorientation
Deterioration of personal care
Incorrect responses
Antisocial behaviour
Complete incapacity to look after self

Epilepsy

Epilepsy appearing for first time in old age is likely to be caused by cerebrovascular disease. Sometimes an epileptic attack may herald a stroke.

The following diseases may cause fits and may present in older people with symptoms and signs similar to a stroke:

- Intracranial tumour – primary or secondary
- Subdural haematoma
- Cerebral abscess
- Post-traumatic encephalopathy
- Meningitis and meningoencephalitis
- Epilepsy (Todd's paralysis)
- Meningovascular syphilis
- Giant-cell arteritis

Intracranial tumours

Types
Meningioma
Gliomas
Metastasis
Acoustic neuroma
Pituitary tumours

Clinical features
General symptoms:
Headache, confusion, behaviour disorders, epilepsy, dementia, vomiting.

Localising features:
Hemiparesis, hemianopsia, diplopia, cranial nerve palsies.

False localising signs:
Secondary to raised intracranial pressure, sixth nerve palsy, cerebellar ataxia.

Parkinsonism

Parkinsonian syndrome consists of different pathological conditions with marked clinical similarities. It is a common disease of the central nervous system, starting during the sixth or seventh decades.

The basic defect consists of dopamine deficiency in the pigmented nuclei of the brain stem.

Aetiology
Idiopathic
Post-encephalitic (extremely rare)
Head injury
Cerebral tumours with midbrain compression
Manganese poisoning
Carbon monoxide poisoning
Drugs – phenothiazines, butyrophenones, reserpine, methyldopa

Clinical features
Pill-rolling tremor – not common in older patients.
Tremor of tongue, lips, lower jaw and head.
Hypokinesia – this is the most important cause of disability
Immobile face, infrequent blinking, impaired chest expansion, difficulty in protruding tongue, loss of synergic movements, loss of balance, positive glabellar tap.
Muscular rigidity – appears early in neck, cogwheel or lead pipe rigidity, characteristic posture with adducted flexed limbs.
Festinant gait, micrographia, turning in bed becomes difficult, stooping posture, impairment of postural control and righting reflexes, falls, complete immobility.
GIT symptoms – dysphagia, excessive salivation, constipation, hiatus hernia, weight loss.
Mental disturbances – depression and irritability, dementia in advanced cases.
Other features – feeble and monotonous speech with loss of phonation, contractures, increased flushing and sweating.

Prognosis
Idiopathic parkinsonism in the elderly is a chronic progressive incurable disease. About 60% of patients are dead within 10 years of first being diagnosed. The causes of death are bronchopneumonia, pressure sores, urinary tract infections, fractured femur, and other complications of postural instability, wasting and falls.

107

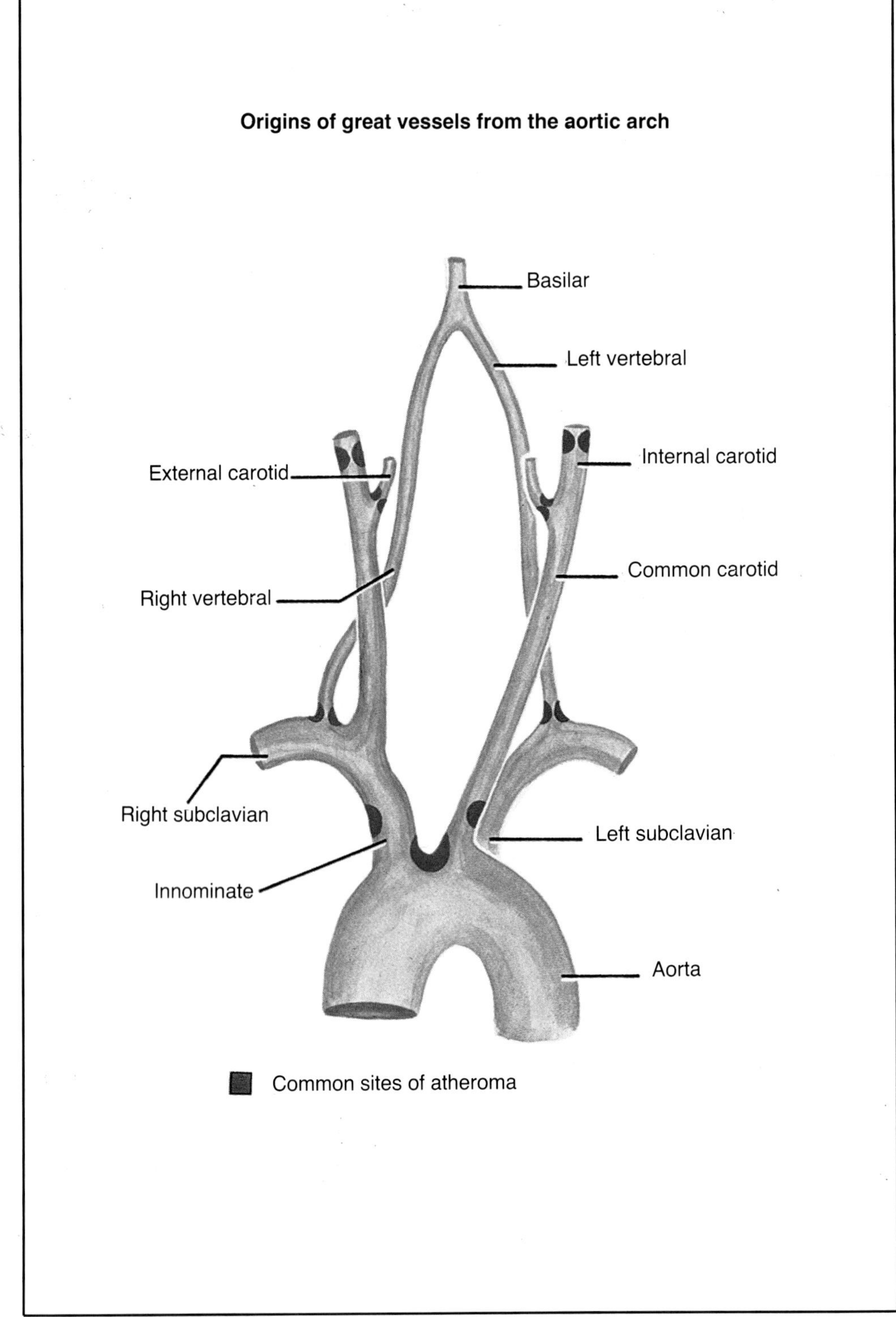

107 and 108 Atheroma. Aortic arch with great vessels of the neck and Circle of Willis, showing common sites of arteriosclerosis.

108

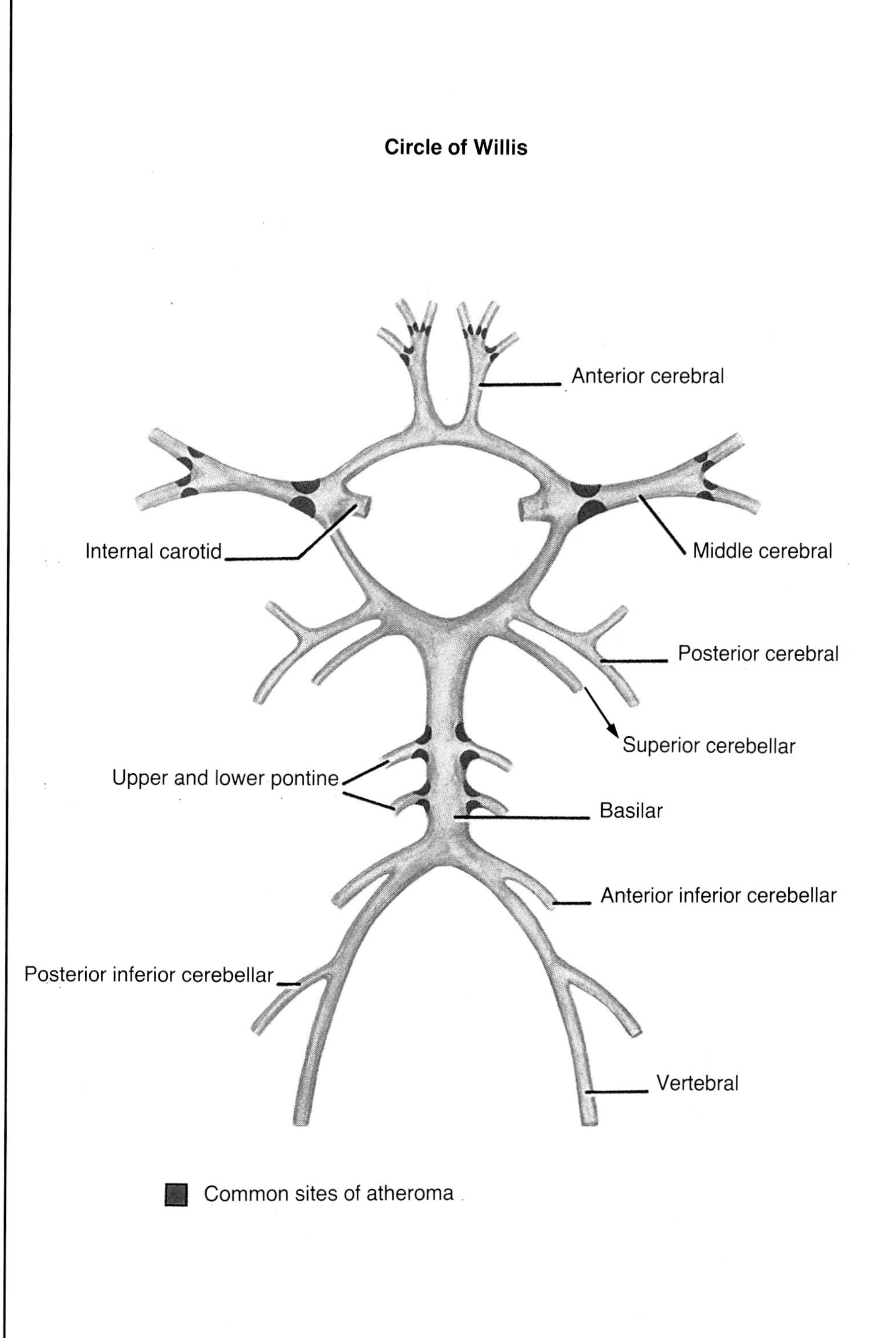
Circle of Willis
Anterior cerebral
Internal carotid
Middle cerebral
Posterior cerebral
Superior cerebellar
Upper and lower pontine
Basilar
Anterior inferior cerebellar
Posterior inferior cerebellar
Vertebral
Common sites of atheroma

109

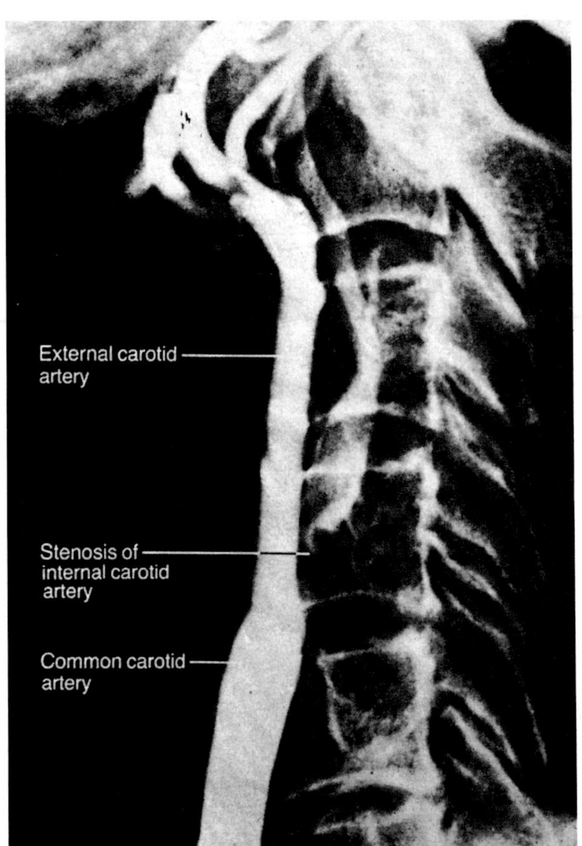

109 Stenosis of internal carotid artery. Revealed by arteriography. A bruit in the neck may be audible and there is risk of a cerebrovascular accident.

110 Stenosis of internal carotid artery. A more severe case shown by arteriography. Doppler ultrasonography is a useful and non-intrusive way of investigating stenosis. Arteriography is only indicated if surgery is seriously contemplated.

110

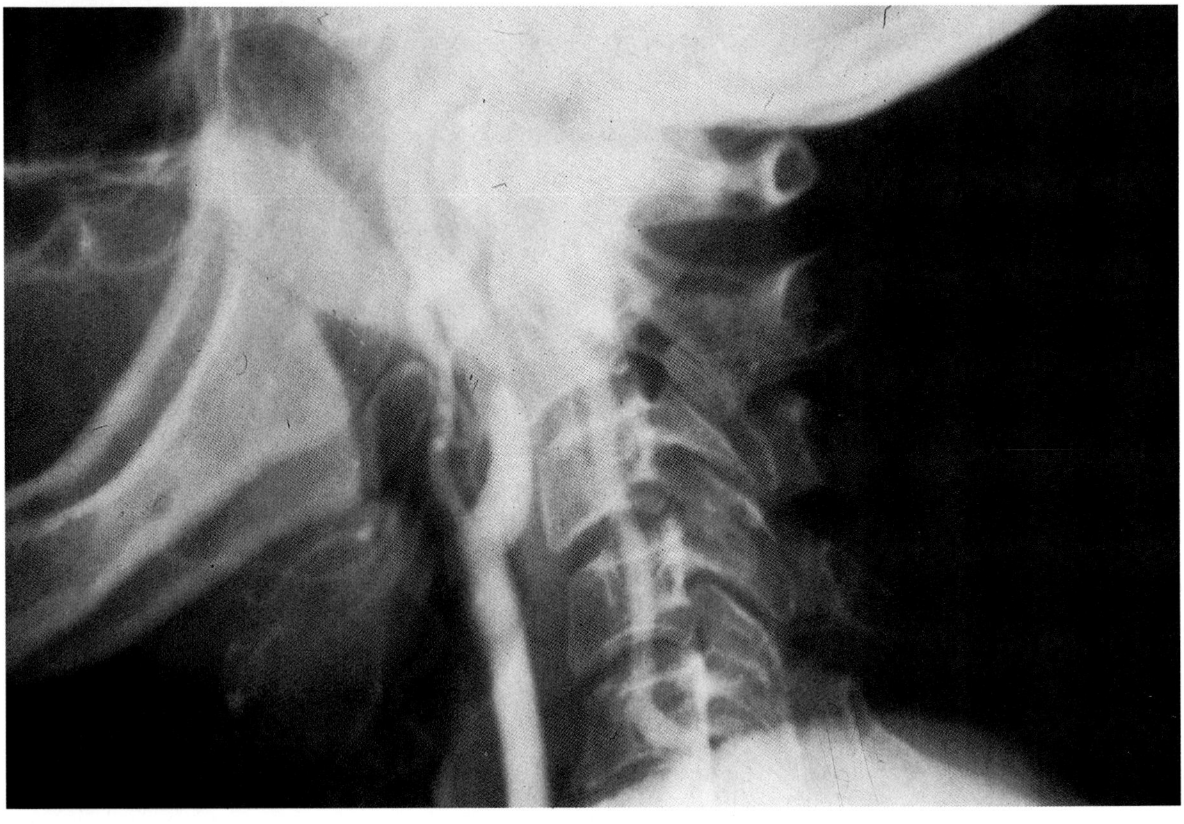

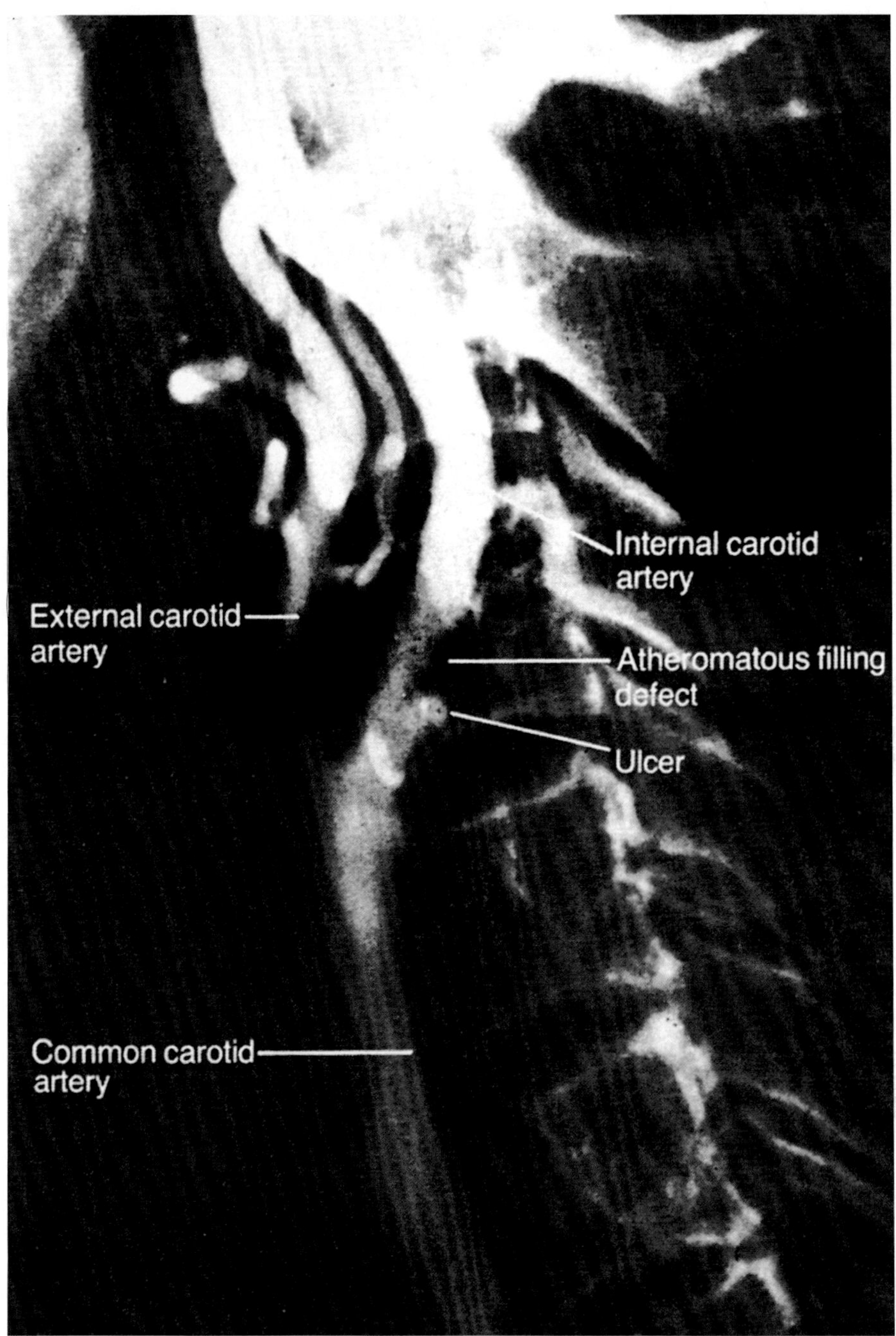

111 Atherosclerosis. Carotid angiogram showing an atheromatous filling defect in the internal carotid artery. Such lesions may cause transient cerebral ischaemic attacks.

112

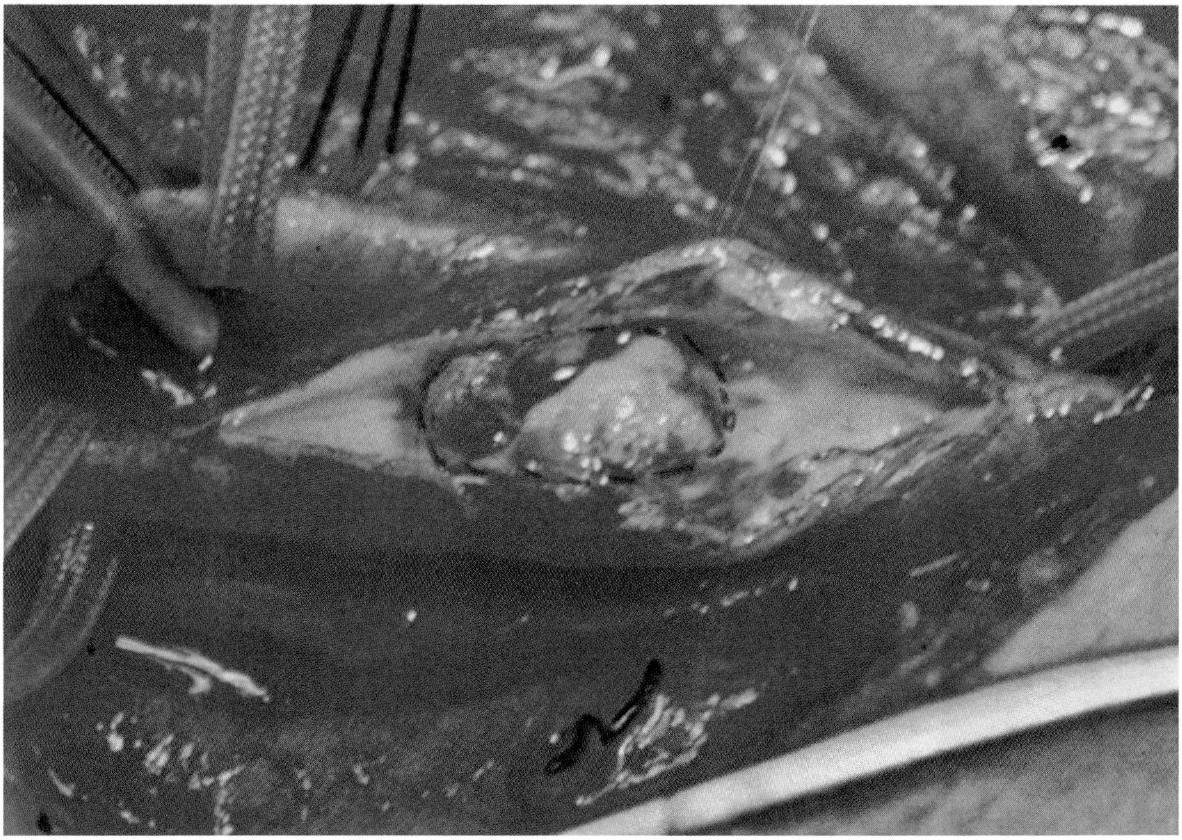

112 Carotid thrombosis. Thrombus in the internal carotid artery revealed at surgery.

113

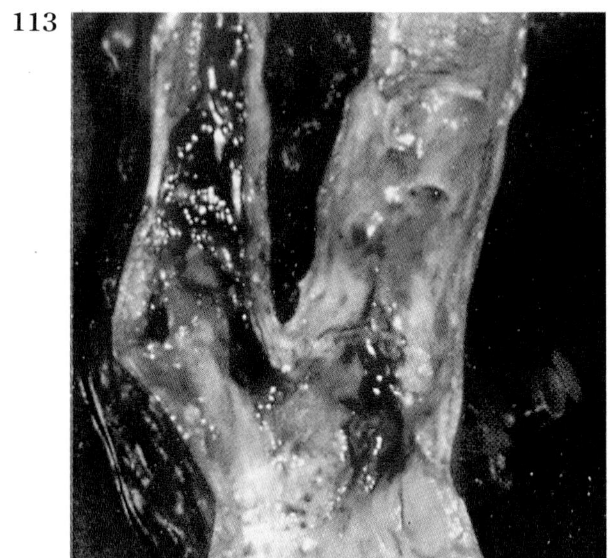

113 Atheroma. Intimal atheroma in a patient with prolonged hypertension. Such patients are at increased risk from developing cerebral infarction. (Courtesy of Pharmaceutical Division, Ciba-Geigy.)

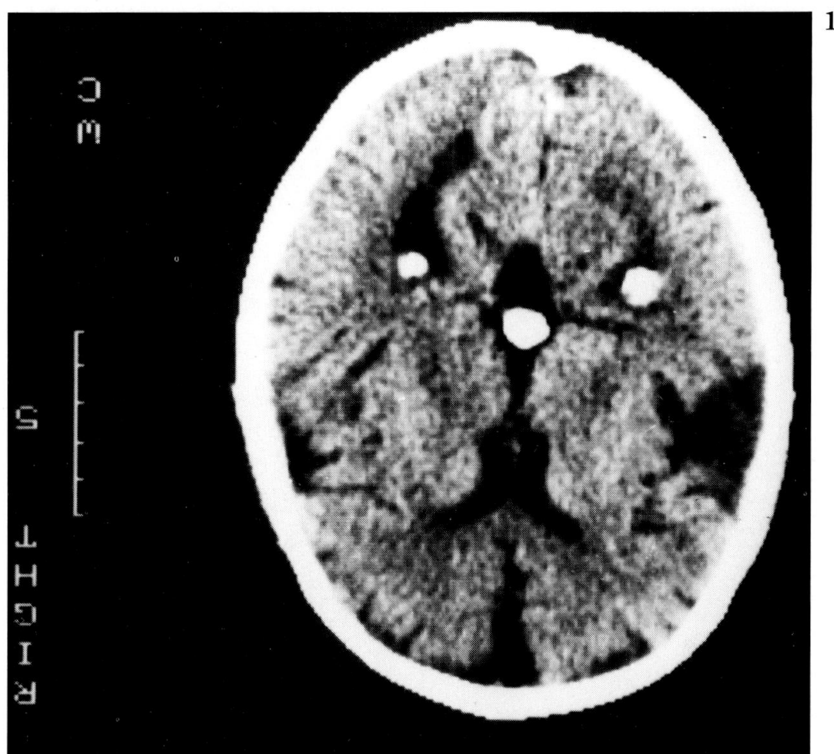

114

114 Cerebral infarction. A CAT scan showing recent left parietal cerebral infarction in a patient presenting with right hemiplegia.

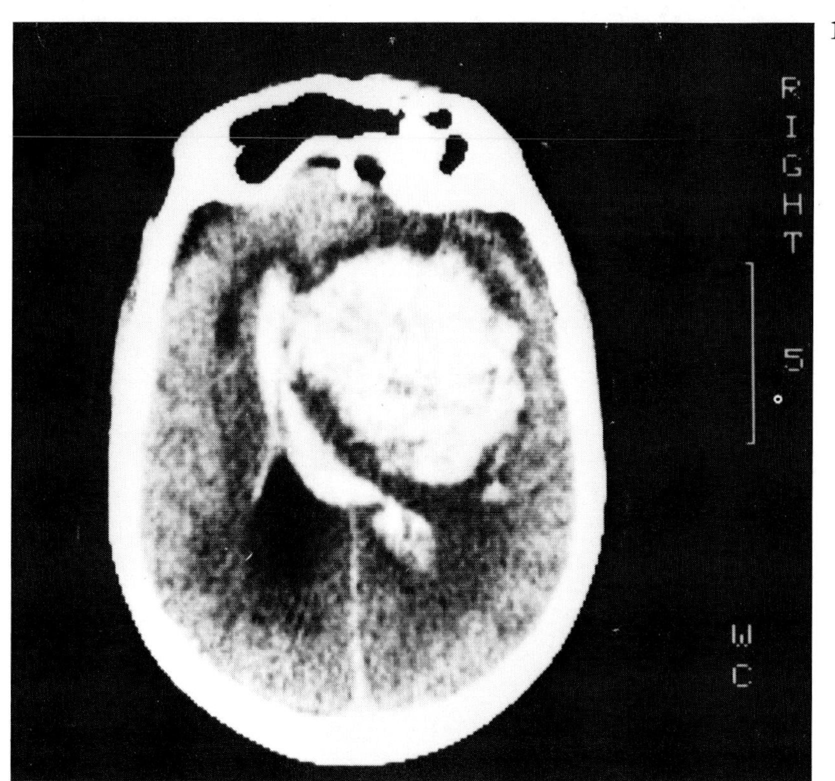

115

115 Cerebral haemorrhage. A CAT scan showing massive cerebral haemorrhage with leakage of blood into the lateral ventricle.

116

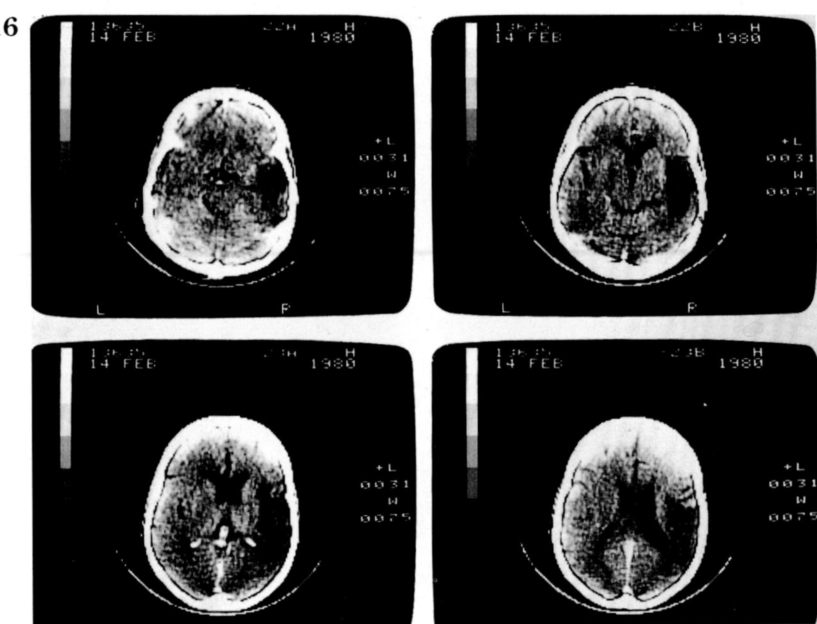

116 Cerebral infarction. A CAT scan showing mature right middle cerebral artery infarct.

117

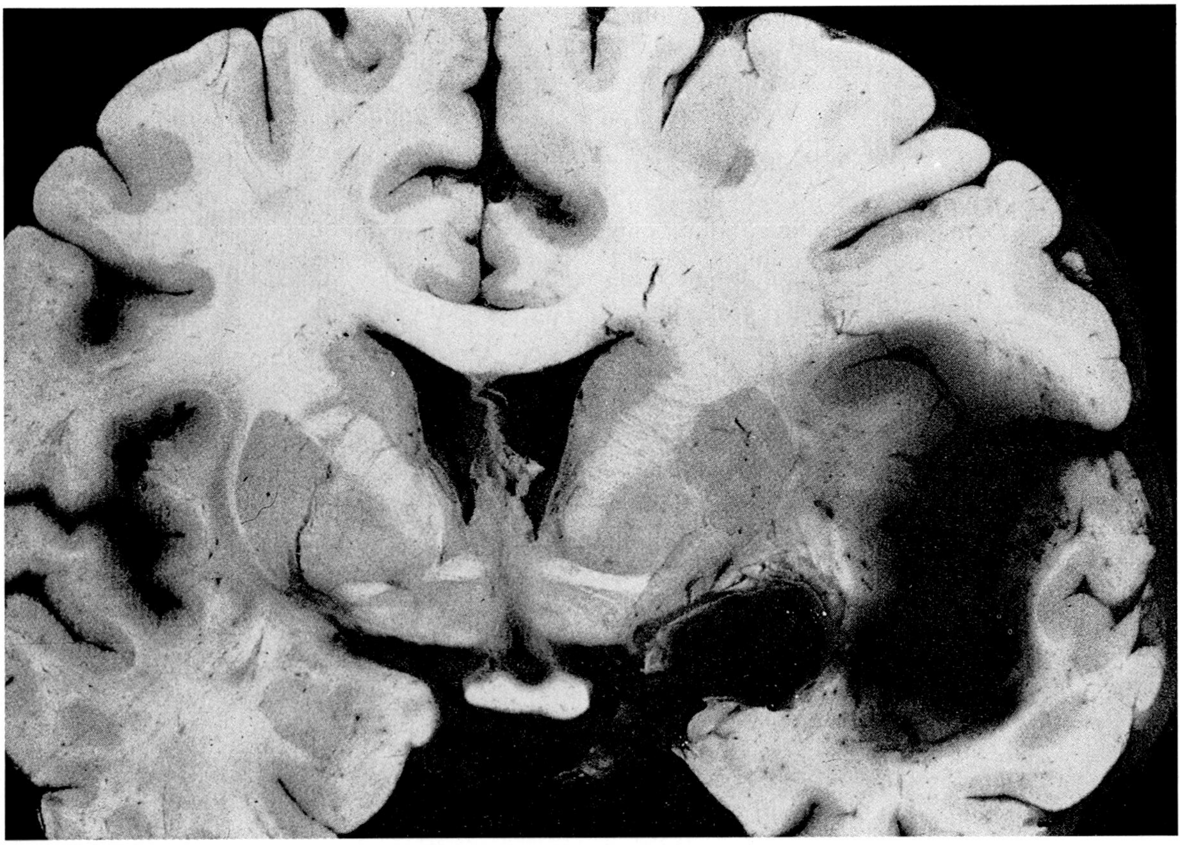

117 Meningocerebral haemorrhage. Subsequent to rupture of a middle cerebral artery aneurysm.

118

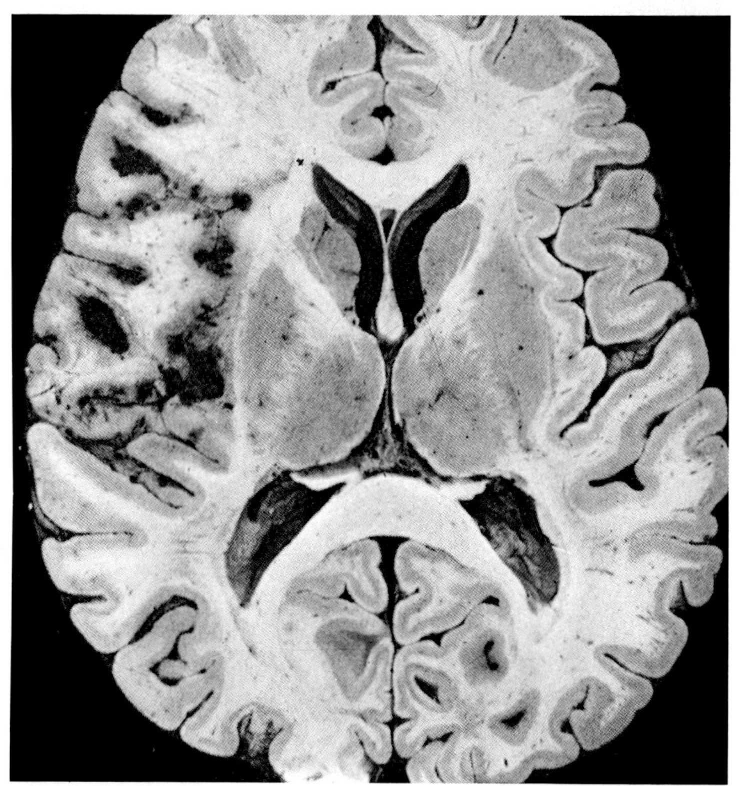

118 Haemorrhagic infarct. An infarct in the territory of the supply of the middle cerebral artery. Usually presents with a sudden hemiplegia.

119

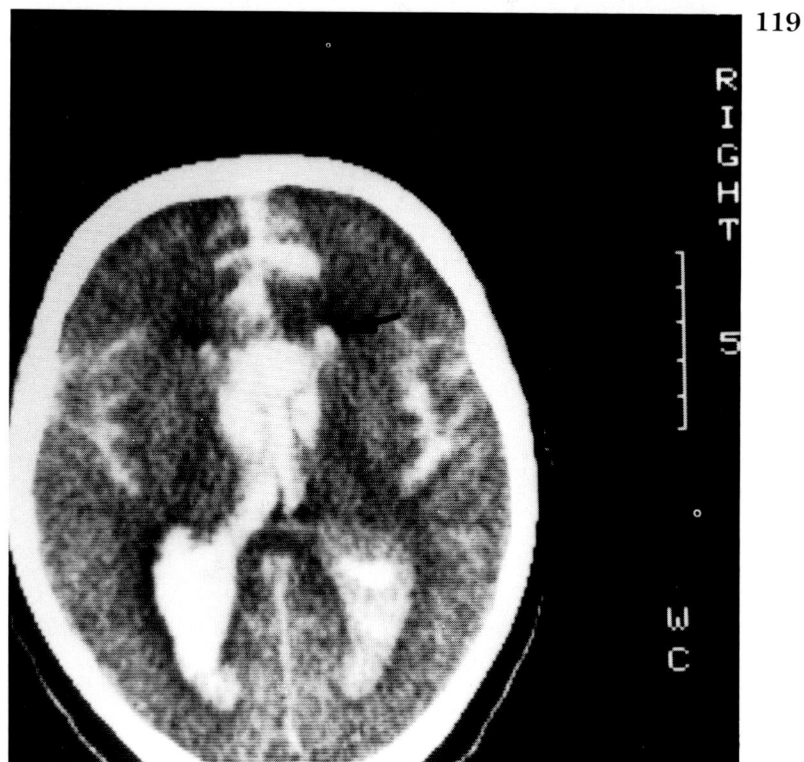

119 Subarachnoid haemorrhage. A CAT scan showing subarachnoid haemorrhage in an elderly woman presenting with severe headache. The arrow points at bleeding into the ventricles and subarachnoid space from the aneurysm.

120

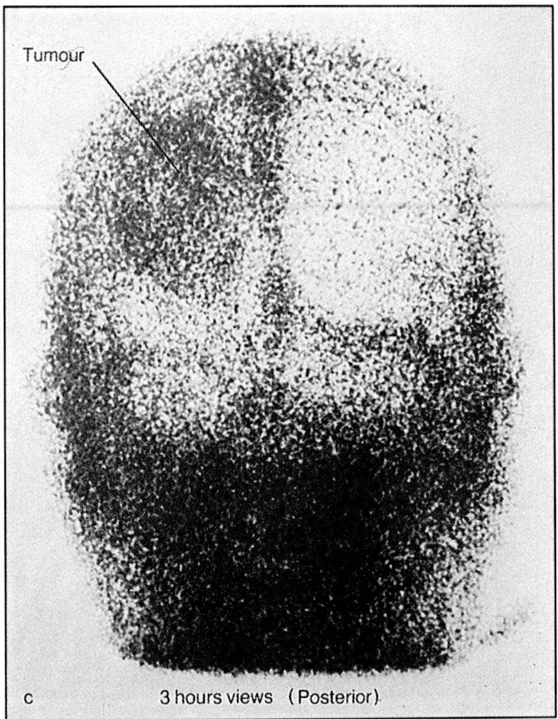

120 Brain tumour. An isotope scan showing space-occupying lesion in the left cerebral hemisphere. Sudden haemorrhage into such a tumour may present as a cerebrovascular accident.

121 and 122 Meningioma. Isotope scans showing anterior and right lateral views of a dense round lesion, which is very suggestive of a meningioma. The patient presented with confusion, falls, incontinence, dysphasia and ataxia. Isotope scanning has become outdated; most centres now use CAT scanning.

121

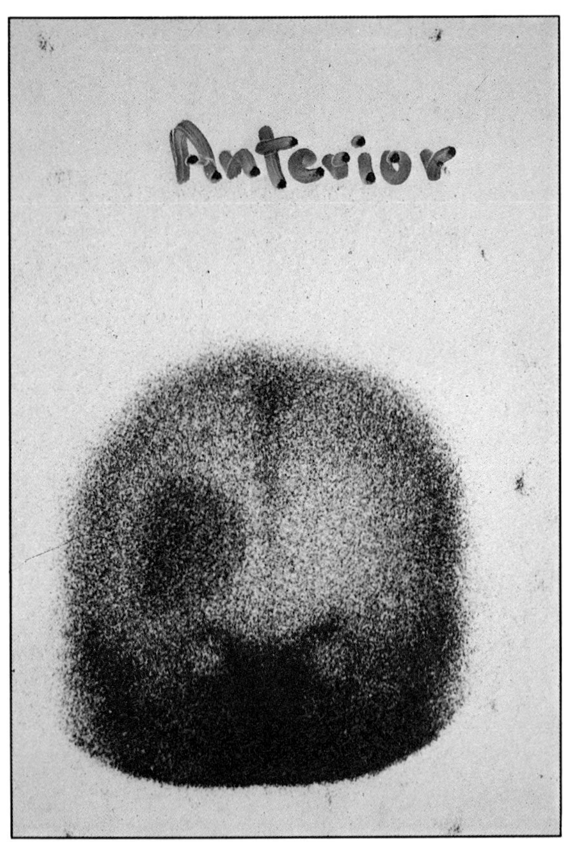

12

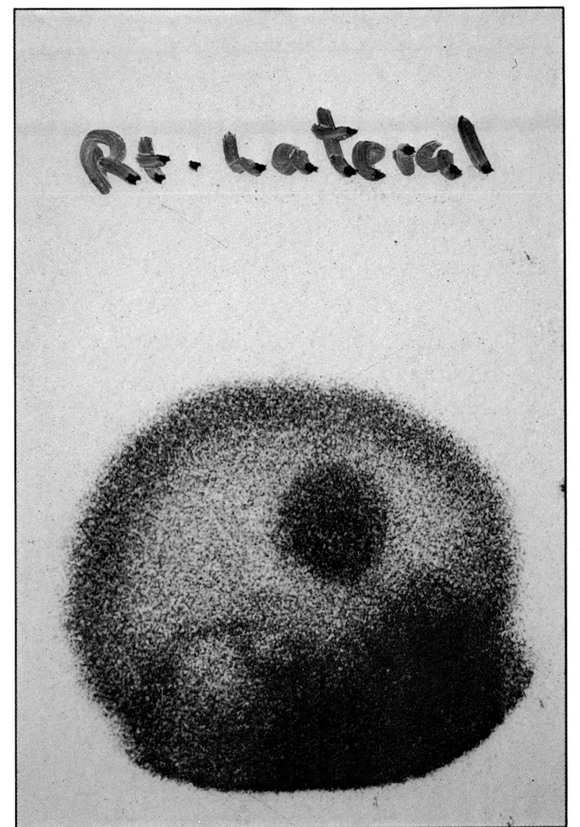

123

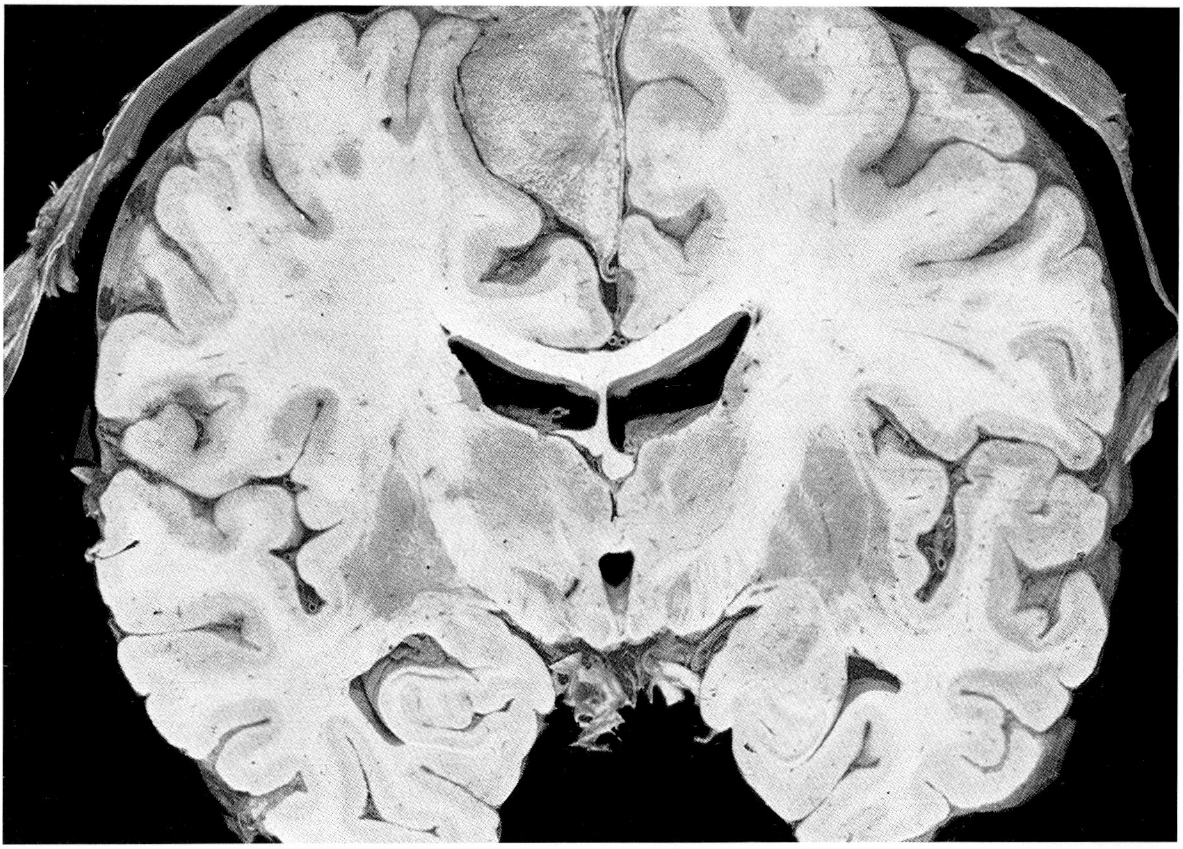

123 Parasagittal meningioma. Slow-growing tumour presenting with neurological signs in the trunk and lower limbs.

124 Convexed meningioma. A CAT scan showing left convexed meningioma. The patient had right-sided upper motor neurone signs.

124

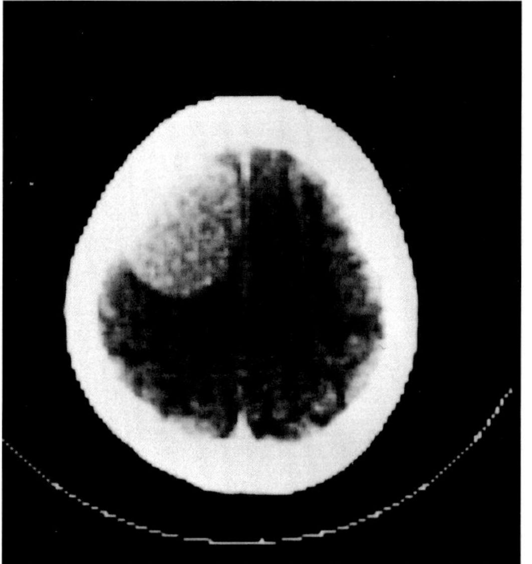

125

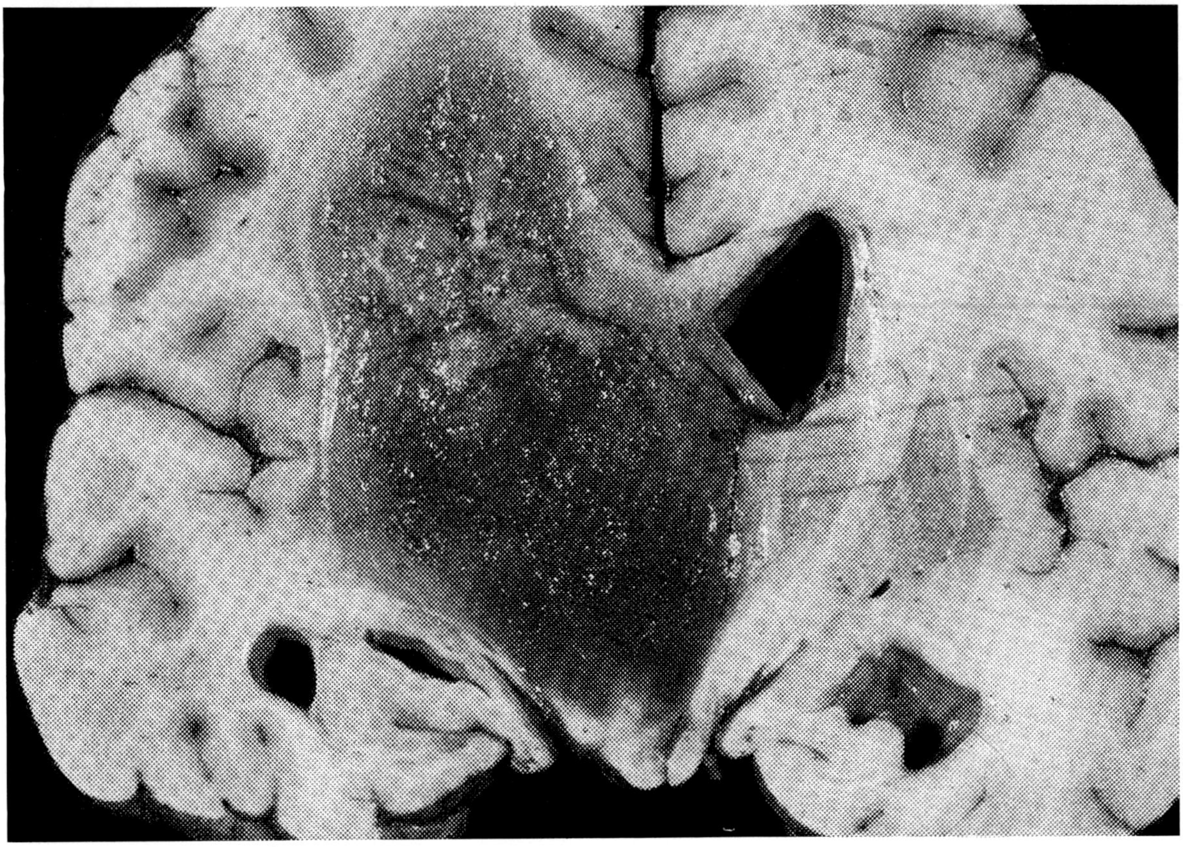

125 Astrocytoma Grade IV. Highly malignant brain tumour. Often seen in the elderly and may present with stroke-like illness or dementia.

126

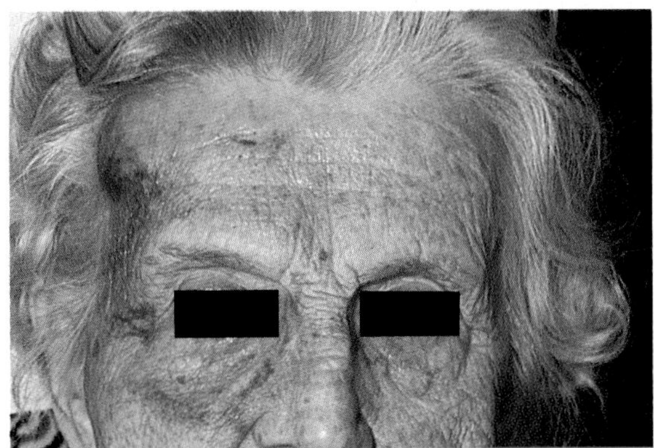

126 Head injury. An area of bruising on the right temporal region. The patient felt well and x-rays revealed an intact skull. After a few days the patient developed symptoms suggestive of subdural haematoma.

127

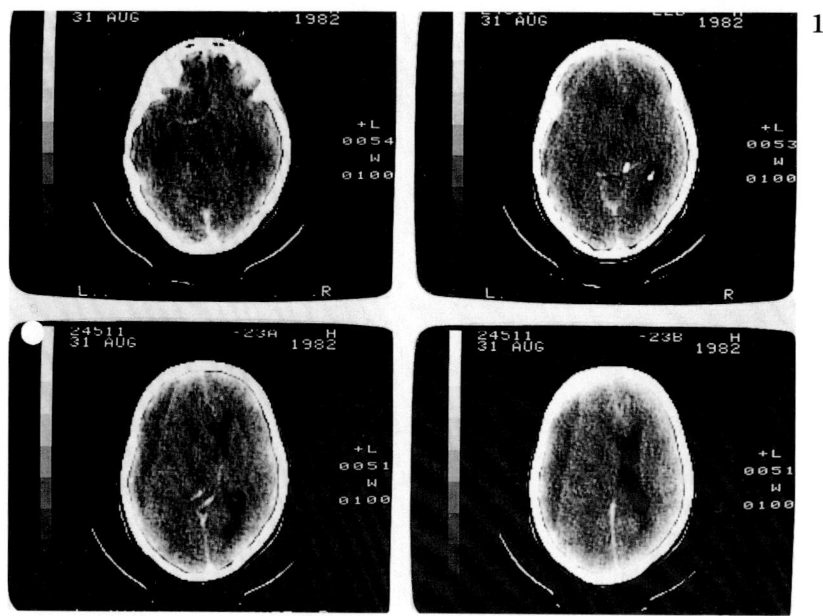

127 Subdural haematoma. A CAT scan showing chronic left subdural haematoma.

Subdural haematoma

Collection of blood between dura and arachnoid space caused by trauma or spontaneously. The head injury in the elderly may be trivial. Early neurological intervention (drainage) is extremely important if permanent neurological damage is to be avoided.

Clinical features

Fluctuating level of consciousness
Confusion
Headaches
Hemiparesis
Ptosis and dilated pupil on affected side
Lateralising signs
Dementia-like picture
Skull x-rays may show a fracture displaced pineal or displaced choroid plexus
CAT will localise the haematoma
CSF may be clear or xanthochromic

128

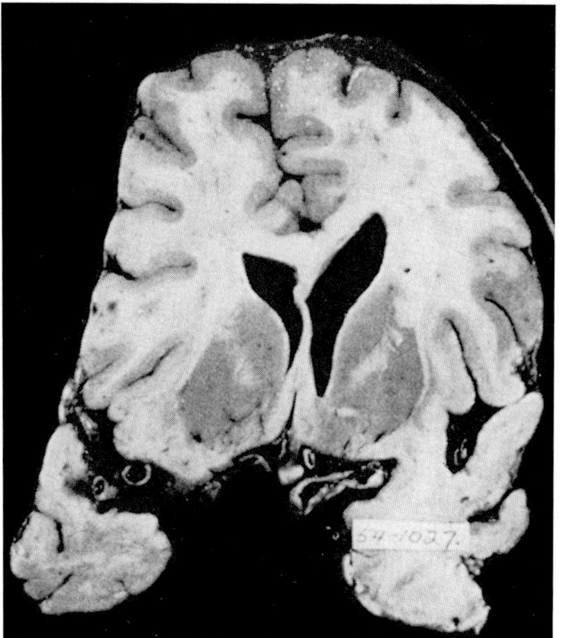

128 Subdural haematoma. The dura and clot have been removed from the specimen and the compression of brain by a subdural haematoma is apparent.

129

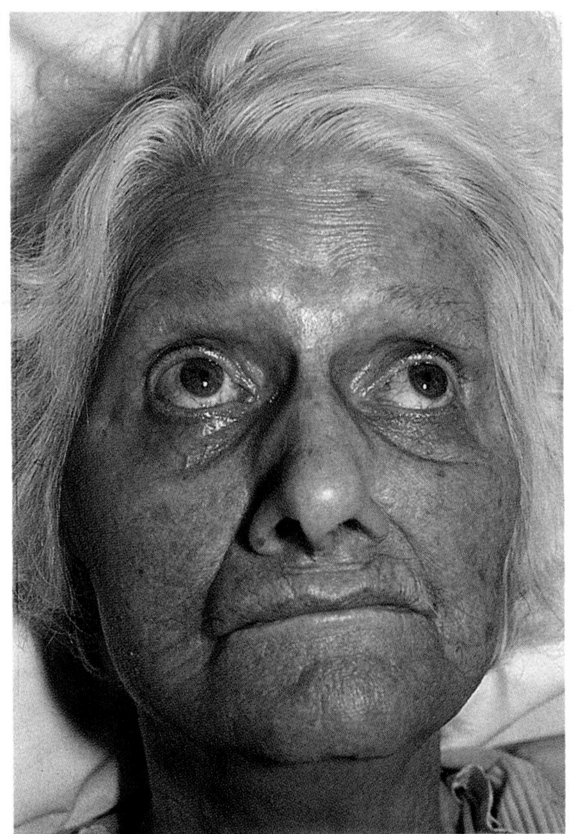

130

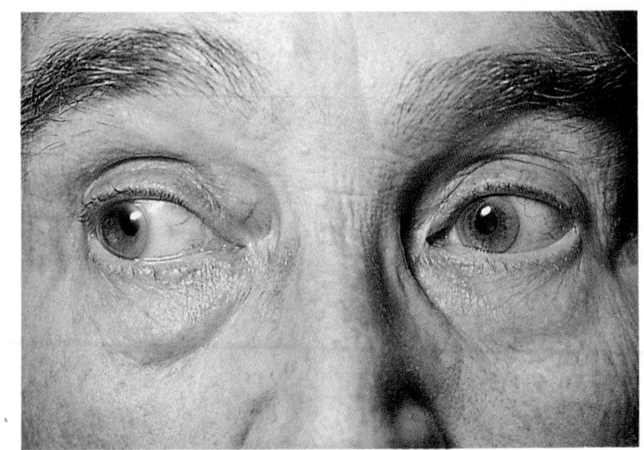

131

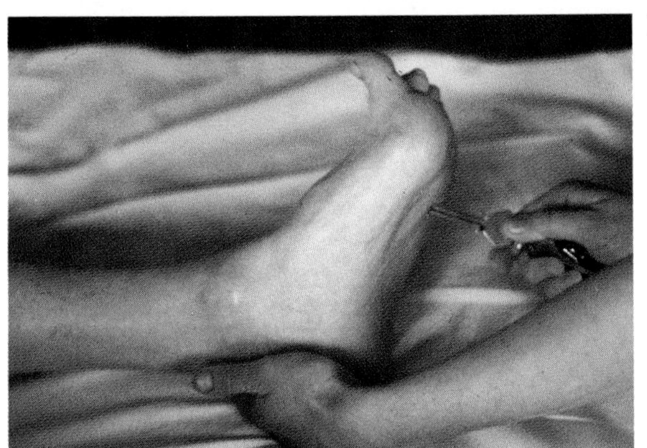

132

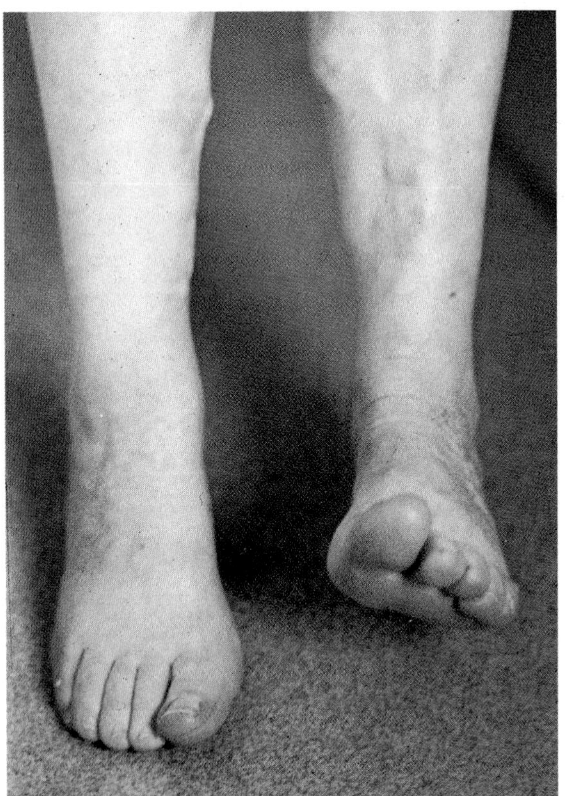

129 Fixed gaze. The eyes are fixed in an upward direction and there is paralysis of gaze. This is thought to be caused by brain-stem compression and can occur with intracerebral haemorrhage.

130 Stroke. A case of acute stroke causing left hemiplegia. The eyes are deviated to the side of the lesion.

131 Babinski's reflex. Upgoing plantar reflex, a typical sign of a recent upper motor neurone lesion. May sometimes be absent in elderly hemiplegics.

132 Foot drop. In a case of right hemiplegia. The patient is unable to dorsiflex the right foot and will require a footboard or other support to prevent permanent disability.

133 Increased spasticity. Spasticity of the arm after recent hemiplegia. Early physiotherapy is required to prevent contractures and further disability.

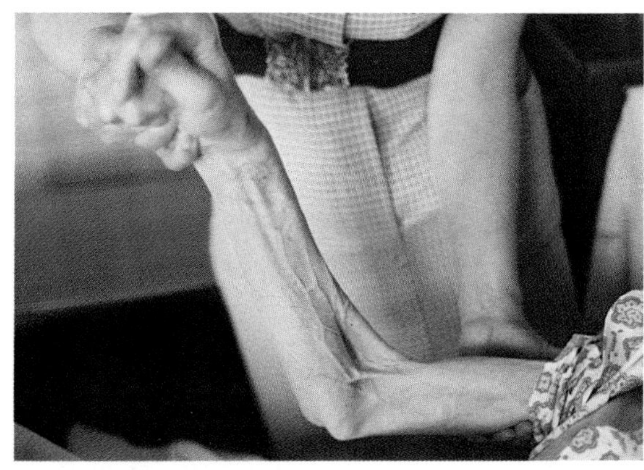
133

34

134 Loss of postural stability. In cerebrovascular accidents involving the non-dominant hemisphere, walking apraxia and loss of postural control are usually apparent. The patient is unable to sit upright and tends to fall sideways. Patients should not be left in that position.

135

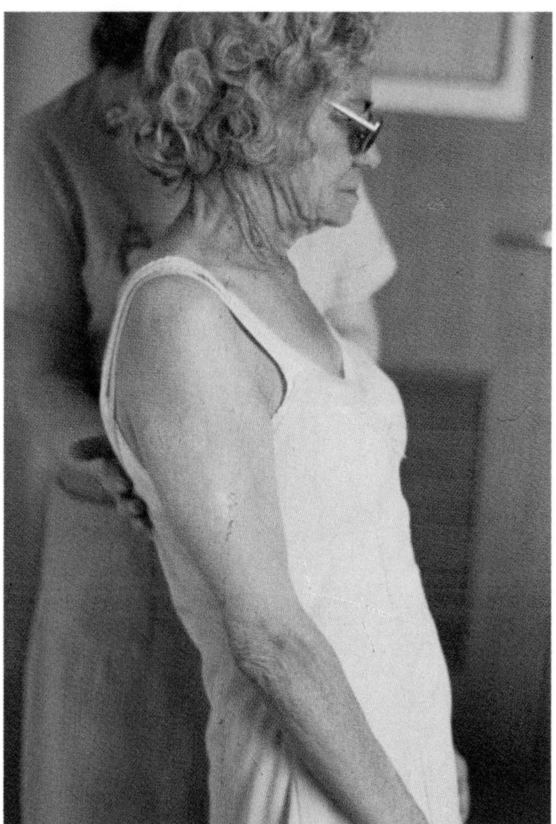

135 Backward falling. A tendency to lean and fall backwards is a frequent problem in vertobrobasilar ischaemia and global cerebral syndromes.

This patient should improve with regular physiotherapy and walking exercises. A special weighted walking frame may reduce the tendency to lean backwards.

136

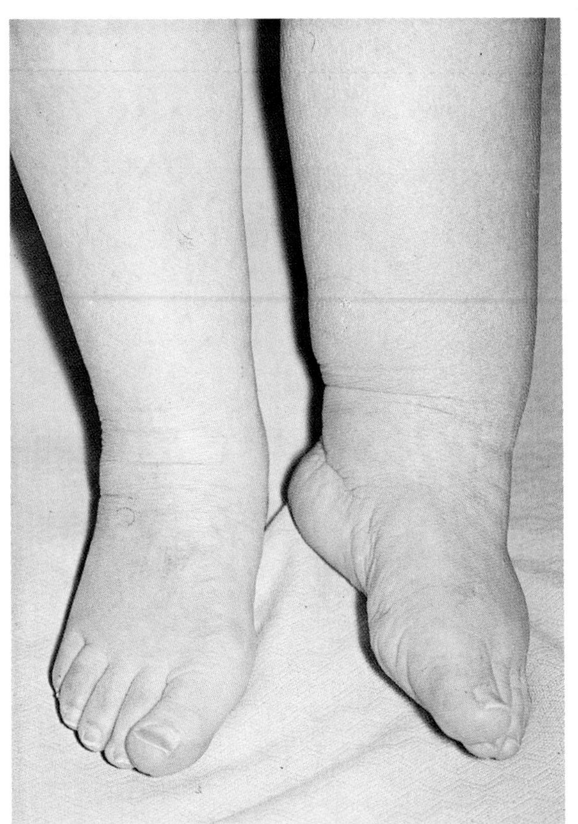

136 Hemiplegic oedema. Oedema of the left foot. Prescribing diuretics is of little benefit but physiotherapy, mobilisation and limb elevation should improve the condition. Flotran splints may also help but have not yet been scientifically evaluated.

137 Hemiplegic hand. Severe contracture of the right hand several months after a dense hemiplegia.

138 Hemiplegic hand. Another case of hemiplegic contracture of the left hand. Such disability can be prevented with early physiotherapy.

139 Hemiplegia. A patient with hemiplegia being taught to walk without mechanical aids.

137

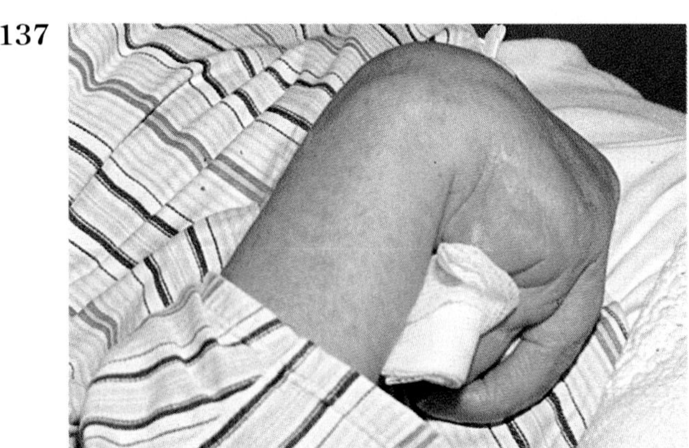

138

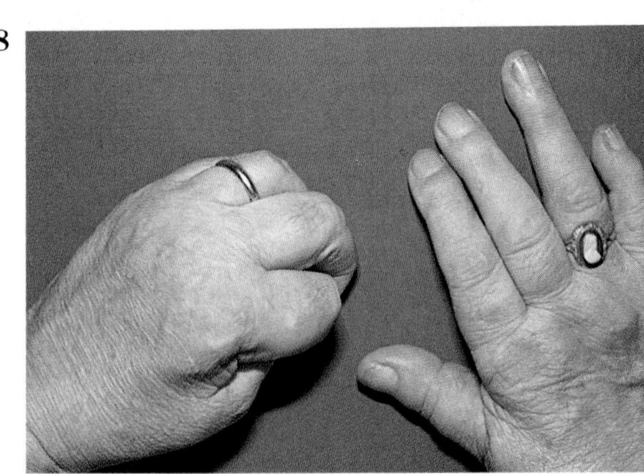

13

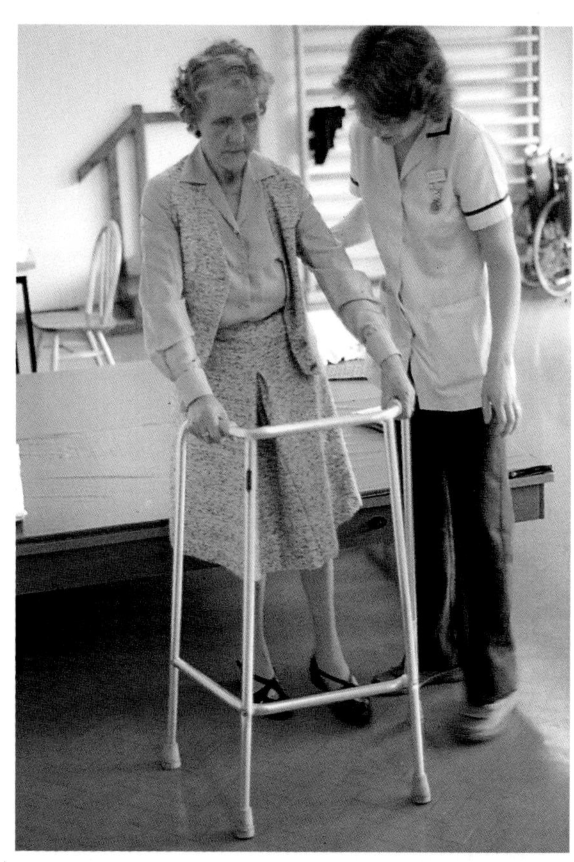

140

140 Hemiplegia. Patient walking with Zimmer frame.

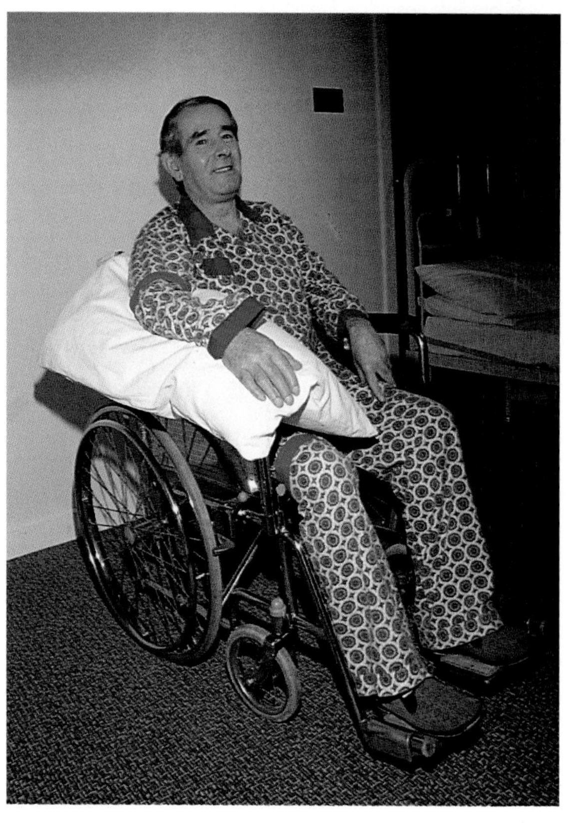

141

141 Hemiplegia. A patient with right hemiplegia in correct sitting posture.

142

143

142 and 143 Perceptual disturbances – spatial neglect. Assessment of spatial neglect in patients with non-dominant hemisphere stroke is most satisfactorily done by getting the patient to draw; the neglect of the left side will be apparent from the drawing. This syndrome is usually accompanied by hemianaesthesia, hemianopia, inappropriate emotions, loss of righting reflex and apathy.

144

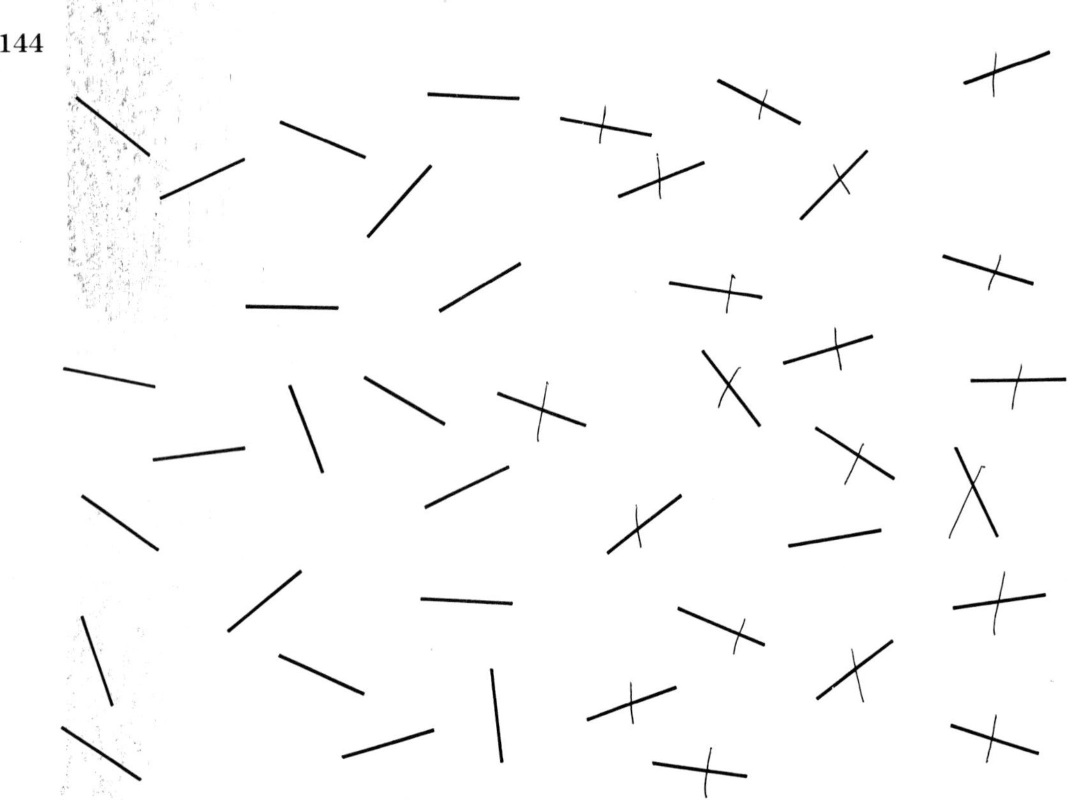

144 Albert's test. This is a very good test for spatial neglect which usually occurs in stroke affecting the non-dominant hemisphere. The therapist scores out one of the lines in the non-affected side and asks the patient to score out all the other lines on the sheet. The test here demonstrates a complete loss of spacial perception on the affected side. The test is useful for monitoring recovery as well as for making the diagnosis.

145 Apraxia. Problems of motor planning (apraxia). The patient has lost the pattern of sequencing a movement. Even if she understands the task and has sufficient movement to perform it, she is unable to plan the required sequence to achieve the goal. Plates **a–f** show sequencing: even a simple task, such as pouring a drink from a bottle, can be too difficult.

146

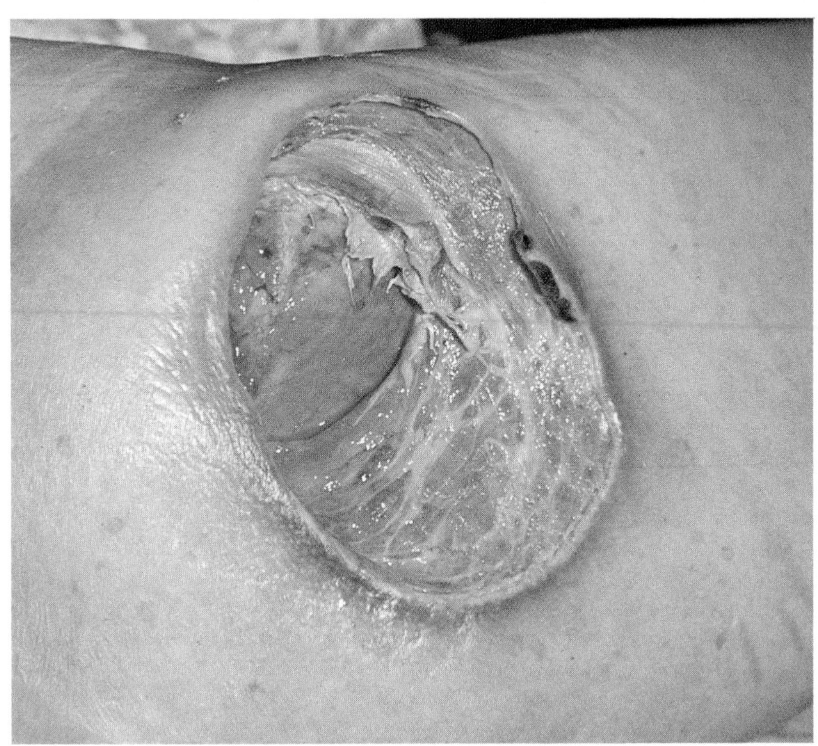

146 Ischial pressure sore. One of the serious but preventable complications of immobility in an elderly patient caused by cerebrovascular accident.

147

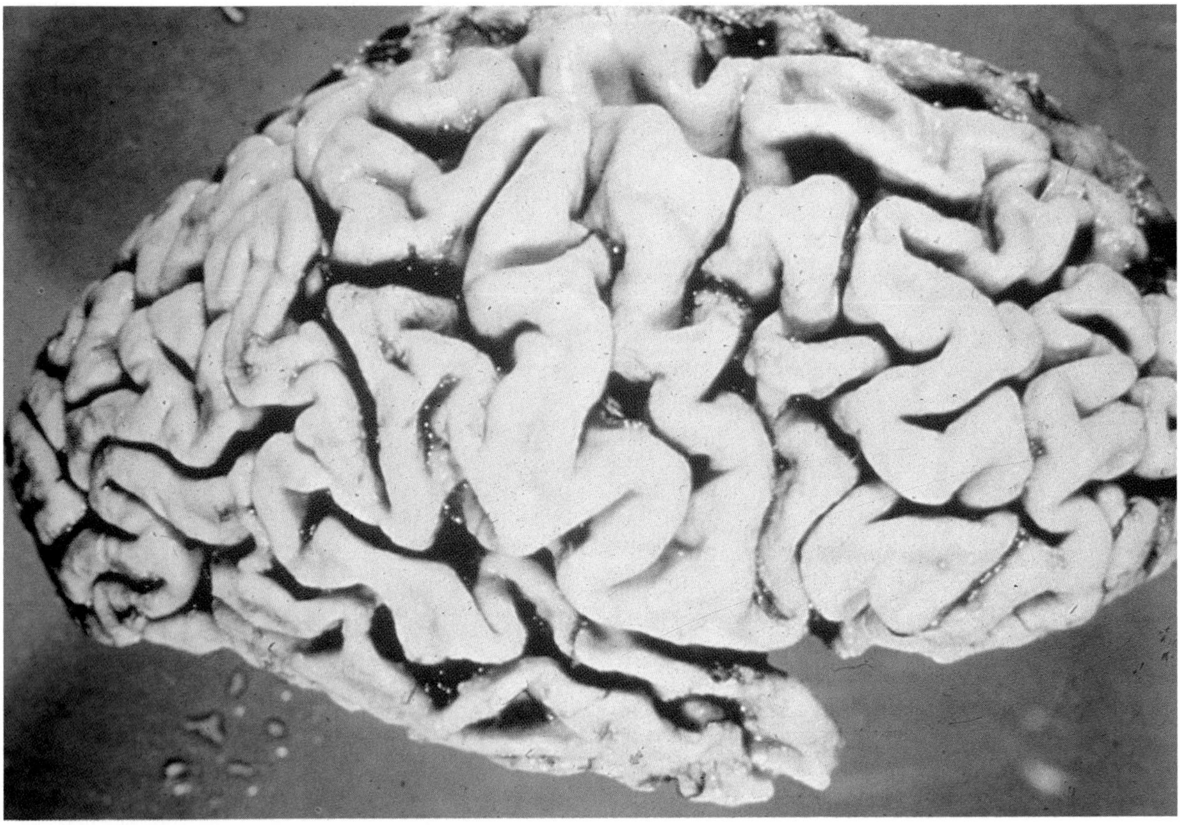

147 Cerebral atrophy. Side view of a fixed brain showing extreme shrinkage of temporal lobe as well as generalised cerebral atrophy more marked anteriorly.

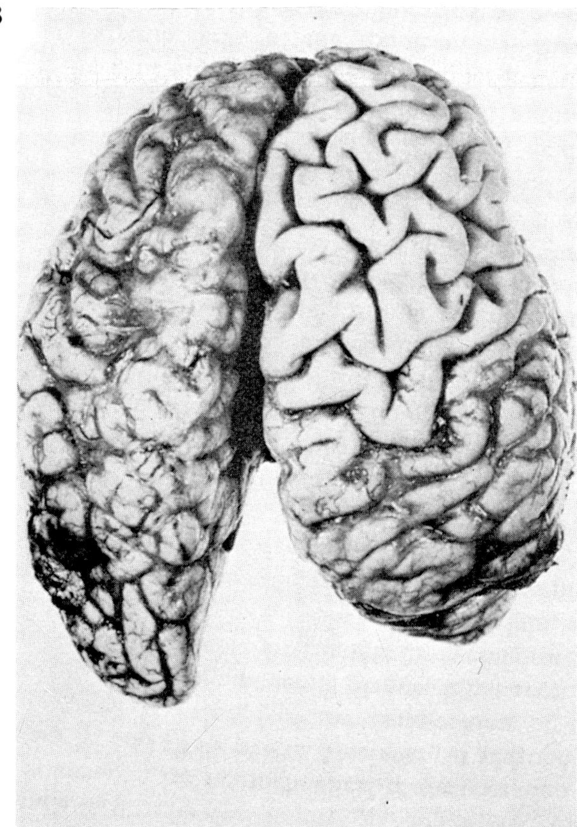

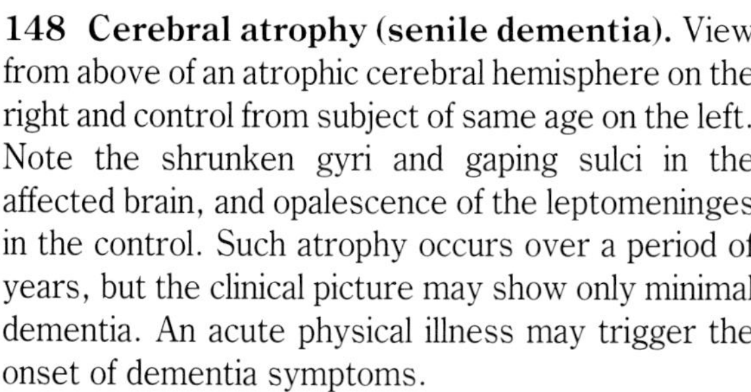

148 Cerebral atrophy (senile dementia). View from above of an atrophic cerebral hemisphere on the right and control from subject of same age on the left. Note the shrunken gyri and gaping sulci in the affected brain, and opalescence of the leptomeninges in the control. Such atrophy occurs over a period of years, but the clinical picture may show only minimal dementia. An acute physical illness may trigger the onset of dementia symptoms.

149 Dementia. A CAT scan showing advanced cerebral atrophy in a case of Alzheimer's dementia.

150 Multi-infarct dementia. Dilated perivascular spaces (etats lacunaires) and scars of small old infarcts in basal ganglia.

151 Senile dementia. Postulated evolution of senile plaques and neurofibrillary tangles. Senile plaques may be found in very small numbers in very old, non-demented patients.

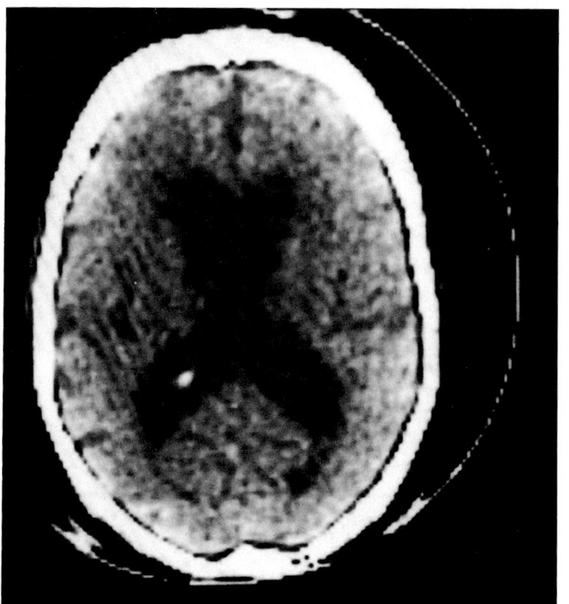

149

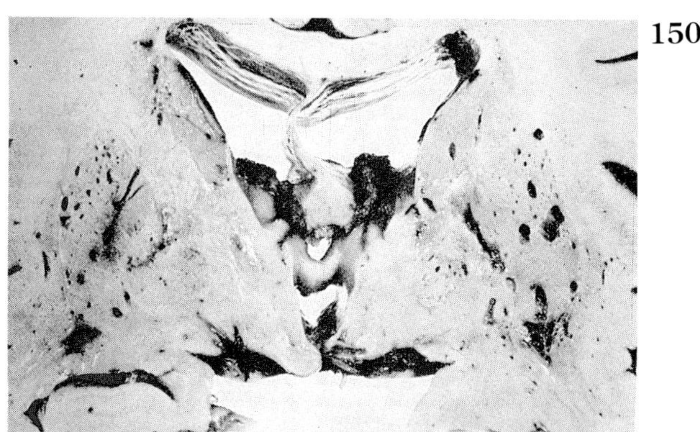

150

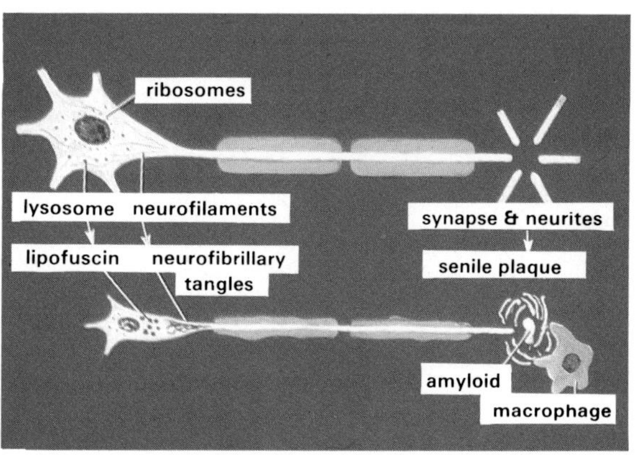

151

152

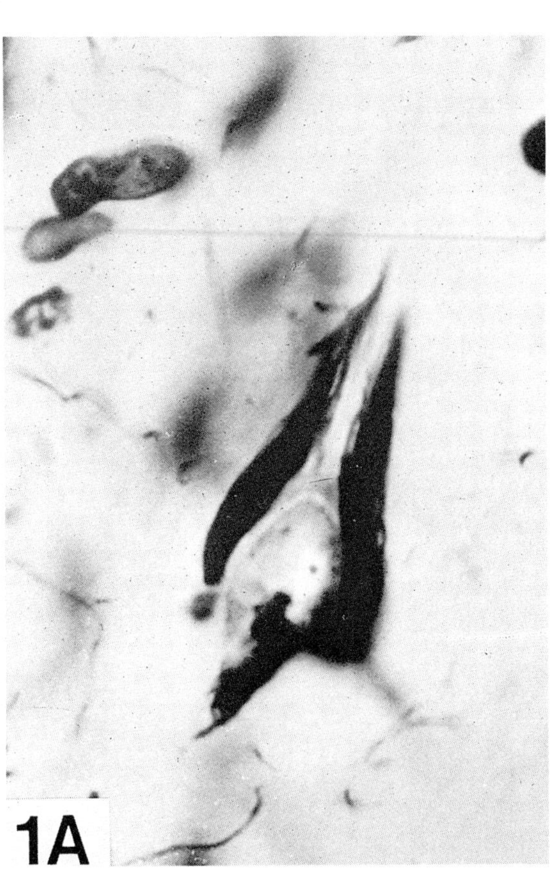

152 Neurofibrillary tangle. Composed of thick strands of argentophilic material largely filling the neuronal cytoplasm and extending into apical dendrite. (*Bodian stain ×560*)

153 Neurofibrillary tangles. Composite picture of neurofibrillary tangles: the almost triangular dense intraneuronal structures. Argyrophilic plaques are also present as larger and more fragmented areas of staining.

153

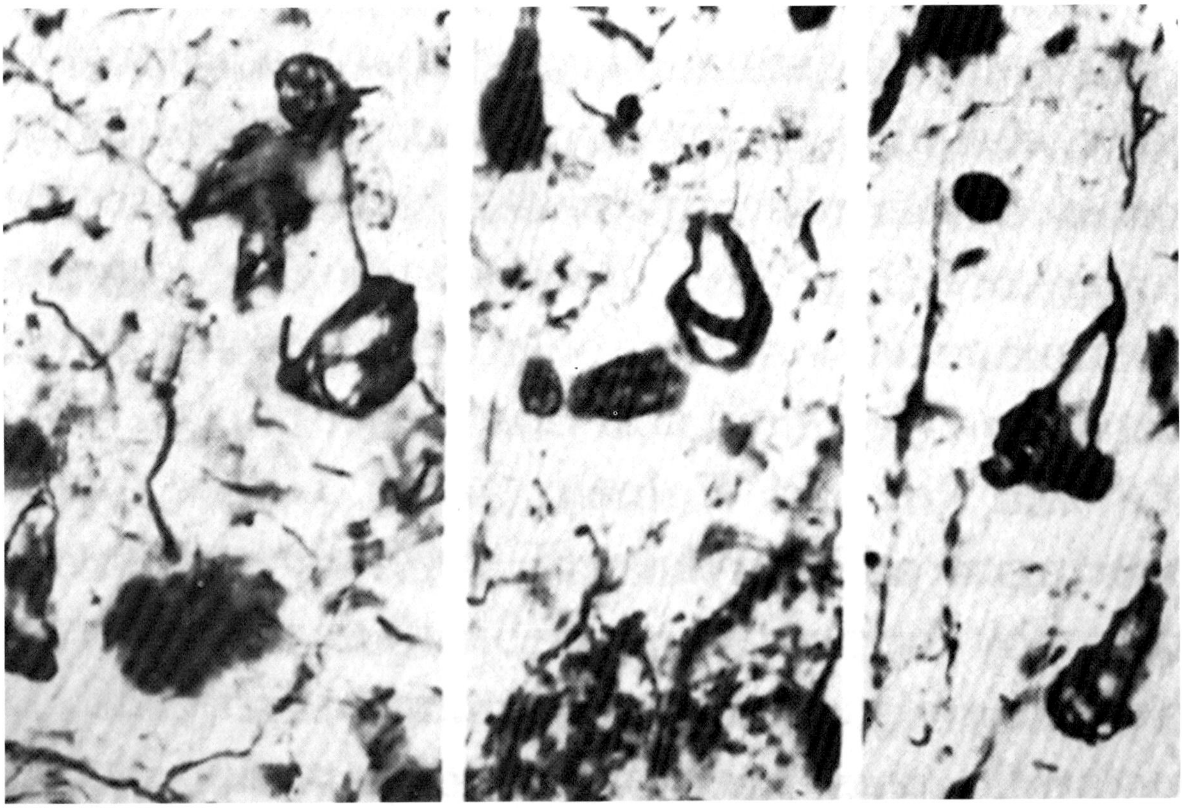

154 Plaque. A typical plaque in thick section reveals its central amyloid core (arrow) surrounded by degenerating neurites.

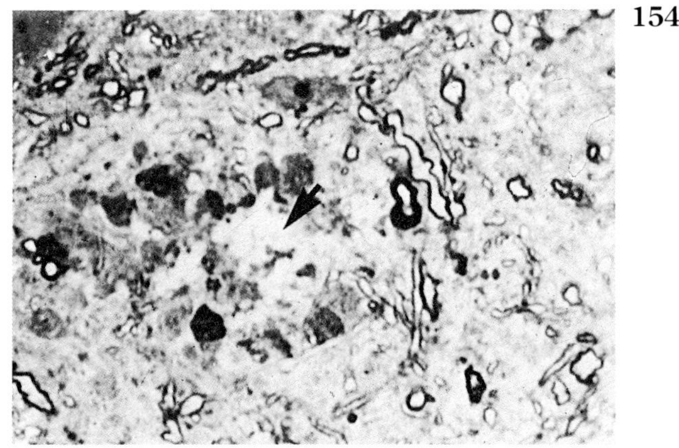

154

155 Plaque. Another typical plaque reveals much dense material derived from degenerating mitochrondria and lysosomes in neuritis. The lighter components around the central core were processes with fibrillar material and wisps of amyloid.

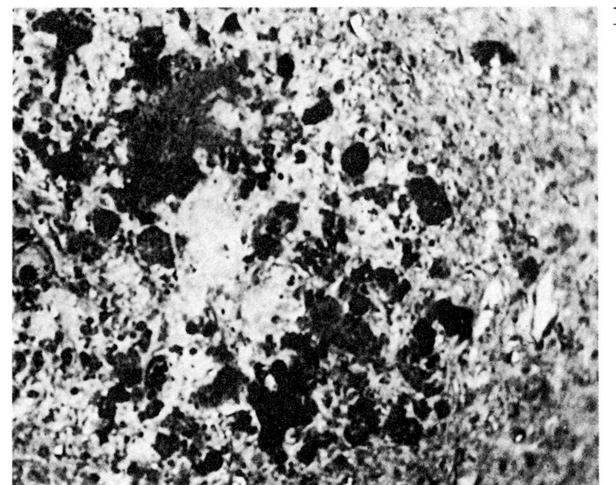

155

156 Plaque. A compact or burned-out plaque consists almost entirely of amyloid. (*Toluidine blue ×560*)

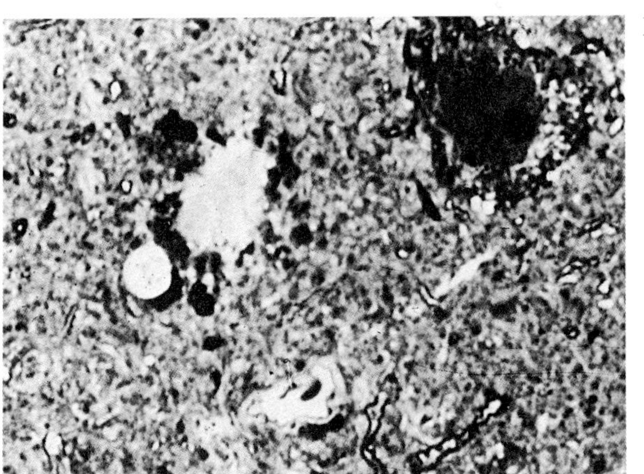

156

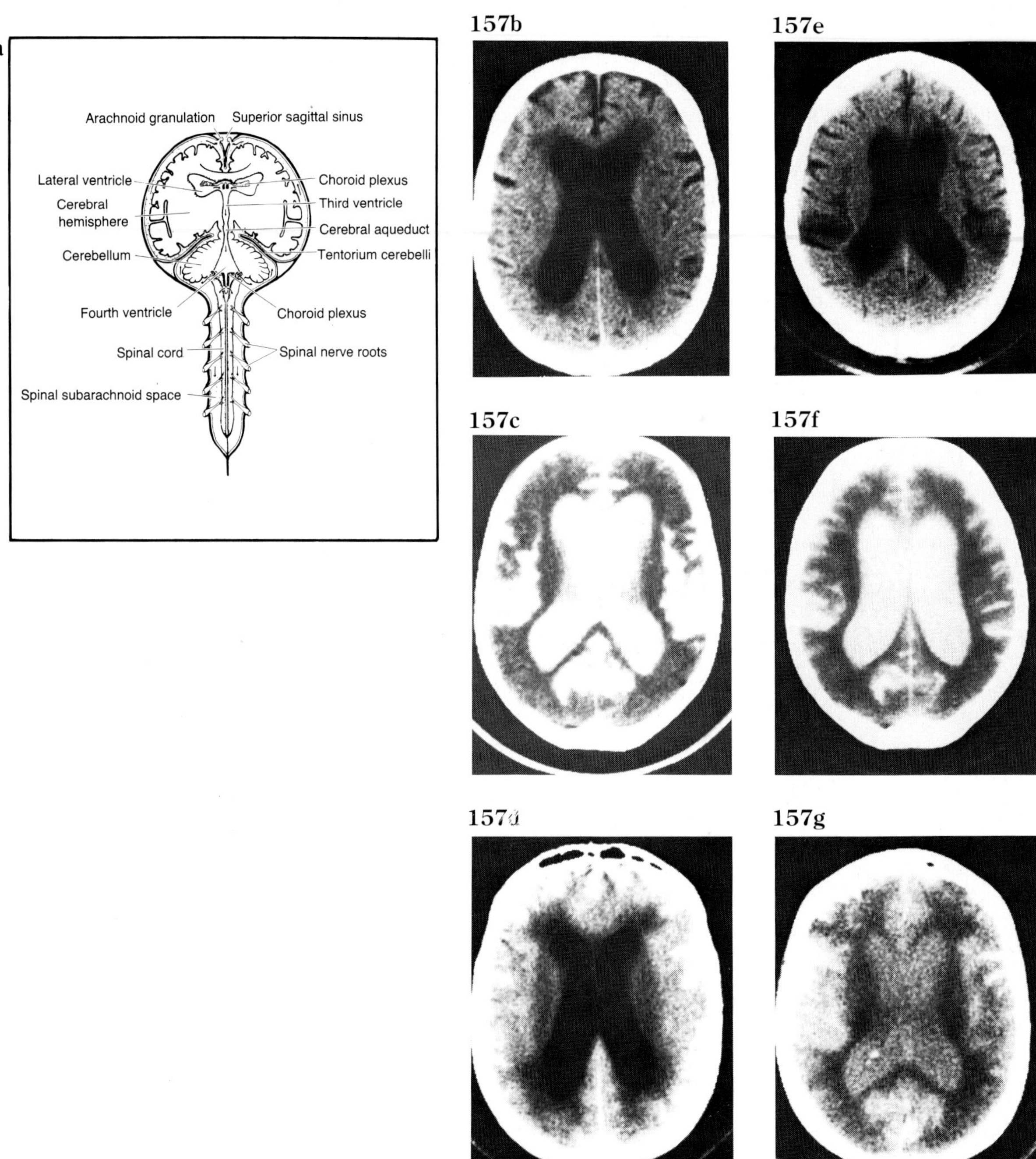

157 Low- or normal-pressure hydrocephalus is a condition in which CSF accumulates in the whole of the subarachnoid space as a result of the failure of the arachnoid granulations to reabsorb the CSF. The condition presents with a triad of mental confusion, incontinence and gait dyspraxia. **a**, Diagram of a subarachnoid space showing the choroid plexuses, where the CSF is formed, and the arachnoid granulations, where it is reabsorbed. *Normal case:* **b**, before contrast; **c**, 6 hours after contrast; **d**, 24 hours after contrast. *Low-pressure hydrocephalus:* **e**, before contrast; **f**, 6 hours after contrast; **g**, 48 hours after contrast. Low-pressure hydrocephalus is characterised by ventricular dilatation but the sign on the CAT scan is non-specific and accurate diagnosis requires intrathecal injection of contrast material. In the normal case (**b–d**) this clears within 24 hours, whereas in low-pressure hydrocephalus (**e–g**) some contrast persists even at 48 hours. Many cases can be cured by inserting a shunt.

158

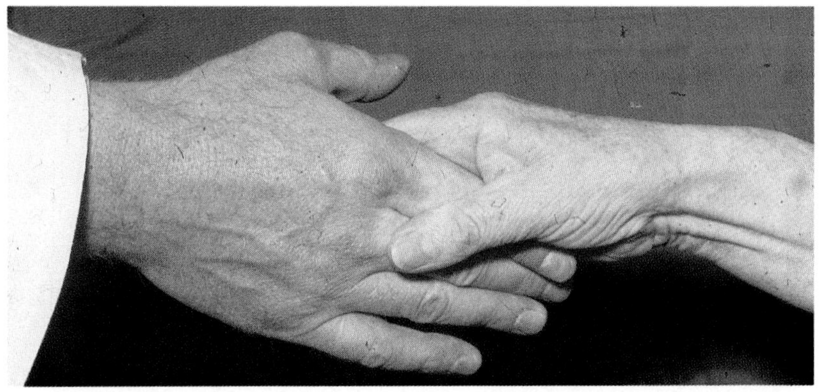

159

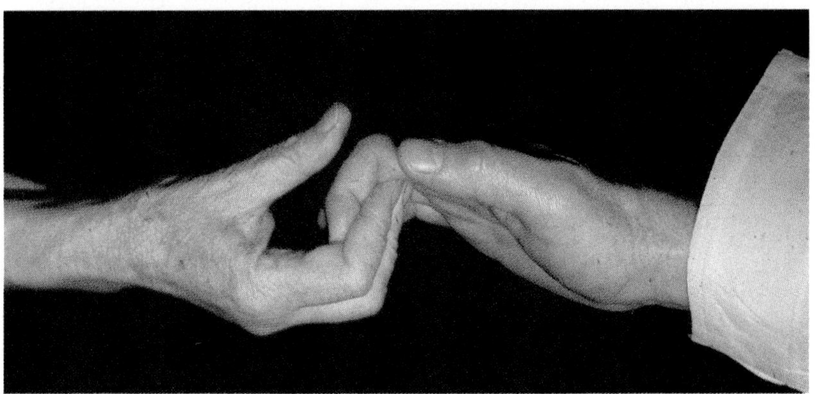

160

158 and 159 Primitive reflexes. Diseases of the frontal lobes – particularly senile and multi-infarct dementias – allow the emergence of primitive reflexes, among which the most easily tested are the grasp reflex and forced groping. In forced groping, the patient's hand follows a moving stimulus inside the palm. In the grasp reflex, a pressure applied by the examiner's fingertips moving towards the patient's fingertips on the flexor tendons causes a grasp which will not be released even if the patient is pulled clear of the bed. Other primitive reflexes seen in dementia are the sucking, snout and palmomental reflexes and the glabellar tap.

160 Dementia. Paratonic rigidity in a case of multi-infarct dementia.

161a

161b

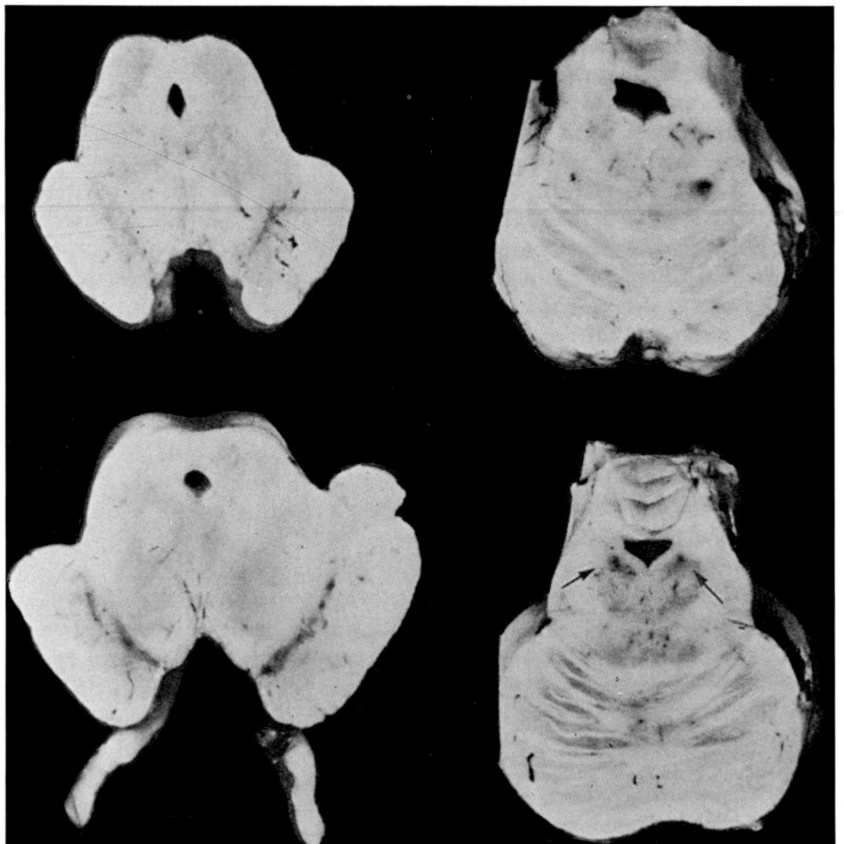

161 Parkinsonism. Patient's brain above, normal control below. **a** Severe pallor of substantia nigra. **b** Disappearance of pigmented neurones of locus caeruleus.

162

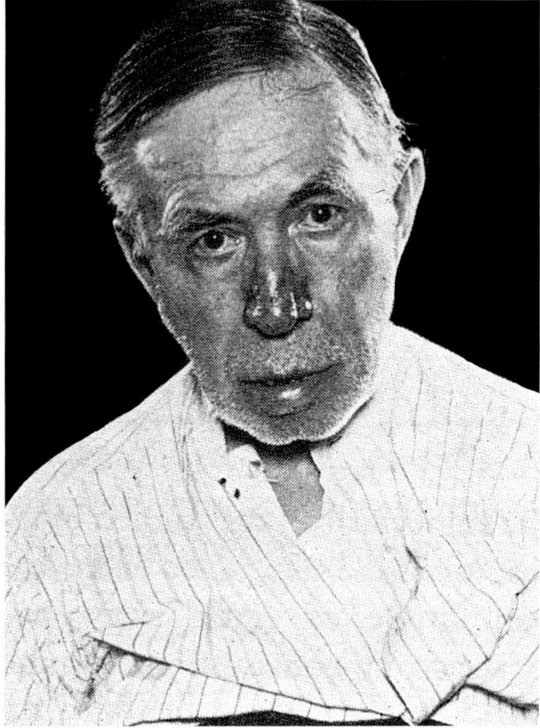

162 Parkinsonism. Showing the classic expressionless face and unblinking stare.

16

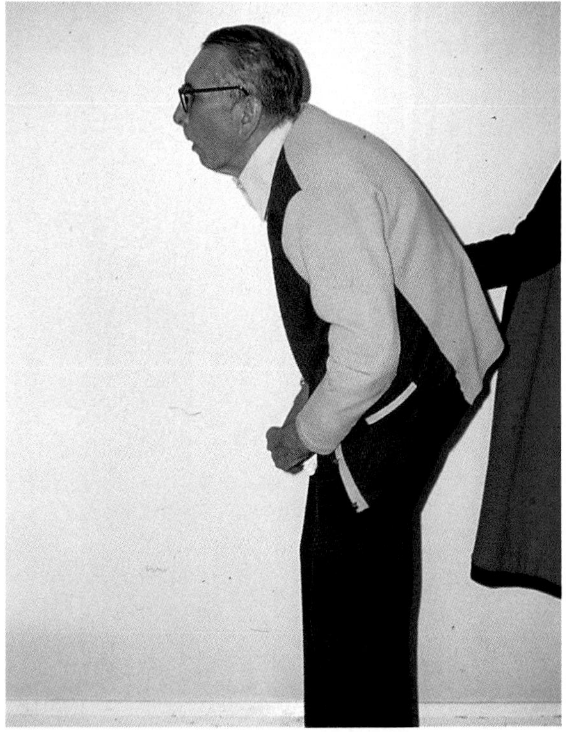

163 Parkinsonism. Typical stooped posture with considerable akinesia and shuffling gait.

164

164 Advanced parkinsonism. With increased muscle tone, dementia and permanent flexion of upper and lower limbs.

165

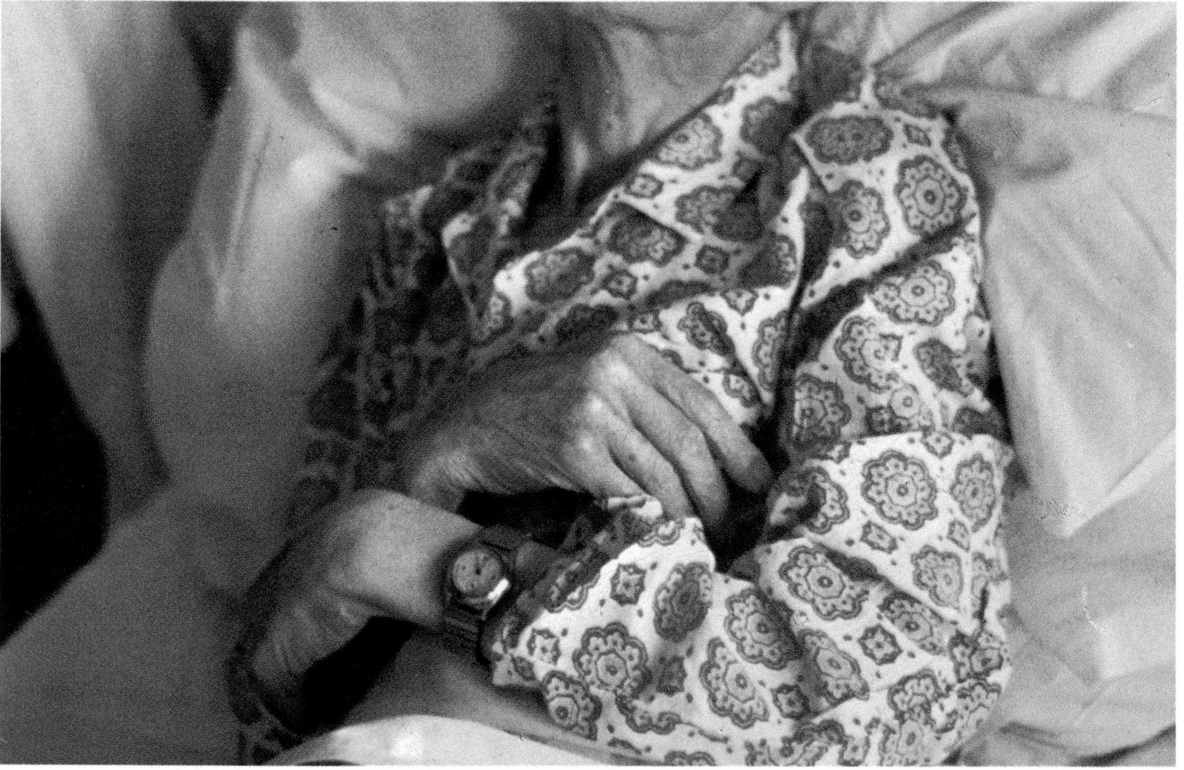

165 Advanced parkinsonism. The arms are flexed with increased rigidity and there is complete akinesia. Such patients are in danger of suffering from pressure sores, faecal impaction, urinary incontinence, dehydration and broncho-pneumonia.

166 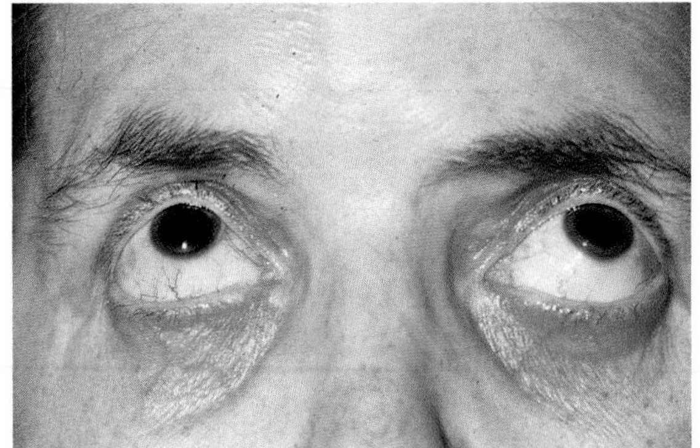

166 Oculogyric crisis. The eyes are deviated and fixed upwards and the patient has pronounced generalised rigidity. This is not the same as Parkinson's disease and does not respond to L-dopa. It is a particular feature of post-encephalitic parkinsonism.

167 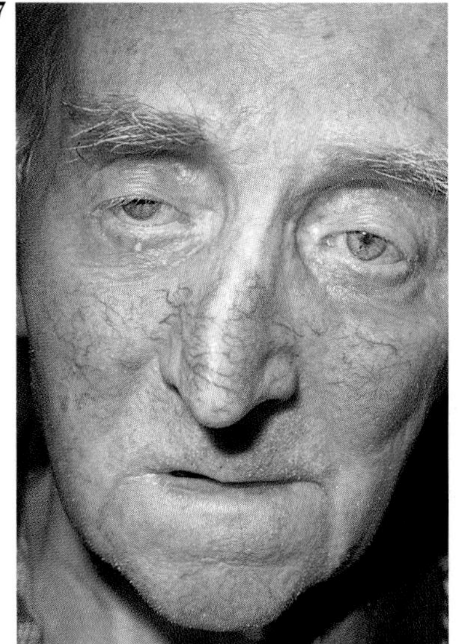

Progressive supranuclear palsy
(Steel–Richardson–Olszewski syndrome)

Clinical features
Pseudodementia – great delay before answering or carrying out instructions
Parkinsonism-like picture
Difficulty in walking and frequent falls
Dystonic rigidity of face, neck and trunk
Supranuclear ophthalmoplegia affecting vertical gaze
Pseudobulbar palsy

167 Progressive supranuclear palsy. The patient has dementia, upper motor neurone signs and an inability to look upwards.

168 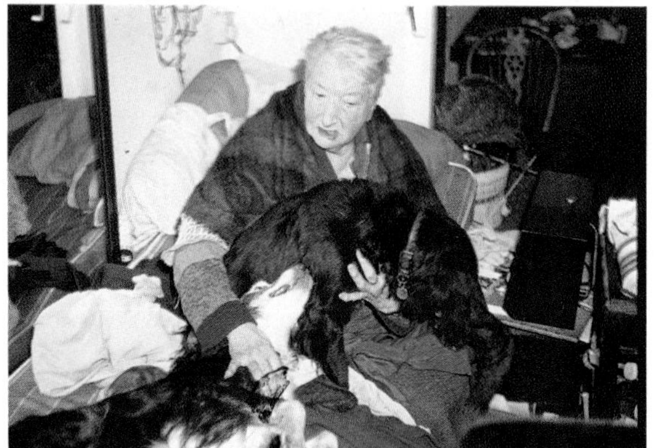

168 Diogenes syndrome. A form of self-neglect occasionally seen in the elderly. The patients are usually single and spend their money on pets or buying food and other household items which they never use. They may have an odd personality, but there are no signs of dementia.

 169

169 Senile self-neglect. Usually due to an underlying illness, e.g. brain failure, hypothyroidism, depression.

6 Disorders of the Chest

170

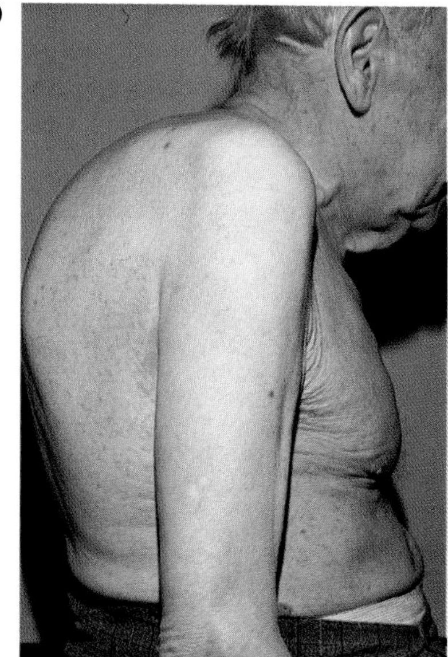

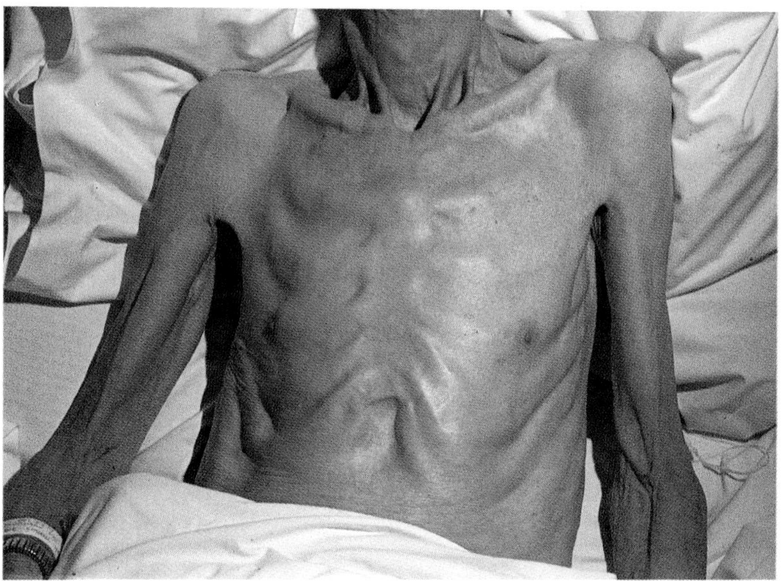

171

170 Barrel-shaped chest. This elderly man had chronic obstructive airways disease and suffered with persistent dyspnoea. Note the dorsal kyphosis.

171 Cachexia. Wasted chest with weight loss caused by carcinoma of the stomach.

172 Dyspnoea. Chest of a patient with chronic asthma. Breathing required considerable effort and the accessory muscles of respiration are being fully used.

Common causes of wasting in the elderly

Malignant disease
Previous gastric surgery
Dementia
Depression and bereavement
Chronic renal failure
Chronic obstructive airways disease
Tuberculosis
Hyperthyroidism
Bacterial endocarditis
Severe social deprivation combined with physical or mental illness

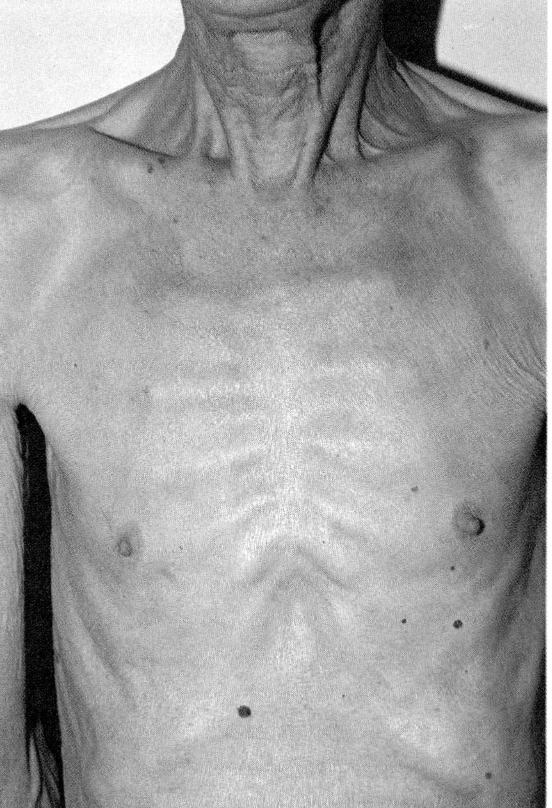

172

173

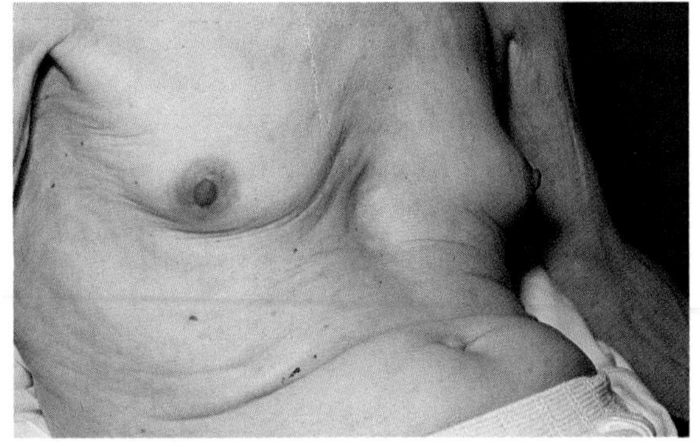

173 Gynaecomastia. Enlargement of breasts in an elderly male who was found to have bronchogenic carcinoma.

174

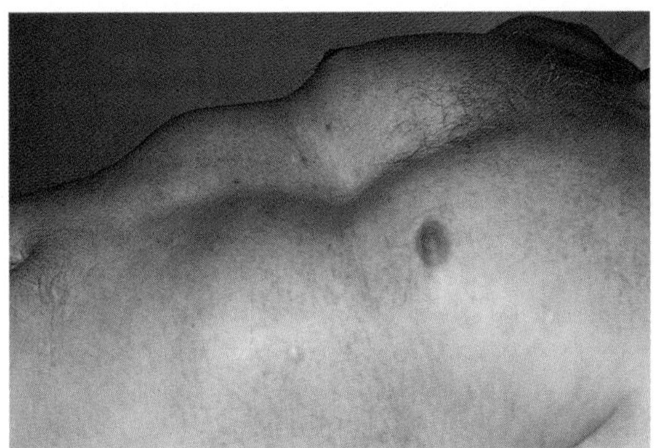

174 Pectus excavatum. Depressed sternum caused by an association of rickets and whooping cough in childhood (but often idiopathic). The patient had no respiratory problems.

Causes of gynaecomastia

- Endocrine
  - Hypothyroidism and thyrotoxicosis
  - Acromegaly
  - Hypothalamic lesions
  - Testicular and adrenal tumours
- Drugs
  - Oestrogens
  - Spironolactone
  - Reserpine
  - Methyldopa
- Cirrhosis of the liver
- Carcinoma of the bronchus and lymphoma
- Chronic renal failure treated with dialysis
- Long-standing paraplegia

175

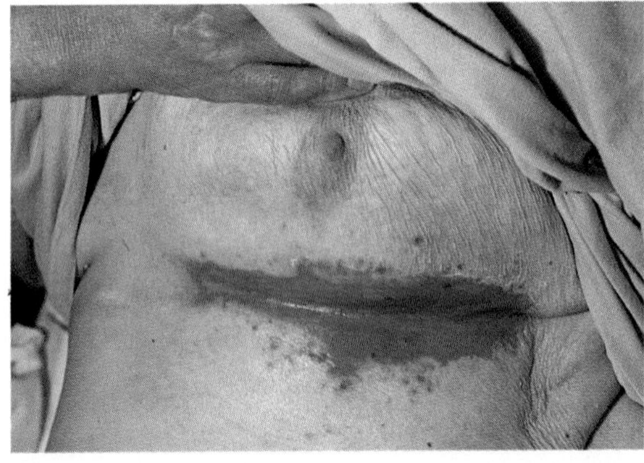

175 Submammary intertrigo. Sore area under the breast of an obese elderly lady. Poor personal hygiene is an important contributory factor.

176

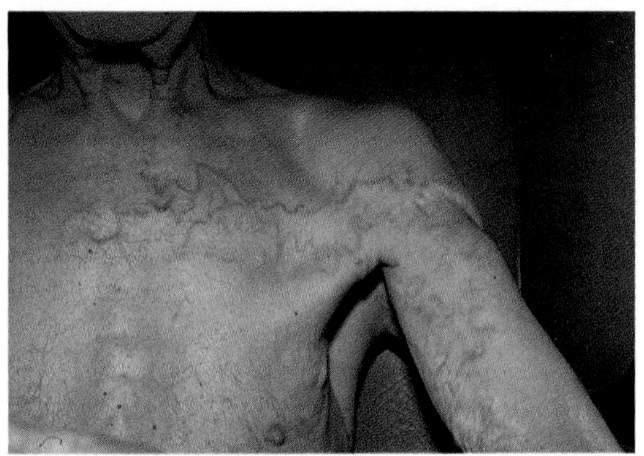

176 Superior vena cava obstruction. Obstruction caused by malignant enlargement of lymph nodes in the superior mediastinum causing dilatation of the superficial veins in the upper chest wall and arm. The patient was found to have carcinoma of the lung.

177 Superior vena cava obstruction. Note the prominence of veins on the chest, and facial congestion. This patient also felt that his collar was too tight around his neck.

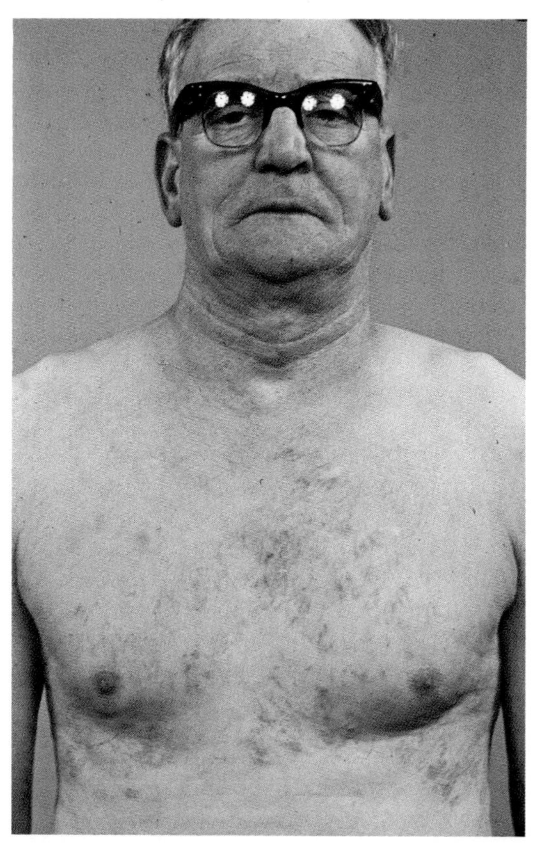

177

178 Winging of scapula. Result of paralysis of serratus magnus muscle caused by a lesion involving the long thoracic nerve. There is inability to raise the arm over the head from a forward position, with winging of medial border of scapula on pushing forward against resistance. The patient had diabetes mellitus.

Causes of mononeuritis multiplex

Diabetes mellitus
Carcinoma
Rheumatoid arthritis
Polyarteritis nodosa
Sarcoidosis

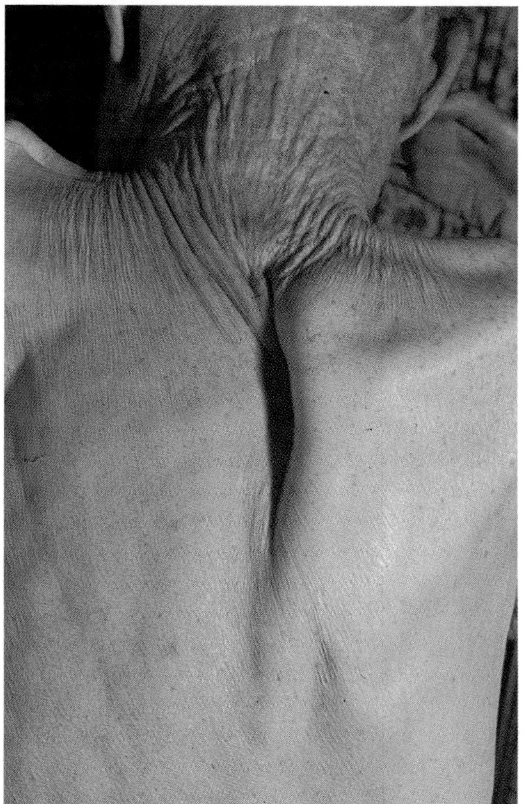

178

179

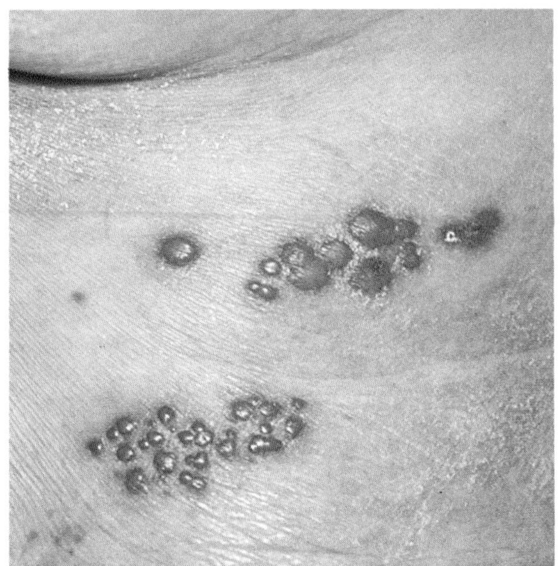

179 Herpes zoster. An early case of herpes zoster showing painful bullous eruption on the chest wall. It is important to identify lesions at the pre-vesicular stage if treatment (with idoxuridine, acyclovir, steroids) is to be fully effective.

180

181

180 and 181 Herpes zoster. Herpes on the lateral chest wall involving the mid-thoracic dermatomes. The patient had chronic lymphatic leukaemia and subsequently developed post-herpetic neuralgia.

182 Carcinoma of the breast. Painless fungating carcinoma in an 85-year-old woman. The condition had been present for several months, but the patient simply ignored it. Carcinoma of the breast tends to run a chronic course in the very elderly. The approximate incidence is 190 per 100,000 per year in females.

182

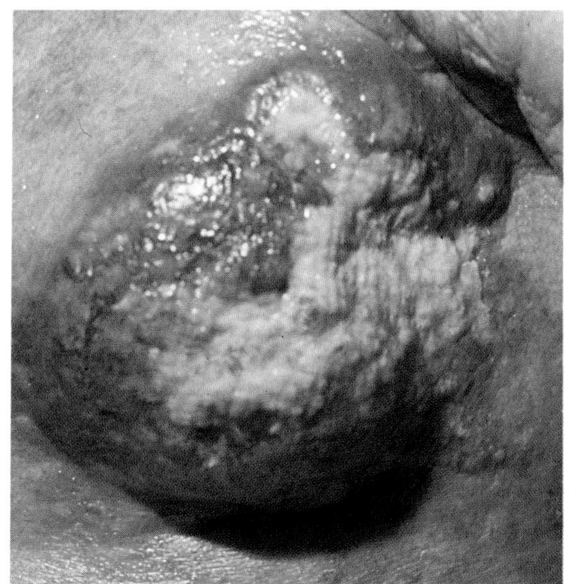

183

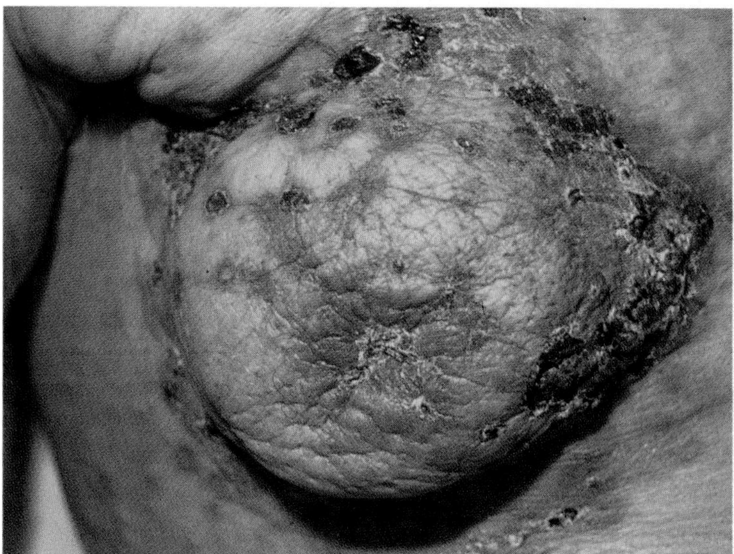

183 Carcinoma of the breast. In this case there is more widespread infiltration by the malignant tissue. The lesion was again painless and there was no evidence of metastases.

184

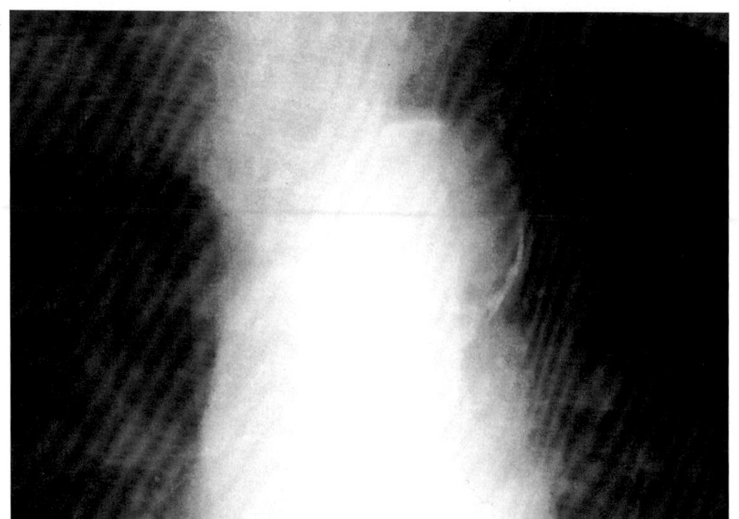

184 Calcified aortic knuckle. A common, benign appearance associated with advancing age.

185

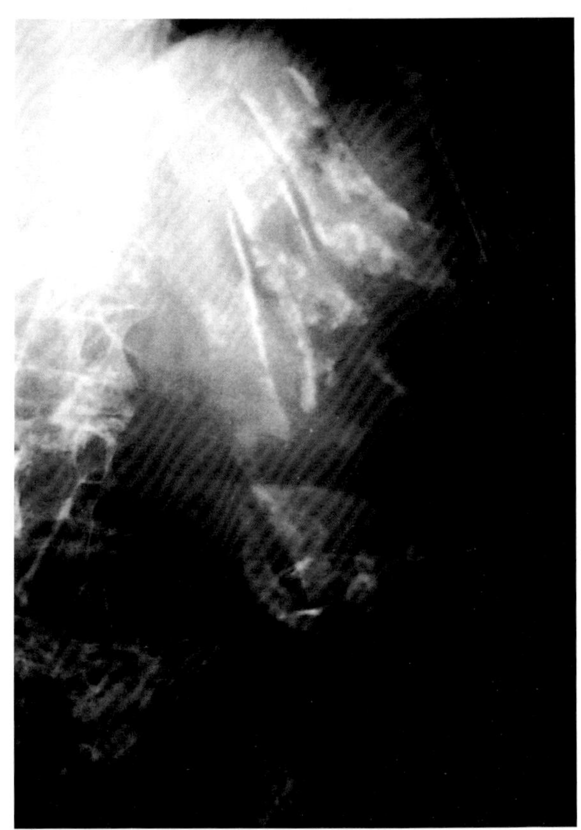

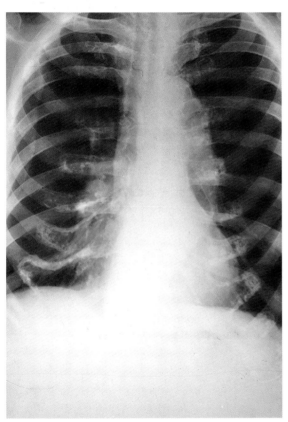

185 Calcified costochondral cartilages. A common, radiological finding in the elderly. May be confused with intrapulmonary or pleural calcification.

186 Calcified costochondral cartilages. A close-up view.

187

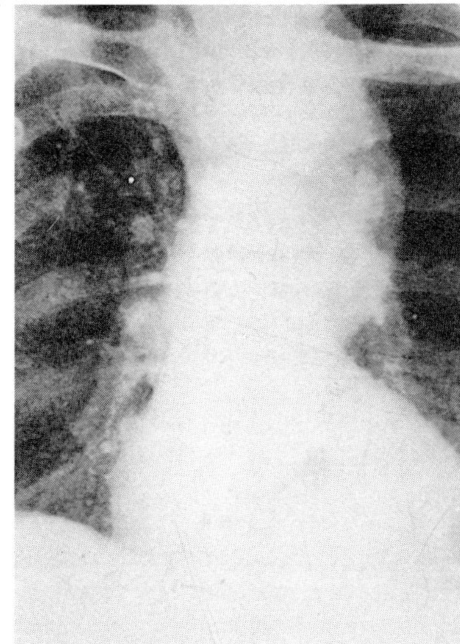

Aneurysms of the aorta aetiology
Aneurysms of the abdominal aorta
Atherosclerosis plus hypertension
Aneurysms of the ascending aorta
Arteriosclerosis
Cystic medial necrosis
Syphilis
Aneurysms of the descending aorta
Arteriosclerosis
Non-penetrating chest trauma

187 Unfolded aorta. A common radiological finding in the elderly, caused by a combination of arteriosclerosis and hypertension. The condition is symptomless but may be confused with aortic aneurysm.

188 Aortic aneurysm. An aneurysm involving the aortic arch. The patient had previously contracted syphilis and had symptoms of mediastinal obstruction.

189 Aortic aneurysm. An aneurysm involving the descending aorta and caused by arteriosclerotic changes in the vessel wall. Note streaks of calcification in the aortic wall.

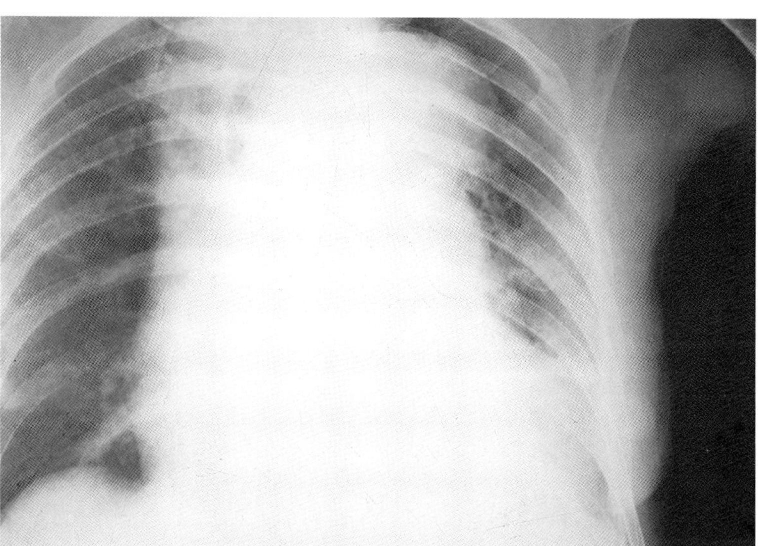

188

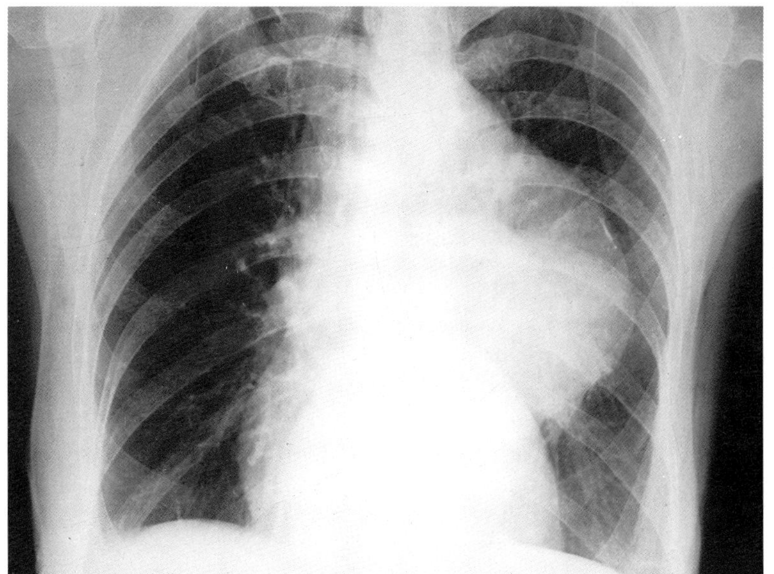

190

191

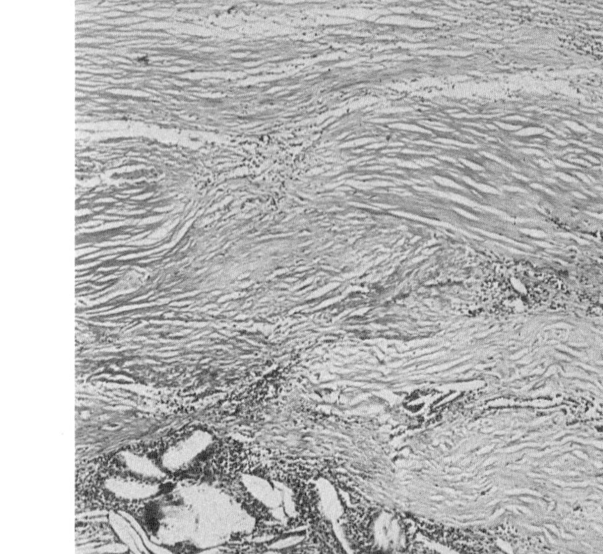

190 and 191 Aortic arteriosclerosis. Early arteriosclerotic changes in the aortic wall. This may eventually lead to the development of an aneurysm. **190** shows a fatty streak in the aortic wall; **191** shows a fibro–fatty plaque in the aorta.

Arteriosclerosis in the elderly may present as cerebrovascular accident, ischaemic heart disease, ischaemic colitis, peripheral vascular disease, or it may remain completely silent.

2

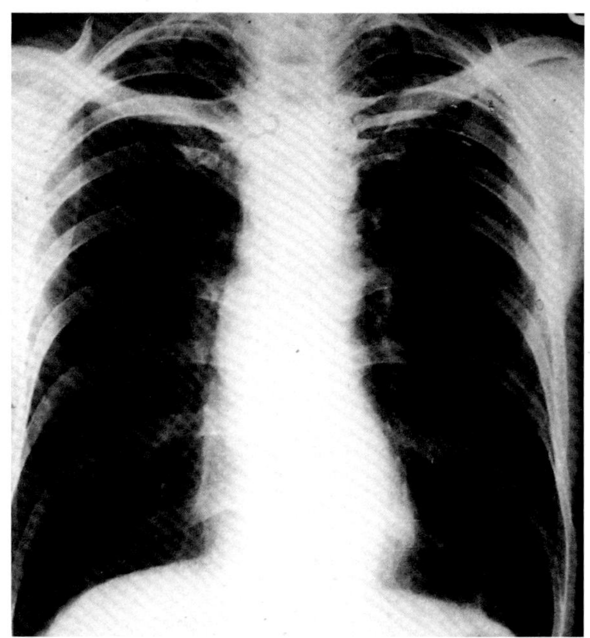

193

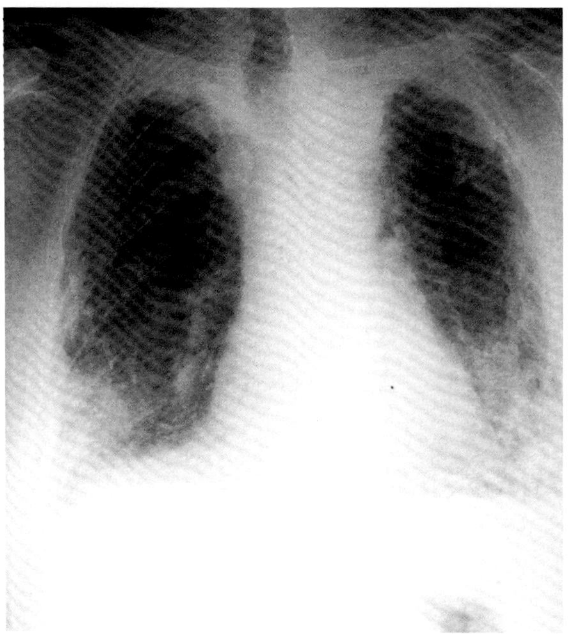

192 Emphysema. Chest x-ray showing hyper-inflated lungs with longitudinal cardiac shadow in an advanced case of emphysema.

193 Pulmonary fibrosis. Chest x-ray showing bilateral basal lung shadows in a case of recurrent chest infections with some bronchiectasis.

Hypertension in the elderly

Treatment of hypertension in the elderly remains controversial. However, a number of studies in recent years indicate that some elderly patients do derive benefit, with reduction in symptoms and increased well-being when their hypertension is treated. Also, there may be a reduction of certain complications such as strokes and heart disease.

WHO defines hypertension as:

> Systolic pressure equal to or higher than 160 mmHg and diastolic pressure equal to or higher than 95 mmHg. Isolated systolic hypertension is defined as systolic pressure of 160 mmHg or more with a diastolic pressure lower than 95 mmHg.

The incidence and prevalence of hypertension in the elderly is between 25% and 60% depending on the level of blood pressure used to define hypertension, the type of population studied and the number of blood pressure measurements taken.

Hypertension in the elderly is an important risk factor for myocardial infarction and cerebrovascular accidents. Isolated systolic hypertension is the single most important risk factor for cardiovascular disease in the elderly. There is evidence that treatment reduces the incidence of fatal and non-fatal strokes by about 39% and also there is overall reduction in cardiac mortality.

It is generally agreed that hypertensive elderly patients below the age of 80 years should receive treatment. The decision whether to treat or not should be made on an individual basis, balancing risks of the disease against compliance and other disabilities.

A list of selected studies that describe some of the benefits of treating hypertension in elderly patients is as follows:

- Effects of treatment in hypertension, Veterans Administration Co-operative Group, *JAMA*, **213**, 1143–52, 1970.
- Five-year findings of the Hypertension Detection Follow-up Program: Hypertension Detection Follow-up Co-operative Group, *JAMA*, **242**, 2562–71, 2572–7, 1979.
- Management Committee of the Australian Therapeutic Trials in Mild Hypertension: the Australian Therapeutic Trial, *Lancet*, **2**, 1261–7, 1980.
- Mortality and morbidity results from the European Working Party on High Blood Pressure in Elderly Trial, *Lancet*, **1**, 1349–54, 1985.
- Coop, J. and Warrander, T.S., Randomised trial of treatment of hypertension in elderly in primary care, *Brit. Med. J.*, **293**, 1145–51, 1986.

Guidelines for treating hypertension in the elderly

1. Blood pressure should be measured three times at least 24 hours apart at the same time each day with the patient in a relaxed state.
2. Treat systolic blood pressure above 180 mmHg and diastolic blood pressure above 110 mmHg. It must be said that some authorities would treat hypertension with slightly lower readings.
3. Advise the patient to adopt a healthier life style first, i.e. reduce weight in obese patients, reduce sodium intake to 1.5–2.5 g daily, reduce alcohol intake to below 30 ml per day, take regular aerobic exercise and stop smoking.
4. Treatment of hypertension in elderly patients should be tailored to the individual patient's needs.
5. Choose drugs that do not adversely affect the quality of life.
6. Reduce the blood pressure gradually.
7. Check the blood pressure lying and standing.
8. Treat hypertension in over eighties only if blood pressure is causing complications; for example, left ventricular failure.
9. Treatment should start with a thiazide, beta-blocker or calcium antagonist.
10. Acetylcholinesterase inhibitors and other vasodilators are useful in patients who do not respond to, or cannot tolerate, other drugs.

194

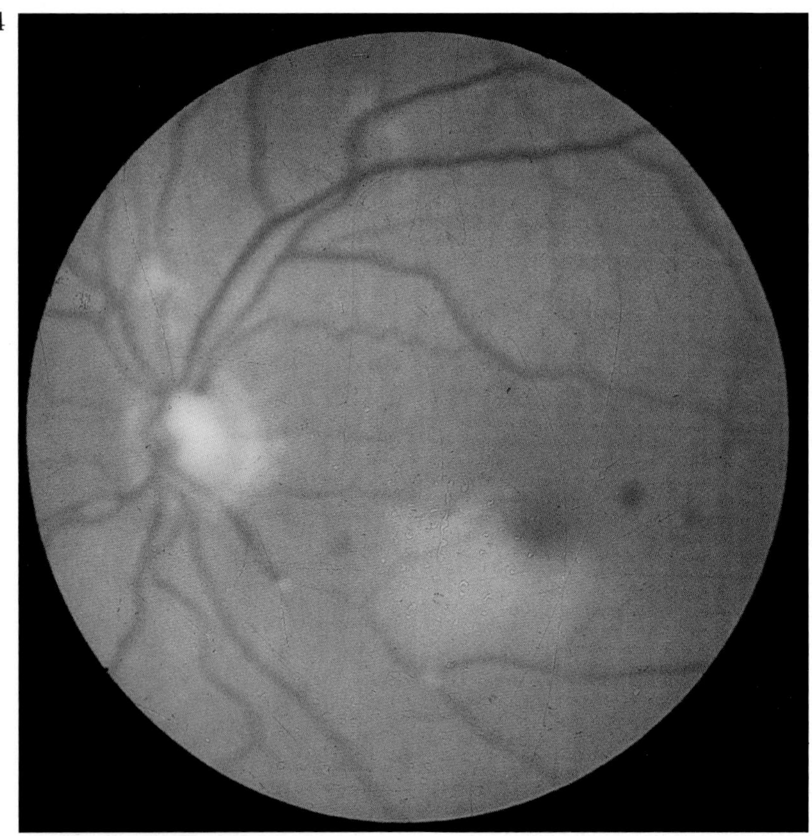

194 Hypertensive fundus. Grade three fundus with haemorrhages and exudates. (Courtesy of *A Colour Atlas of Hypertension*, K.M. Fox and L.M. Shapiro, Wolfe Publishing Ltd.)

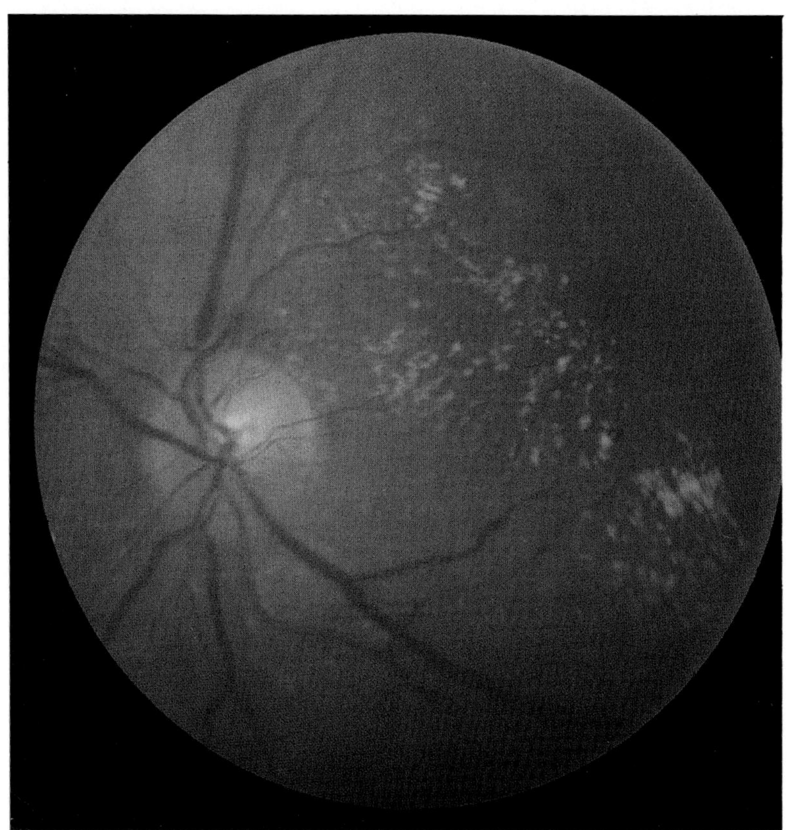

195

195 Hypertensive fundus. Grade three fundus with an extensive area of exudates. (Courtesy of *A Colour Atlas of Hypertension*, K.M. Fox and L.M. Shapiro, Wolfe Publishing Ltd.)

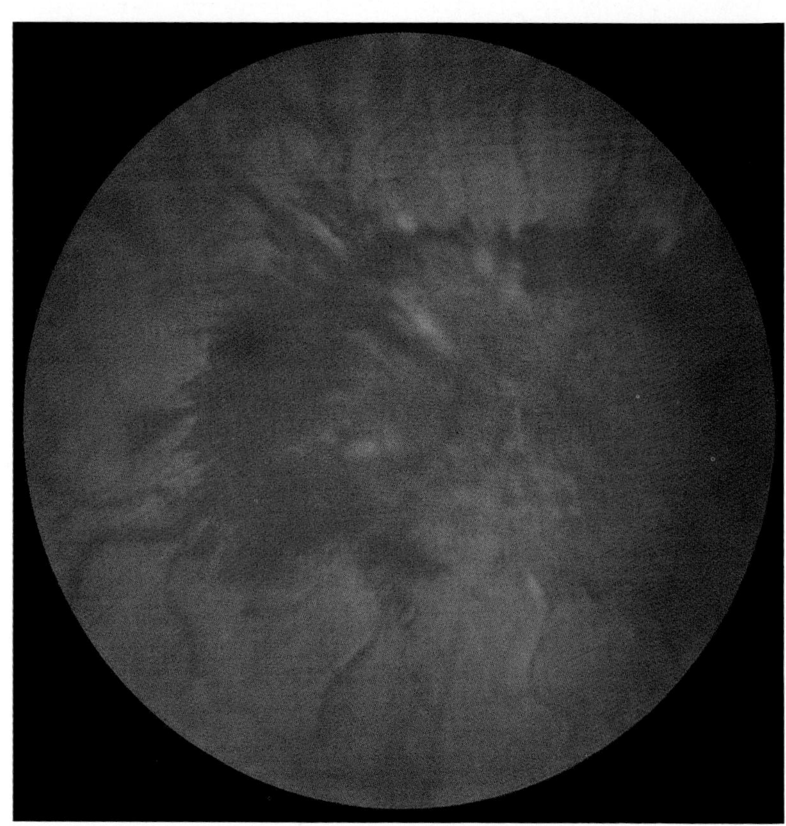

196

196 Hypertensive fundus. Severe grade four fundus with papilloedema, haemorrhages and exudates. (Courtesy of *A Colour Atlas of Hypertension*, K.M. Fox and L.M. Shapiro, Wolfe Publishing Ltd.)

197

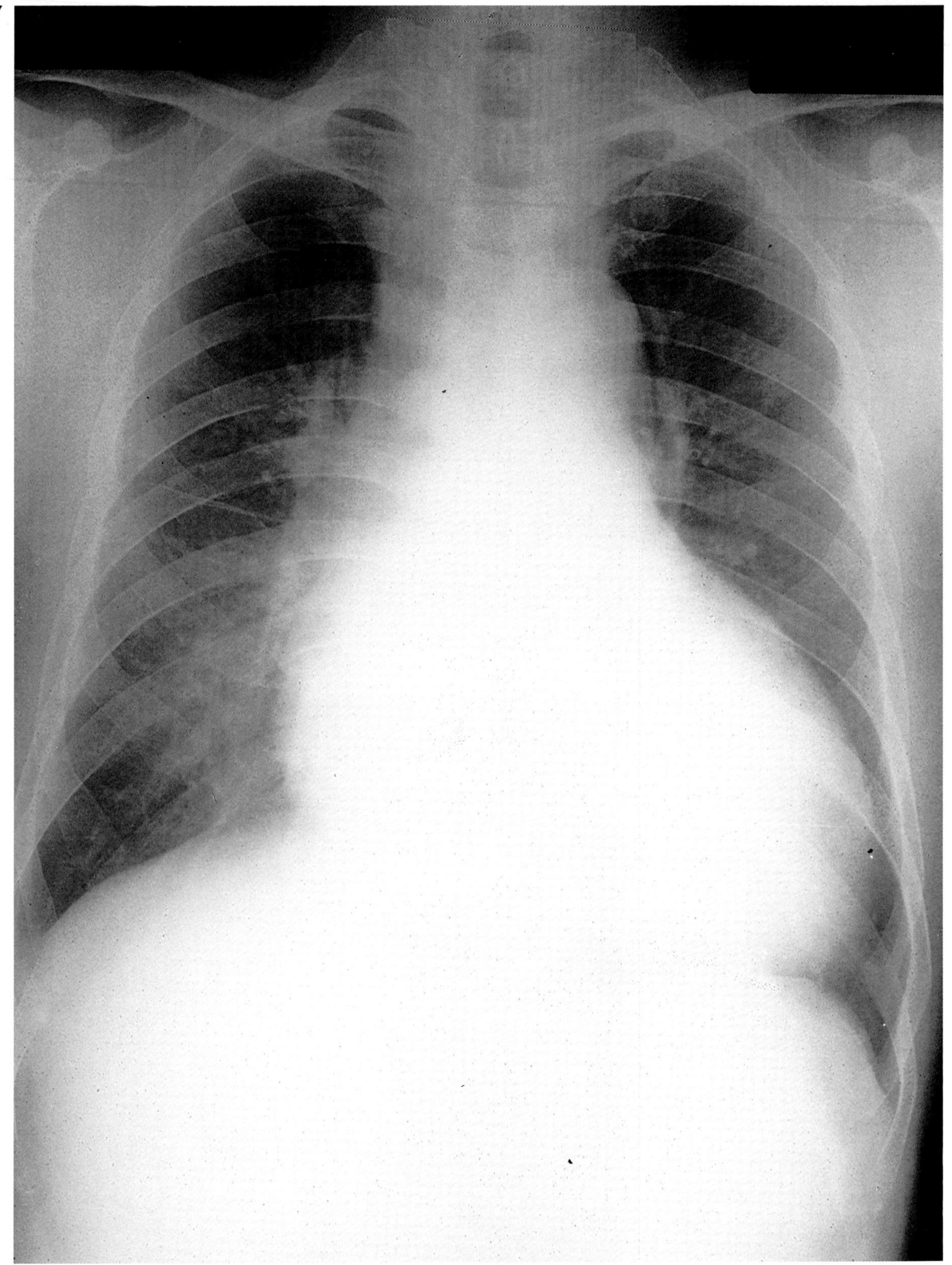

197 Hypertension. Chest x-ray in a patient with severe hypertension, with marked left ventricular dilatation. (Courtesy of *A Colour Atlas of Hypertension*, K.M. Fox and L.M. Shapiro, Wolfe Publishing Ltd.)

198 Pneumonia. A common disease of old age which carries a high mortality rate.

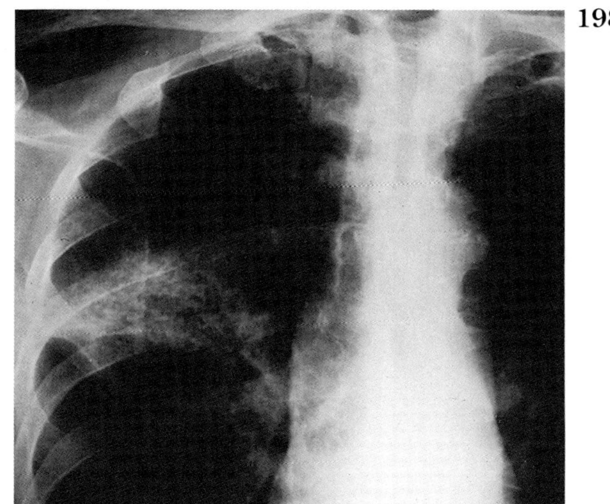
198

199 Chest infection. Plain chest x-ray showing infection at the right lung base. The patient had minimum signs and there was no pyrexia.

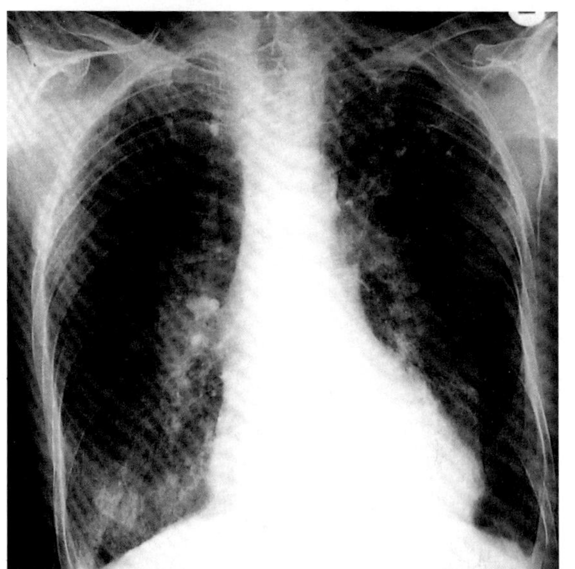
199

200 Chest infection. Plain chest x-ray showing extensive infection in the left lung. Very often such infections are persistent, indicating an underlying bronchogenic carcinoma. In such cases bronchoscopy is generally well tolerated by elderly patients.

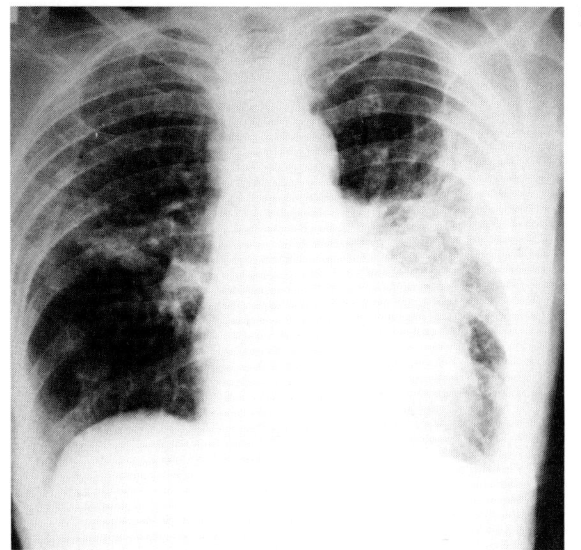
200

201

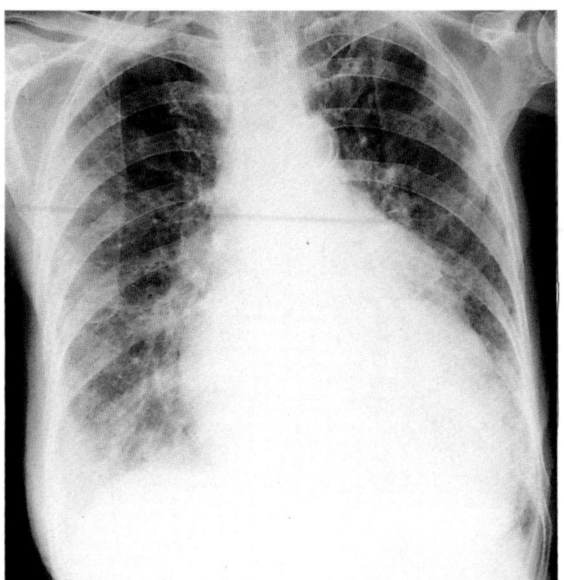

201 Mitral stenosis. Chest x-ray of an elderly patient showing features of mitral stenosis, especially bulging of the left cardiac border. The prevalence of rheumatic mitral valve disease in elderly hospital patients is about 4%.

202

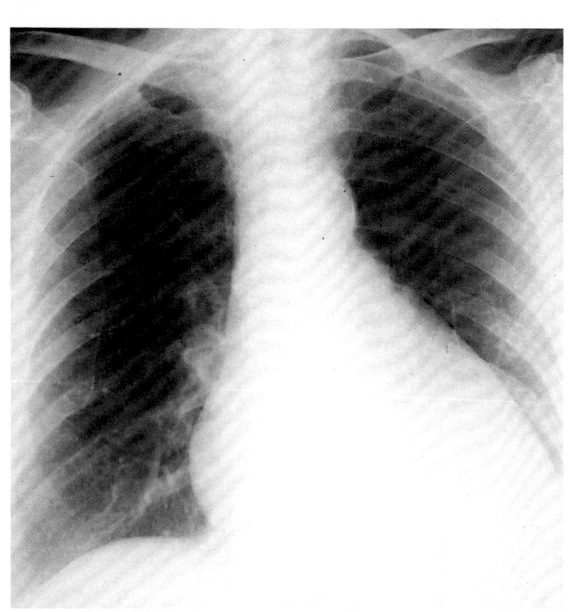

202 Mitral stenosis. A less severe case than **201**. Note straightening of the left cardiac border due to left atrial enlargement. About 33% of patients with this condition have atrial fibrillation.

203

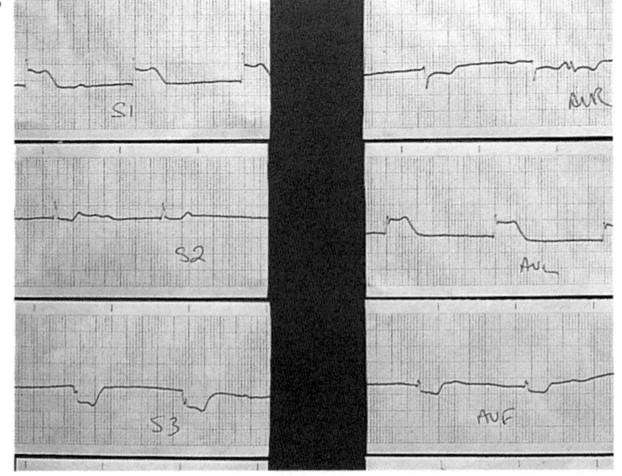

203 Myocardial infarction. ECG showing ST elevation in a case of recent myocardial infarction. In the elderly myocardial infarction often causes no chest pain and the patient presents with collapse, falls, sudden onset confusion or cardiac failure.

204 Atrial fibrillation. ECG showing fast atrial fibrillation. This is a frequent finding in sick, elderly patients and is usually due to underlying ischaemic heart disease. Symptomless atrial fibrillation with normal ventricular rate may not require any specific therapy. However, frequent monitoring is essential.

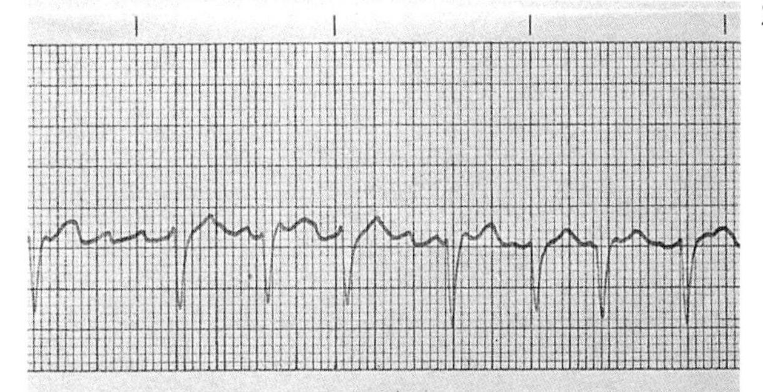

204

205 Ambulatory ECG. This picture shows recording of a 24-hour ambulatory ECG. The recorded tape is later analysed in a computerised playback system which shows up any abnormalities that may have occurred in the ECG over the 24-hour period. This investigation is useful in detecting episodes of cardiac ischaemia and transient cardiac arrhythmias – especially in elderly patients who have unexplained symptoms such as palpitations, dizziness, faints and falls.

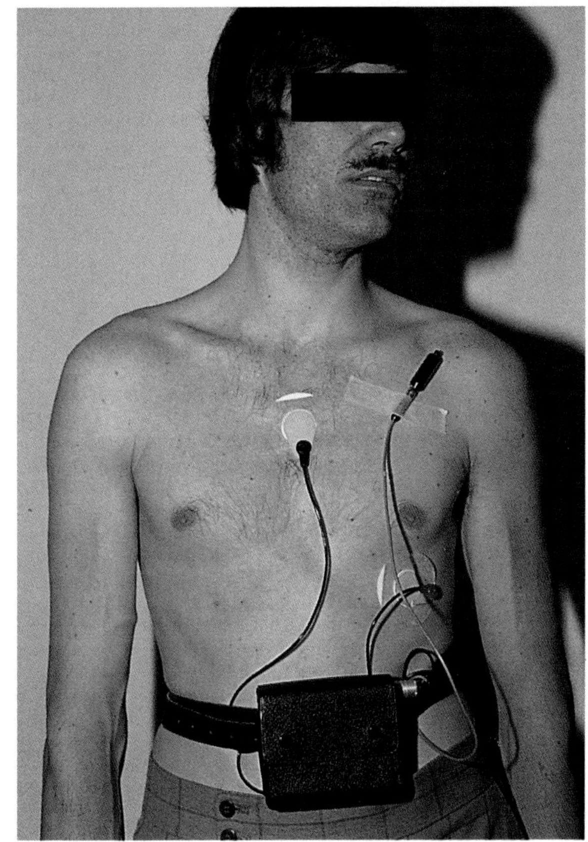

205

206 Transient cardiac arrhythmia. A 24-hour ECG tape analysis showing an episode of transient cardiac arrhythmia which coincided with the patient's symptoms of dizziness and faints. There is tachycardia with ventricular rate above 115/min.

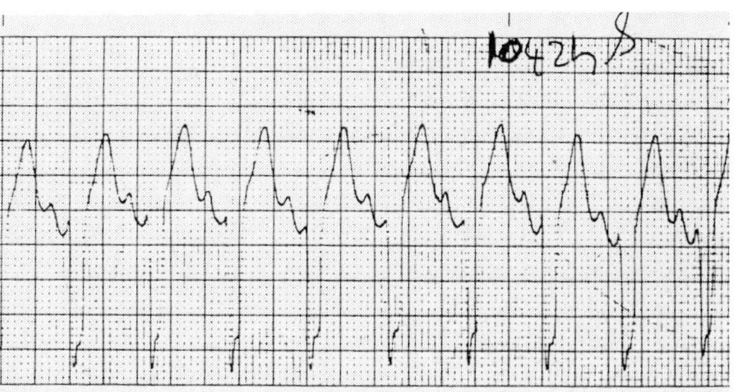

206

207

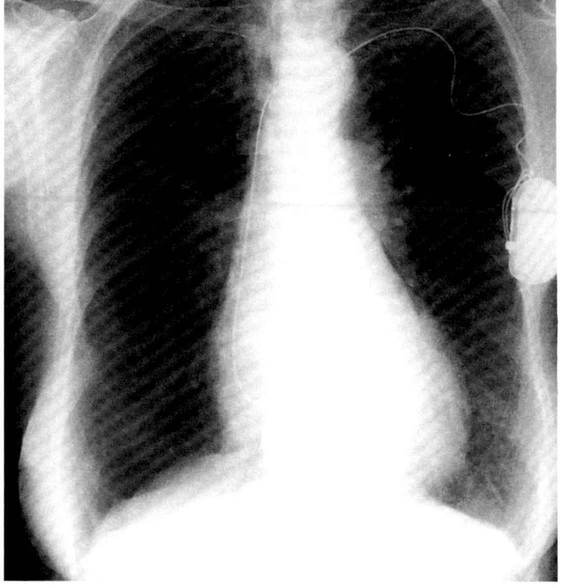

20

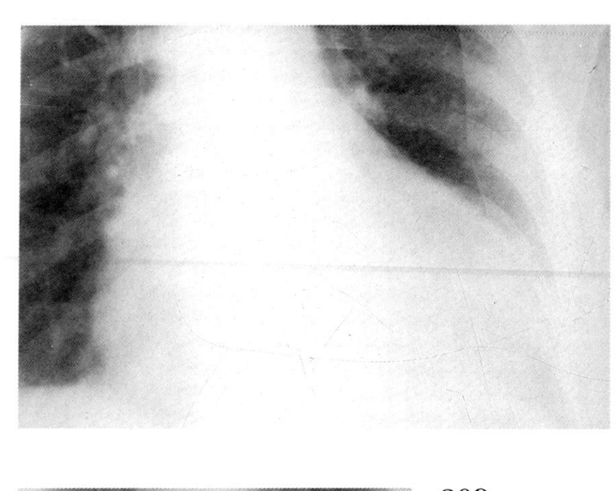

209

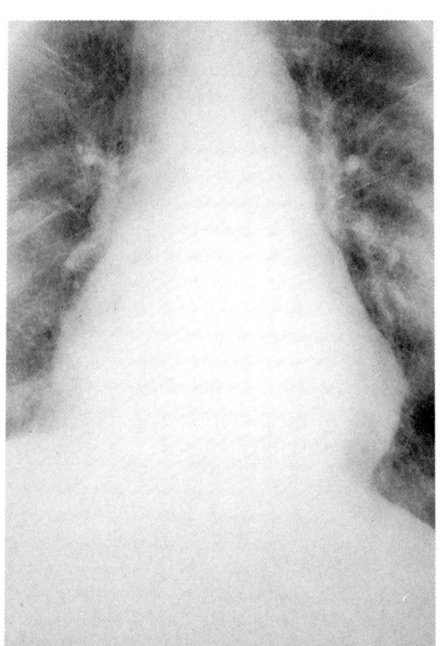

210

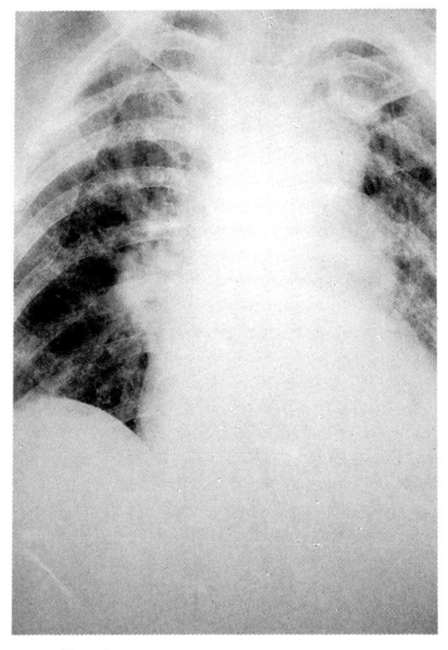

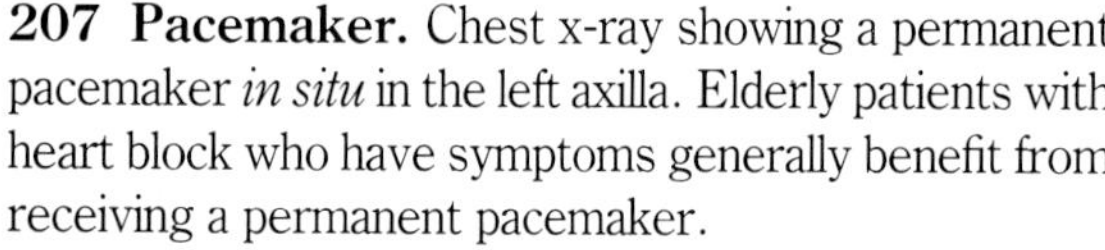

207 Pacemaker. Chest x-ray showing a permanent pacemaker *in situ* in the left axilla. Elderly patients with heart block who have symptoms generally benefit from receiving a permanent pacemaker.

208 Cardiomegaly. Routine chest x-ray in an elderly patient showing cardiac enlargement with left ventricular prominence. The patient had no symptoms of cardiorespiratory disease.

209 Congestive cardiac failure. A frequent cause of admission to geriatric units. Note the gross cardiomegaly and pulmonary oedema.

210 Congestive cardiac failure. There is pulmonary oedema and the cause is hypertensive heart disease.

Cardiac failure in the elderly

Ischaemic heart disease
Hypertension
Degenerative calcific changes in mitral ring or aortic cusp
Corpulmonale
Senile cardiac amyloidosis
Endocarditis – including non-bacterial thrombotic endocarditis
Calcified aortic stenosis
Rheumatic heart disease
Mucoid degeneration of the mitral valve
Myxoedema
High output failure in chronic anaemia, thyrotoxicosis, Paget's disease and beri-beri

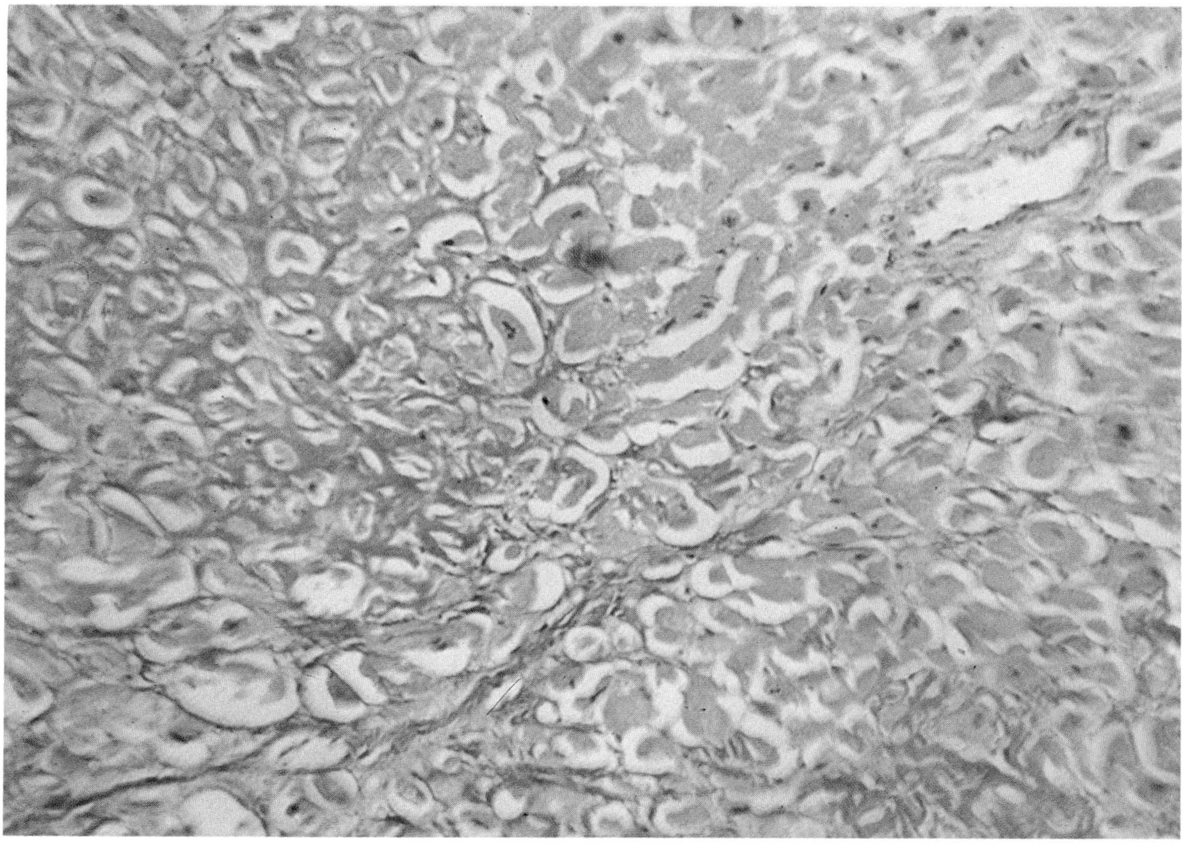

211

211 Cardiac amyloidosis. Found with increasing frequency in the very old and is said to cause congestive heart failure. In the histology picture the amyloid is stained green, muscle yellow, and fibrous tissue red. (*Sulphonated alcian blue technique*)

212 Left ventricular aneurysm. A complication of previous myocardial infarction, involving the left ventricular wall and producing severe left ventricular failure.

It often appears within a few months after the infarct and may give rise to systemic embolism.

212

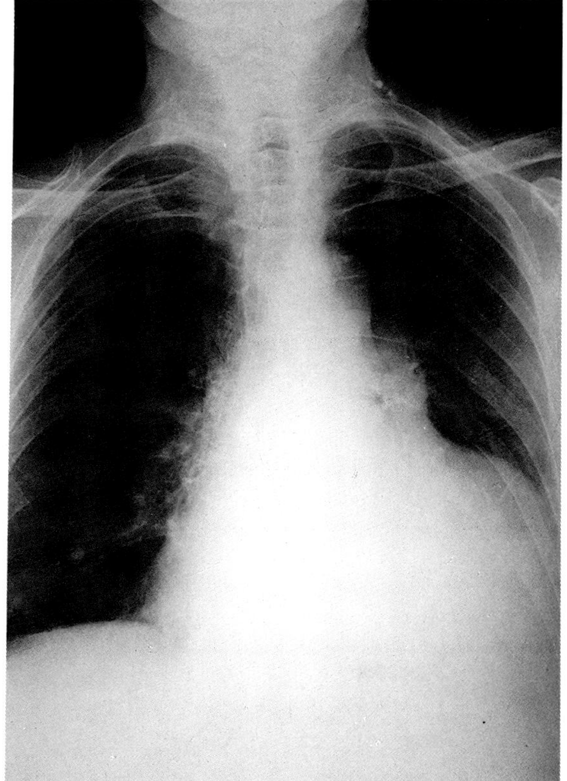

213

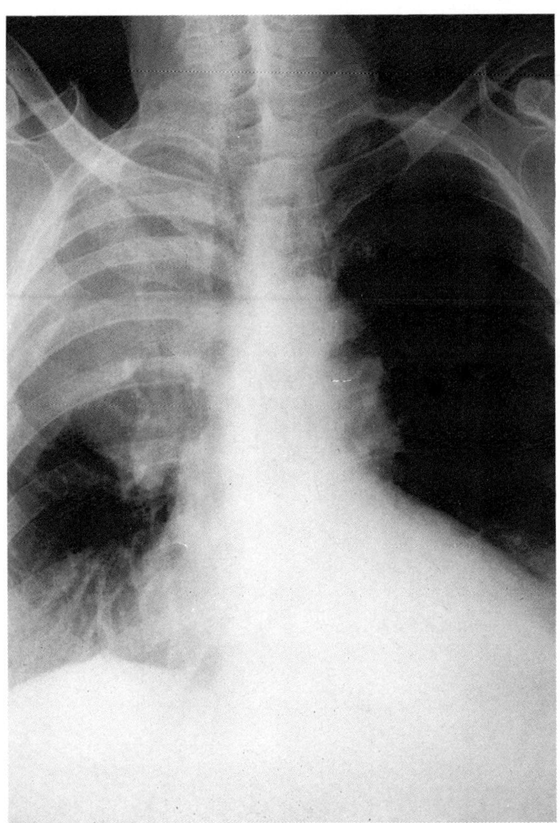

213 Bronchogenic carcinoma. The right upper lung is involved. It is a common malignancy of old age. The incidence is approximately 250 per 100,000 population per year.

Complications of carcinoma of the bronchus

Local complications
Bronchial obstruction, superior vena cava obstruction, pleural effusion, erosion of large blood vessels, cervical sympathetic, recurrent laryngeal or phrenic nerve involvement

Metastasis
Hilar nodes, liver, cerebrum, adrenals, bone

Non-metastatic extra-pulmonary effects
Cachexia, anaemia
Clubbing and hypertrophic pulmonary osteoarthropathy
Encephalopathy, neuropathy and myopathy

Endocrine syndromes:
Inappropriate ADH production
Ectopic ACTH production
Pigmentation
Inappropriate parathormone production
Carcinoid syndrome
Thyrotoxicosis-like disorder
Gynaecomastia
Hypoglycemia
Red-cell aplasia

Skin changes:
Metastasis, pruritis, various types of skin rashes, dermatomyositis, eczema herpeticum, hyperhidrosis

214 Pulmonary metastases. Round, discrete shadows of secondary deposits from carcinoma of the ovary.

Hypernephromas, melanomas and tumours of the breast, pancreas and testicle tend to favour the lungs for the growth of metastases.

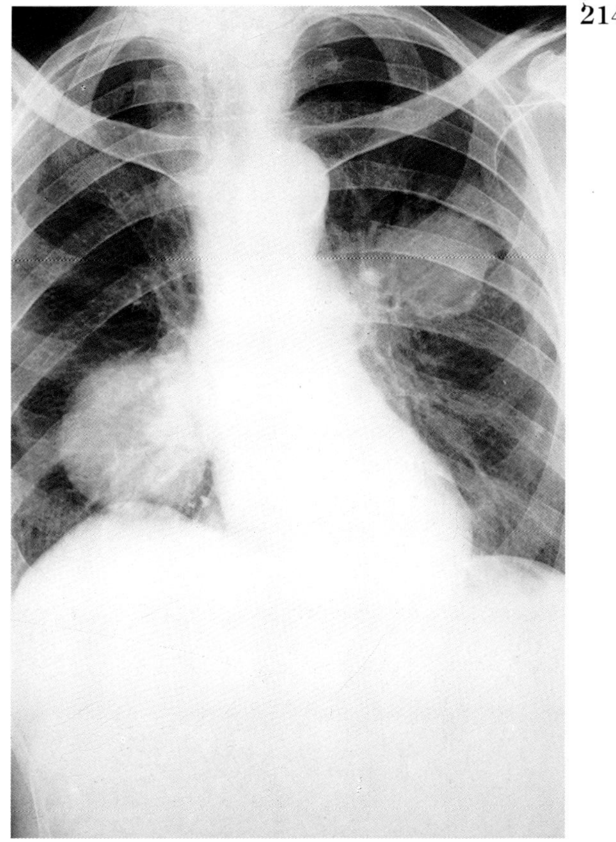

214

215 Pulmonary metastasis. Multiple lung secondaries from carcinoma of the kidney.

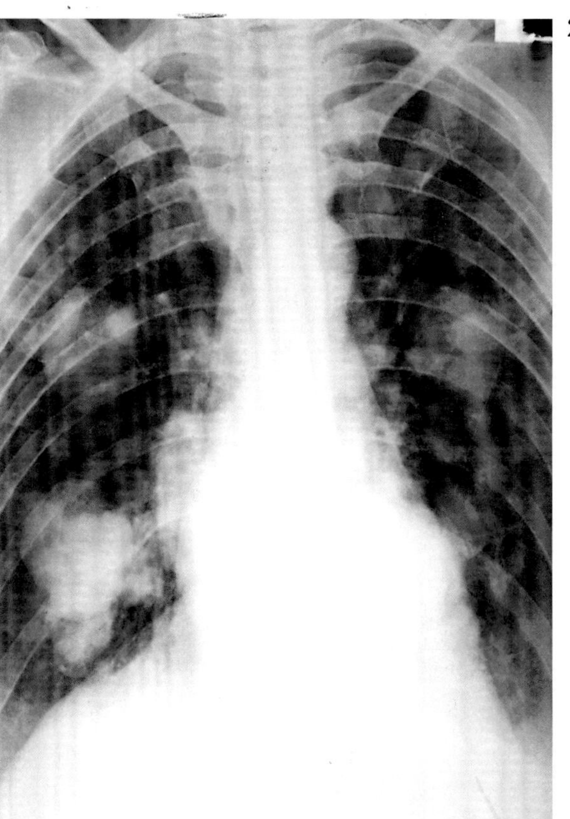

215

216

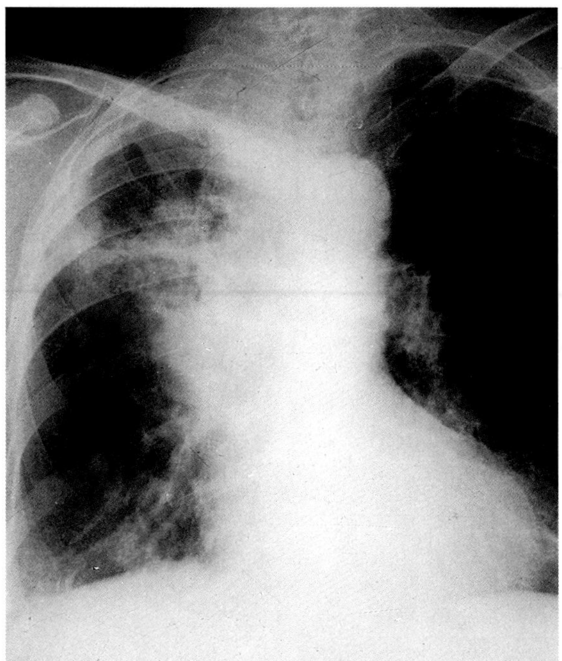

2

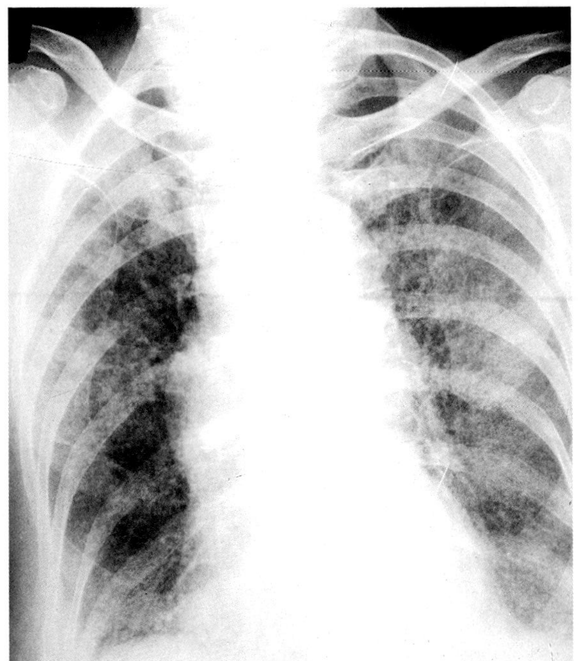

218

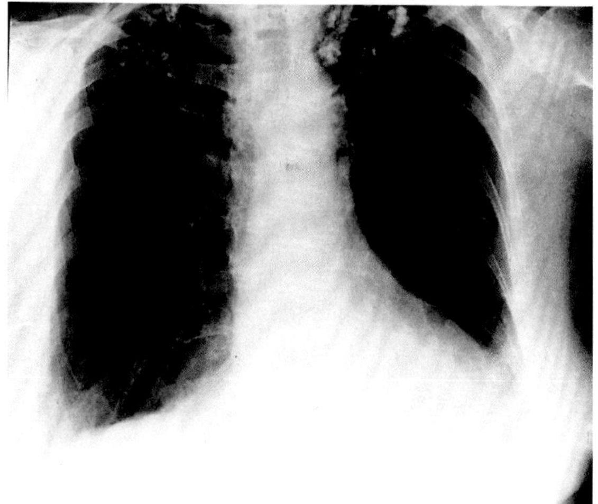

216 Pulmonary tuberculosis. The decline of tuberculosis in the elderly has been much slower than in the younger population. 'Occult tuberculosis' is a frequent finding in geriatric patients. This lady presented with weight loss, weakness, anaemia and elevated ESR.

217 Pulmonary tuberculosis. Chest x-ray showing miliary tuberculosis. This elderly patient presented with acute respiratory illness.

218 Tuberculosis. Chest x-ray showing multiple calcified deposits in both lung apices as a result of old tuberculosis. This is a frequent incidental finding in x-rays of elderly patients.

Special features of TB in the elderly

There has been a relative increase in the incidence of TB among elderly patients. The reasons are:

- Failure or delay in making correct diagnosis
- Reactivation of previously acquired and healed primary TB lesions
- Poor diet and bad living conditions
- Other debilitating diseases with increasing age
- Decline in tuberculin sensitivity with advancing years

Diagnostic features

Tend to be modified in the elderly

Non-specific ill health and weight loss

Pyrexia of unknown origin

Tuberculin test may be negative initially and positive later

Confirmation may be obtained by biopsy of enlarged glands, scalene nodes, liver or bone marrow

In some cases a therapeutic trial of antituberculous agents may be necessary

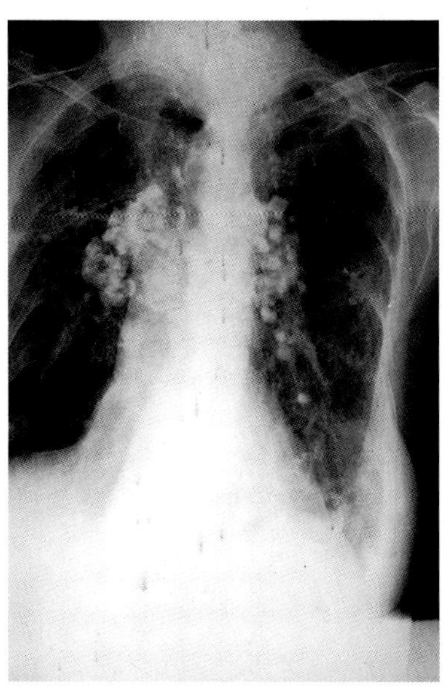

219 **Sarcoidosis.** Chest x-ray of a 75-year-old patient showing bilateral hilar lymphadenopathy with calcification. The Kveim test was positive for sarcoidosis.

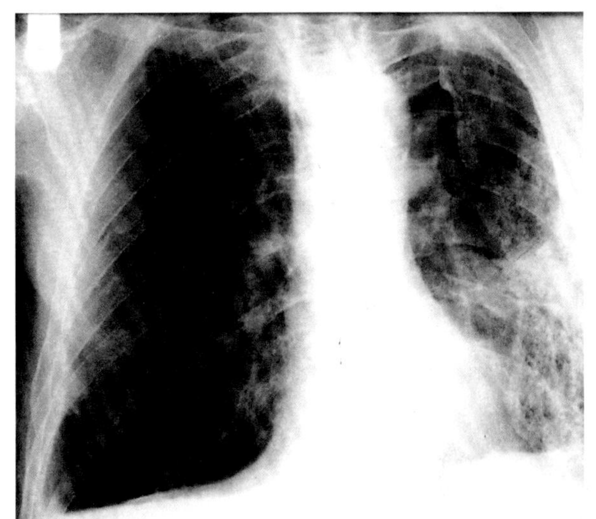

220 **Pleural calcification.** Chest x-ray showing large plaques of pleural calcification on the left side due to an old industrial lung disease (asbestosis). This elderly patient was very incapacitated with dyspnoea.

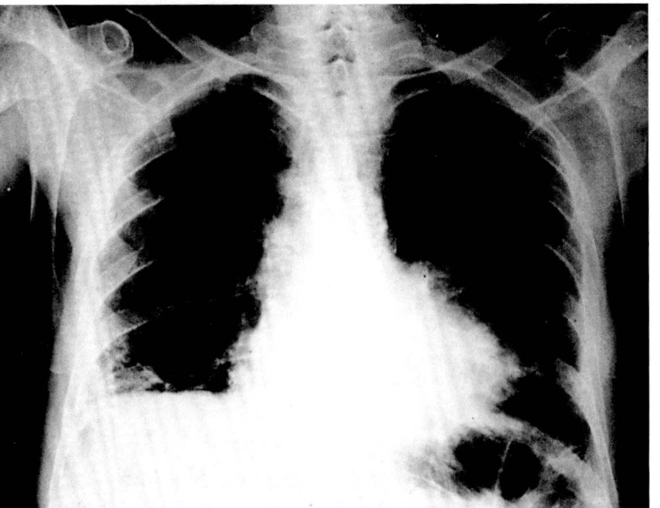

221 **Rheumatoid lung.** Chest x-ray showing 'shaggy' left heart border in a case of chronic rheumatoid arthritis. There is also pulmonary fibrosis and the patient had features of fibrosing alveolitis. Rheumatoid arthritis can cause the following pulmonary problems: fibrosing alveolitis; pleural effusion; nodules in lungs or pleura; Caplan's syndrome (multiple pulmonary nodules on chest x-ray in coal workers); acute pneumonitis; and small airways obstruction in smokers.

222

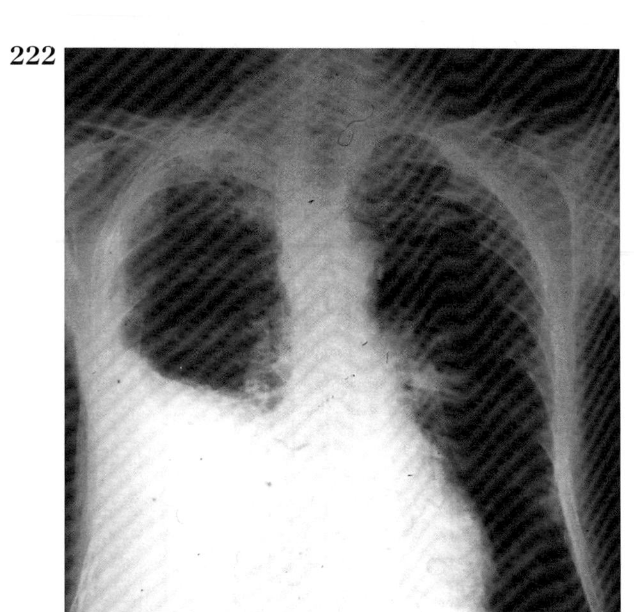

222 Pleural effusion. Chest x-ray showing large right-sided pleural effusion. This elderly patient had very few symptoms. Examination of the aspirate revealed malignant cells.

223

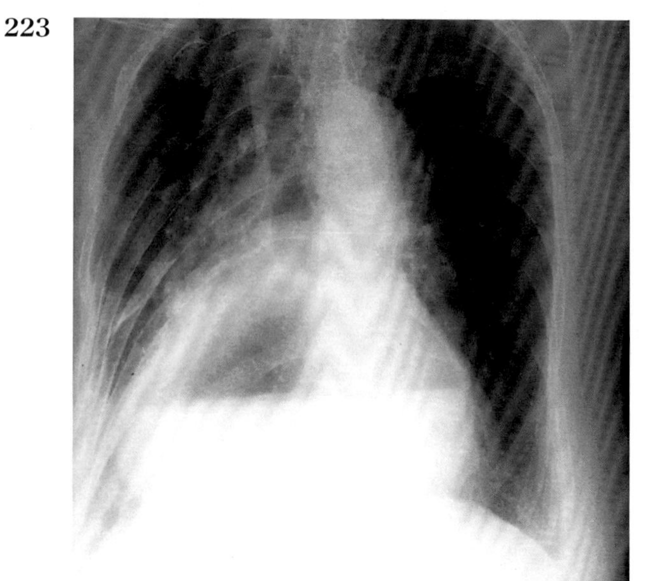

22

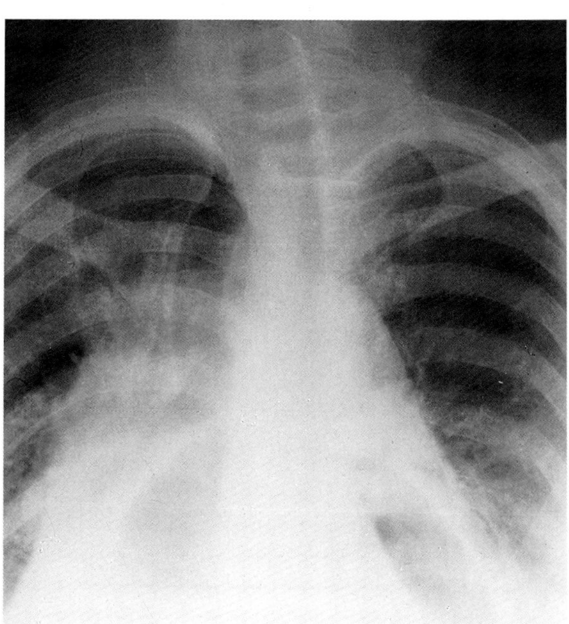

223 and 224 Hiatus hernia. Incidental finding on a routine chest x-ray. Note the shadow containing an air bubble behind the cardiac silhouette. It is usually silent but can produce symptoms of reflux oesophagitis and iron-deficiency anaemia.

225 Hiatus hernia. Barium meal x-ray showing a sliding hiatus hernia. This elderly patient had symptoms of reflux oesophagitis.

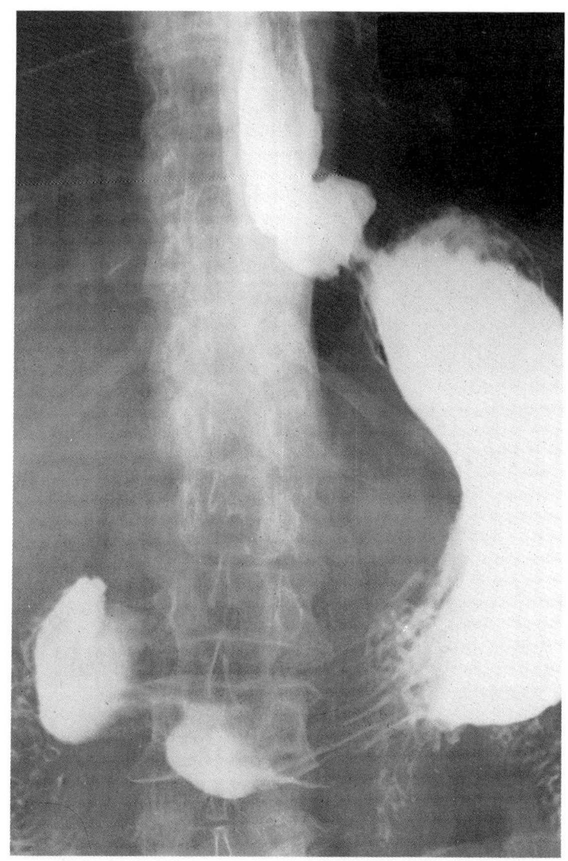

225

Hiatus hernia

Types

Oesophagastric sliding type
Paraoesophageal rolling type
Mixed

Clinical features

- Symptoms caused by oesophagitis
  - Dysphagia
  - Discomfort in chest with bending, stooping or lying down
  - Pain like that of ischaemic heart disease
- Symptoms caused by hernia
  - Usually asymptomatic
  - Retrosternal discomfort
  - Irritation of diaphragm causing coughing and hiccups
- Symptoms caused by haemorrhage
  - Chronic blood loss leading to anaemia
  - Rapid blood loss may result in shock

226 Reflux oesophagitis. Endoscopic view of lower oesophagus showing reflux oesophagitis with inflammatory changes in the mucosa. Note open cardia.

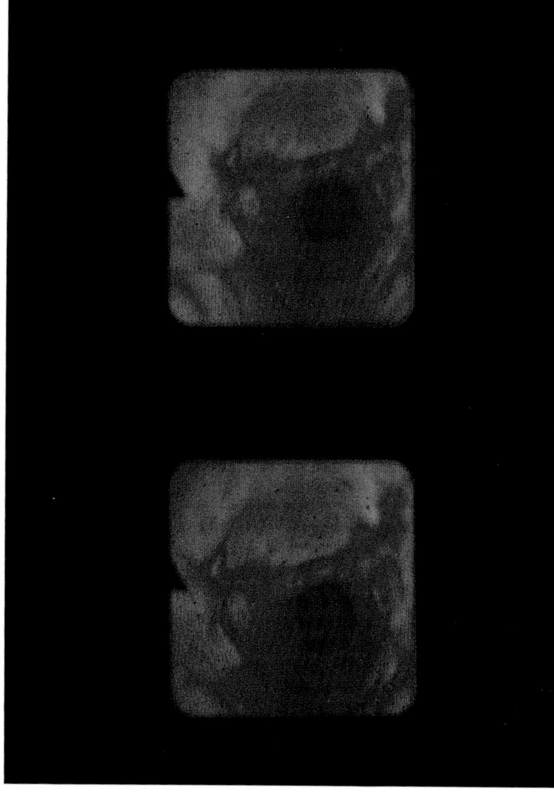

226

227

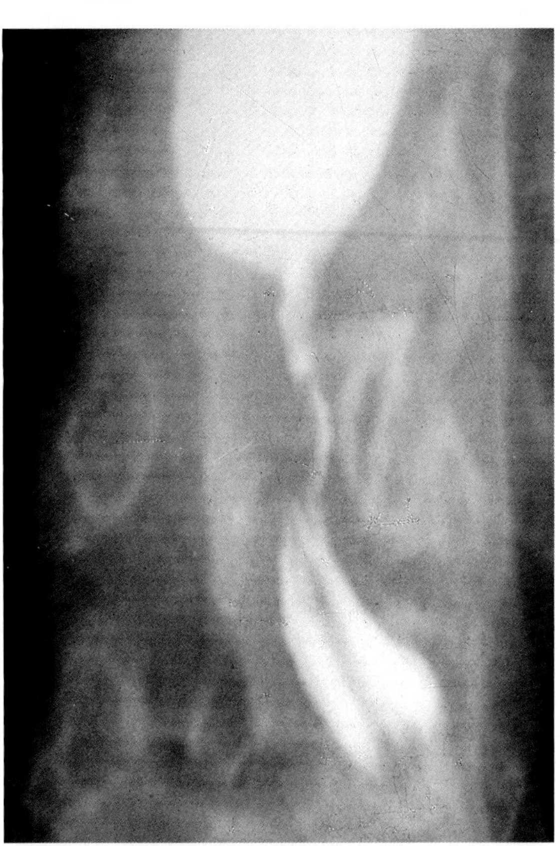

227 Oesophageal stricture. Barium meal x-ray showing an oesophageal stricture. Endoscopy revealed its malignant nature. Strictures also occur in association with chronic gastro-oesophageal reflux disease.

228

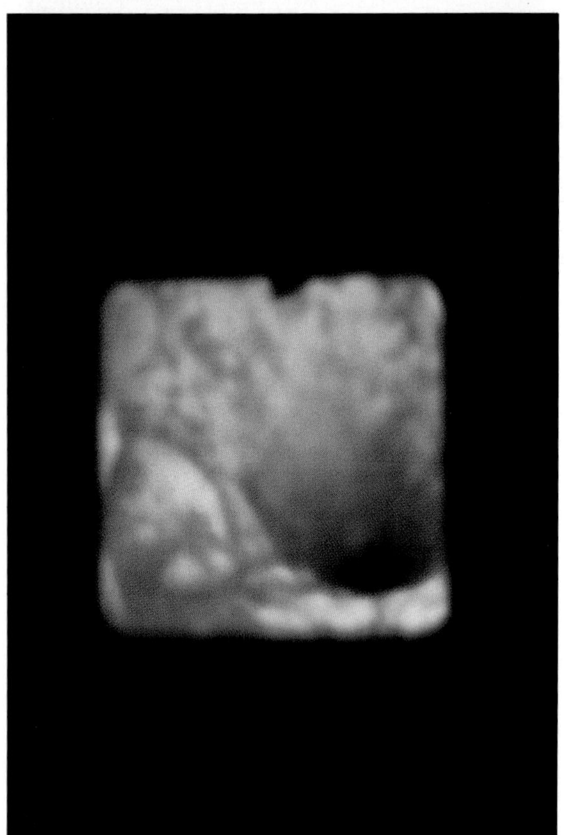

228 Oesophageal candidiasis. Endoscopic view showing typical pale patches of candidiasis. The elderly patient complained of sore throat and dysphagia. Radiologically, it may be confused with oesophageal carcinoma. Oesophageal candidiasis occurs in patients who are severely debilitated, e.g. malignancy.

Osteoporosis

This is a common disorder of old age in which there is a reduced amount of bone per unit volume of bony tissue without any increase in osteoid.

Aetiology
Post-menopausal bone loss in females
Poor skeletal development of females
Prolonged negative calcium balance in some individuals. Eight per cent of UK population have insufficent dietary calcium intake
Nutritional factors – calcium deficiency, gastrectomy and malabsorption
Immobilisation
Hyperadrenocorticism
Hyperthyroidism
Acromegaly
Rheumatoid arthritis
Inadequate exercise

Clinical features
Usually asymptomatic
Backache caused by vertebral collapse
Fractured neck of the femur and Colles' fracture
Nerve-root compression
Increasing kyphoscoliosis and loss of height, marked transverse abdominal crease

Diagnosis
Normal serum calcium, phosphate and alkaline phosphatase
X-rays show reduced bone density (ghost-like bones), hollow vertebral bodies, biconcave (codfish) bodies, compression fracture of vertebrae and sometimes Schmorl's nodes
(Bone biopsy with histological examination of bony tissue will indicate the degree of osteoporosis)

229

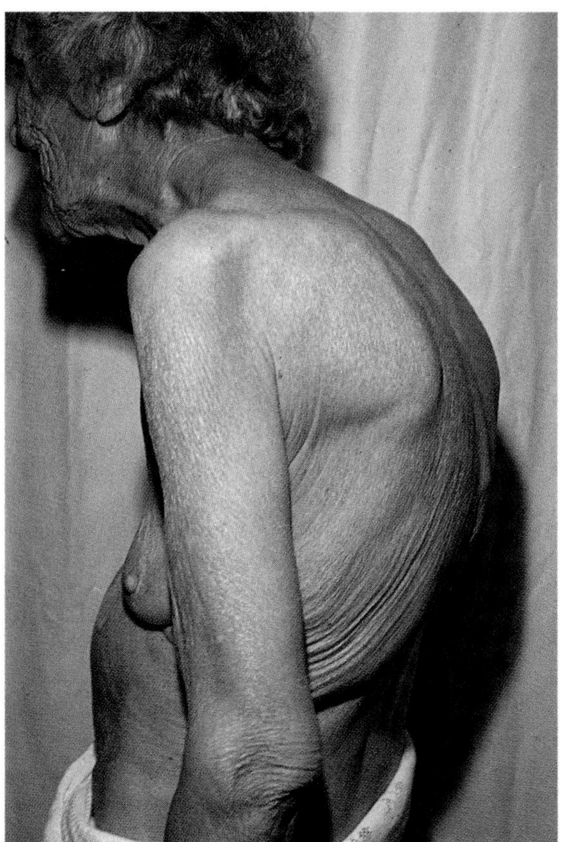

229 Kyphosis. This elderly lady's condition was caused by a combination of spinal osteoporotic vertebral collapse and chronic degenerative changes in the vertebral column.

230

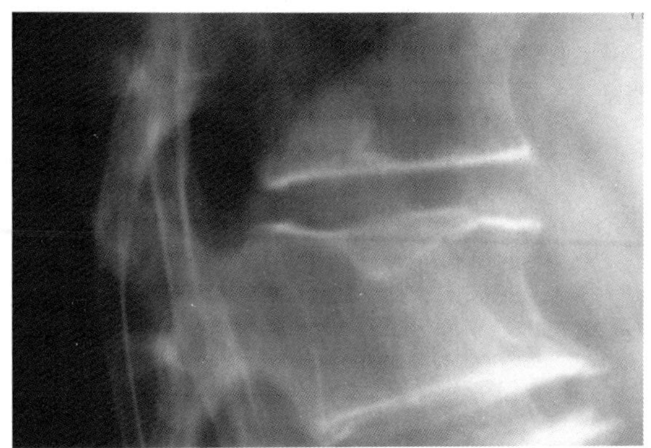

230 Schmorl's node. A sign of advanced spinal osteoporosis. There is herniation of the intervertebral disc into the body of the osteoporotic vertebra.

231

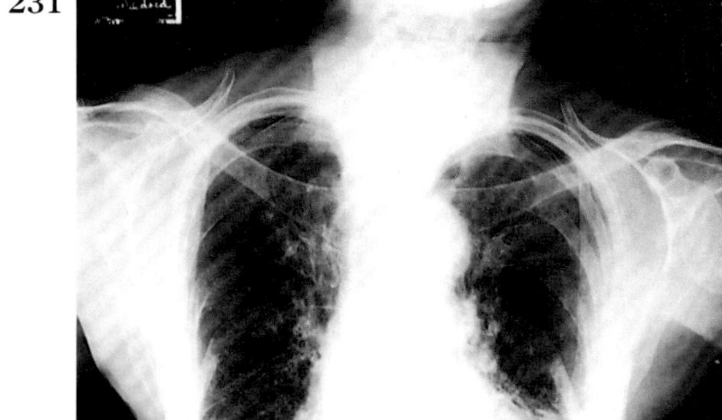

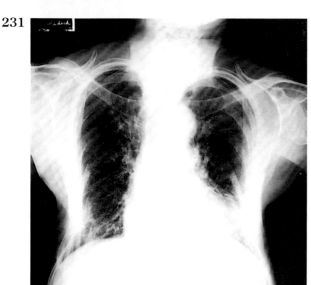

231 Bell-shaped chest. Chest x-ray showing bell-shaped thoracic cage in a case of advanced osteoporosis. A similar picture may also occur in osteomalacia.

232

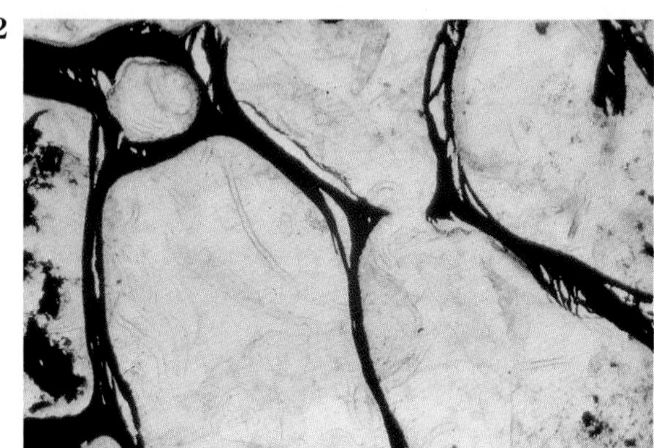

232 Osteoporosis. Bone histology showing reduction of both protein matrix and mineralisation.

233 Osteoporotic spine. Biconcave vertebral bodies with reduced radiographic density. The trabecular bone is particularly affected.

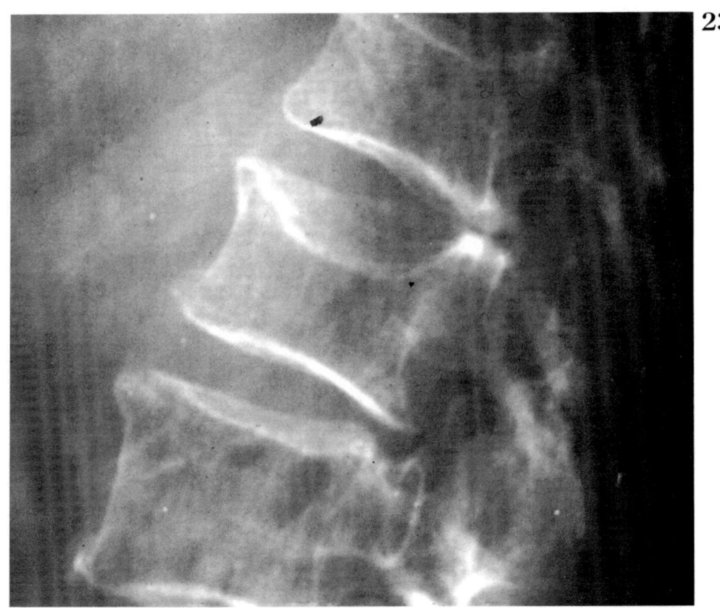
233

234 Osteoporotic spine. Increased translucency of the vertebral bodies with wedging of a midthoracic vertebra.

This patient presented with severe backache, radiating around to the front, with kyphosis and deteriorating mobility.

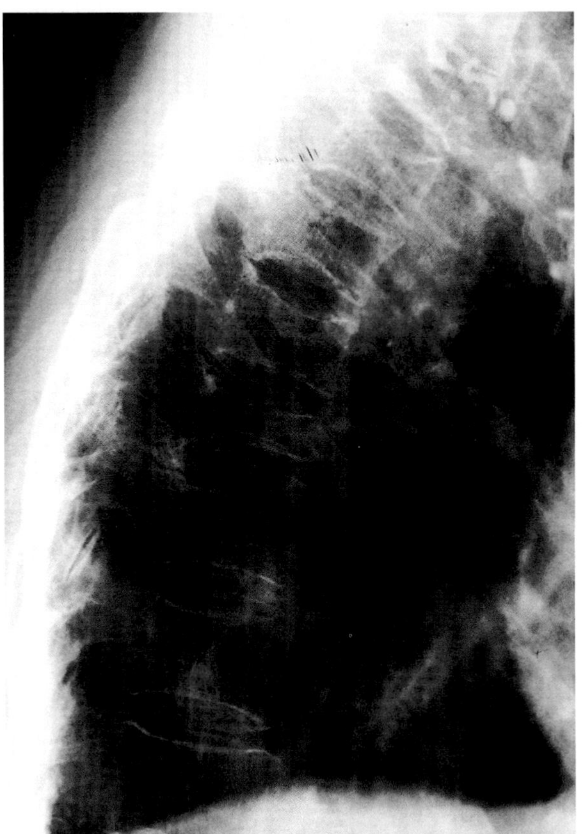
234

235

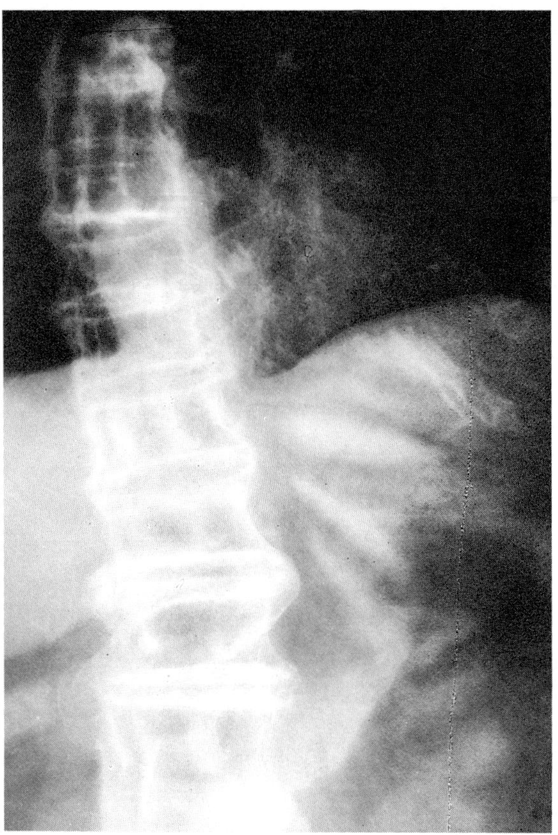

2

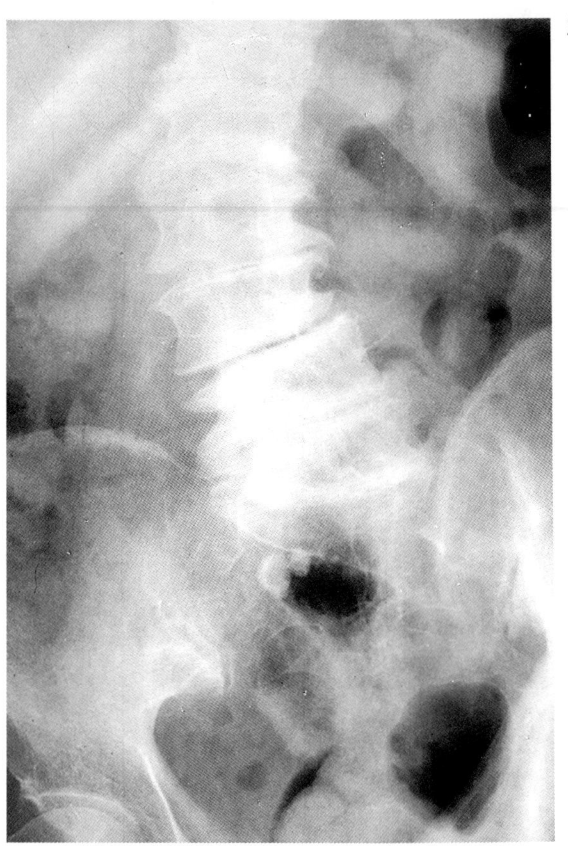

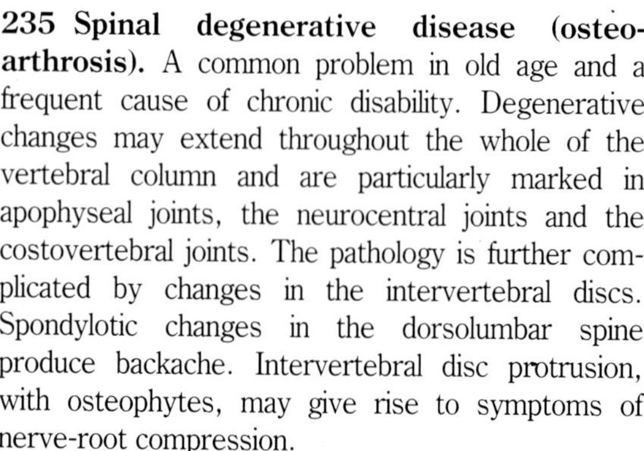

235 Spinal degenerative disease (osteo-arthrosis). A common problem in old age and a frequent cause of chronic disability. Degenerative changes may extend throughout the whole of the vertebral column and are particularly marked in apophyseal joints, the neurocentral joints and the costovertebral joints. The pathology is further complicated by changes in the intervertebral discs. Spondylotic changes in the dorsolumbar spine produce backache. Intervertebral disc protrusion, with osteophytes, may give rise to symptoms of nerve-root compression.

2

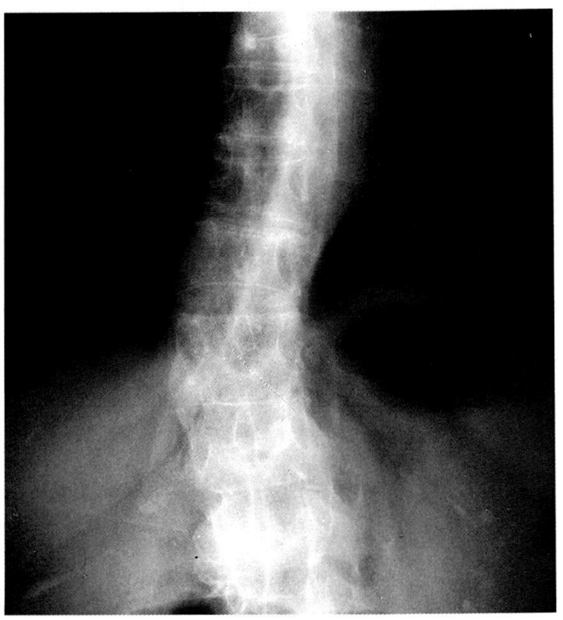

236 and 237 Spinal scoliosis. This is a common radiological finding in the elderly and is usually associated with spinal osteoarthrosis.

7 Disorders of the Abdomen

238 Obese abdomen. Fatty 'apron' of obesity in an elderly lady. She suffered from advanced osteoarthritis and hypertension.

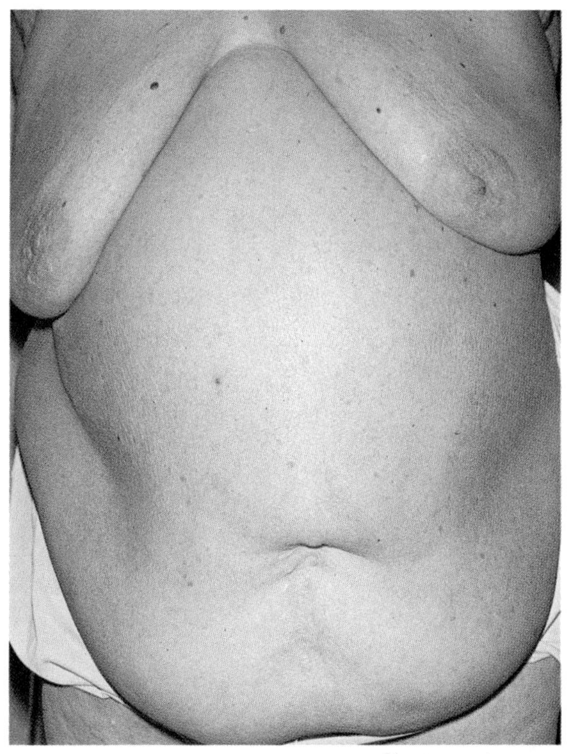
238

239 Cachexia. Wasted abdomen of an 80-year-old man who had carcinoma of the colon with secondary spread. Note the slight generalised hyperpigmentation.

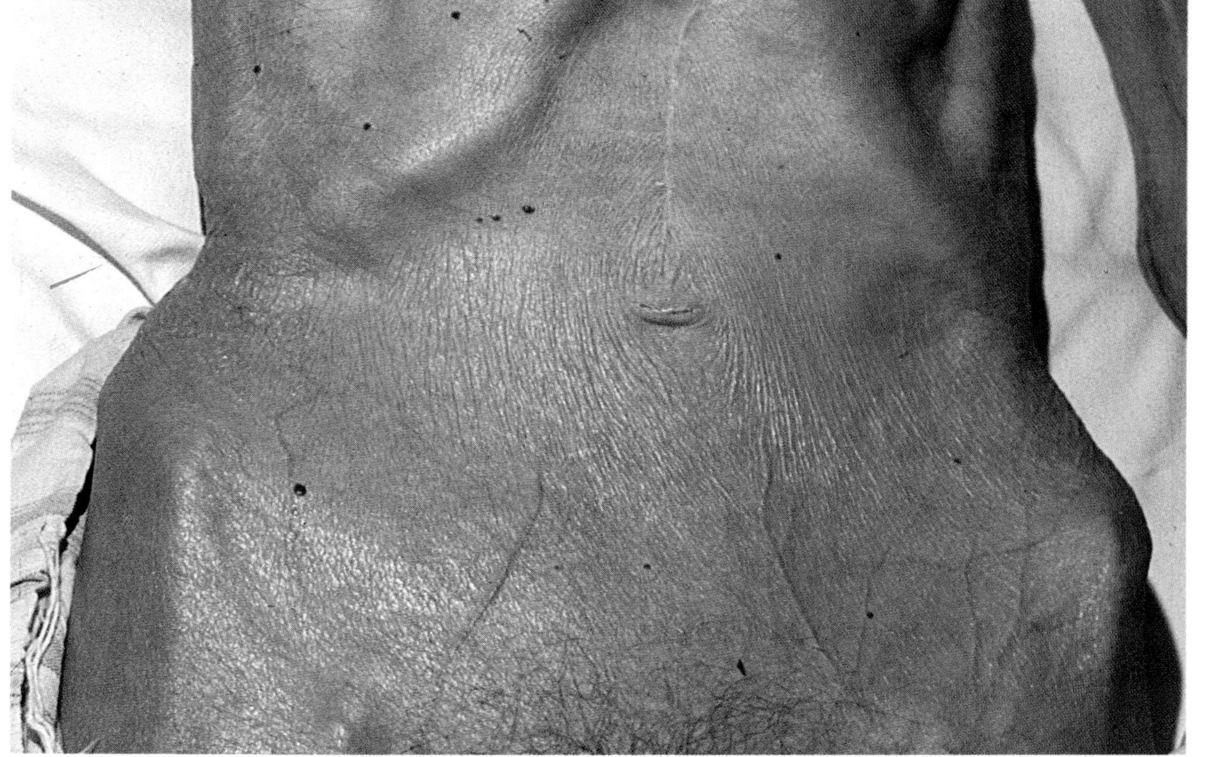
239

240

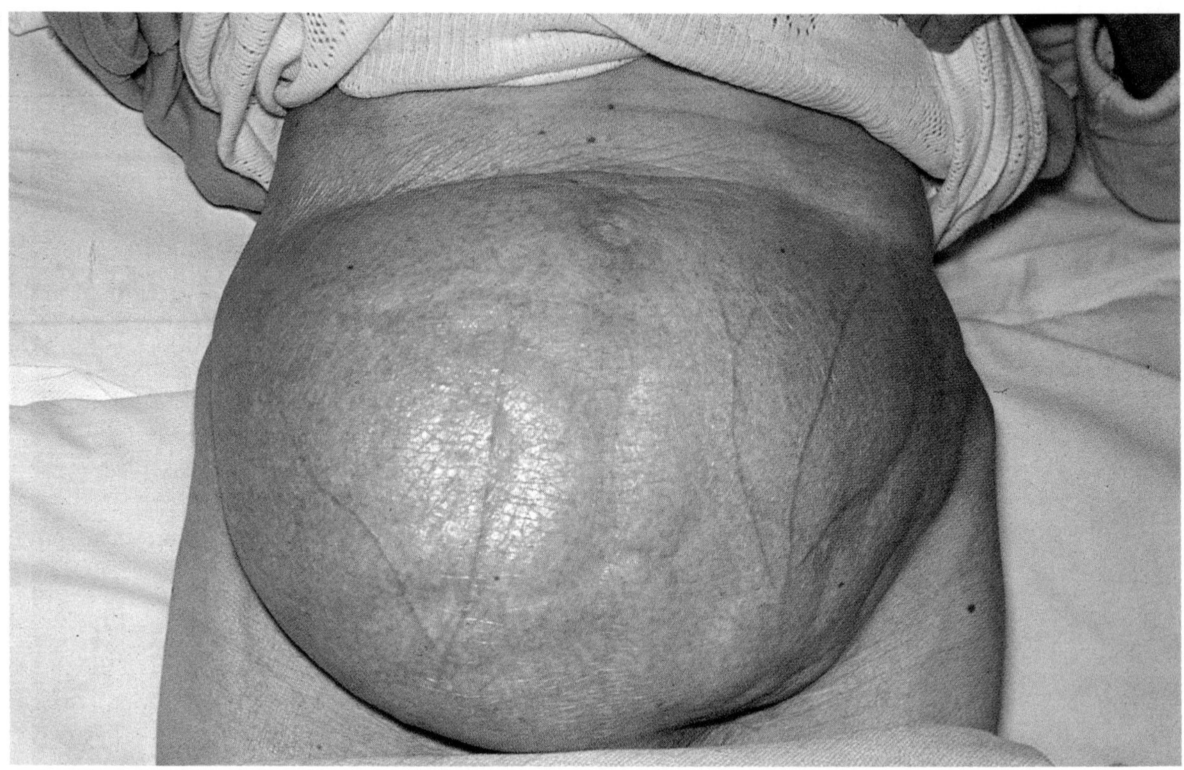

241

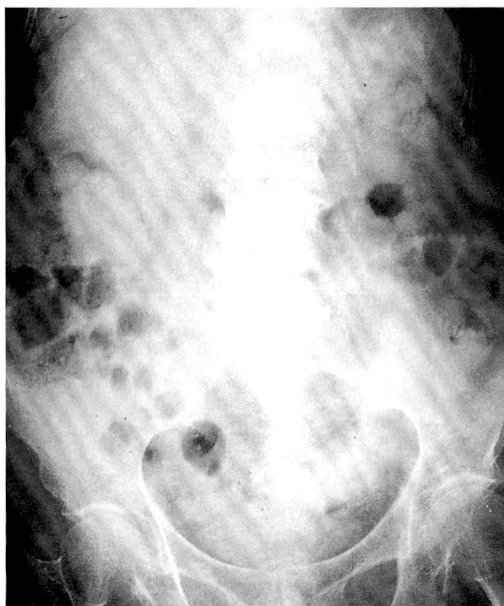

240 Severe constipation. Prominent bowel pattern caused by severe constipation. This parkinsonian patient's bowels were impacted with faeces. Enemas were required to relieve the condition.

241 Constipation. Plain x-ray of the abdomen showing dense faecal shadows distending most of the colon and rectum.

Constipation in the elderly

Aetiology

- Low dietary intake of fibre and roughage
- Immobility and lack of exercise
- Poor bowel habits
- Lack of privacy and new environment
- Drugs – codeine, antidepressants, laxative dependence, iron salts, anticholinergics
- Colonic lesions – diverticular disease, cancer of colon, idiopathic megacolon, obstruction, spastic colon
- Anal lesions – fissure, abscess, haemorrhoids
- Metabolic and endocrine – myxoedema, hypokalaemia, hypercalcaemia, dehydration
- CNS disorders – depression, parkinsonism, autonomic neuropathy, cerebrovascular accidents, spinal cord lesions

Complications of constipation

Impaction and faecal incontinence
Urinary retention and overflow incontinence
Bowel obstruction
Agitation, irritability
Confusion

242 Megacolon. Plain x-ray of the abdomen showing megacolon in an elderly patient. In the elderly it is usually a complication of chronic constipation and cathartic colon syndrome and presents as gross tympanitic abdominal distension, sometimes associated with diarrhoea and faecal incontinence. Sigmoid volvulus is a further complication.

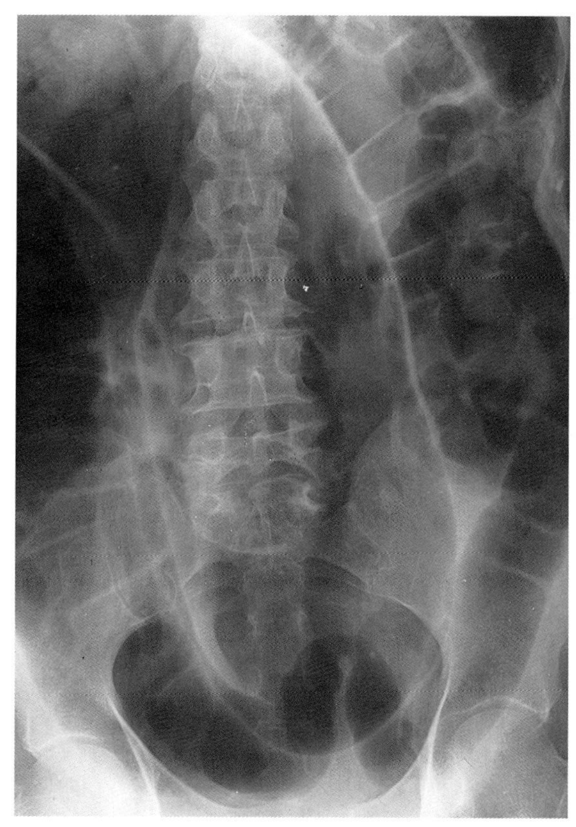
242

Faecal incontinence in the elderly

Overflow incontinence
(Frequent, soft or fluid faecal soiling)
Constipation and faecal impaction

Neurogenic incontinence
(Gastrocolic reflex leads to formed stool once or twice a day)
Cerebral and spinal cord lesions including dementias, CVA, tumour, cervical myelopathy

Anorectal incontinence
('Stress' incontinence due to pudendal nerve damage and lax pelvic floor muscles)
Childbirth trauma, life-long straining at stools, rectal prolapse

Symptomatic incontinence
(Any cause of diarrhoea)
Carcinoma of the colon
Diverticular disease
Inflammatory bowel disease
Ischaemic colitis
Antibiotics and laxatives

243 Oedema of the abdominal wall. Secondary to hypoalbuminaemia associated with nephrotic syndrome.

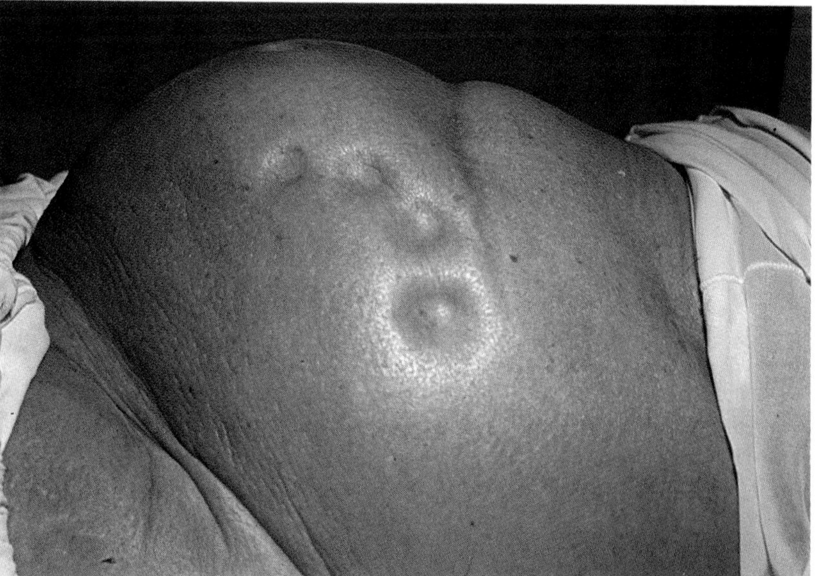
243

244

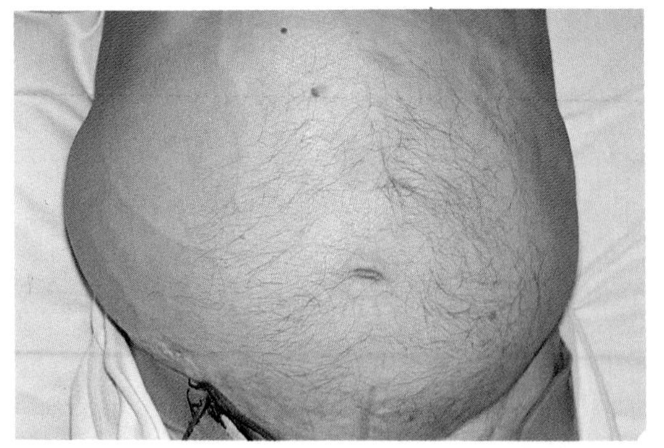

244 Ascites. Tense, distended abdomen caused by gross ascites. The patient had hepatic cirrhosis, with features of portal hypertension and hepatocellular failure.

245

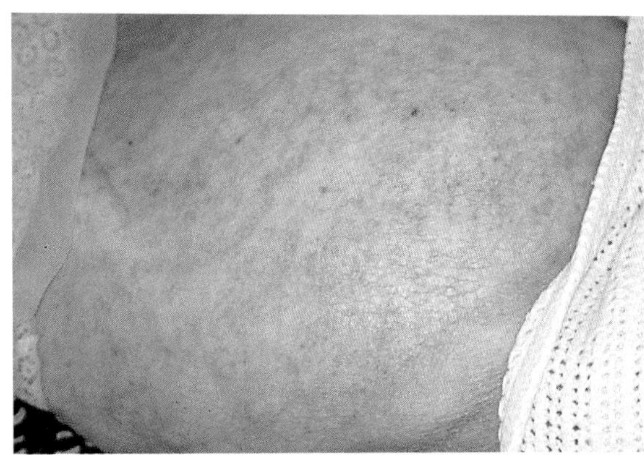

245 Ovarian cyst. Distended abdomen of an elderly patient who had a long-standing ovarian cyst but displayed very few symptoms.

246

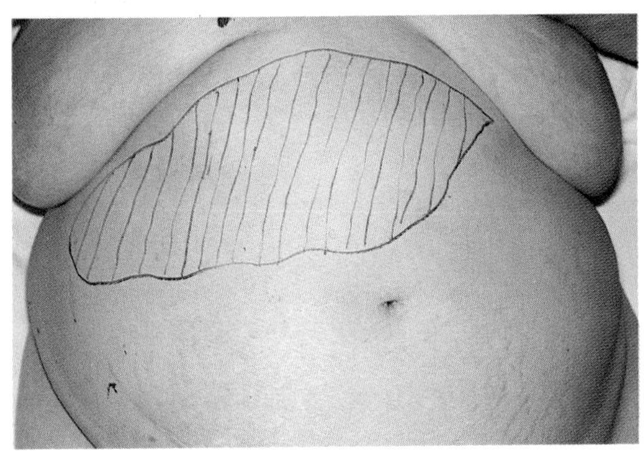

246 Hepatomegaly. Caused by hepatic metastases from carcinoma of the rectum. The liver is enlarged, hard and painless, with a nodular surface.

Common causes of hepatomegaly in the elderly

Congestive cardiac failure
Myeloproliferative disorders
Neoplastic, especially metastasis

247 Spider naevus. This patient had alcoholic liver cirrhosis and presented with confusion, incontinence and hepatic failure.

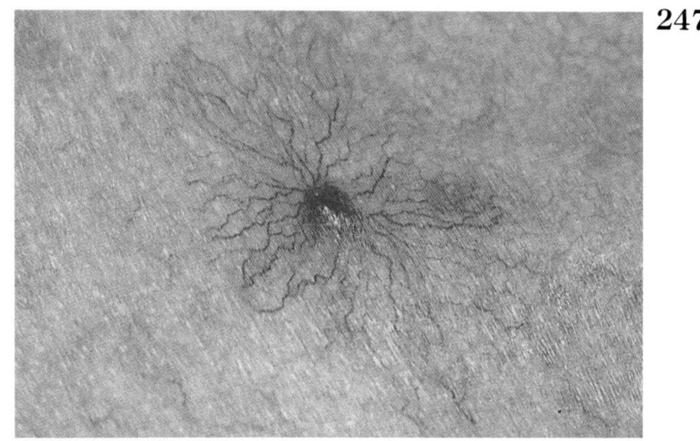

247

248 Ultrasound of the abdomen. The liver is enlarged and of patchy echogenicity, consistent with liver metastatic disease. There is some ascitic fluid beneath both the hemidiaphragms. This elderly patient had a past history of breast cancer and presented with weight loss, anorexia, vomiting and abnormal liver function tests. Ultrasound of the abdomen confirmed the diagnosis of secondaries in the liver.

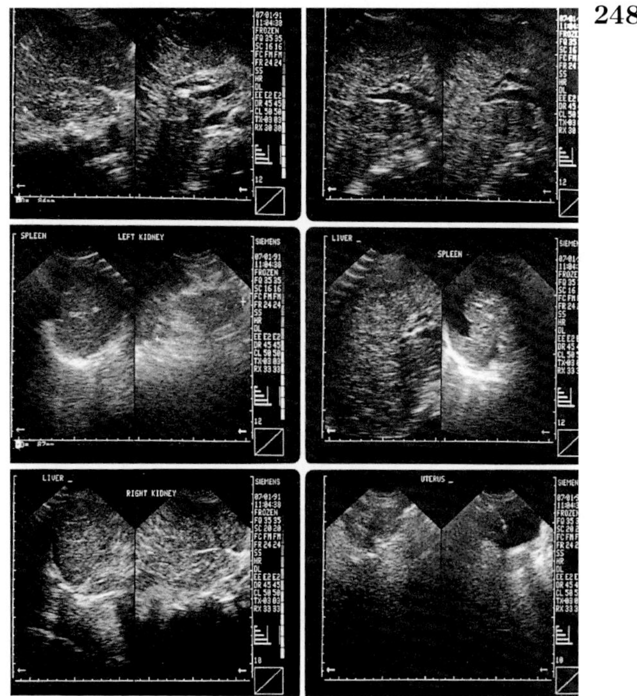

248

249 Caput medusae. Visible venous collateral circulation over the anterior abdominal wall in a patient with advanced cirrhosis of the liver.

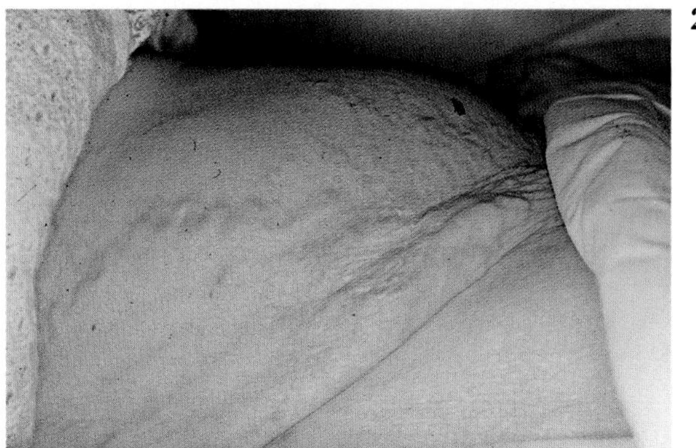

249

250

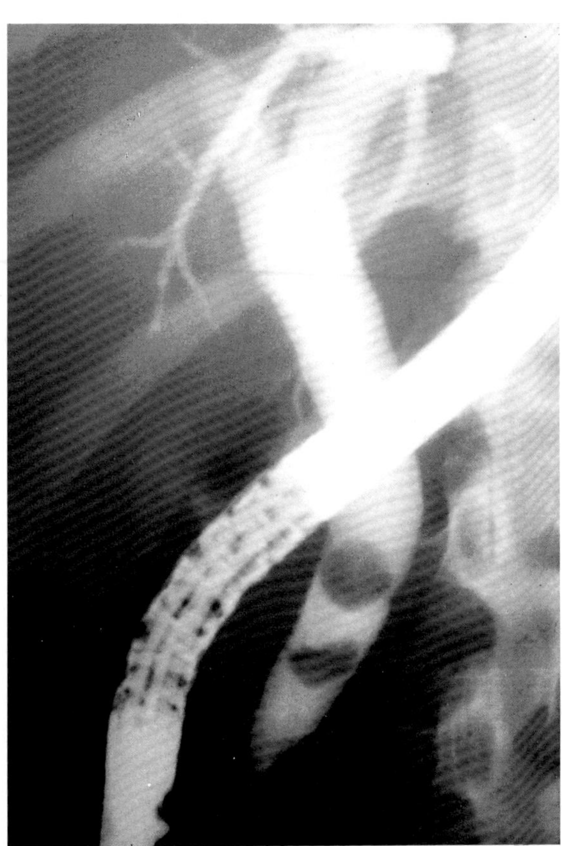

250 Gallstones. A dilated bile duct containing gallstones, demonstrated by the technique of endoscopic retrograde chole-pancreatography (ERCP) in which the contrast is injected through Vater's ampulla using a gastroscope.

251

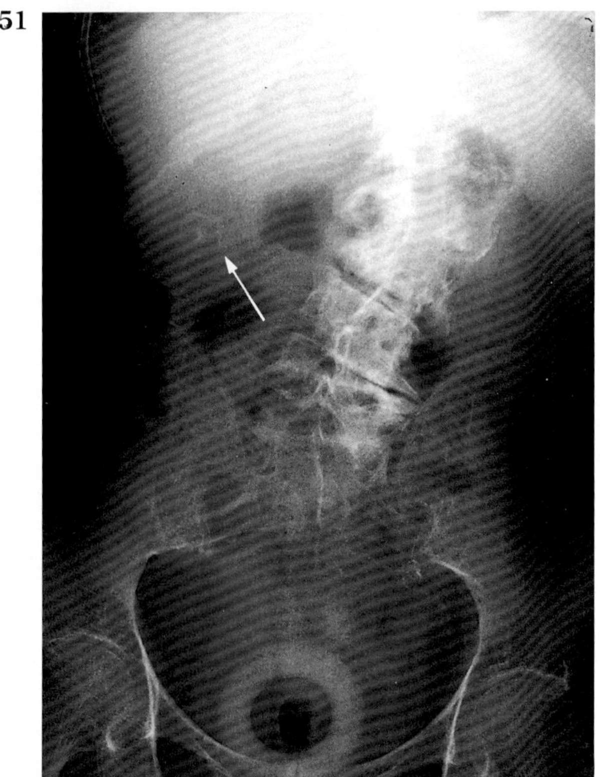

251 Multiple problems. Plain x-ray of abdomen of an elderly patient showing gallstones (arrowed) causing pain, spinal scoliosis causing backache and an old ring pessary causing urinary incontinence.

252

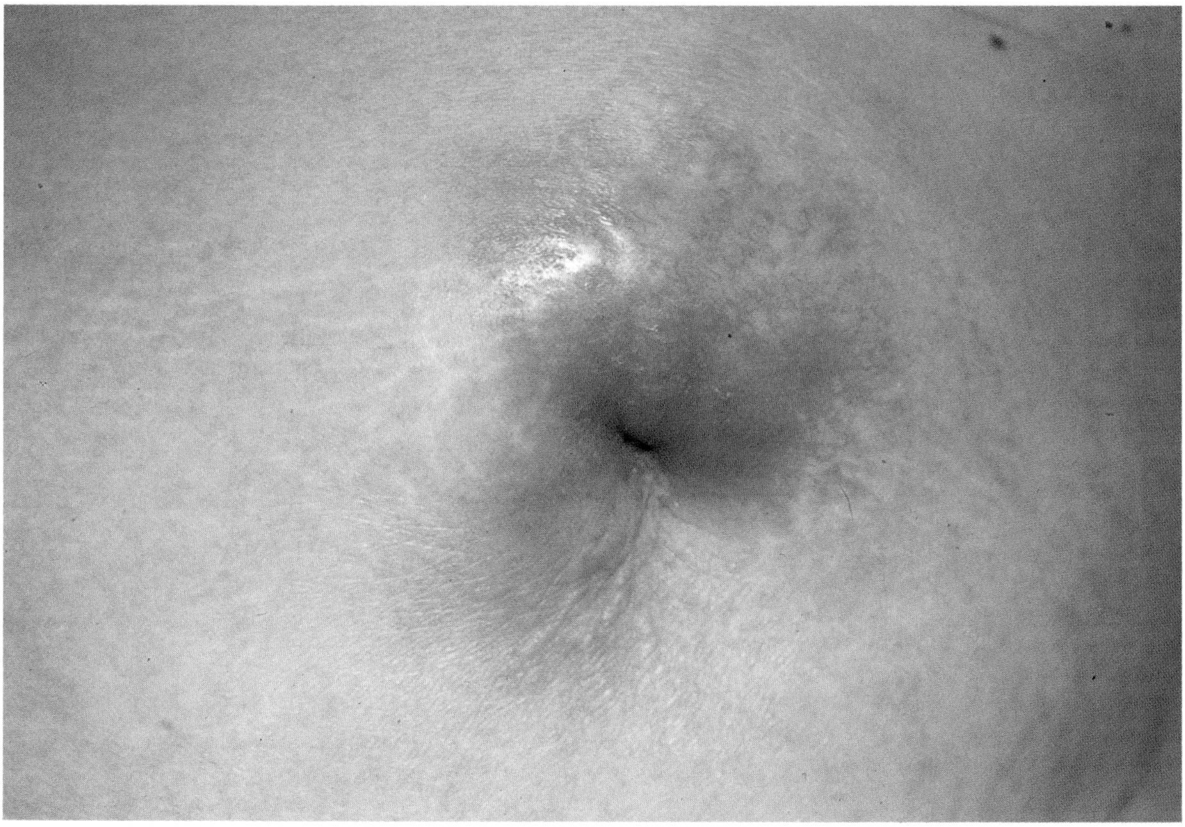

252 Umbilical infection. A result of self-neglect and poor hygiene.

253

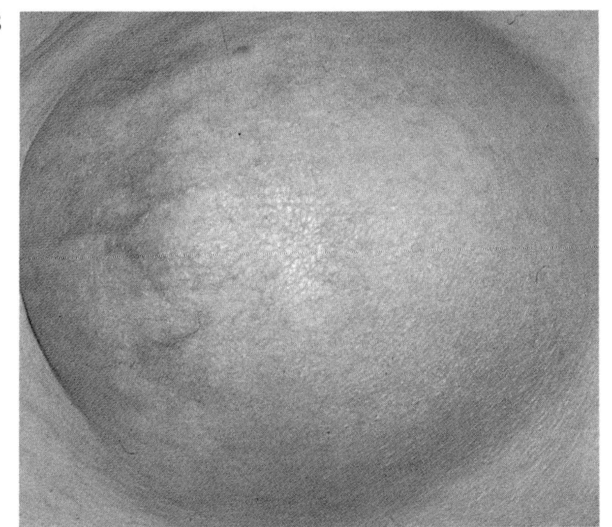

253 Umbilical hernia. A common finding in old age. Usually symptomless.

254

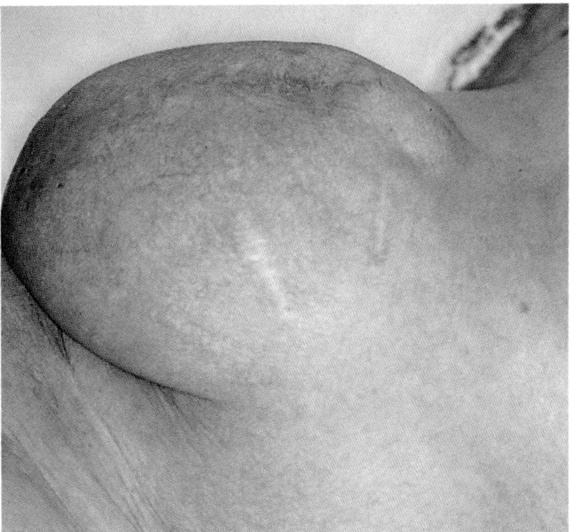

254 Incisional hernia. Occurred after a laparotomy for bleeding duodenal ulcer. Patient presented with increasing abdominal discomfort and constipation.

255

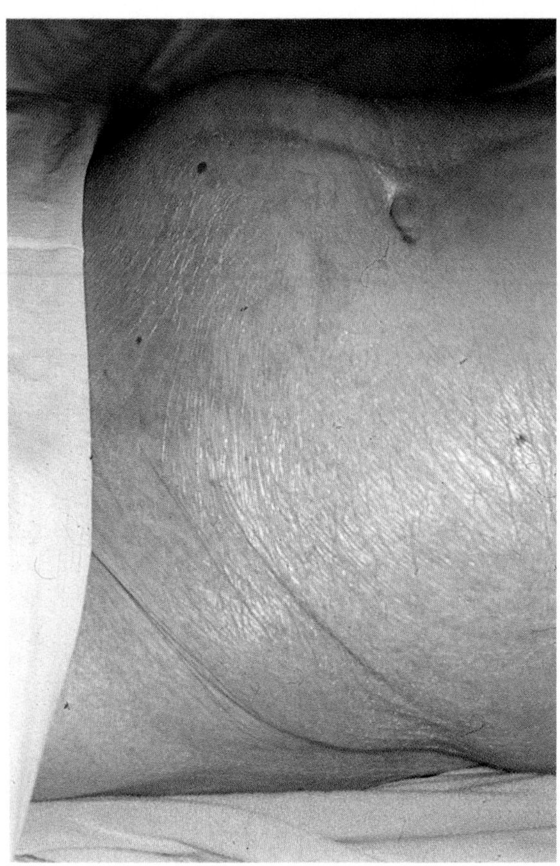

255 Urinary retention. Distended bladder in an elderly man who had prostatic hypertrophy and had developed urinary retention with overflow incontinence.

Common causes of urinary retention in old age

Abdominal operations
Prostatism
Faecal impaction
Pelvic tumours
Urethral stricture
Drugs – anticholinergics, diuretics, psychotropic agents, antidepressants
Anxiety and fear
Atonic neurogenic bladder
Spinal lesions

2

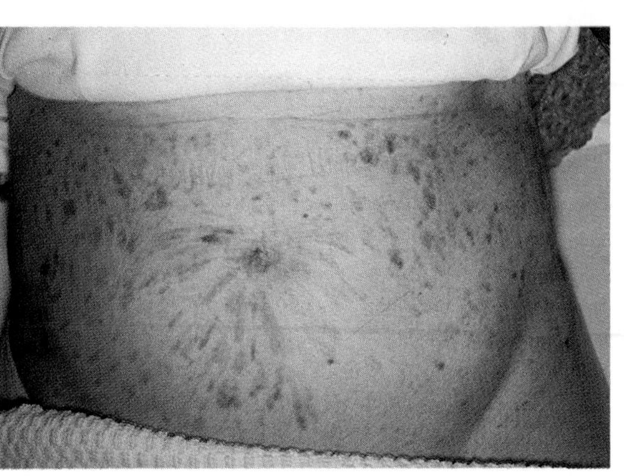

256 Seborrhoeic warts. These warts are benign lesions which become increasingly common with ageing. They appear as brownish macules on the head and trunk. Darkness and size tend to increase with advancing age.

25

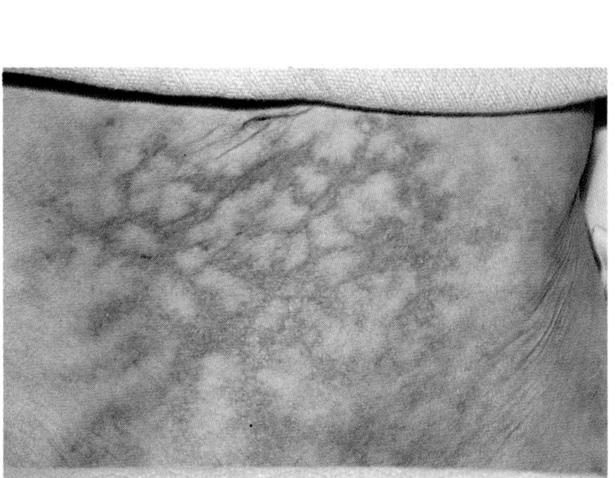

257 Erythema ab igne on the anterior abdominal wall. This patient had recurrent abdominal pain caused by peptic ulcer disease. She used hot-water bottles to relieve her symptoms.

258 Aortic aneurysm presenting as a pulsatile abdominal mass. Nearly all aneurysms in the abdominal aorta are caused by atherosclerosis; most occur in men over 60 years of age. However, this patient is a female.

258

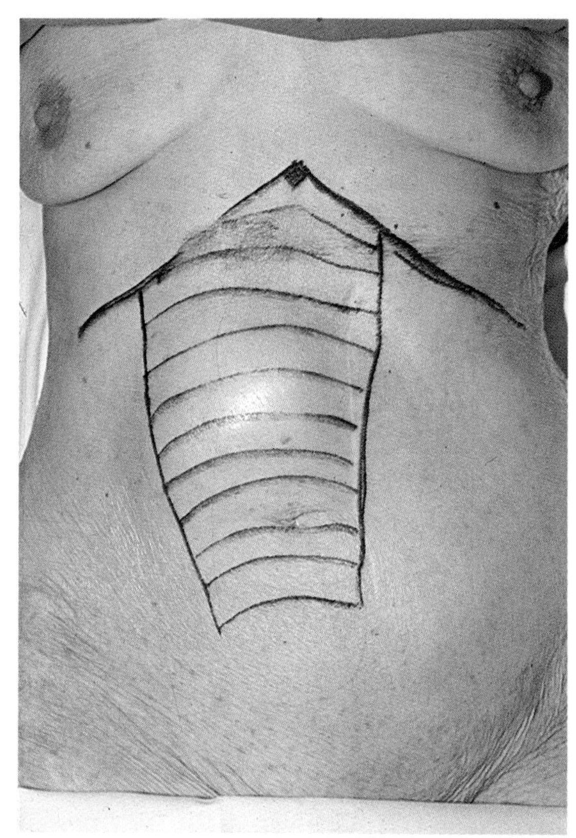

259 Aortic aneurysm. Calcified abdominal aortic aneurysm. May need to be differentiated from other causes of intra-abdominal calcification. The main complication is rupture of the aneurysm. Note spinal osteoporosis.

259

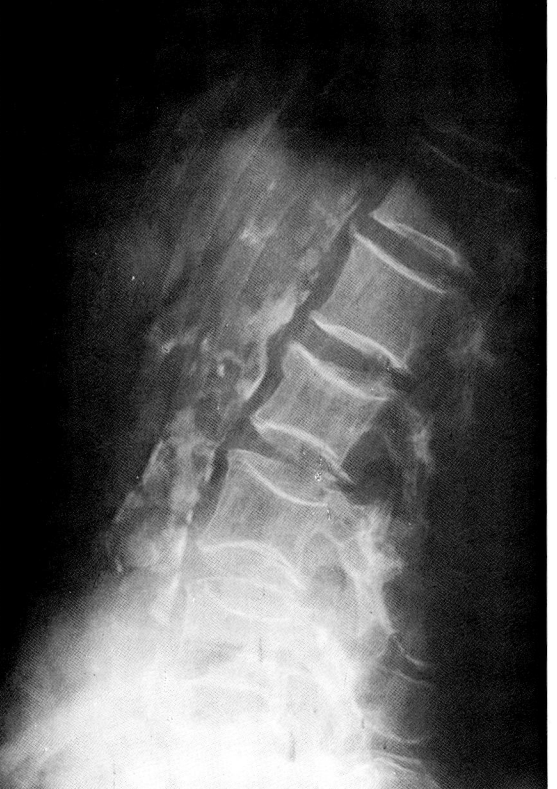

260

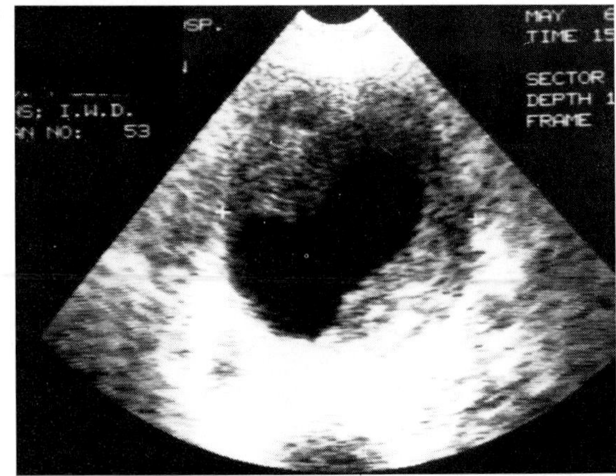

260 Aortic aneurysm. Ultrasound scan of aneurysm of the abdominal aorta showing area of blood clot. It is usually recommended that asymptomatic aortic aneurysms greater than 6 cm in diameter should be treated surgically.

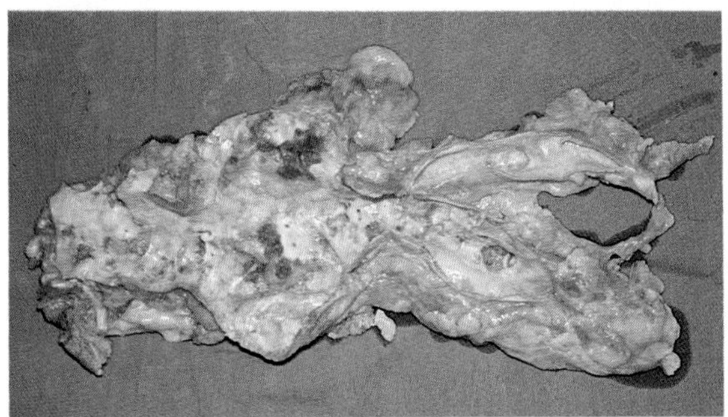

261 Aortic aneurysm. Autopsy specimen showing a ruptured abdominal aortic aneurysm.

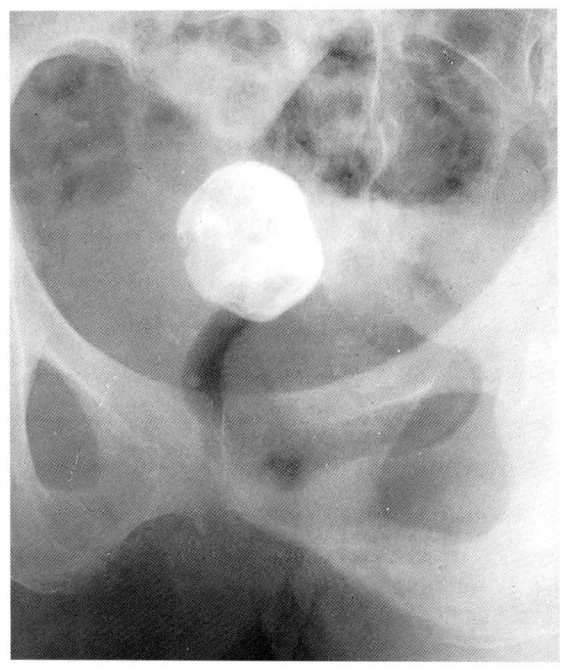

262 Calcified fibroid. A frequent cause of intra-abdominal calcification in elderly women. Usually benign and found incidentally.

263 Scrotal hernia. A large scrotal hernia causing considerable discomfort. This elderly man refused surgical intervention.

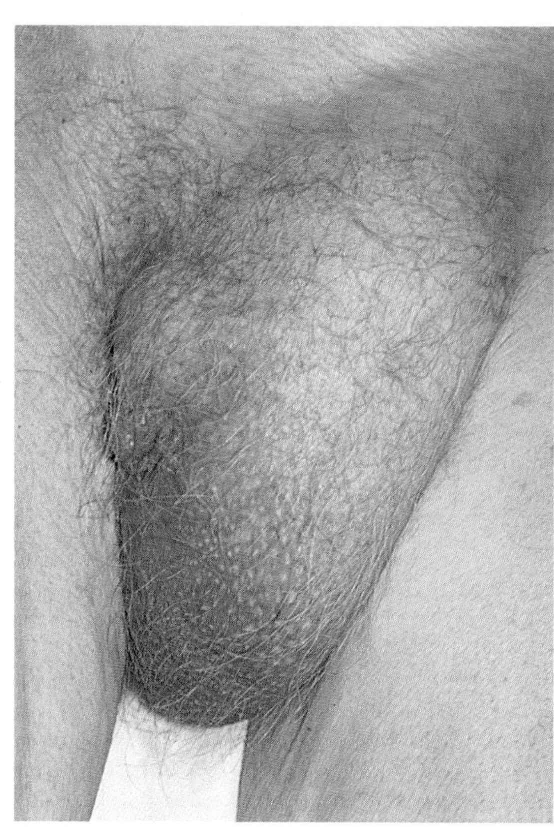

263

264 Splenomegaly. Caused by chronic lymphatic leukaemia whose incidence rises with advancing age. Usually asymptomatic in the elderly.

264

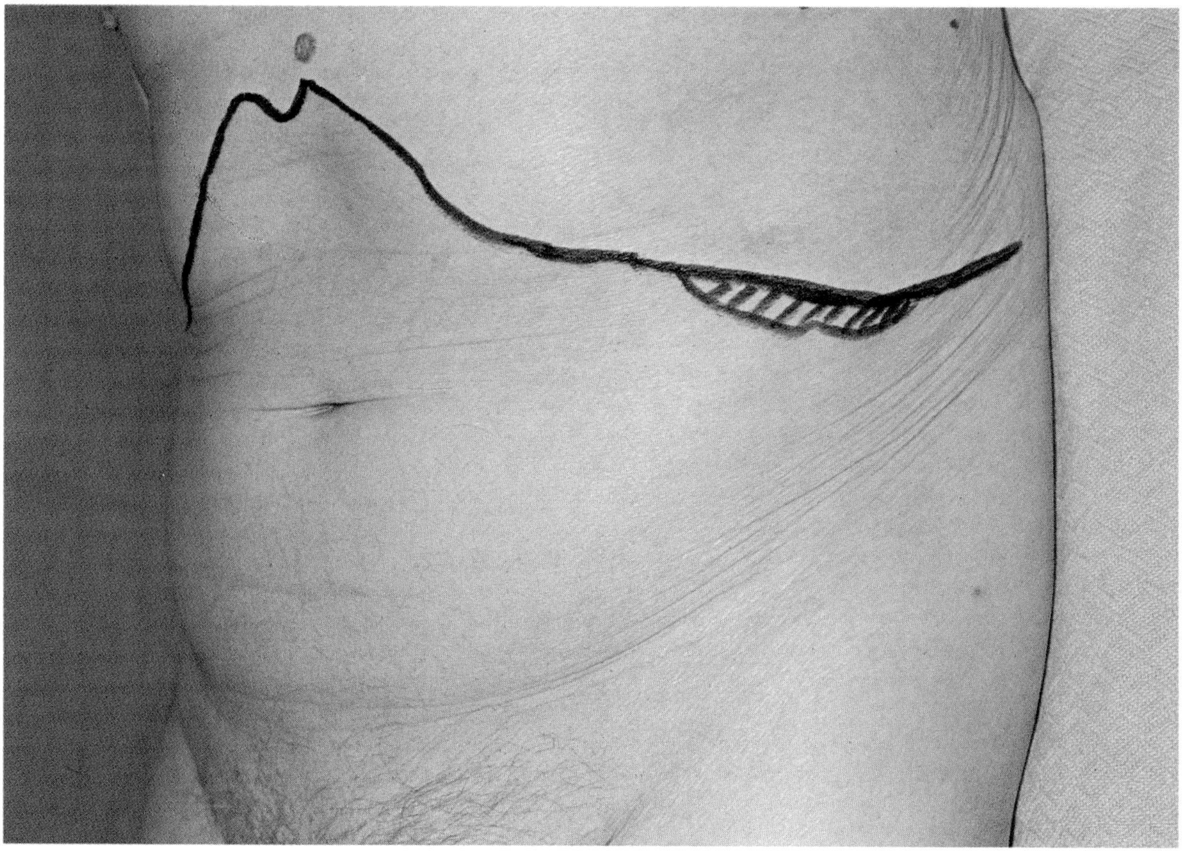

265

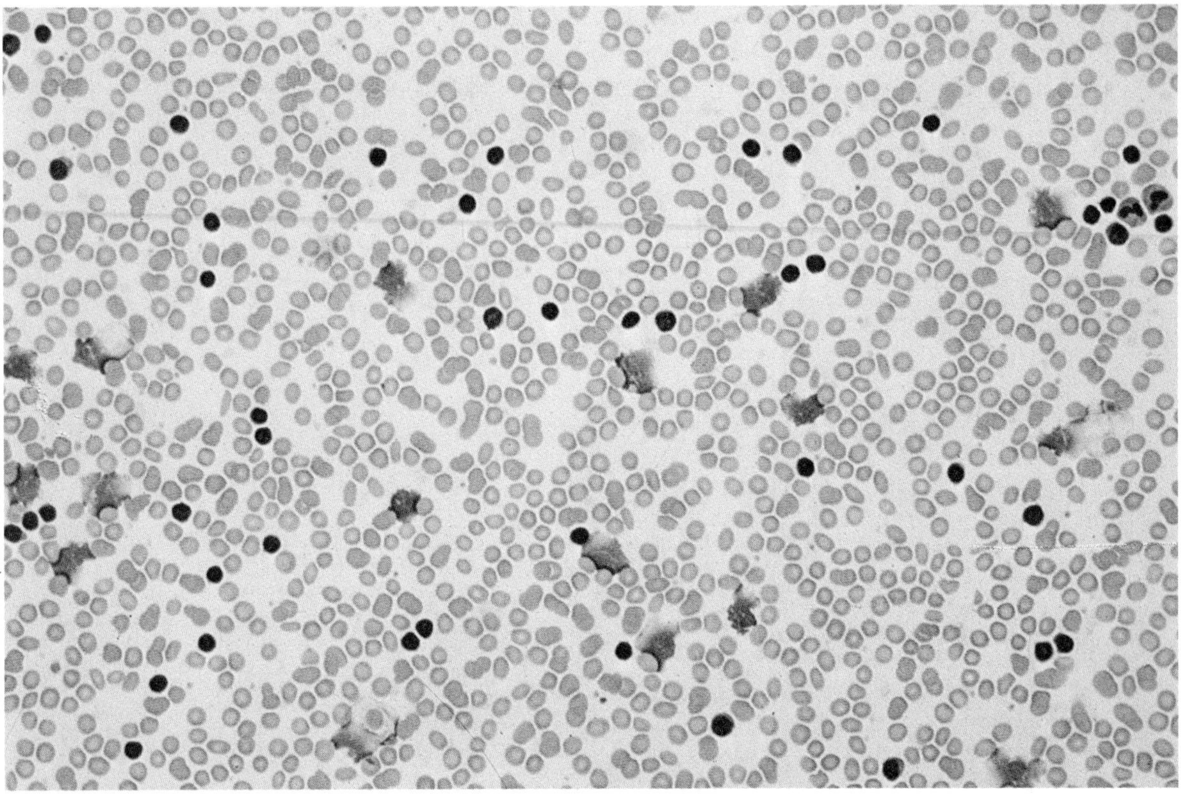

266

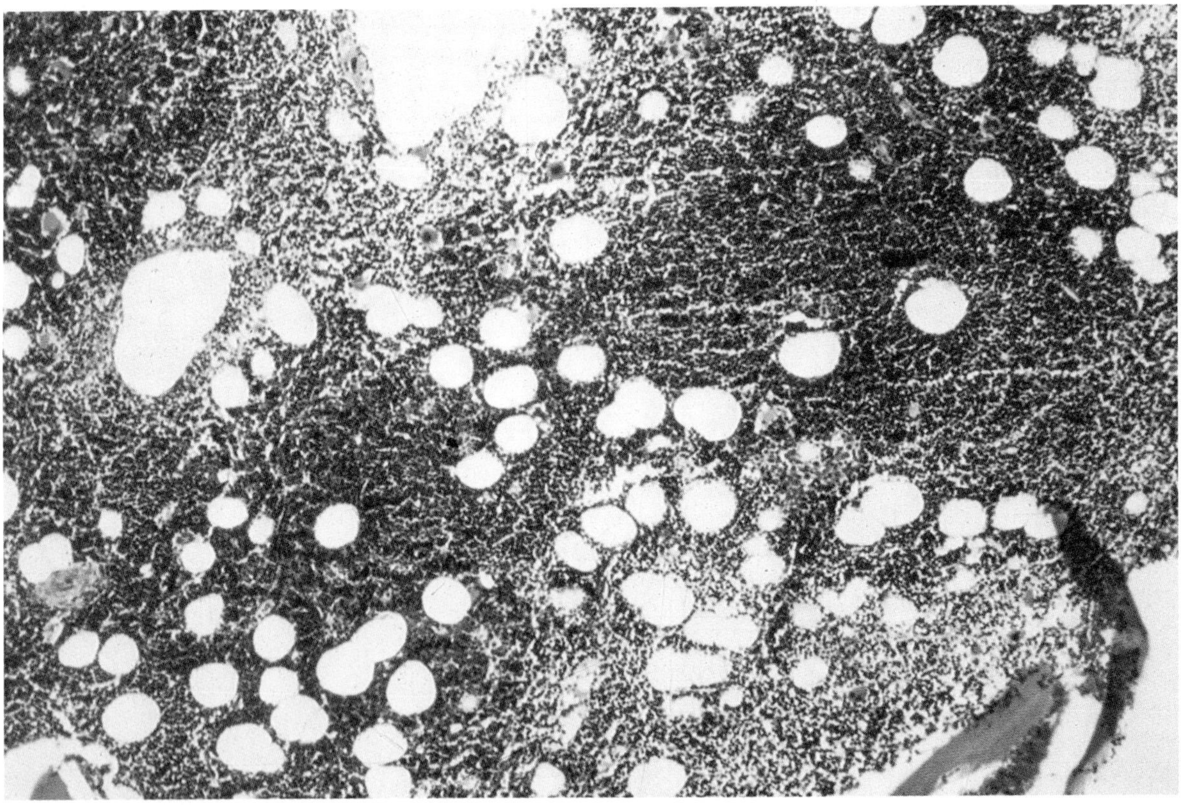

265 and 266 Chronic lymphatic leukaemia. Bone-marrow section showing lymphocytic infiltration, with some focal pattern and paratrabecular sparing. (×*100*)

267 Renal failure. Intravenous urogram showing a filling defect in the bladder due to a malignant tumour, which causes dilatation and deformity of the pelvicalyceal system on the left side. The patient presented with haematuria, anaemia and raised blood urea. Common causes of high blood urea in the elderly are dehydration, drugs, prostatic hypertrophy, bladder tumours, urinary tract infections, pyelonephritis, septicaemia and hypertensive renal disease.

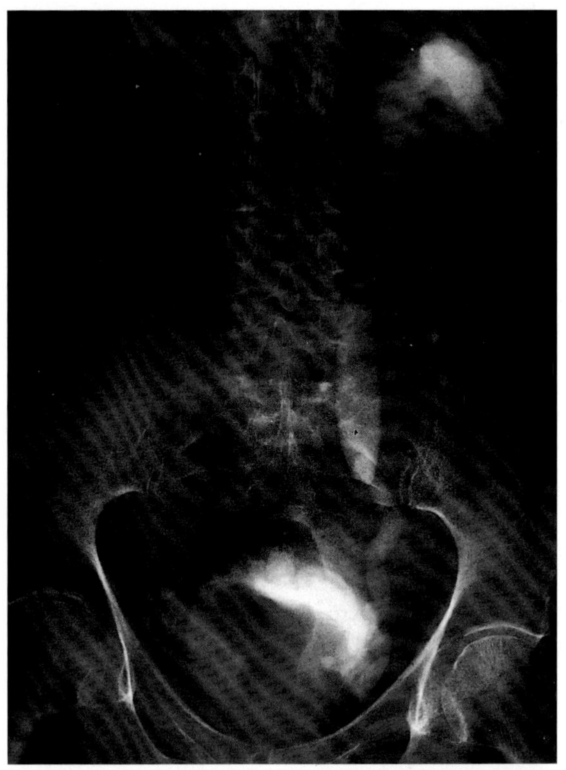

267

268 Bony metastases. X-ray of pelvis and lumbar spine showing areas of increased bone density due to secondary deposits from carcinoma of the prostate, the most common malignancy of men over age 65 years.

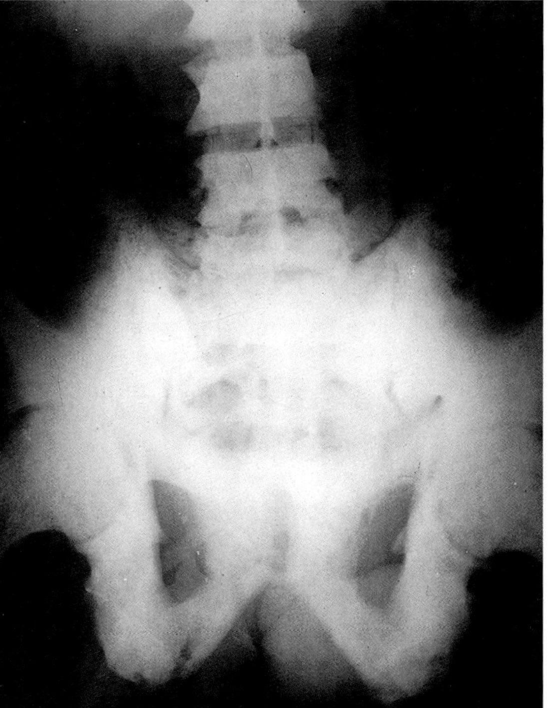

268

269

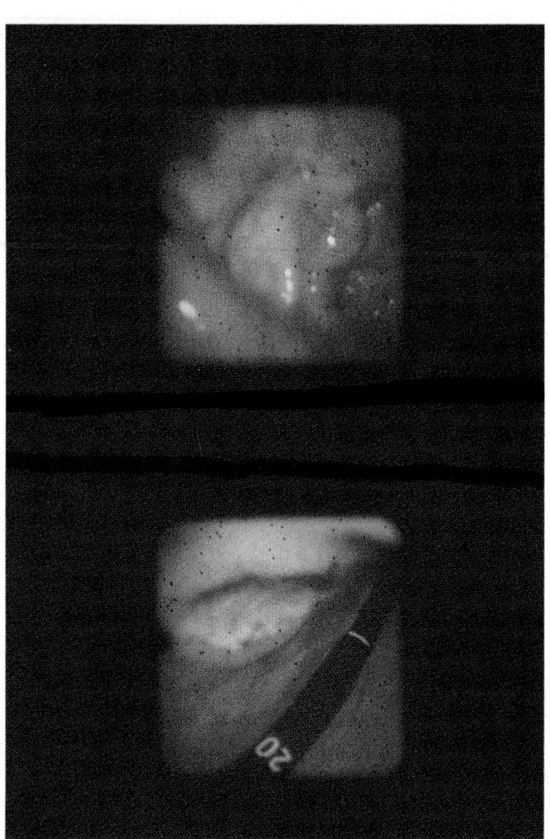

269 Benign gastric ulcer. Endoscopic view of a benign gastric ulcer. In the elderly the symptoms may be less acute and the patient may present with weight loss, mild indigestion and anaemia. The condition may be symptomless.

270

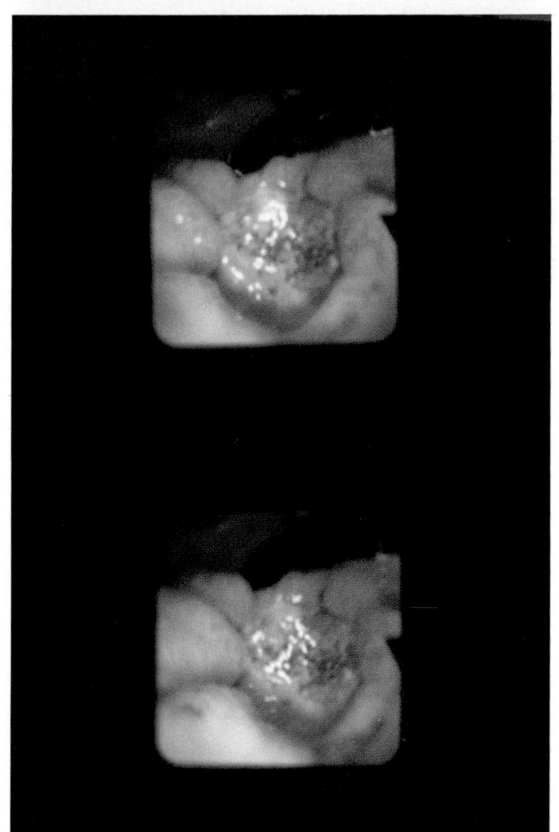

270 Malignant gastric ulcer. Endoscopic view of a malignant gastric ulcer.

271 Duodenal ulcer. Ulcer in duodenal bulb seen through an endoscope.

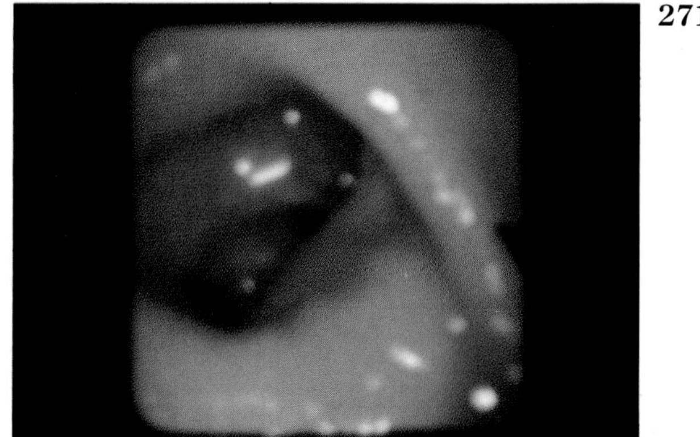
271

272 Bleeding gastric ulcer. Endoscopic view shows clearly the haemorrhage from the ulcer.

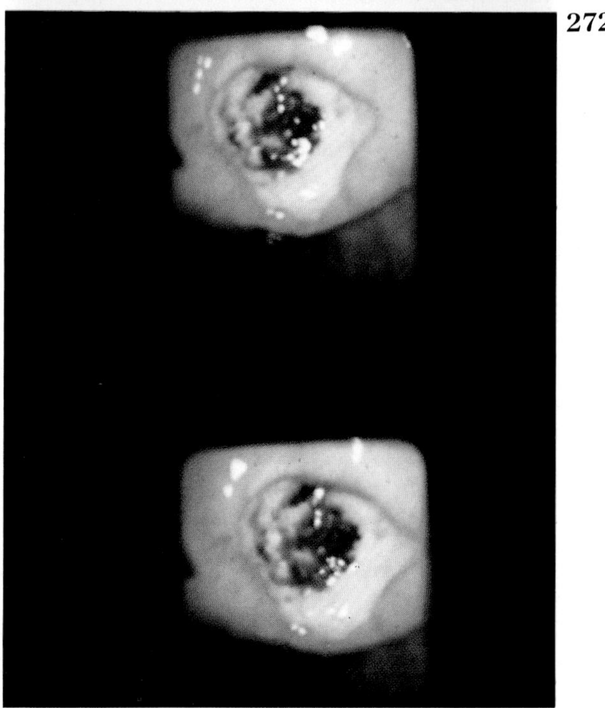
272

273 Duodenal ulcer. Barium meal x-ray showing an active duodenal ulcer. The patient had mild anaemia but no symptoms of pain or indigestion.

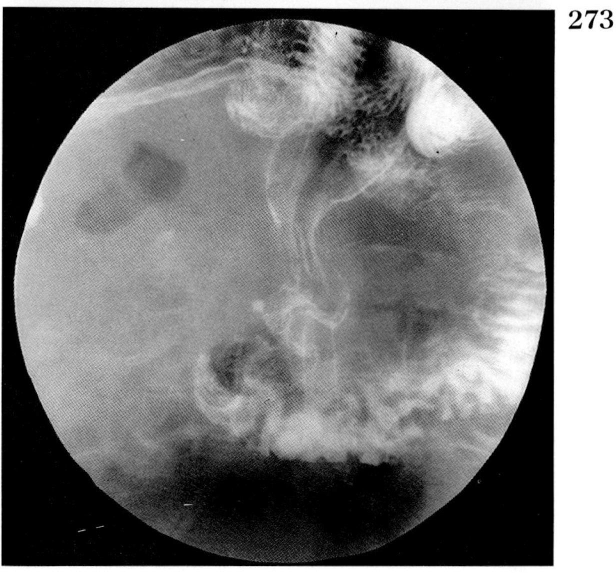
273

274

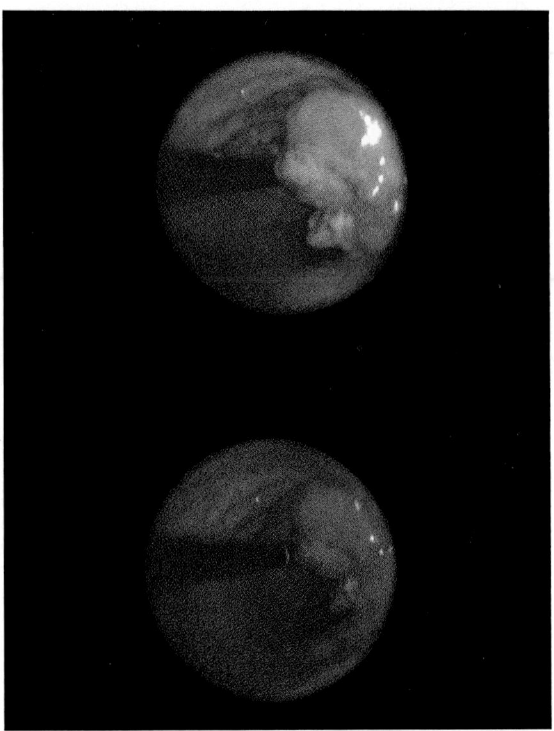

274 Polypoid carcinoma. Endoscopic view of polypoid carcinoma in gastric fundus.

Diverticular disease of the colon

Incidence
Diverticulosis can be demonstrated in up to 50% of people over 80 years of age, by barium enema radiology

Aetiology
Several different factors play a part, including lack of fibre in the diet

Clinical features
Usually asymptomatic
Pain in left iliac fossa
Constipation
Diarrhoea
Flatulence
Rectal bleeding
Nausea and loss of appetite

Complications
Diverticulitis
Haemorrhage
Abscess formation
Perforation – peritonitis, pericolic abscess, fistula formation into other viscera
Anaemia

275

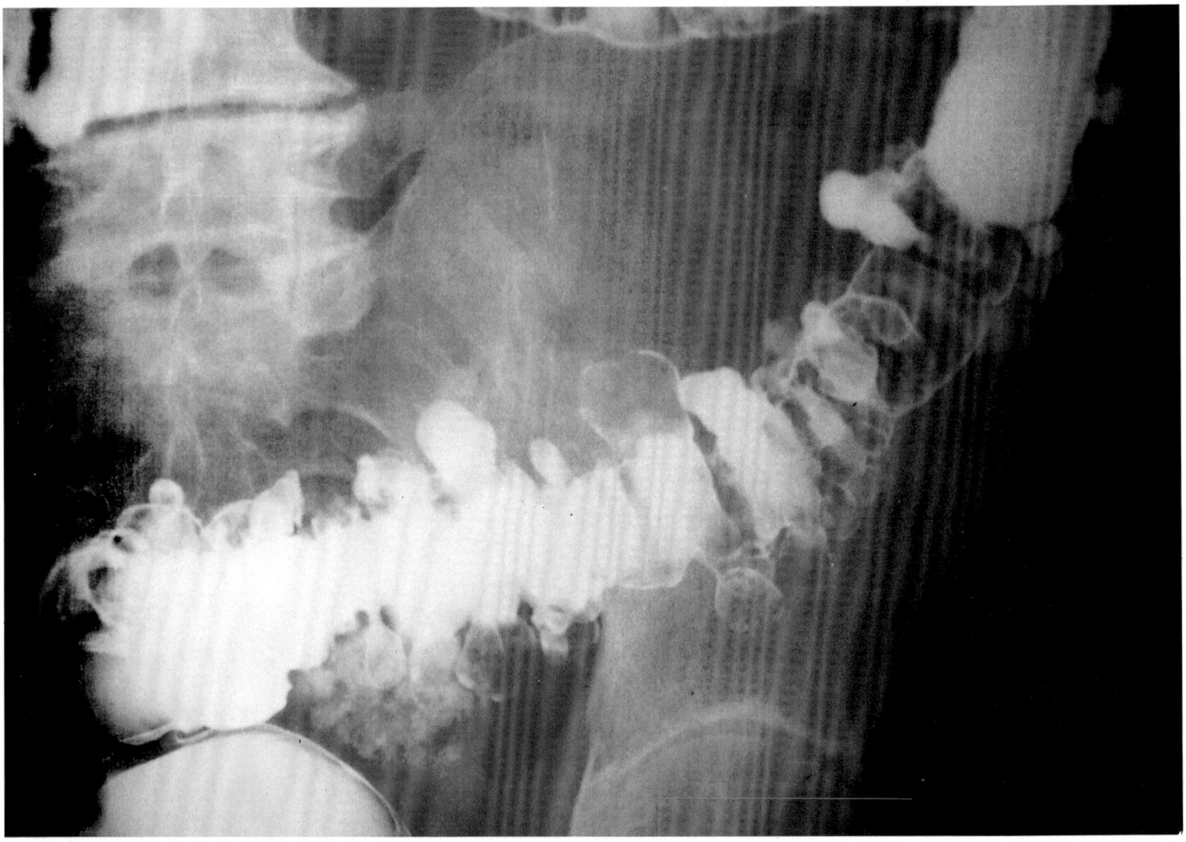

276

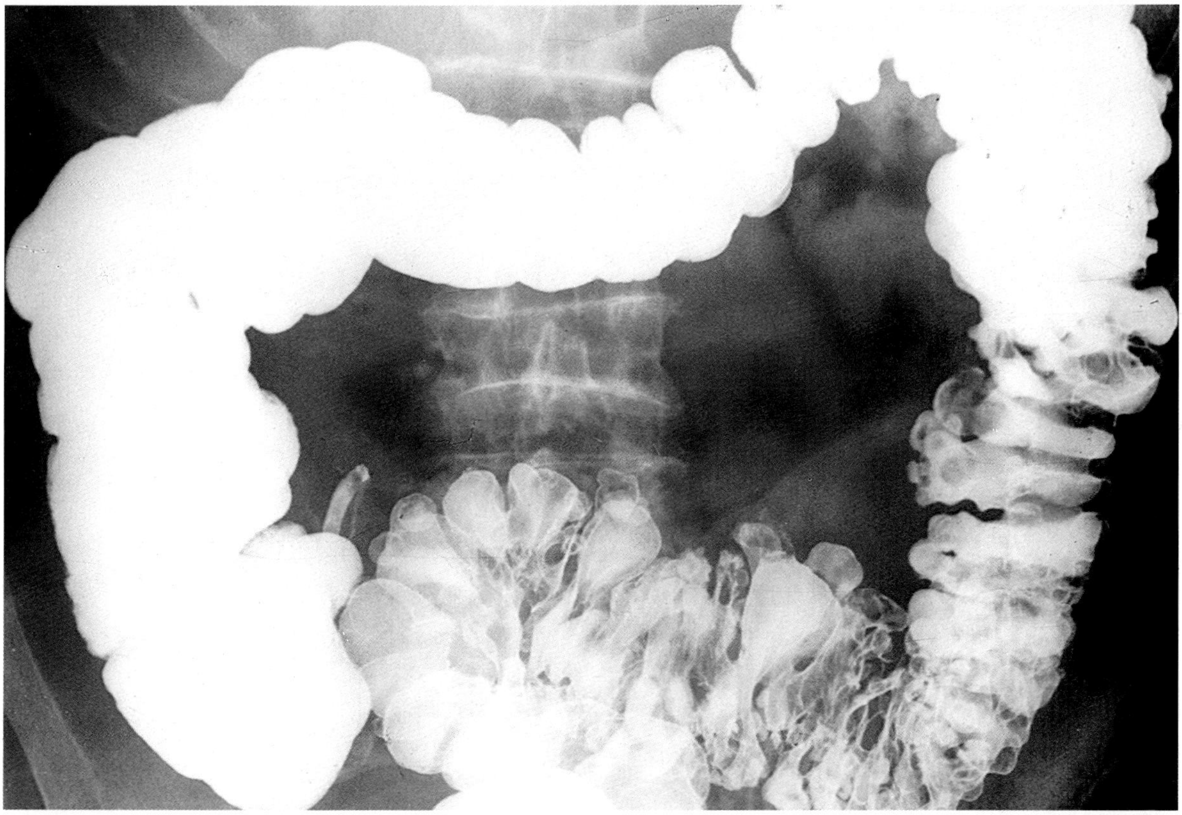

7

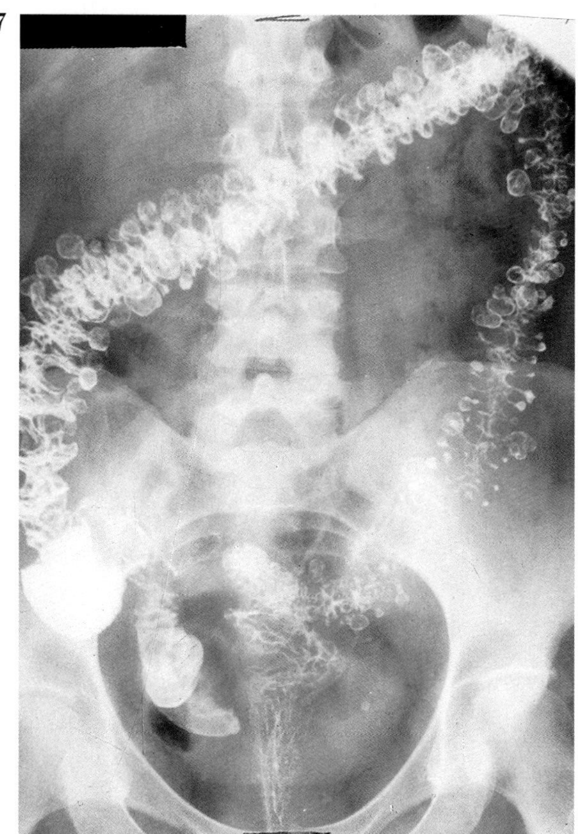

278

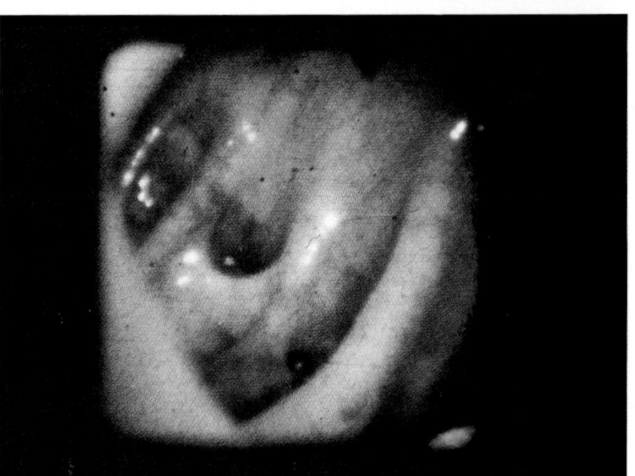

275–277 Diverticular disease. A frequent radiological finding in the elderly that produces various large-bowel problems, including constipation, diarrhoea, anaemia and acute diverticulitis. However, it is mostly symptomless.

278 Diverticular disease. Colonoscopy showing the mouth of a diverticulum with some surrounding muscle spasm.

279

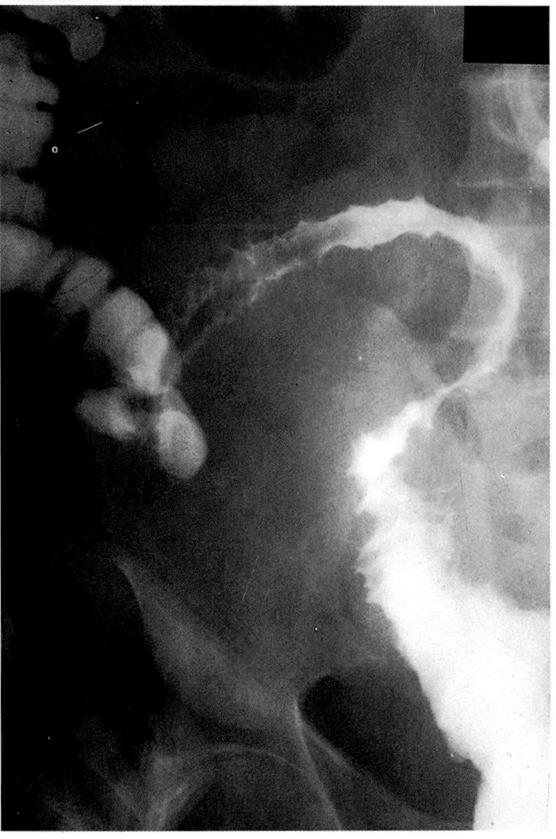

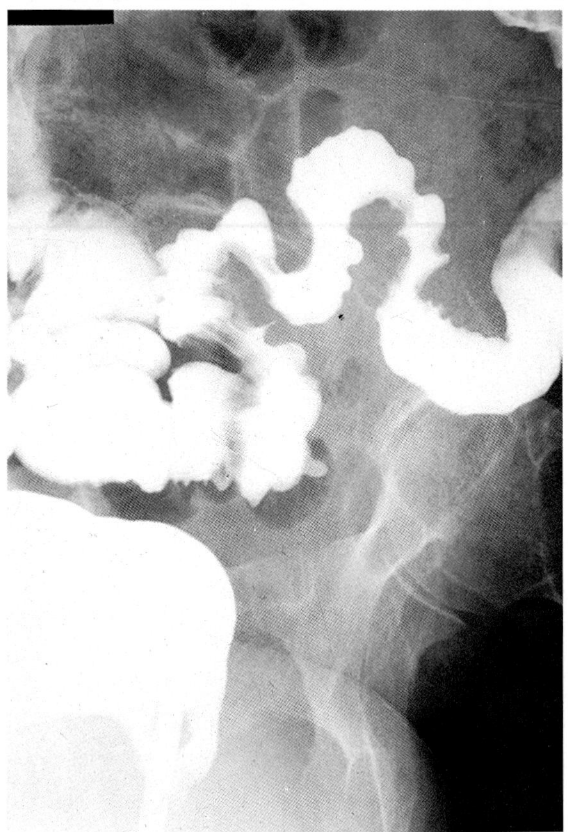

279 Ischaemic colitis. Typical radiological appearance in the region of a splenic flexure. 'Saw-tooth' and 'thumb-printing' signs are clearly shown. These are caused by oedema of the bowel wall.

280 Ischaemic colitis. This barium enema x-ray shows both 'thumb printing' and sacculation caused by the formation of pseudodiverticula.

281

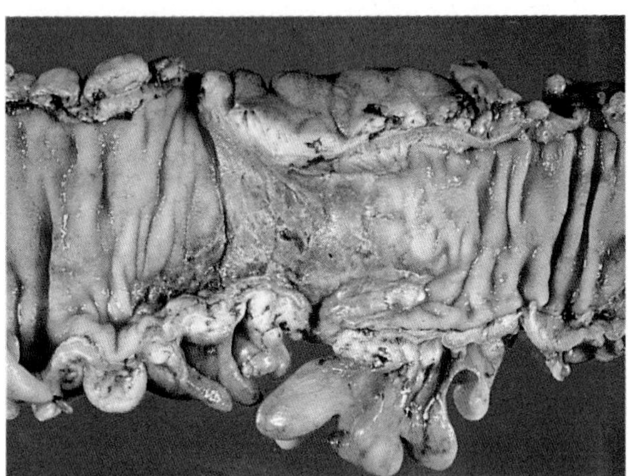

281 Ischaemic colitis. Pathology specimen of the colon showing narrowed ischaemic segment.

Ischaemic colitis occurs in later life and the causative factors are atherosclerosis, congestive heart failure, use of cardiac glycosides and haemorrhage caused by bleeding from a duodenal ulcer.

The clinical presentation may be acute or chronic and consists of abdominal pain and diarrhoea, which may be bloodstained. In some cases, an ischaemic area causes bowel constriction, which results in obstruction.

2

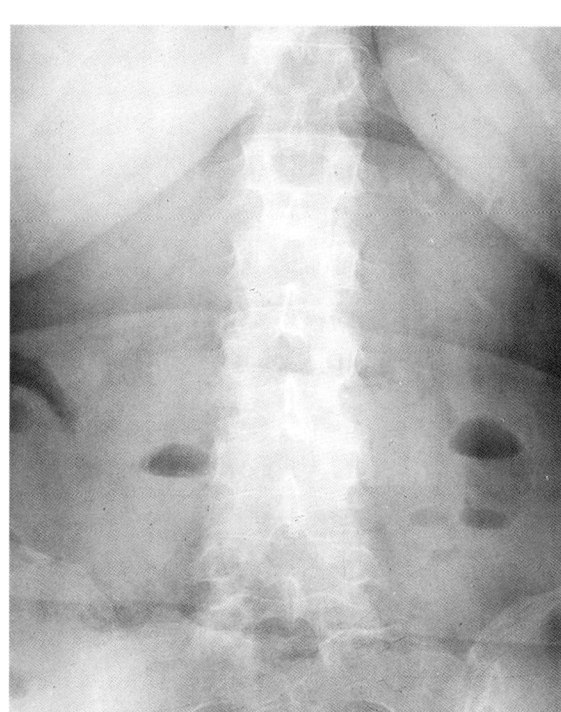

283

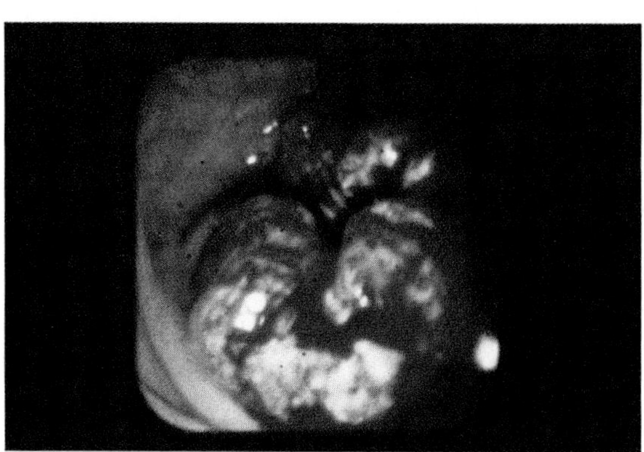

283 Carcinoma of the colon. Colonoscopy showing a neoplasm which may present with recurrent diarrhoea, weight loss and anaemia. Carcinoma of the colon is the most common form of malignancy in old age.

282 Intestinal obstruction. Plain x-ray of the abdomen (erect) showing multiple fluid levels in a case of intestinal obstruction. This elderly patient was found to have a carcinoma of the colon.

34

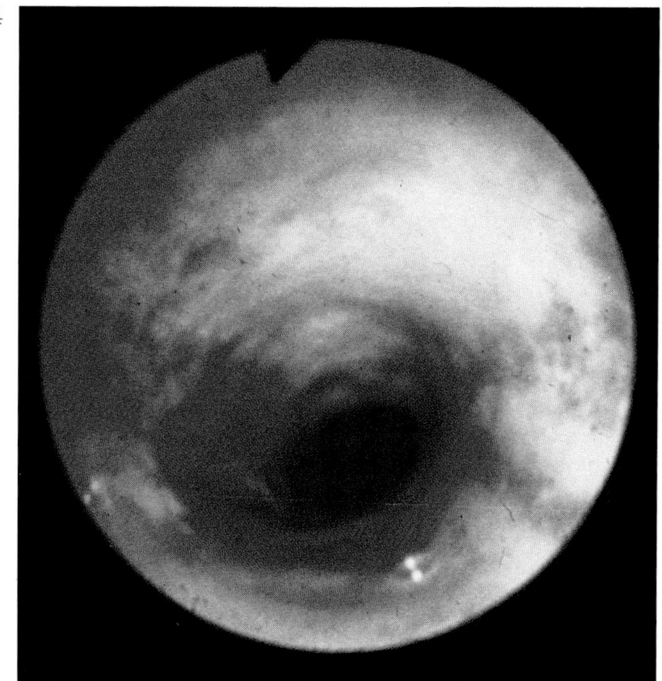

285

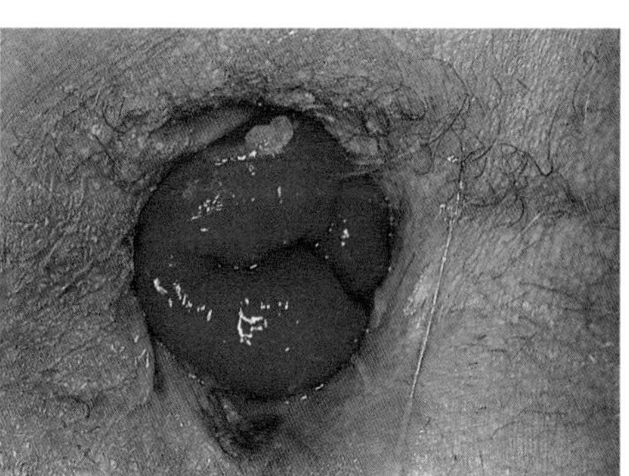

285 Haemorrhoids. A common problem in elderly patients, haemorrhoids are a frequent cause of recurrent constipation and may cause anaemia. General medical assessment of an elderly person must include a rectal examination.

284 Ulcerative colitis. Colonoscopy. The mucosa is red and inflamed and bleeds easily on contact. This disease is uncommon in old age.

Incontinence of urine

It is estimated that there are about 140,000 elderly people in the United Kingdom who suffer from incontinence. Precipitating factors are a combination of restricted mobility, distant or awkward toilet and increased frequency or urgency.

Incontinence of urine may be caused by lesions at four different anatomical levels:

The muscles of the pelvic diaphragm
The urethra
The bladder
The brain, spinal cord and autonomic nerves controlling micturition.

Weakness of the pelvic diaphragm leads to 'genuine-stress incontinence' – called 'genuine' to distinguish it from pseudo-stress incontinence in patients with detrusor instability. In this latter case coughing or moving may fire off a bladder contraction because of an unstable bladder.

Disorders of the urethra include atrophic urethritis in females in association with atrophic vaginitis (to be treated with oestrogens) and obstruction as a result of constipation or prostatic enlargement.

Diseases of the bladder include cystitis and, rarely, tumours or calculi.

Disorders in the central nervous system depend on whether they involve the reflex arc of micturition (through the second, third or fourth sacral segments of the spinal cord), in which case it will be of a 'lower motor neurone' type or the spinal cord above the sacral segments, brainstem or cerebral cortex, in which case it will be of an 'upper motor neurone' type. The first is often called a neurogenic atonic bladder and the second a neurogenic reflex, uninhibited or unstable bladder. Full diagnosis requires cystometry.

Urinary incontinence can also be classified as transient or established urinary incontinence.

Transient urinary incontinence – reversible
Infective – urinary tract infections
Retention with overflow – faecal impactions, anticholinergic drugs
Increased diuresis – diuretics, diabetes mellitus
Toxic confusional states – oversedation and psychological
Senile vaginitis
Environmental causes

Established urinary incontinence
Uninhibited neurogenic bladder – dementias, cerebrovascular accidents, parietal and frontal lobe lesions
Neurogenic, reflex, uninhibited or unstable bladder – paraplegia and spinal cord lesions
Retention with overflow – tabes, diabetes, prostatism, spinal cord thrombosis
Idiopathic unstable bladder – psychosomatic

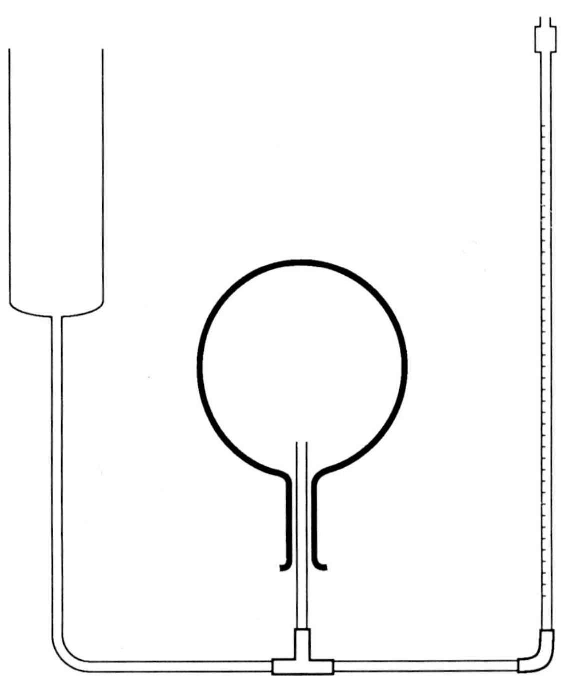

286 Simple cystometer. Cystometry records the reaction of the bladder to increasing distension. The simplest cystometer involves a catheter attached to a T-tube, one limb going to a reservoir from which the bladder is filled and the other to a manometer which records changes in intravesical pressure as the bladder is filled from the reservoir.

287

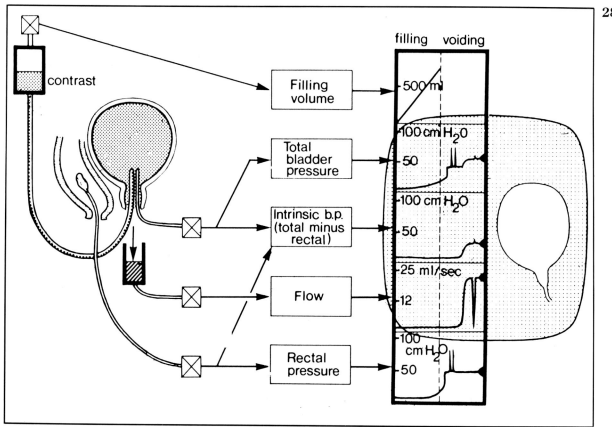

287 Cystometry. Diagrammatic representation of equipment for simultaneous cystometry and cystourethrography, with video-tape recording as first described by Bates and his colleagues in the *British Journal of Urology*, 1970. The equipment shown includes a reservoir which fills the bladder with radio-opaque fluid, and a second line from the bladder through a transducer which records intravesical pressure. To distinguish intrinsic bladder contractions from those that are transmitted from the abdominal cavity, a second pressure recording line is taken from the rectum, and by subtracting this pressure from that of the bladder, the pure bladder muscle contraction is shown as 'subtracted' pressure. This sophisticated system also allows the recording of the degree of filling, the degree of emptying and a simultaneous picture of the shape of the bladder and urethra taken by x-ray.

288

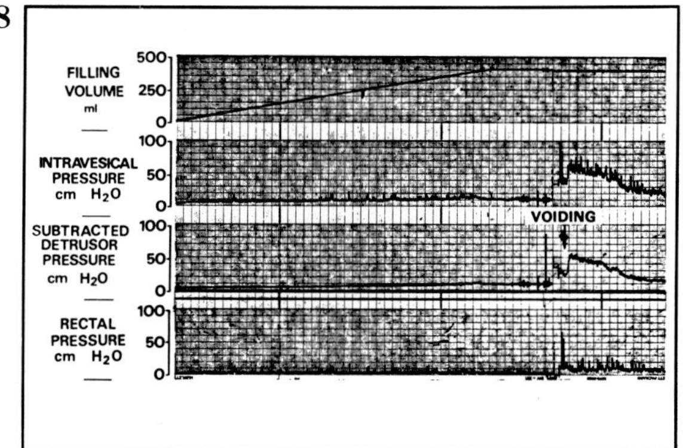

288 Normal cystometrogram. Bladder filling up to 450 ml of fluid, with no intrinsic contractions occurring until the patient attempts to void.

289

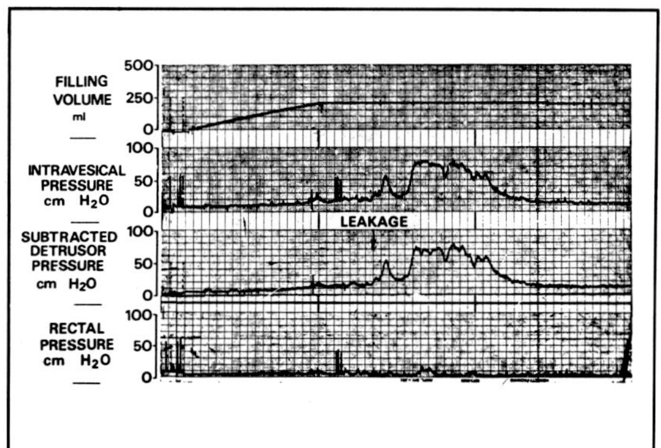

289 Uninhibited neurogenic bladder. In this cystometrogram tracing the bladder contractions occur at 250 ml filling, followed by a series of contractions associated with leakage.

Cystography

Changes which may be demonstrated in the bladder by cystography are associated either with bladder outlet obstruction (for example, enlargement of the prostate) or with functional outlet obstruction in the uninhibited or reflex neurogenic bladder in which intrinsic bladder contractions occur against a closed outlet. The findings which may then be seen include (these three x-rays, **290**, **291** and **292**, are all of females and such findings are not uncommon in aged incontinent women):

290 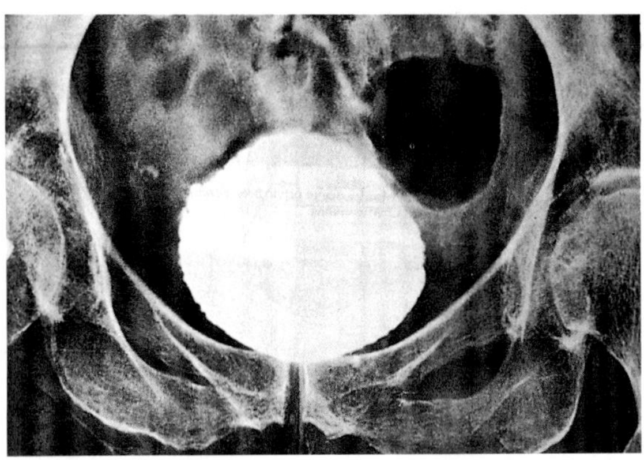

290 Trabeculation.

291 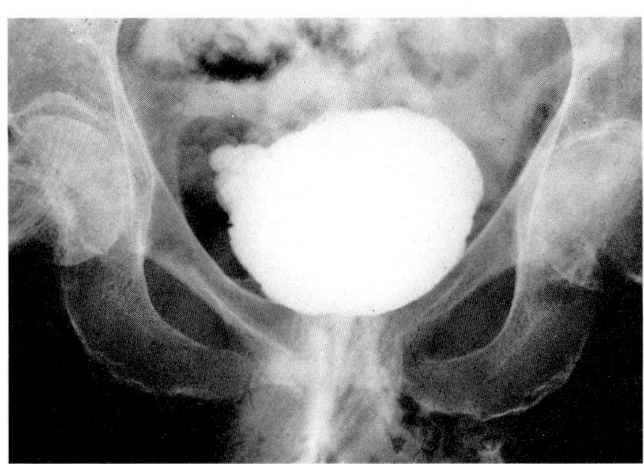

291 Formation of cellules or pseudodiverticula.

292 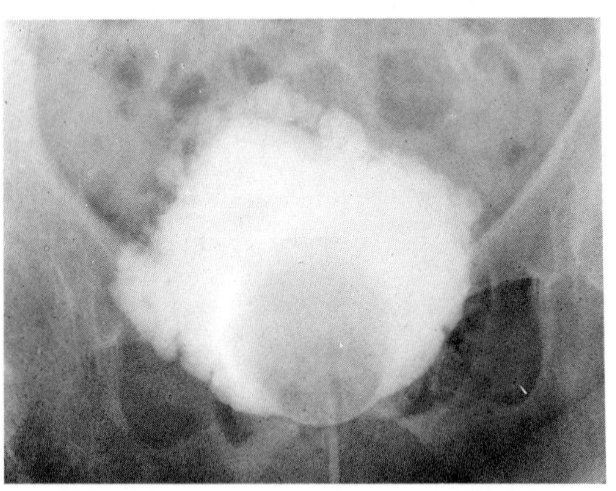

292 Formation of diverticula.

)3

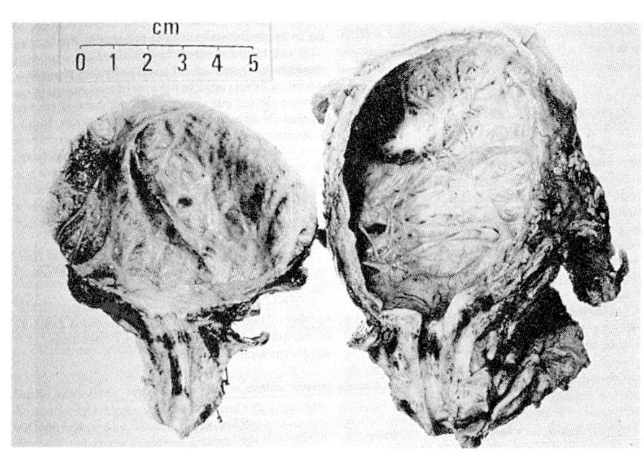

294

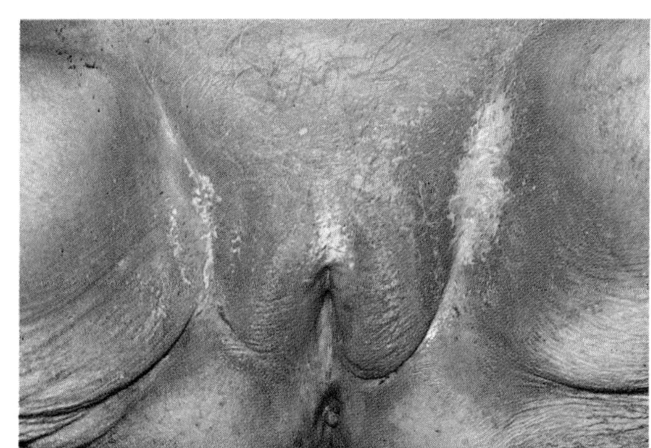

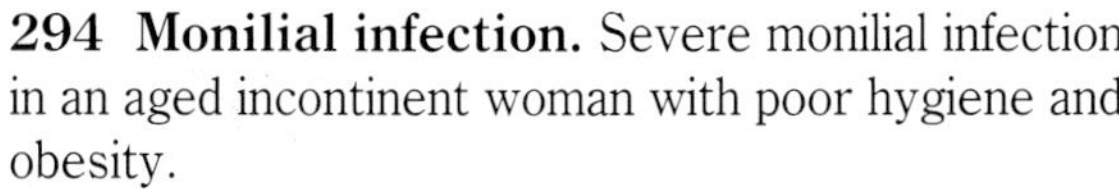

293 Bisected female bladder showing trabeculation and cellule formation.

294 Monilial infection. Severe monilial infection in an aged incontinent woman with poor hygiene and obesity.

295 Caruncle. This is a granulomatous and ulcerating lesion, presumably the end stage of a urethrocele. This anatomical abnormality is seen frequently in elderly incontinent women.

296 Rash caused by urinary incontinence. Early stages. Contributory factors consist of immobility, ill-health, pressure and lack of nursing care.

297 Rash caused by urinary incontinence. Advanced stages with cellulitis, excoriation and a serious risk of a pressure sore.

295

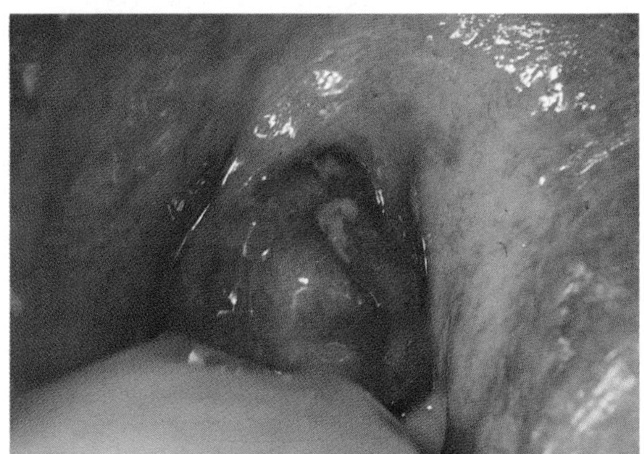

296

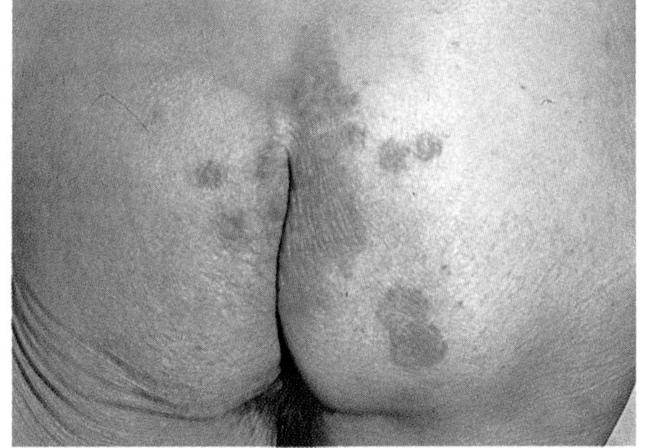

297

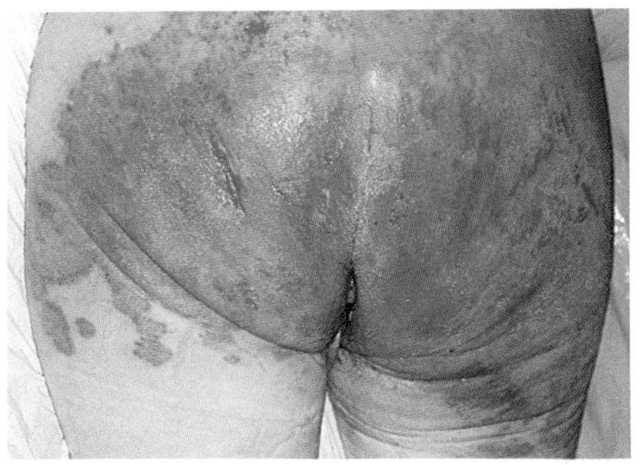

298 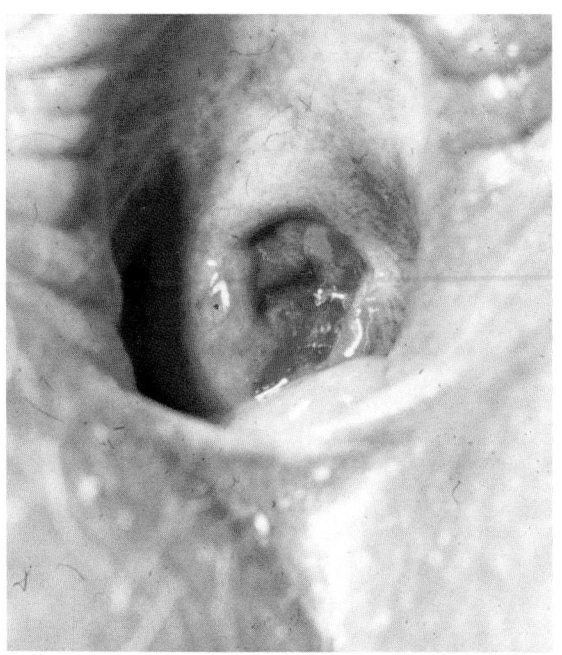

298 Slight urethral prolapse. There is minimal prolapse of the urethral mucosa. This is a fairly common condition in elderly women, probably associated with age changes affecting the supporting tissues of the urethra, and a frequent cause of incontinence.

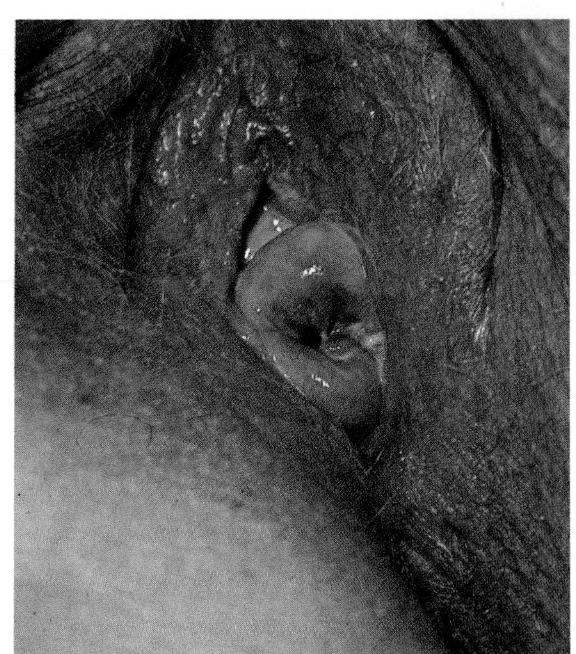 29

299 Uterovaginal prolapse. A more advanced case than the one considered in **298**. Vaginal atrophy, weakness of vaginal walls and ageing skeletal muscle can cause this condition which can result in urinary incontinence.

300 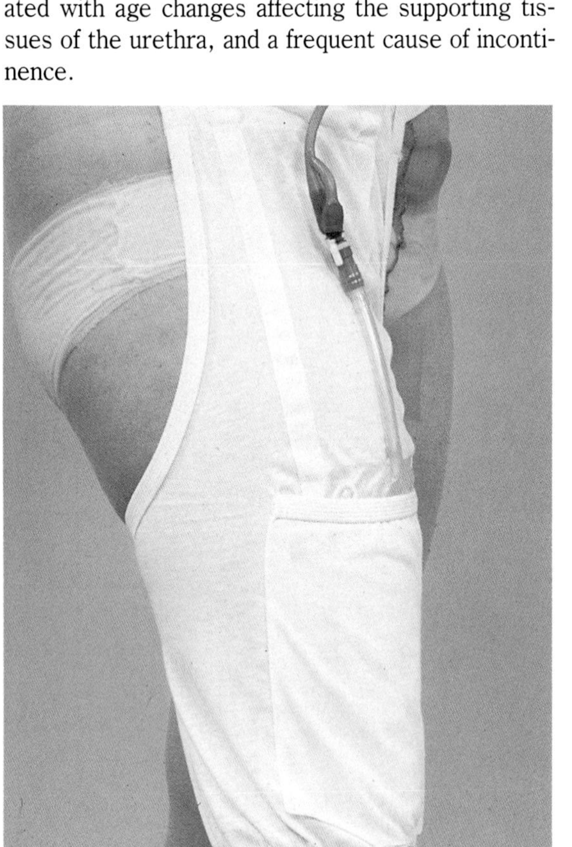

300 Urinary drainage bag. Catheterised patient wearing a one-leg pant garment with a pocket on the outside to hold the urinary drainage bag. There are several types of supports for drainage bags in these circumstances, including the sporran and holster types suspended from waistbands and those worn around the leg. In general, those supported from the waistband are more likely to stay in position when the drag occurs from weight of urine in the bag as it fills up.

8 Disorders of the Upper Limbs

Causes of wasting of the small muscles of the hand

Cord lesions:
Tumour, e.g. meningioma
Motor neurone disease
Cord compression
Trauma
Vascular lesions
Syringomyelia

Root lesions:
Cervical spondylosis
Neurofibroma

Brachial plexus lesions:
Cervical rib
Pancoast's tumour
Scalenus anterior syndrome

Nerve lesions:
Carpal tunnel syndrome (median nerve)
Ulnar nerve lesion
Polyneuropathy

Miscellaneous:
Shoulder–hand syndrome
Arthritis – e.g. rheumatoid arthritis
Disuse atrophy, e.g. paralysis
Extreme old age

301

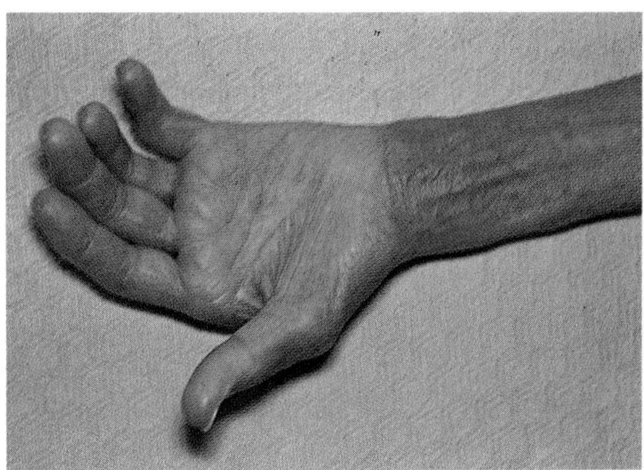

301 Thenar eminence wasting. This patient has mild wasting of hand muscles, especially of thenar eminence. He was found to have motor neurone disease.

302

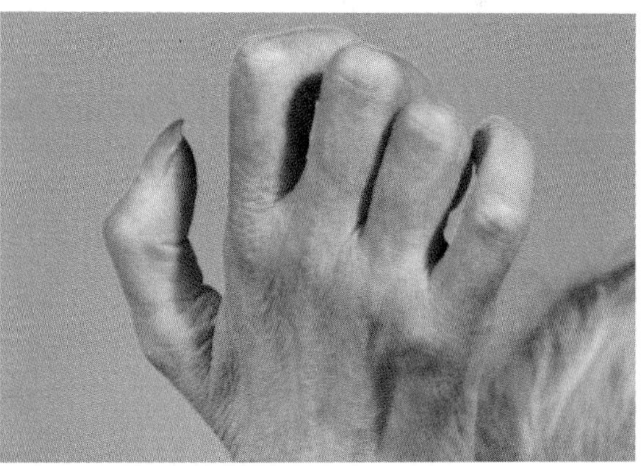

302 Claw-hand deformity. Wasting of small muscles of the hand with 'claw-hand' deformity caused by ulnar nerve palsy.

303

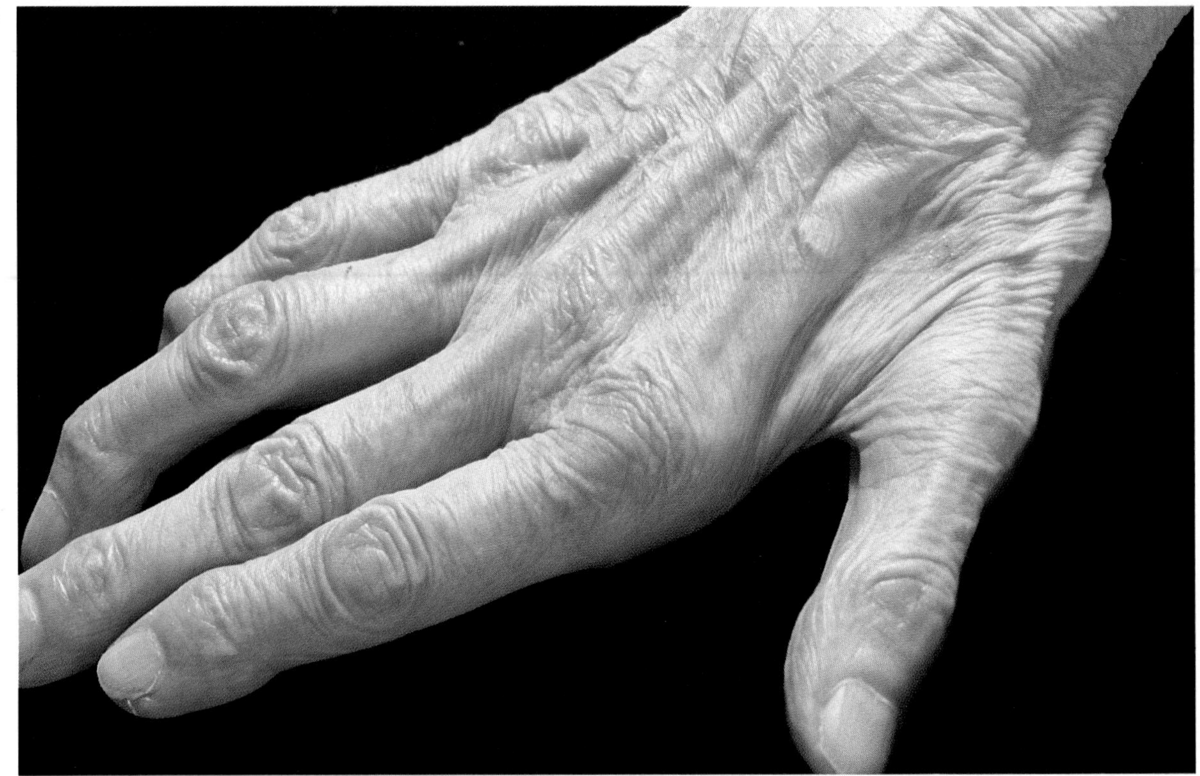

304

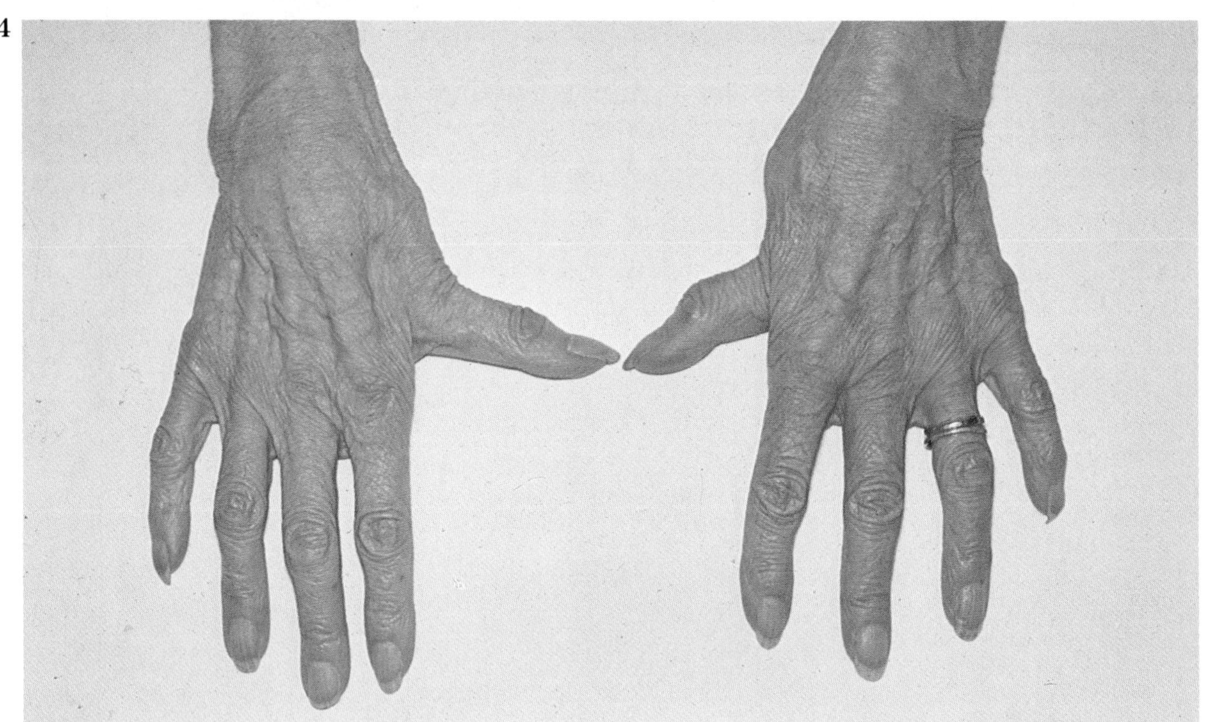

303 and 304 Wasting of the small muscles of the hand. This is caused by a lesion involving the lower brachial plexus (eighth cervical and first thoracic roots). There is paralysis and wasting of the small muscles of the hand. **304** shows a patient who had bilateral incomplete cervical ribs causing bilateral brachial plexus compression.

305 Osteoarthritis. Primary generalised osteoarthrosis showing both Heberden's and Bouchard's nodes.

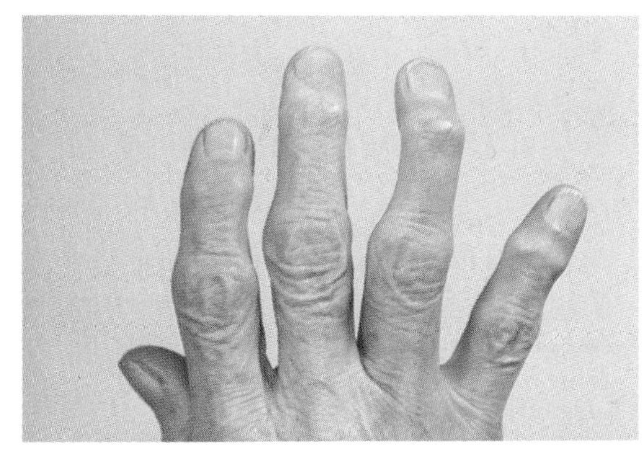
305

306 Osteoarthritis. Common destructive arthropathy in the elderly. In this case the distal interphalangeal joints, the carpometacarpal joints of the thumbs and the proximal interphalangeal joints show changes of osteoarthritis. Note the associated wasting of the small muscles of the hands.

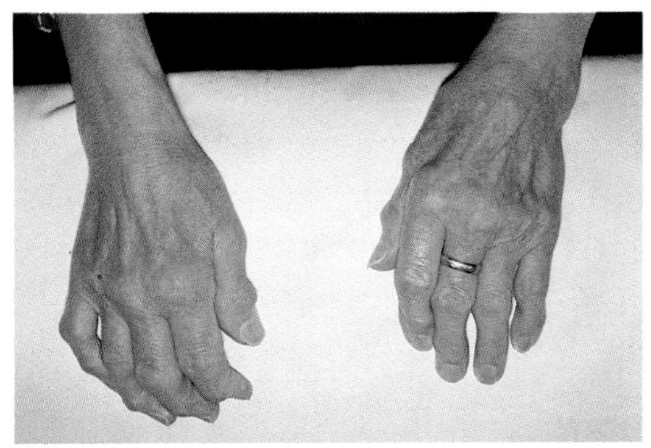
306

307 Heberden's nodes. Bony swellings in the distal interphalangeal joints; a typical feature of longstanding osteoarthritis. Women are affected much more frequently than men.

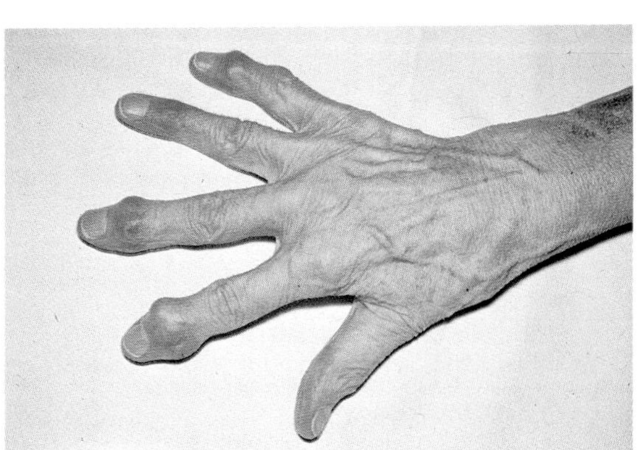
307

308 Bouchard's nodes. Also a feature of osteoarthritis. They are similar to Heberden's nodes but occur in the proximal interphalangeal joints.

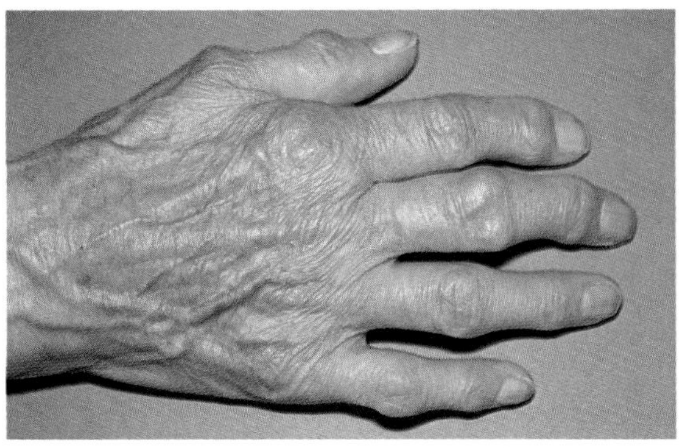
308

Osteoarthritis in old age

Osteoarthritis is a chronic degenerative joint disease. Radiological surveys have indicated an incidence in old age of over 80%. It affects the spine, hips, knees and, less frequently, the joints of the upper limbs. It is more common in obese, relatively immobile people.

The disease is usually primary, with symmetrical involvement of the distal interphalangeal joints, the first metacarpal joint and other joints including the spine, but secondary osteoarthritis can occur with congenital anatomical abnormalities of joints, trauma and mechanical problems, crystal deposition disease, avascular necrosis, septic arthritis and often recurrent haemarthrosis in haemophiliacs. In secondary osteoarthritis there is usually asymmetrical involvement of weight-bearing joints.

Symptoms

Pain in one or more joints, worst towards the evening and increased by particular activity. Eighty per cent of patients have morning stiffness. Other symptoms are immobility-associated obesity, depression, falls and insomnia.

Signs

Knee – bony swelling, effusions, tenderness, crepitus, painful limitation of movement and Baker's cyst.

Distal interphalangeal joints – bony swelling and deformity and Heberden's nodes.

Chronic stages – slowly progressive course with exacerbation and remissions. Joints develop painful restriction of movement, sometimes with deformity such as hip flexion, knee valgus or laxity. There are no extra-articular manifestations.

X-ray features

Loss of joint space, sclerosis of adjacent bone, marginal osteophytes and subarticular cysts.

Laboratory tests

No specific diagnostic test. ESR is normal and latex test is negative. Synovial fluid is clear, viscous and non-inflammatory.

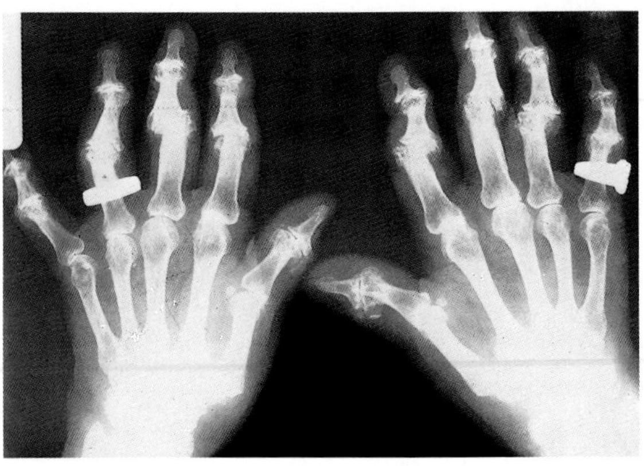

309 Osteoarthritis. X-ray of hands showing an advanced case of osteoarthritis. There is bony overgrowth and loss of joint space in distal interphalangeal and proximal interphalangeal joints.

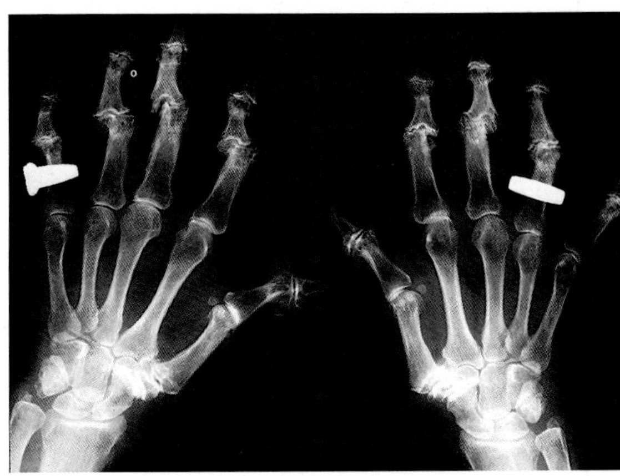

310 Osteoarthritis. X-ray of a moderately advanced case of osteoarthritis showing typical changes in distal interphalangeal and proximal interphalangeal joints.

Rheumatoid arthritis in old age

There are three main groups:

- 1st Group – those patients who carry their rheumatoid arthritis with them into old age
- 2nd Group – those who have fresh joint damage in later years
- 3rd Group – those who have symptoms of rheumatoid arthritis for the first time in old age

Features of rheumatoid arthritis appearing for the first time in old age:

The male:female ratio is altered.
In old age – male:female ratio 1:25
In younger age groups – 1:5

Distribution of joint involvement is similar but synovitis of ankles and wrists is less frequent in older age. Involvement of the hip also tends to be less frequent in elderly males.

Radiological changes tend to be more severe but there is relatively less deformity. Response to gold therapy is better in the elderly.

Systemic features such as weight loss, lymphadenopathy, splenomegaly and prolonged morning stiffness are of less intensity.

Onset tends to be abrupt.

Nodules are slightly less frequent.

Anaemia is common and ESR is usually high.

Osteoporosis is frequent.

Rheumatoid factor tests tend to show high titres.

Rheumatoid arteritis is rare.

Complications of rheumatoid disease

Chronic ill health
Weight loss, depression, pressure sores, immobility, constipation, social isolation.

Locomotor
Deformity, joint subluxations, tendon rupture, nerve compression (carpal tunnel syndrome), cervical subluxation, Baker's synovial cyst, rupture of synovial sac, cricoarytenoid arthritis, arthritis of auditory occicles, osteoporosis, muscle atrophy.

Cardiopulmonary
Pleural effusion, pulmonary nodules, fibrosing alveolitis, Caplan's syndrome with pneumoconiosis, pericarditis.

Ocular
Scleritis, uveitis, Sjogren's syndrome, scleromalacia perforans.

Arteritis
Raynaud's phenomenon, leg ulcers, mesenteric ischaemia.

Miscellaneous
Peripheral and autonomic neuropathy, amyloidosis, Felty's syndrome and complications of drug therapy.

311

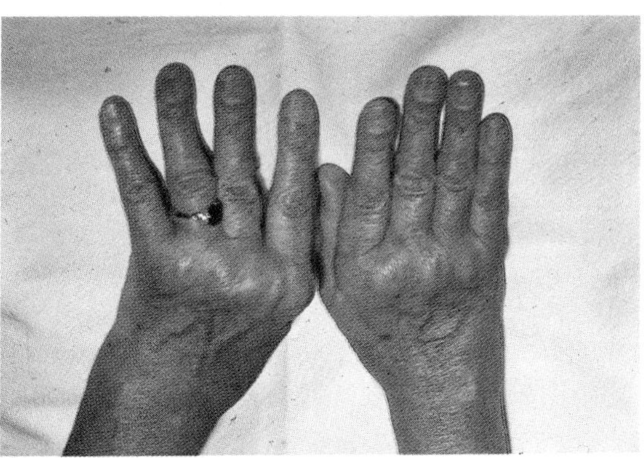

311 Rheumatoid arthritis. Changes of rheumatoid arthritis in the hand of an elderly lady. There is considerable destruction of the proximal interphalangeal and metacarpophalangeal joints. The rheumatoid disease had started in middle age and was still active, with pain, anaemia and high ESR.

312

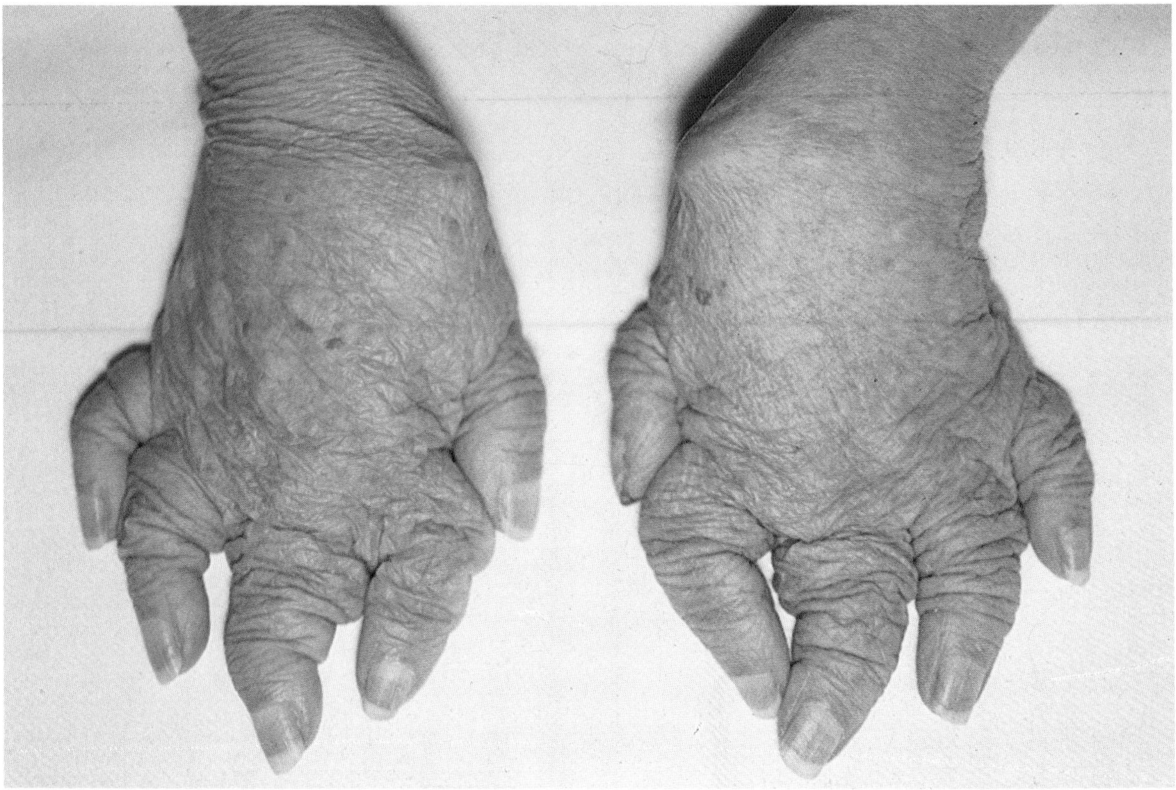

313

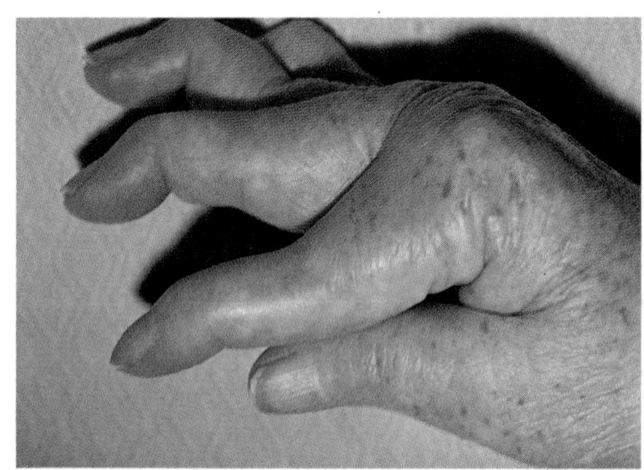

314

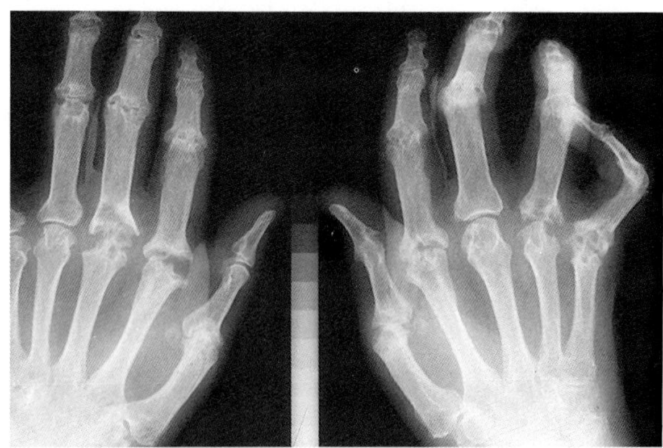

312 Severe rheumatoid arthritis. Chronic burnt-out rheumatoid disease. All the joints, including wrists, are affected and there is gross deformity with shortening and subluxation and complete loss of function.

313 Swan-neck deformity. Hyperextension at proximal interphalangeal joint caused by rheumatoid disease producing the classic swan-neck deformity.

314 Rheumatoid arthritis. X-ray of the hands of an elderly patient showing extensive joint destruction. There are marked erosions in metacarpophalangeal and proximal interphalangeal joints. Also, osteoarthritic changes in the distal interphalangeal joints.

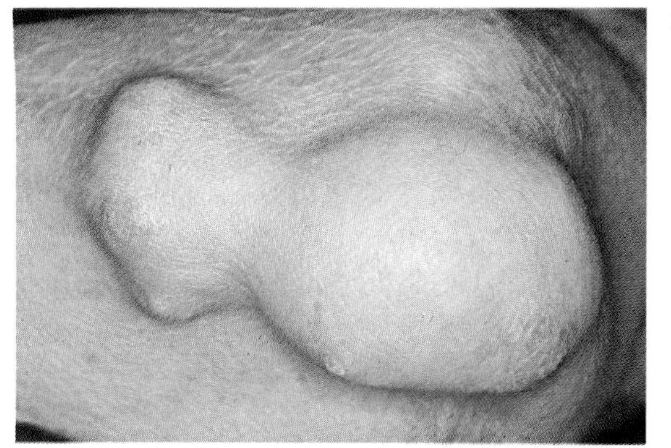

315

315 and 316 Rheumatoid nodules. Periarticular soft-tissue swellings occurring below the elbow on the extensor surface. Nodules are thought to form around an area of vasculitis. They may become necrotic and ulcerate.

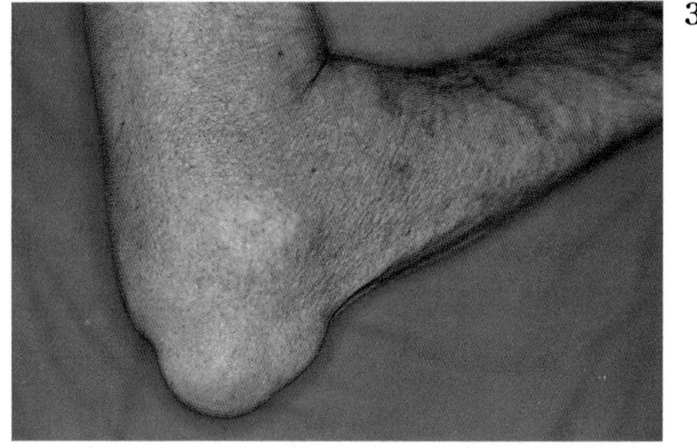

316

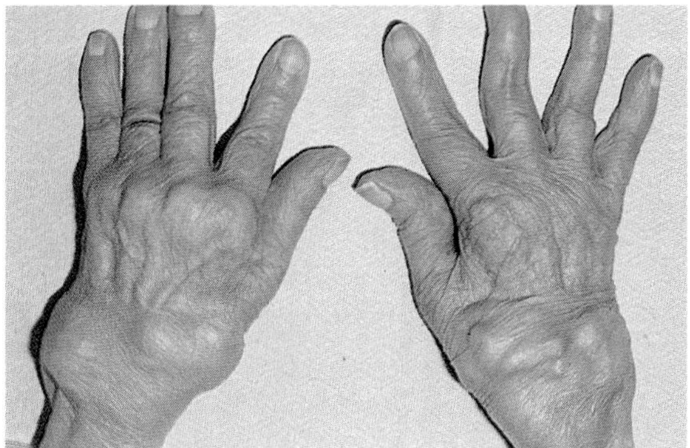

317

317 Rheumatoid arthritis. A case of advanced rheumatoid arthritis in an elderly lady – involving mainly the wrists and surrounding soft tissues.

318

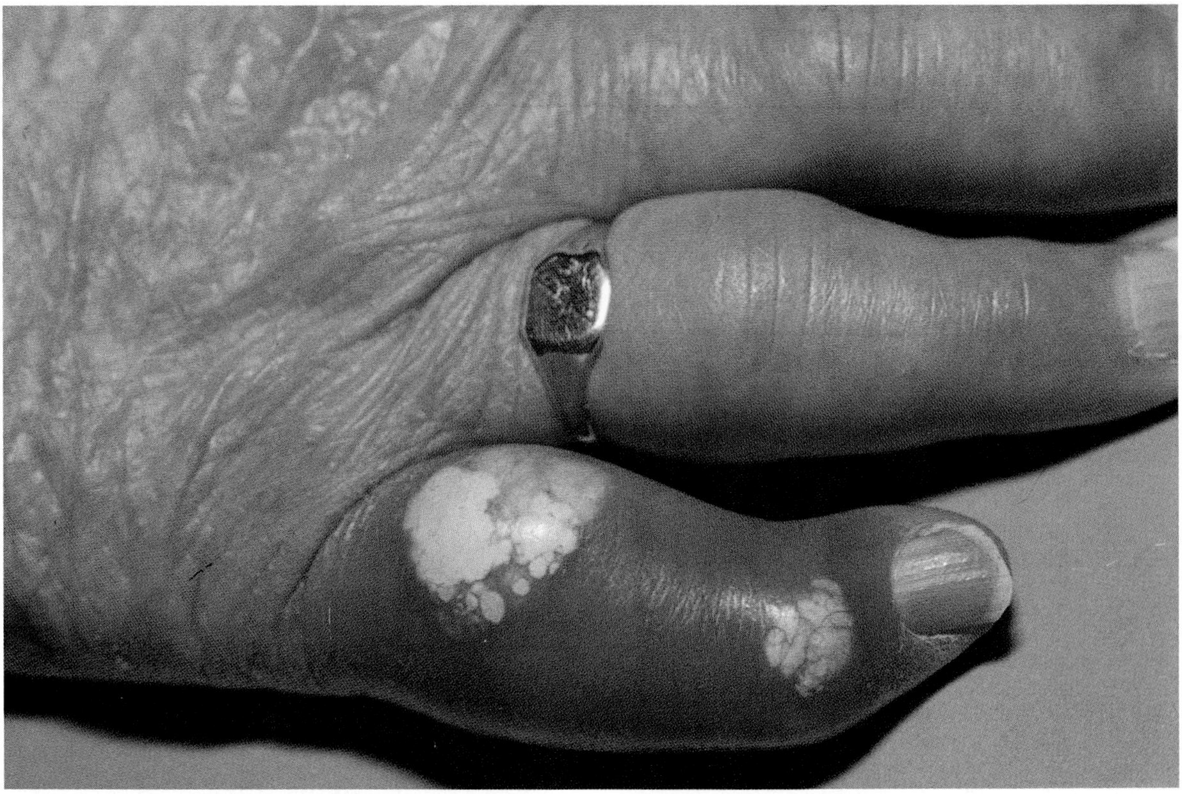

319

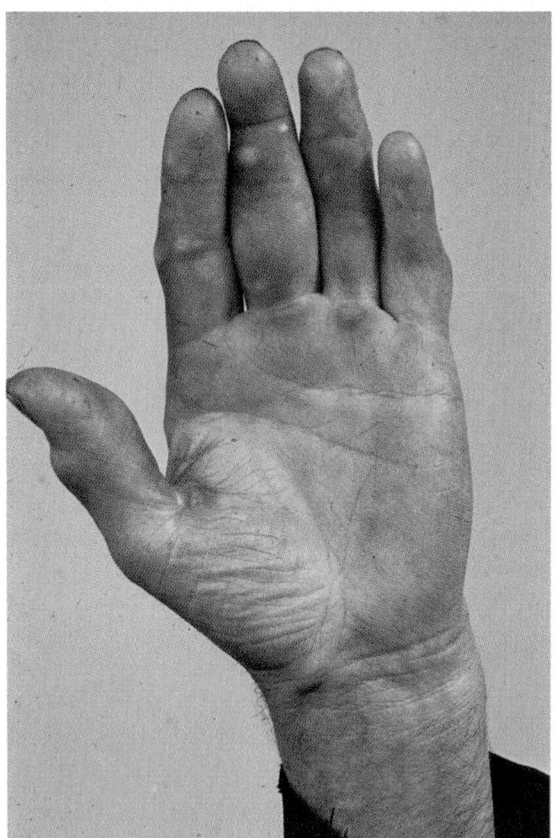

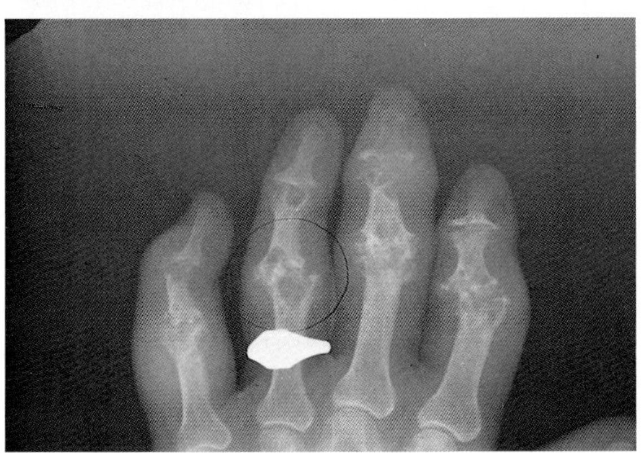

318 Tophaceous gout. This elderly lady, who had a long-standing history of 'rheumatism' and gout, was only diagnosed when tophi appeared on the fingers. The feet were not involved but the serum uric acid level was elevated. She responded rapidly to appropriate therapy.

319 Tophaceous gout. Gouty tophi seen on the palmar surface of the fingers.

320 Gout: hand x-ray. Note the destructive changes in proximal interphalangeal and distal interphalangeal joints with punched-out radiolucent areas in the bones.

321 Paget's disease. X-ray of the hands showing Paget's disease of the right fourth proximal phalanx. Note the increased density and thickening of the bone.

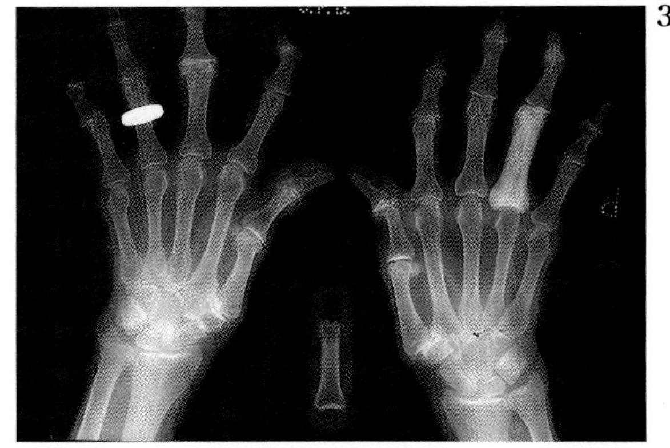
321

322 Dupuytren's contracture. Painless flexion contracture affecting the ring finger first and then involving the other fingers. It is caused by progressive fibrosis of the palmar fascia. About 25% of people over 60 years of age have some thickening of the palmar fascia. Some cases are familial. There is an increased incidence in patients with alcoholic liver disease and epilepsy. Note the incidental wasting of the thenar eminence.

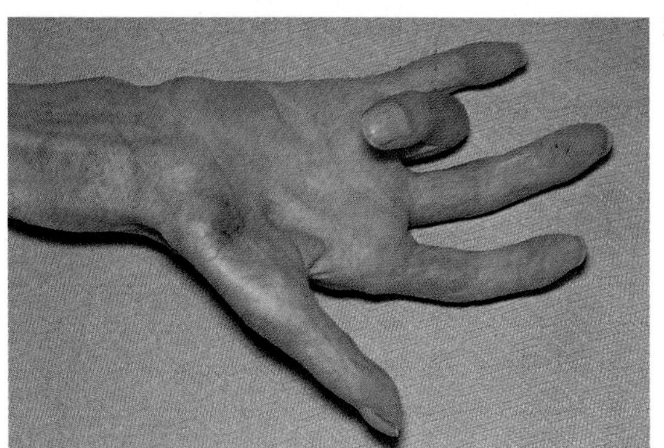
322

323 Dupuytren's contracture. In this case there is almost symmetrical involvement of both hands.

323

324

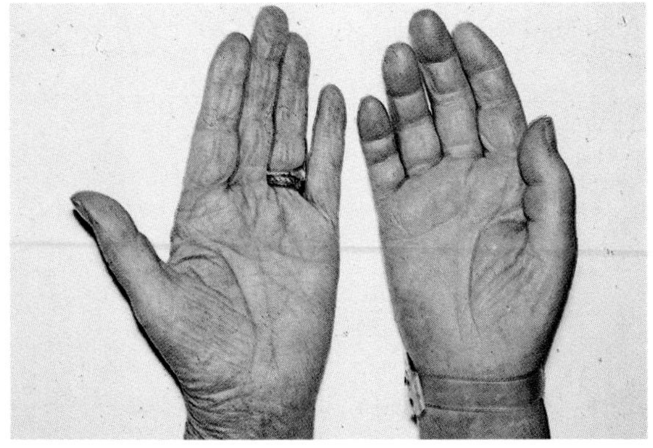

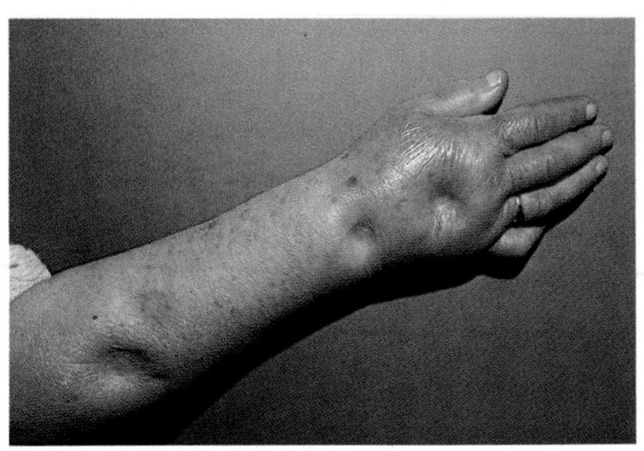

324 Hemiplegic oedema. Right hand showing non-pitting oedema caused by disuse and autonomic changes associated with hemiplegia.

325 Oedema. This elderly lady had gross pitting oedema of the arms and hands (also legs) caused by hypoalbuminaemia resulting from a protein-losing enteropathy.

326

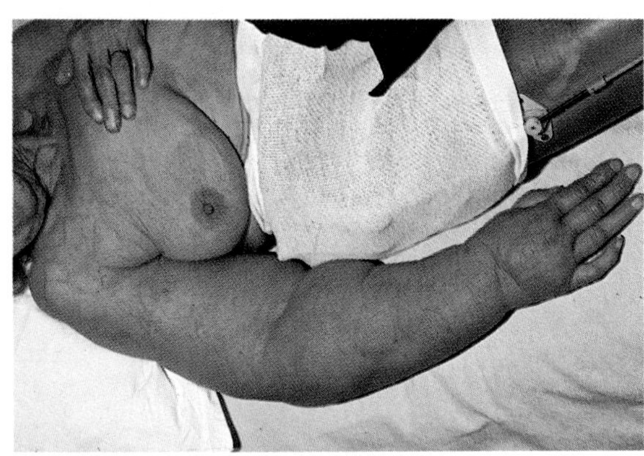

326 Lymphoedema arm. Caused by malignant lymph nodes in the axilla. This patient was found to have carcinoma of the breast. Note the artificial right leg.

327

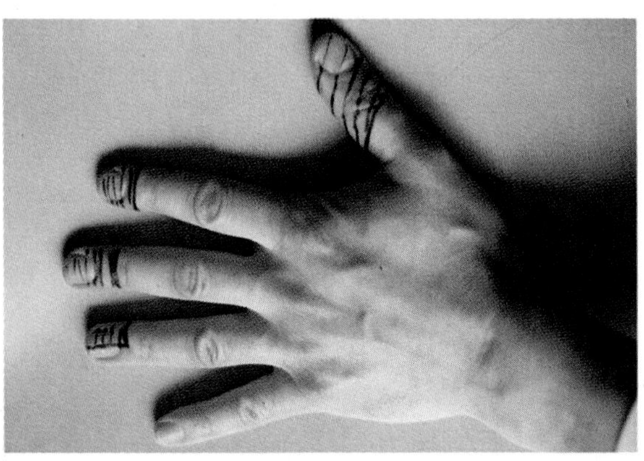

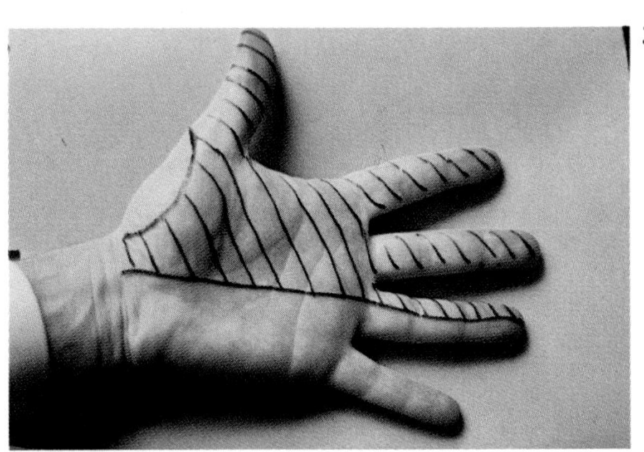

327 and 328 Carpal tunnel syndrome. Areas of sensory impairment as a result of a median-nerve lesion at the wrist. The median nerve also innervates the pronators of the forearm, long finger flexors and abductor and opponens muscles of the thumb. Myxoedema is a frequent cause of carpal tunnel syndrome in older patients.

329 Claw hand. Ulnar nerve palsy showing typical claw-hand deformity.

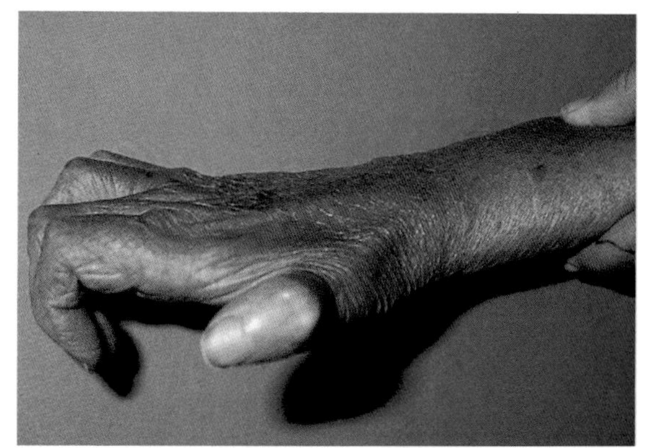

329

330 Burns. This elderly man had recurrent burns on the fingers. Examination of the central nervous system revealed sensorimotor neuropathy caused by cervical spine disease.

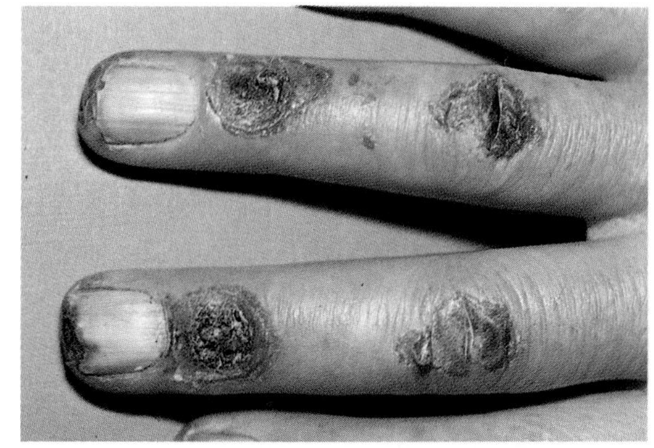

330

331 Peripheral cyanosis. Note the bluish discoloration of fingers and nails. The cyanosis in this case was of central origin and caused by corpulmonale.

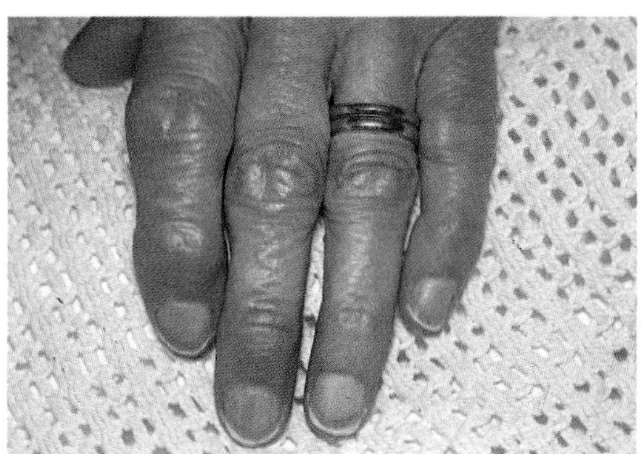

331

332 Palmar erythema. A peripheral ring of erythema around the palmar surface of the hand is a frequent finding in the elderly. It is usually 'innocent', but other causes are liver disease, polycythaemia and thyrotoxicosis.

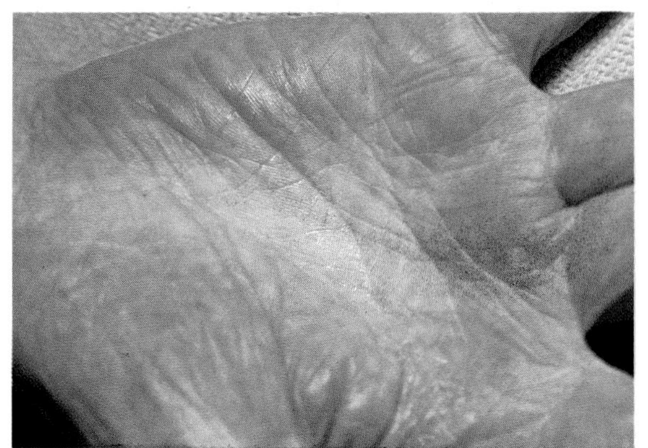

332

333

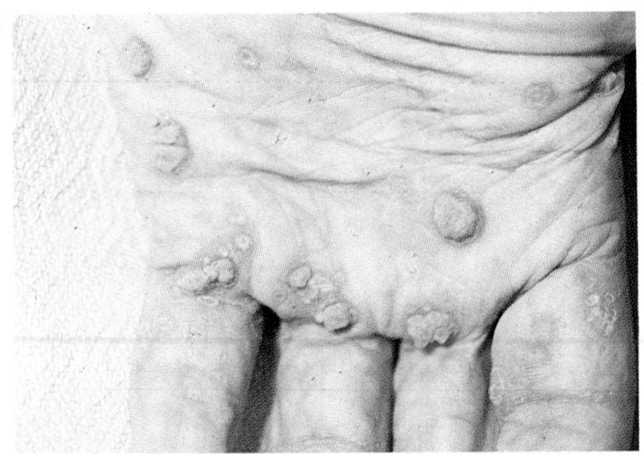

333 Palmar warts. These are deep, painful, flat lesions covered by a thick layer of cornified epithelium and occurring on the palms and soles. They are caused by a virus and are occasionally seen in the elderly.

334

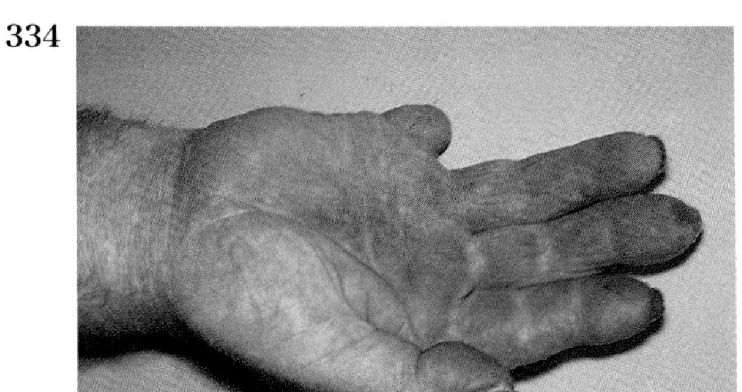

334 Faecal staining of the hands. This elderly patient was grossly confused and disorientated. He had chronic brain failure and was found to have faecal impaction. His hands and clothes were smeared with faeces because he had been attempting manual disimpaction.

335

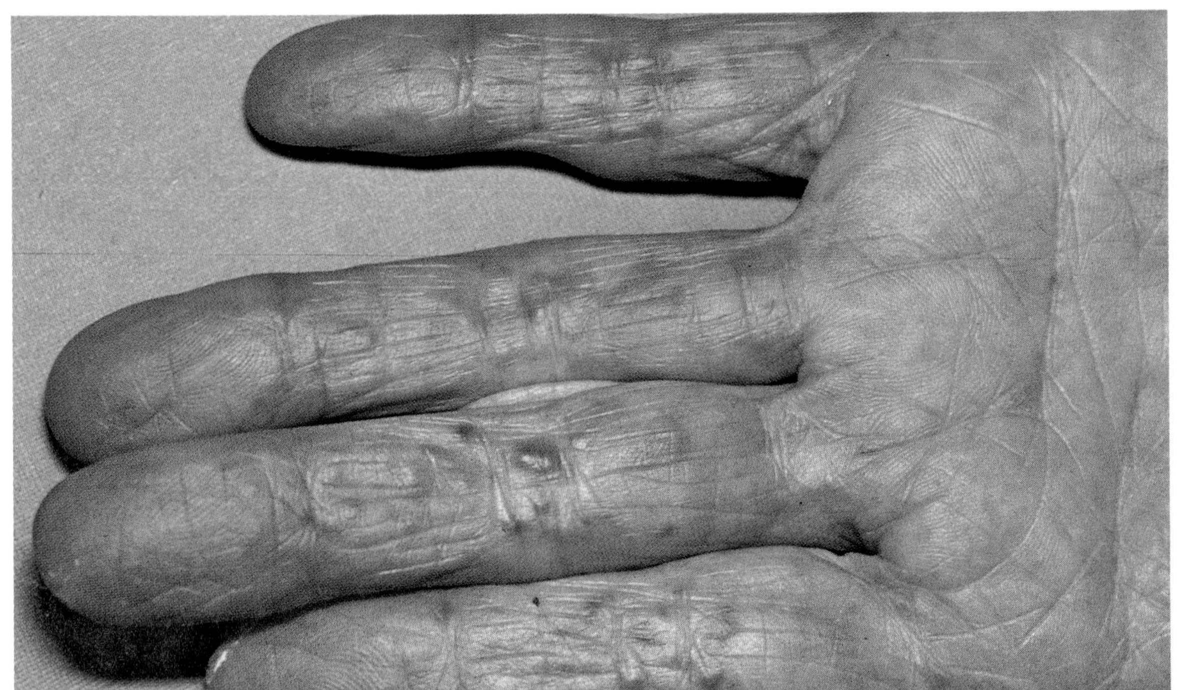

335 Finger varicosities. Dilated veins occur on the palmar aspects of the fingers in over 50% of people over 70 years of age. There is no known relation with any venous abnormalities elsewhere in the body and the finding has no clinical significance.

336 Pathological fracture. X-ray of the humerus showing a pathological fracture caused by secondary deposits from carcinoma of the colon. Note the destruction and sclerosis of bone around the fracture.

Elderly patients with osteoporosis, osteomalacia, Paget's disease and bony metastasis are more prone to fractures.

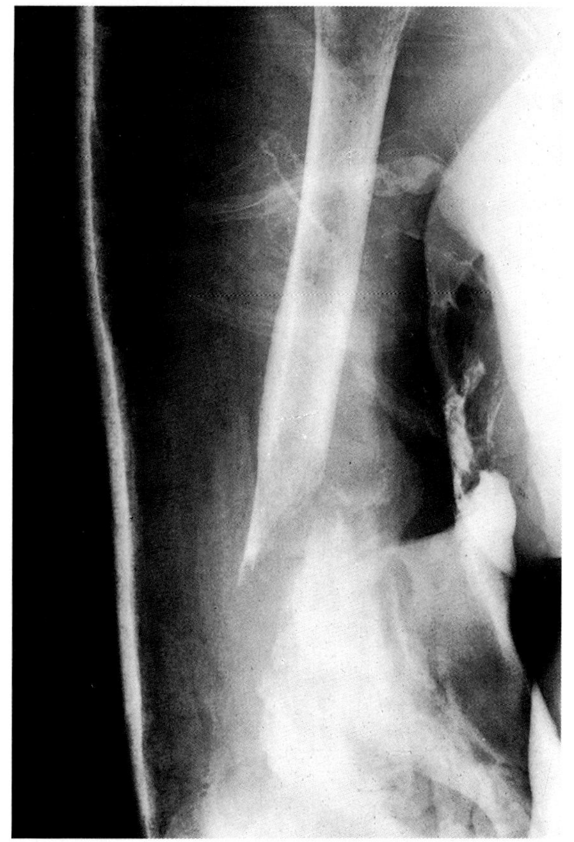

336

337 Cryoglobulinaemia. Purpuric spots and sores on the forearms that appeared recurrently with exposure to cold and were thought initially to be senile purpura. Investigations revealed the presence of cryoglobulinaemia with macroglobulins.

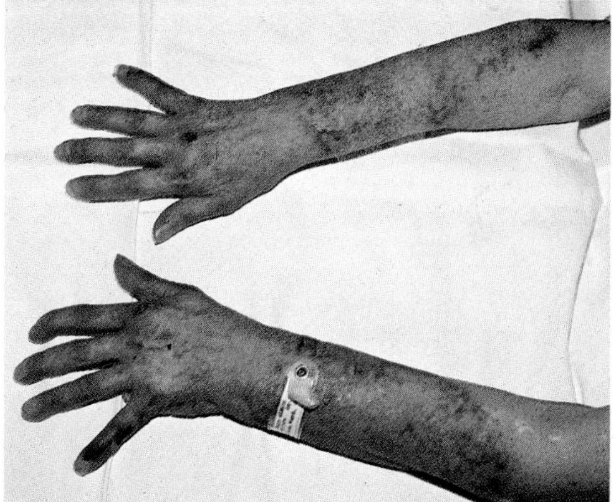

337

338

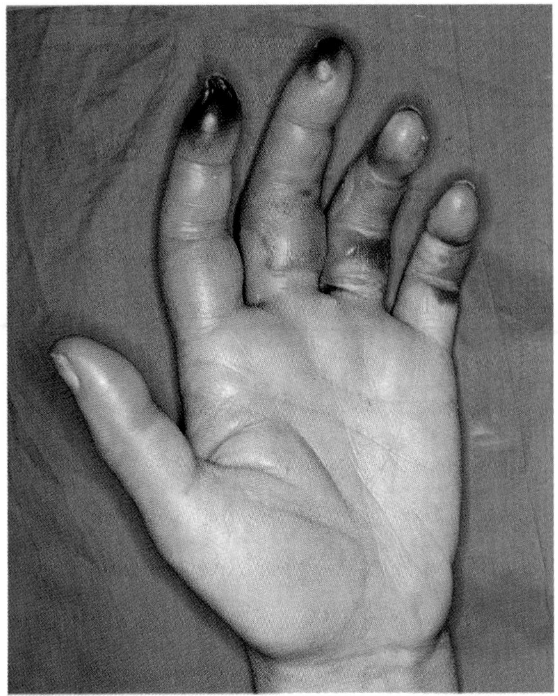

339

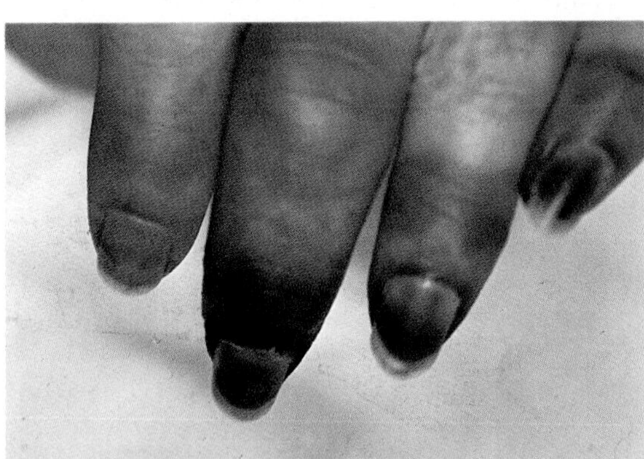

339 Vasculitis. Severe ischaemia of the fingers caused by polyarteritis nodosa.

338 Raynaud's phenomenon. Note the finger-tip ischaemia and necrosis. This elderly female patient had severe cervical spondylosis.

Raynaud's phenomenon

Paroxysmal digital ischaemia usually accompanied by pallor, cyanosis and followed by erythema.

Causes

- Reflex vasoconstriction
  - Raynaud's disease
  - Cervical spondylosis
  - Shoulder–hand syndrome
  - Use of vibrating machinery
- Arterial occlusion
  - Thoracic outlet syndrome
  - Arteriosclerosis
  - Embolus
  - Buerger's disease
- Collagen diseases
  - Systemic sclerosis
  - Polyarteritis
  - Systemic lupus erythematosis
  - Rheumatoid arthritis
- Increased blood agglutination
  - Cold agglutinins
  - Dysproteinaemias
  - Polycythaemia, leukaemia
- Miscellaneous
  - Cold injury – frostbite
  - Toxins – ergot, tobacco
  - Beta-blocker drugs
  - Amyloidosis
  - Myxoedema

340

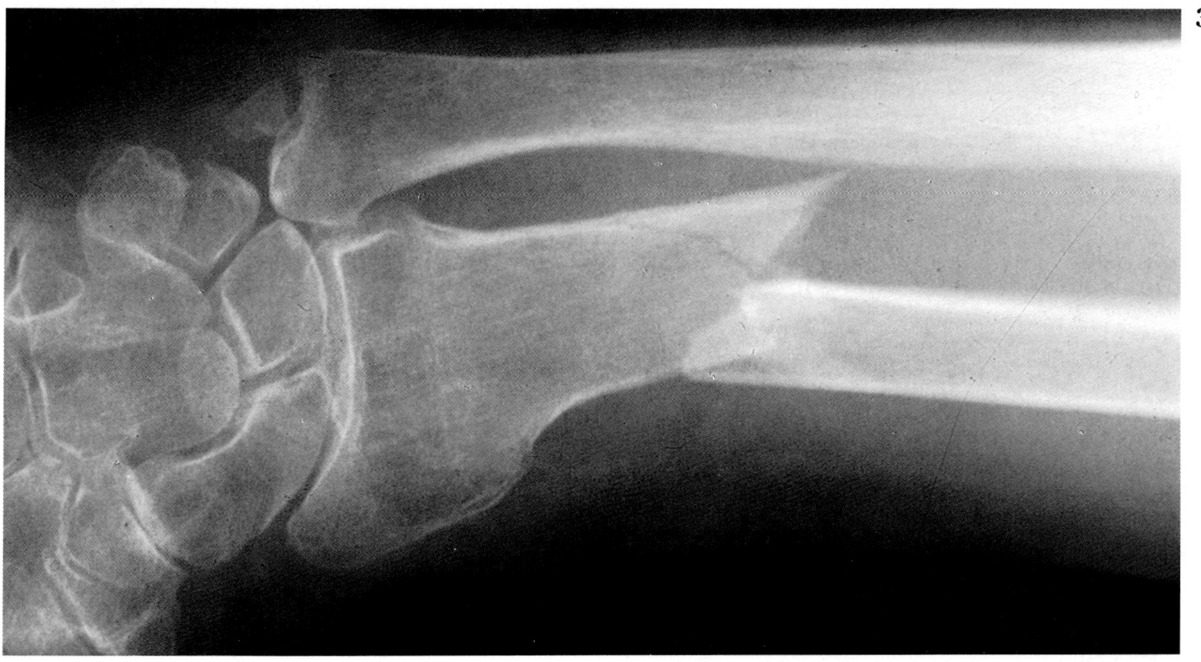

340 Fractured wrist. Common orthopaedic problem in the elderly. May result with slight trauma and cause considerable disability.

341

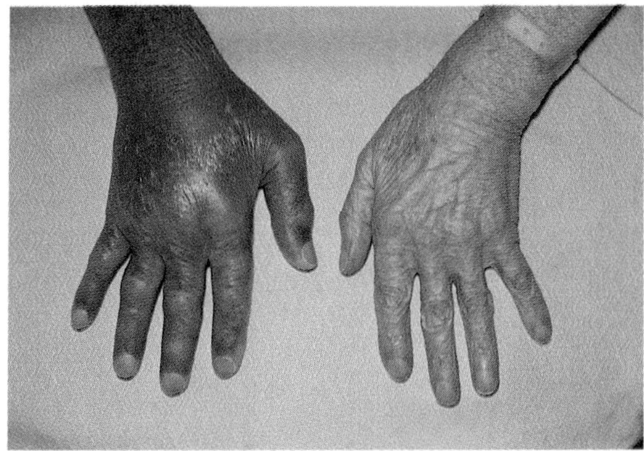

341 Ecchymosis. Severe ecchymosis of the right hand in an 82-year-old widower who had a tendency to bruise excessively. Investigations revealed the presence of hypovitaminosis-C plus anaemia and painful joints. Leucocyte ascorbic acid levels were below normal.

342
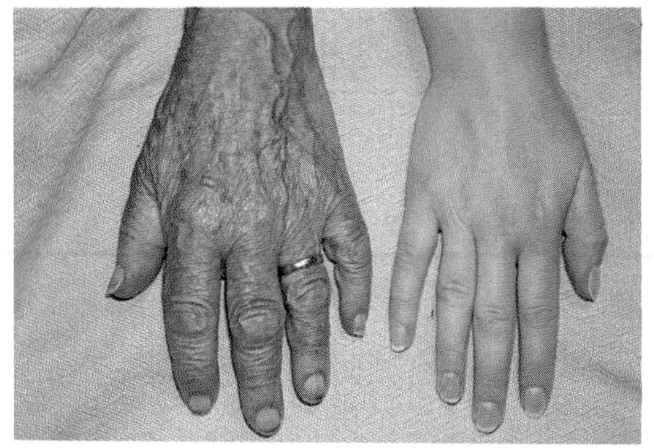

343
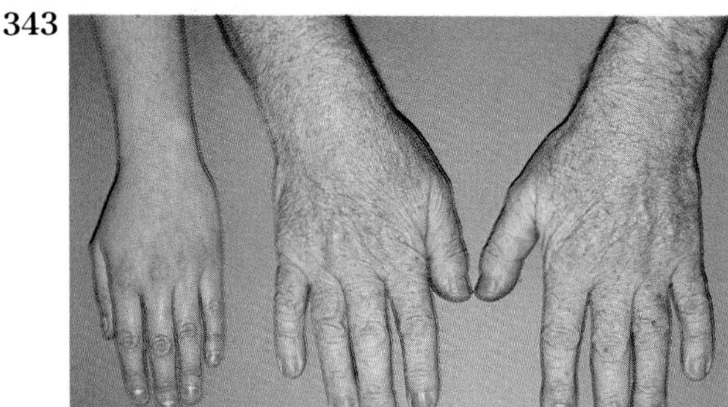

342 and 343 Acromegaly. Acromegalic hands compared with normal hands. Note the enlargement; the ends of the digits are square.

344
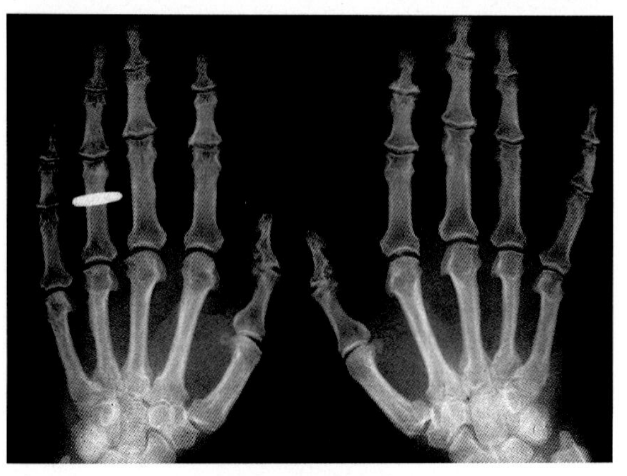

344 Acromegaly. X-ray showing generalised bony enlargement and tufting of the terminal phalanges.

345
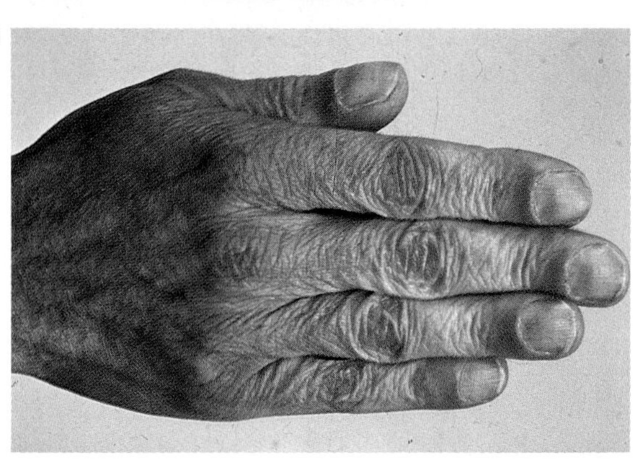

345 Bronchiectasis. Note the clubbing of the fingers.

Clubbing – common causes in the elderly

- Thoracic
  - Carcinoma of the lung
  - Chronic pulmonary suppuration
  - Fibrosing alveolitis
  - Mediastinal tumours
- Cardiovascular
  - Bacterial endocarditis
- Extrathoracic
  - Cirrhosis of the liver
  - Ulcerative colitis
  - Pyelonephritis

346 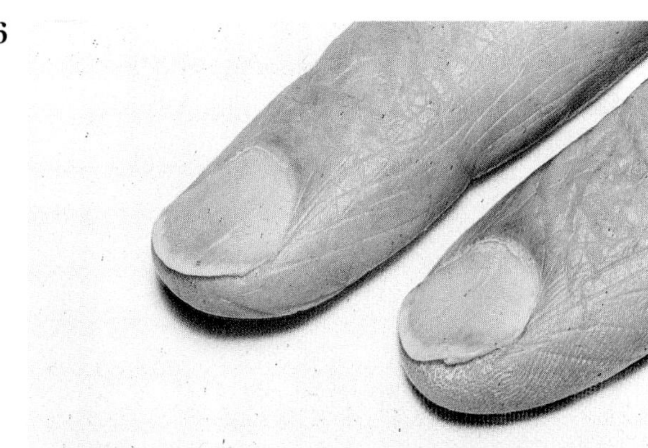

347 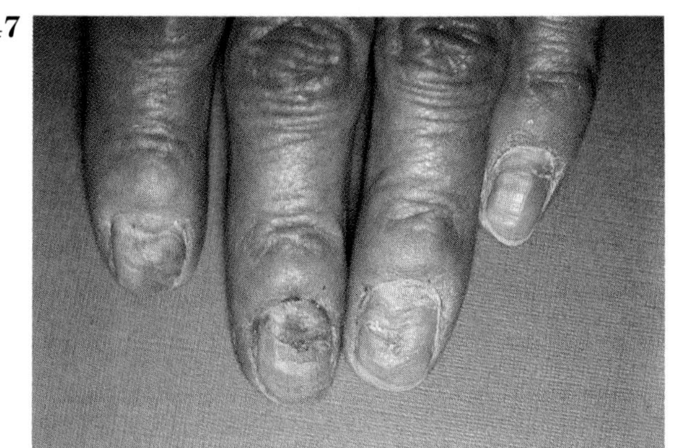

346 and 347 Koilonychia. Early and severe. Such nail changes may occur with anaemia, but sometimes they are quite 'innocent' in the elderly.

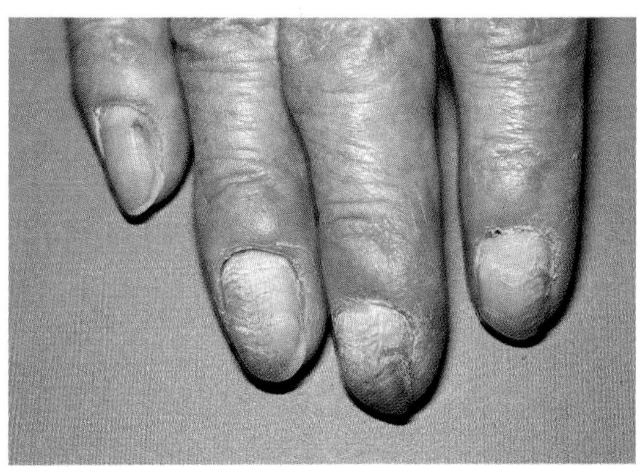 348

348 Psoriasis. Psoriatic changes in the nails. The patient also had extensive skin disease and arthropathy.

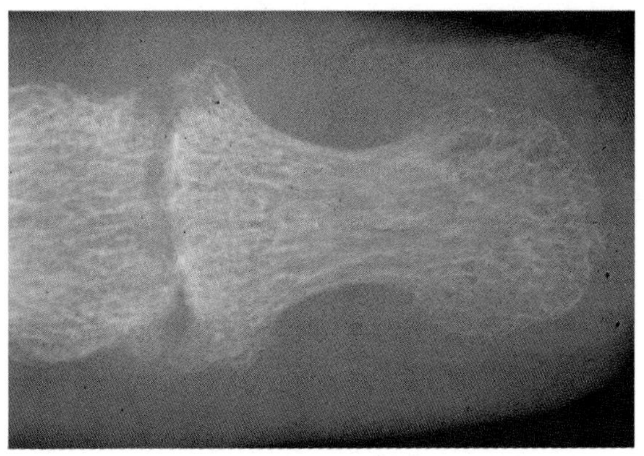 349

349 Psoriatic arthropathy. X-ray showing typical erosive changes at distal interphalangeal joint.

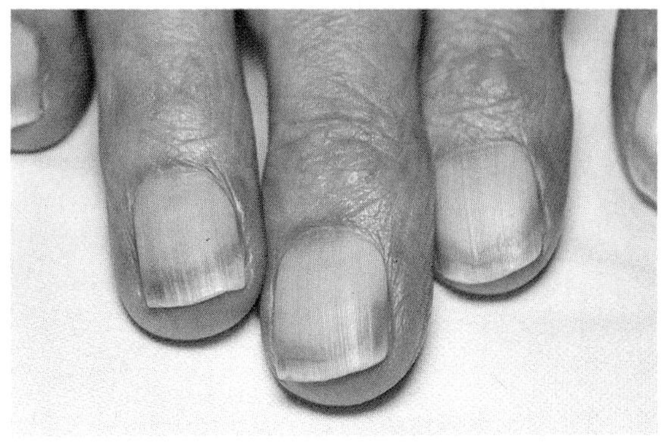 350

350 White nails. Note the marked pallor of the nail-bed caused by hypoalbuminaemia, secondary to chronic liver cirrhosis. Occasionally, three distinct zones are visible – white, pinkish and opaque. This pattern is called 'neopolitan' nails and is said to occur with collagen degeneration and osteoporosis in the very old.

351

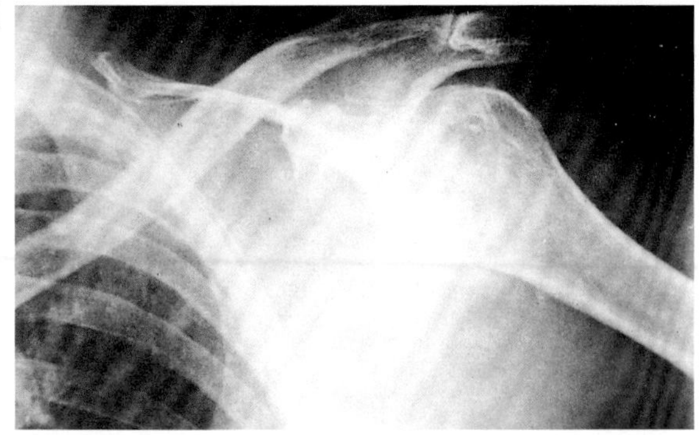

351 Osteoarthritis. X-ray of the shoulder, showing changes of advanced osteoarthritis. The elderly patient had generalised arthritis with pain and stiffness in the hips and shoulders.

352

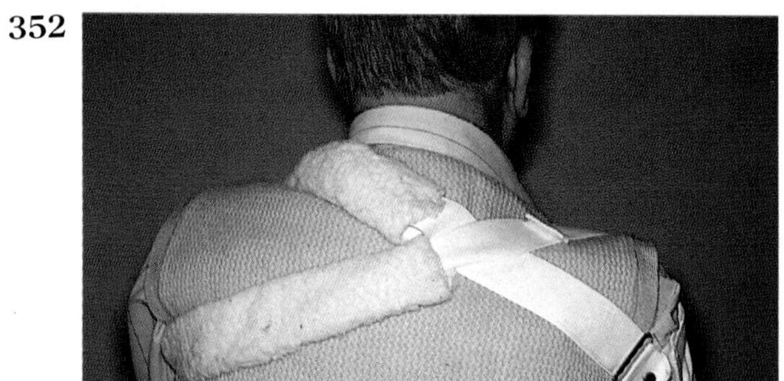

352 Subluxation. A figure-of-eight bandage being used to treat sublaxation of the right shoulder. This occurred following a stroke when the patient was receiving physiotherapy for right hemiplegia. Subluxation can be prevented by specialist physiotherapy and correct techniques of handling and moving the patient.

353

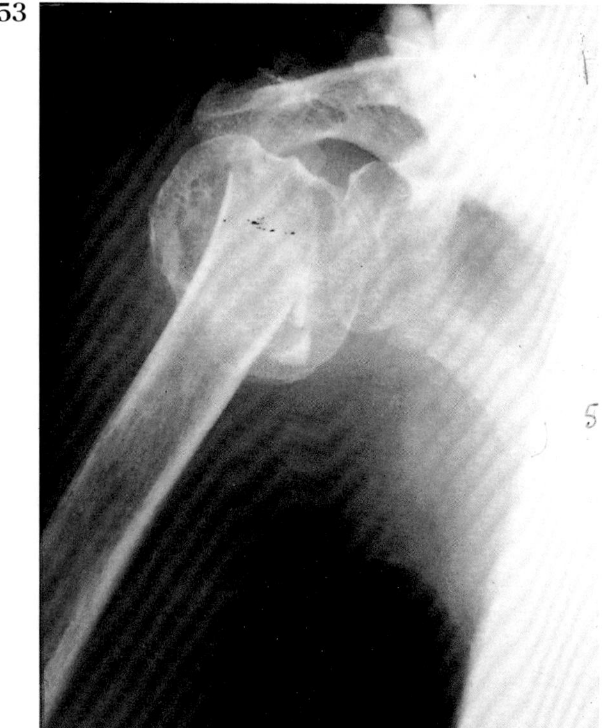

353 Fracture of humerus. X-ray showing impacted fracture of the neck of the humerus. This had occurred due to a fall and the shoulder had become very painful and stiff. The patient was unable to perform daily living activities and required long-term residential care.

354 Frozen shoulder. Right side. The patient is unable to abduct the arm at the shoulder joint, which is painful and stiff. It is caused by adhesive capsulitis, which is a common complication of hemiplegia.

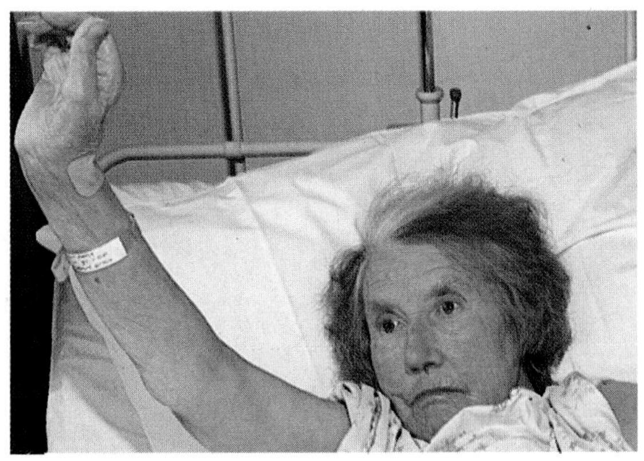

354

355 Supraspinatus tendinitis. A form of frozen shoulder. Note the calcification in the supra-spinatus tendon.

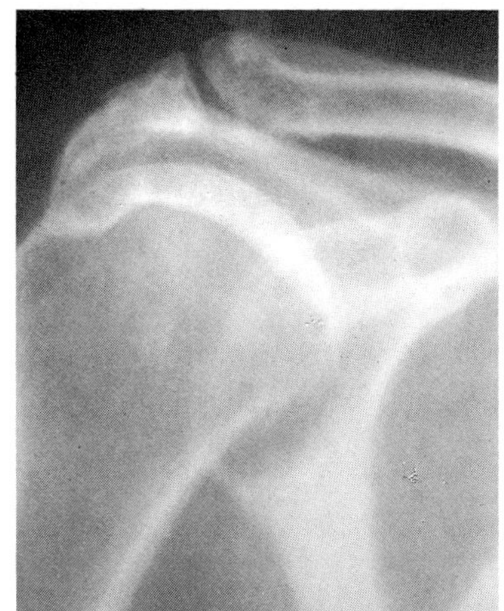

355

Shoulder–hand syndrome

Occurs in association with:
- Myocardial infarction
- Hemiplegia
- Pulmonary lesions
- Epilepsy
- Cervical spine lesions
- Herpes zoster
- Brain tumour
- Paniculitis
- Vasculitis
- Trauma

Causes of painful and stiff shoulder
Shoulder–hand syndrome
Adhesive capsulitis
Supraspinatus tendinitis
Impacted fracture of the neck of the humerus
Rotator cuff injury
Diastasis of the shoulder joint
Contracture
Reflex sympathetic dystrophy
Brachial plexus injury

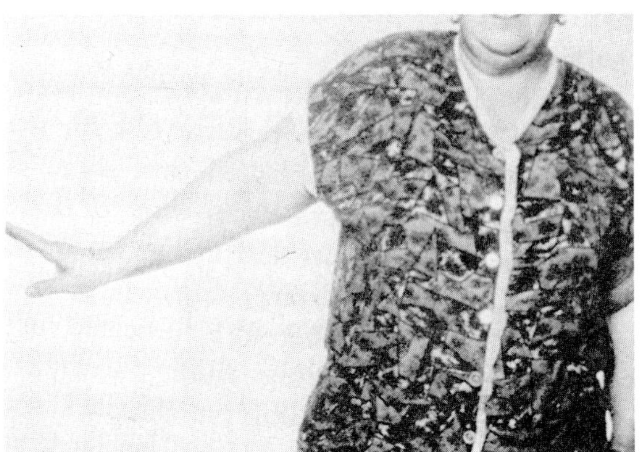

356

356 Adhesive capsulitis of the shoulder.

357

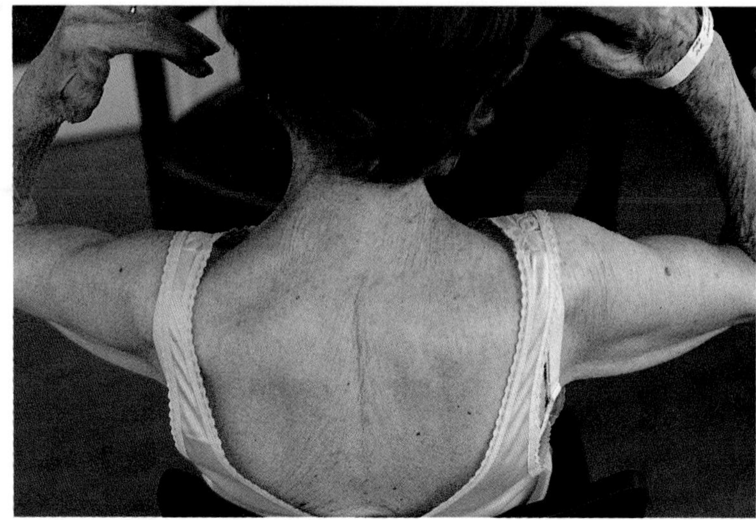

357 Polymyalgia rheumatica (PMR). An elderly female patient presenting with chronic aches and pains, weight loss, anaemia and episodes of pyrexia. Her ESR was elevated and she had pain and stiffness of the muscles around the neck, shoulder and pelvic girdles. She was unable to lift her arms and could not comb her hair.

About 15–20% of the patients presenting with PMR also develop temporal arteritis. In differential diagnosis one should consider rheumatoid arthritis, osteoporosis, septic arthritis, polymyositis, viral myalgia occult malignancy, osteomalacia and cervical spondylosis.

9 Disorders of the Lower Limbs

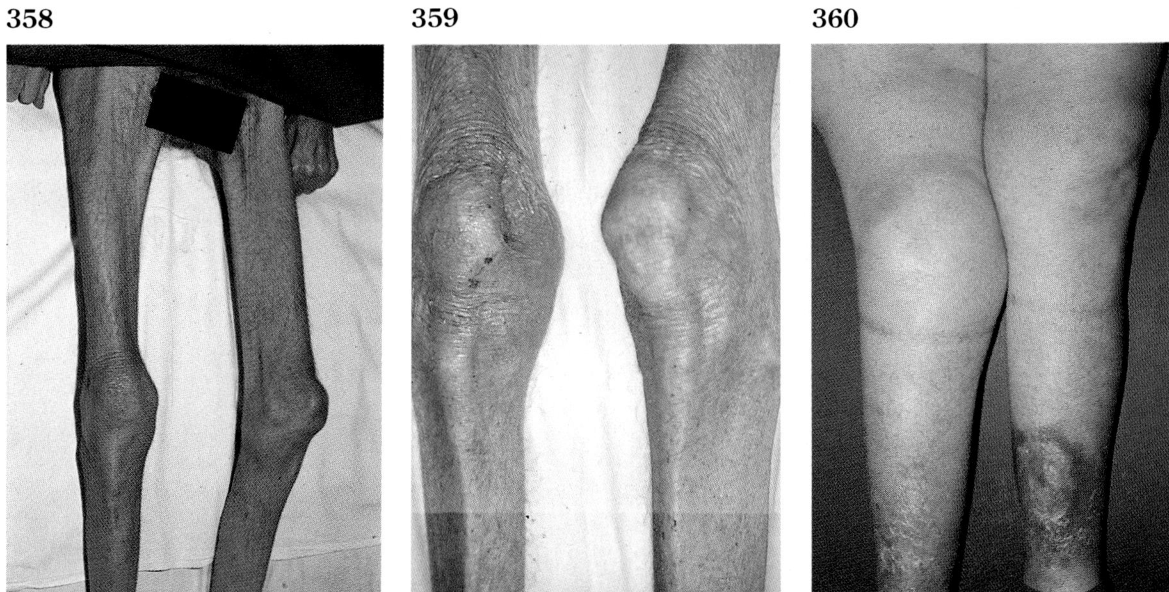

358 359 360

358 Wasting. Carcinomatous wasting of the legs with involvement of all muscle groups. This 76-year-old patient was found to have carcinoma of the stomach.

359 Motor neurone disease. Severe wasting of the legs due to advanced motor neurone disease. In some elderly patients this disorder may run a chronic course.

360 Osteoarthritis of the knees. Both knees are affected by the arthritis with pain, swelling, deformity and reduced mobility. The left leg is shorter than the right as a result of arthritic destruction of the left hip joint.

361

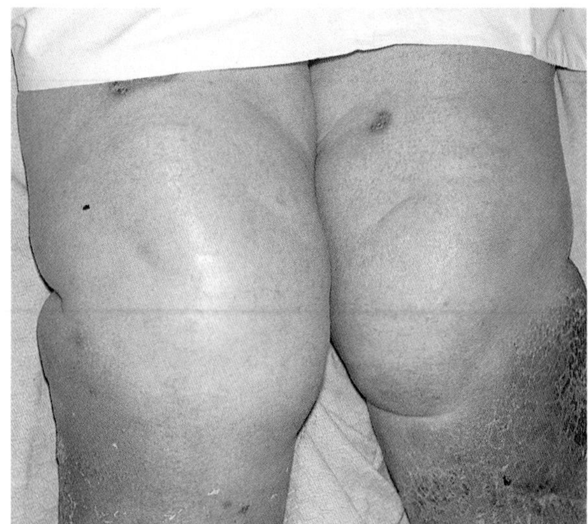

361 Multiple problems. This patient has both severe osteoarthritis of the knees and varicose eczema.

362

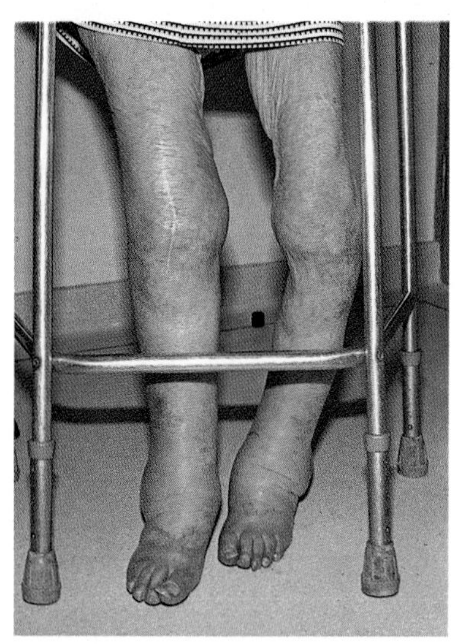

362 Osteoarthritis of the knees. Advanced osteoarthritis affecting both the knees. The left knee shows secondary genu varus with joint instability and subluxation. Note the associated muscle atrophy about the knees, with postural oedema of the ankles. Note the arthrodesis.

363

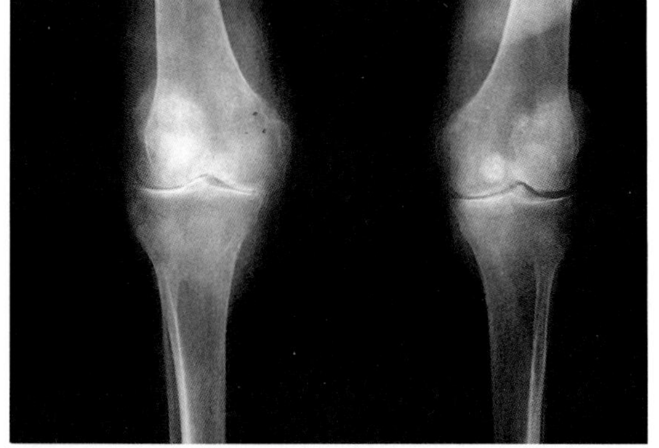

363 Osteoarthritis. X-ray of the knees showing loss of joint space and subchondral bony sclerosis.

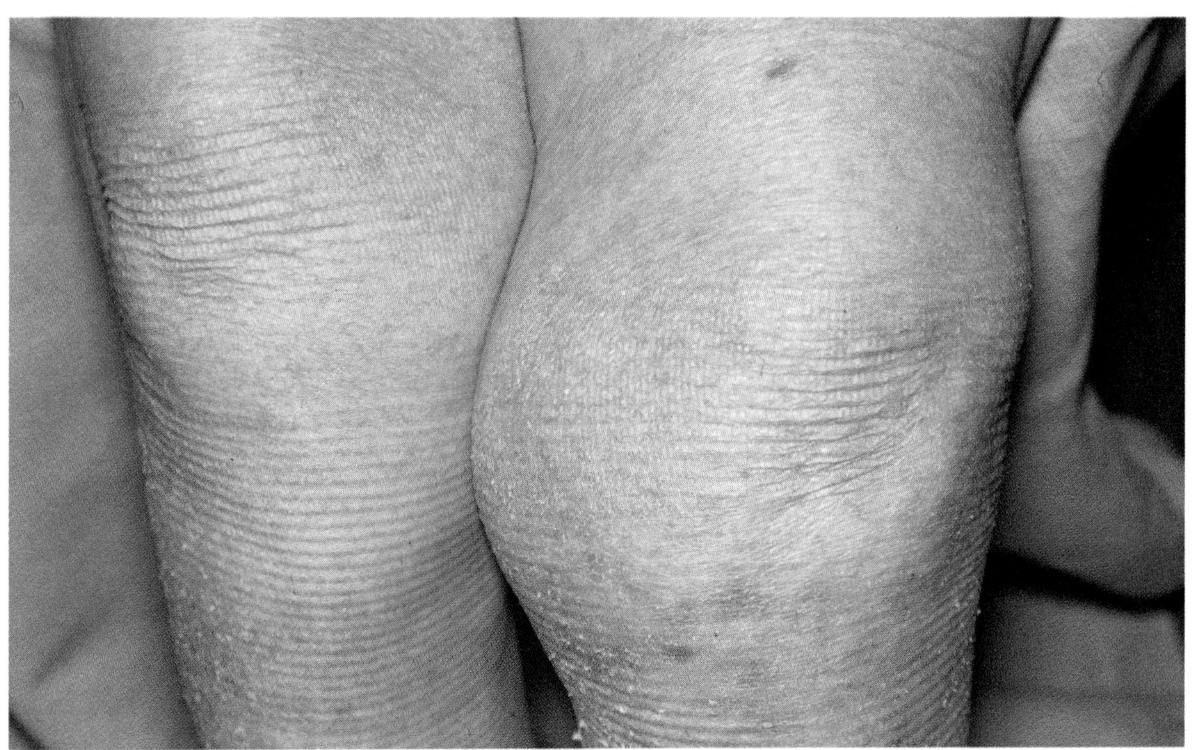

364

364 **Pseudogout.** Painful swelling of the left knee joint. X-rays revealed the presence of chondrocalcinosis. Aspiration of fluid from the knee showed typical birefringent microcrystals of calcium pyrophosphate dihydrate. The patient also had maturity onset diabetes mellitus and hypertension.

365 **Pseudogout.** Anteroposterior and lateral x-rays of the knee showing typical linear deposits of calcium pyrophosphate arthropathy in the menisci and articular cartilage, with degenerative changes indistinguishable from osteoarthritis.

Calcium pyrophosphate arthropathy (pseudogout)

Associated conditions
Osteoarthritis
Chronic renal failure
Hyperuricaemia
Hyperparathyroidism
Paget's disease of the bone
Diabetes mellitus
Hypertension
Haemochromatosis
Acromegaly

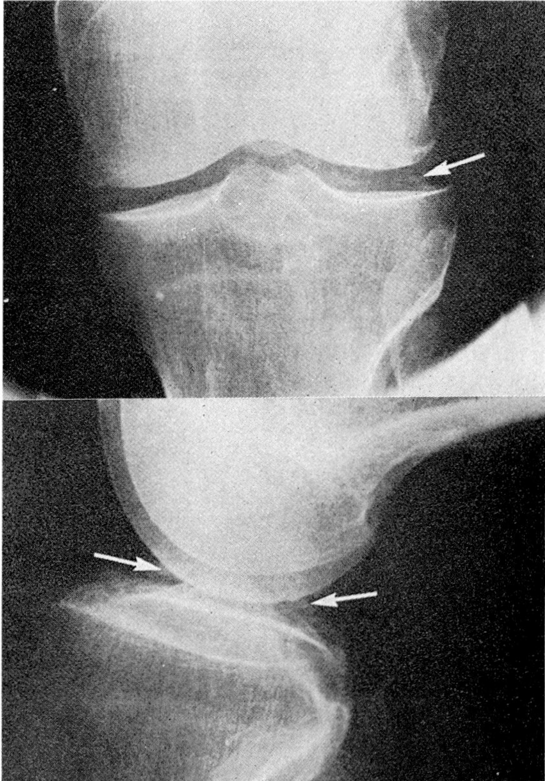

365

366

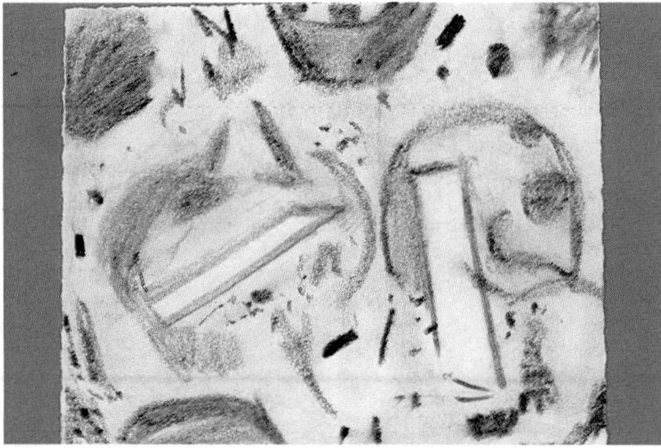

366 Chondrocalcinosis (diagrammatic). Calcium pyrophosphate dihydrate crystals seen in the leucocytes show positive birefringence under a polarised microscope.

367

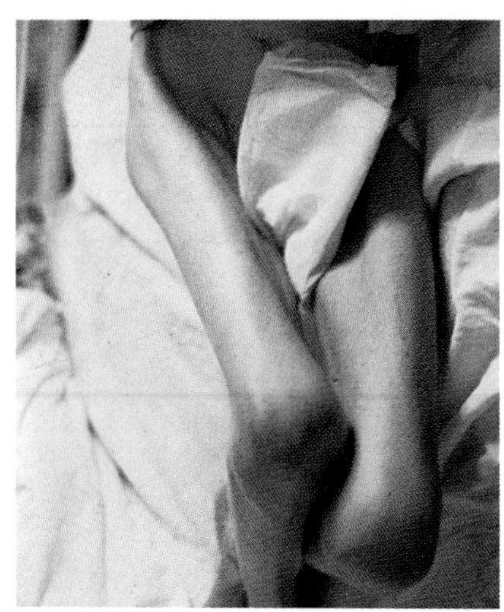

367 Quadriceps wasting. Marked wasting of the quadriceps muscles caused by immobility and bilateral cerebrovascular disease. Such cases may go on to develop contractures.

368

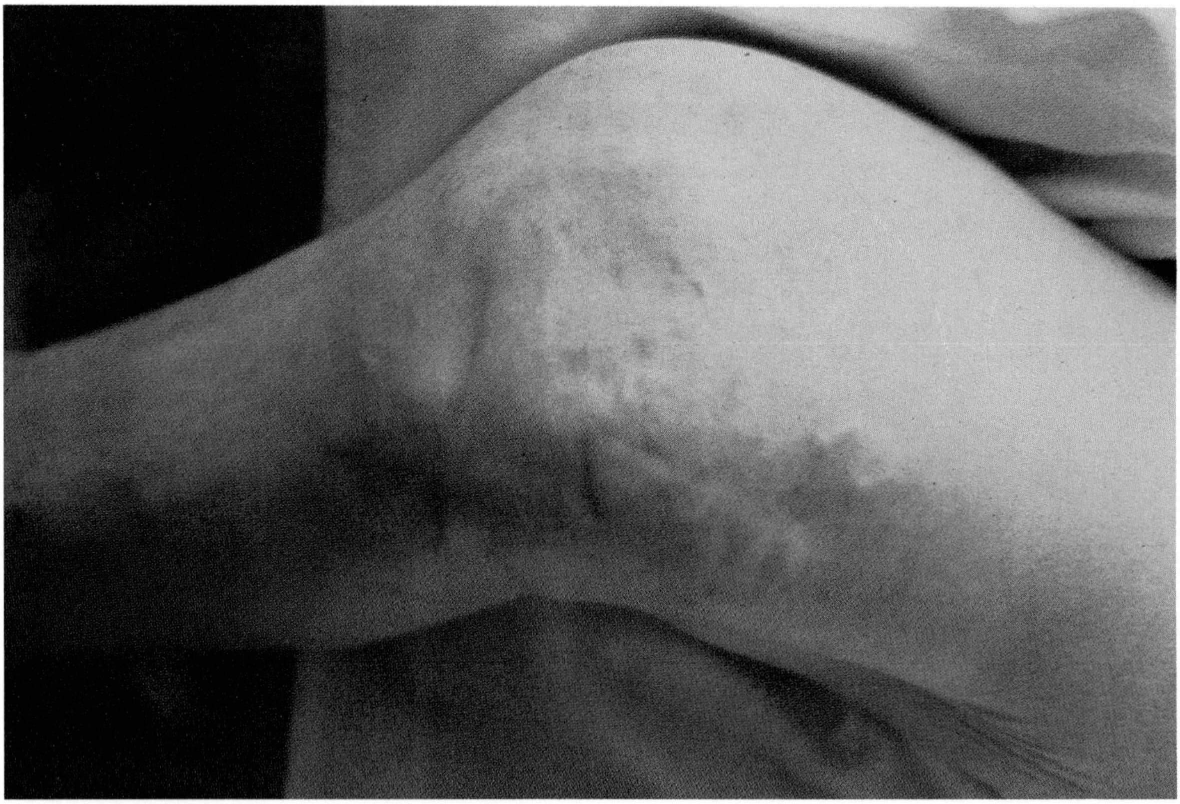

368 Knee-joint effusion in a case of chronic degenerative joint disease.

Fractures in the elderly

Aetiology
Falls or sudden mechanical stress *plus:*
- Osteoporosis
- Osteomalacia
- Paget's disease
- Bony metastasis

Types
Femur – commonest type of fracture in the elderly: Subcapital or pertrochanteric
- Humerus – usually impacted
- Colles' fracture
- Pelvic fracture
- Rib fracture
- Pathological fractures
- Compression fractures of vertebrae in osteoporosis

369

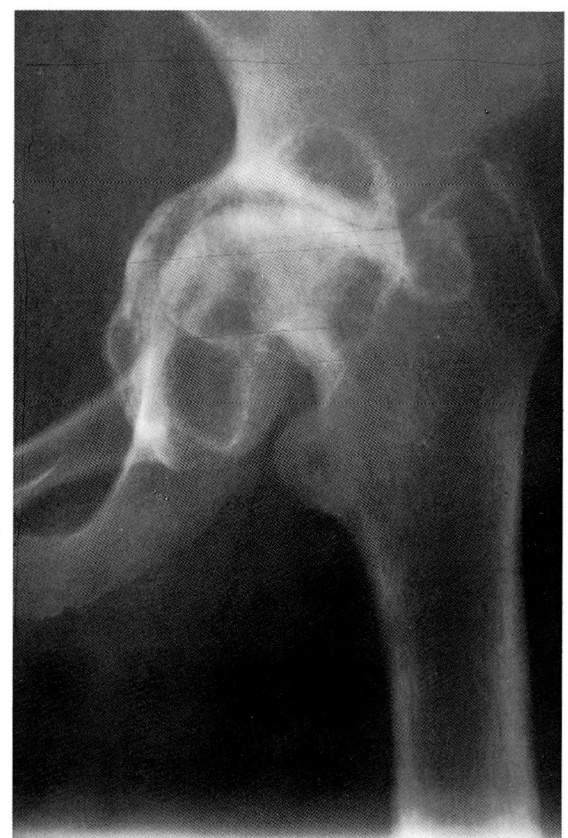

370

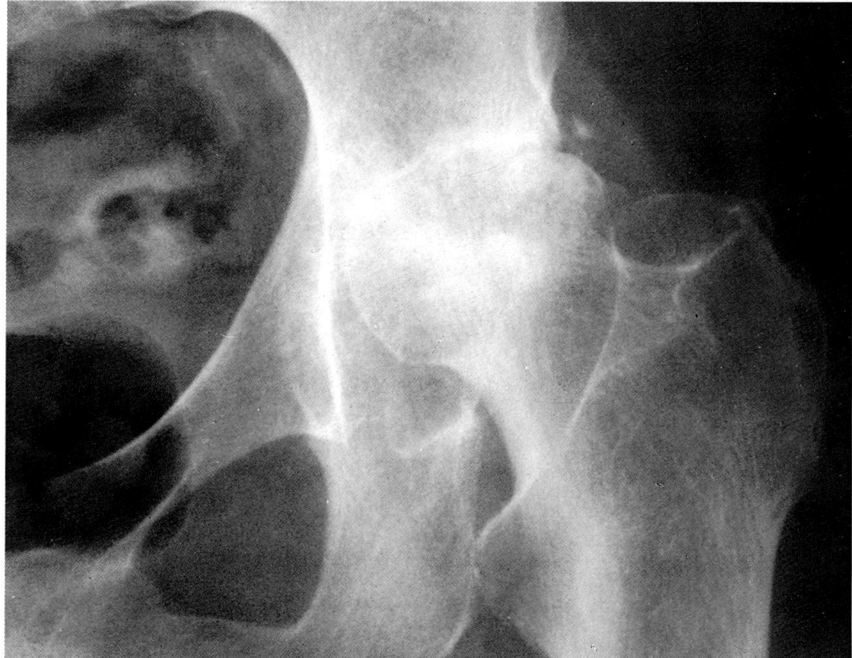

369 and 370 Osteoarthritis of the hip joint. Note the almost complete loss of articular cartilage with flattening of the femoral head and small cystic areas in the head and neck of the femur. Subchondral bone has areas of sclerosis, and protrusio acetabuli is developing.

371

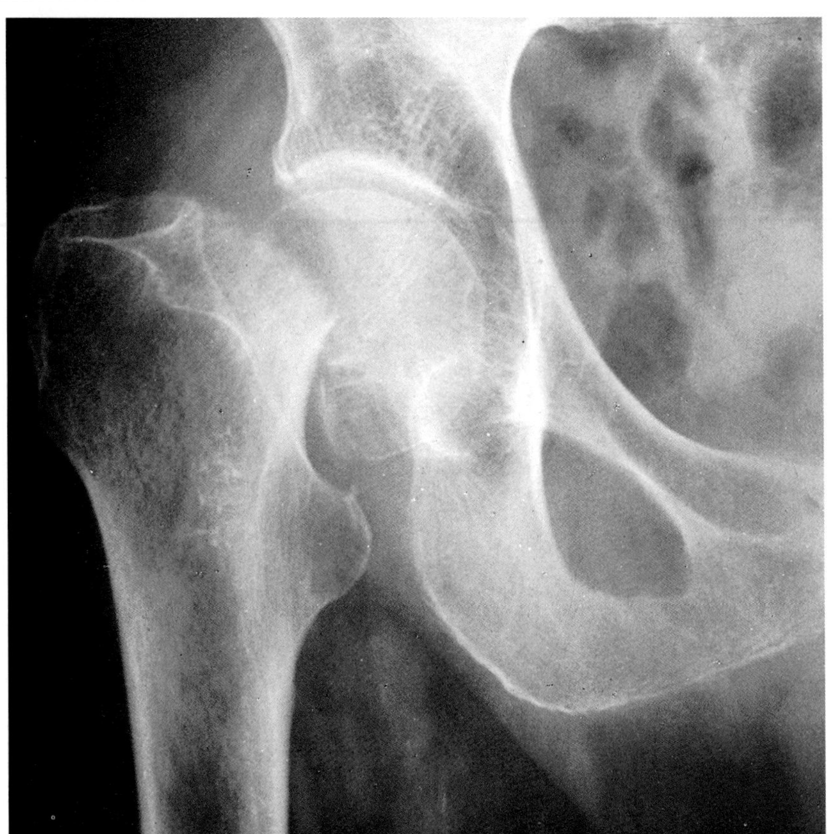

371 Fracture of the neck of the femur. X-ray showing a recent subcapital fracture through the neck of the femur. This is a serious and disabling 'disease' of the elderly, especially women, and is associated with osteoporosis. Combined orthopaedic–geriatric units can do much in tackling this rapidly increasing disorder.

372 Bilateral fractures. This patient suffered from recurrent falls and sustained fractures of both necks of femurs, within months of each other. The right fracture is treated with Thompson's prosthesis and the left one with nail and plate.

372

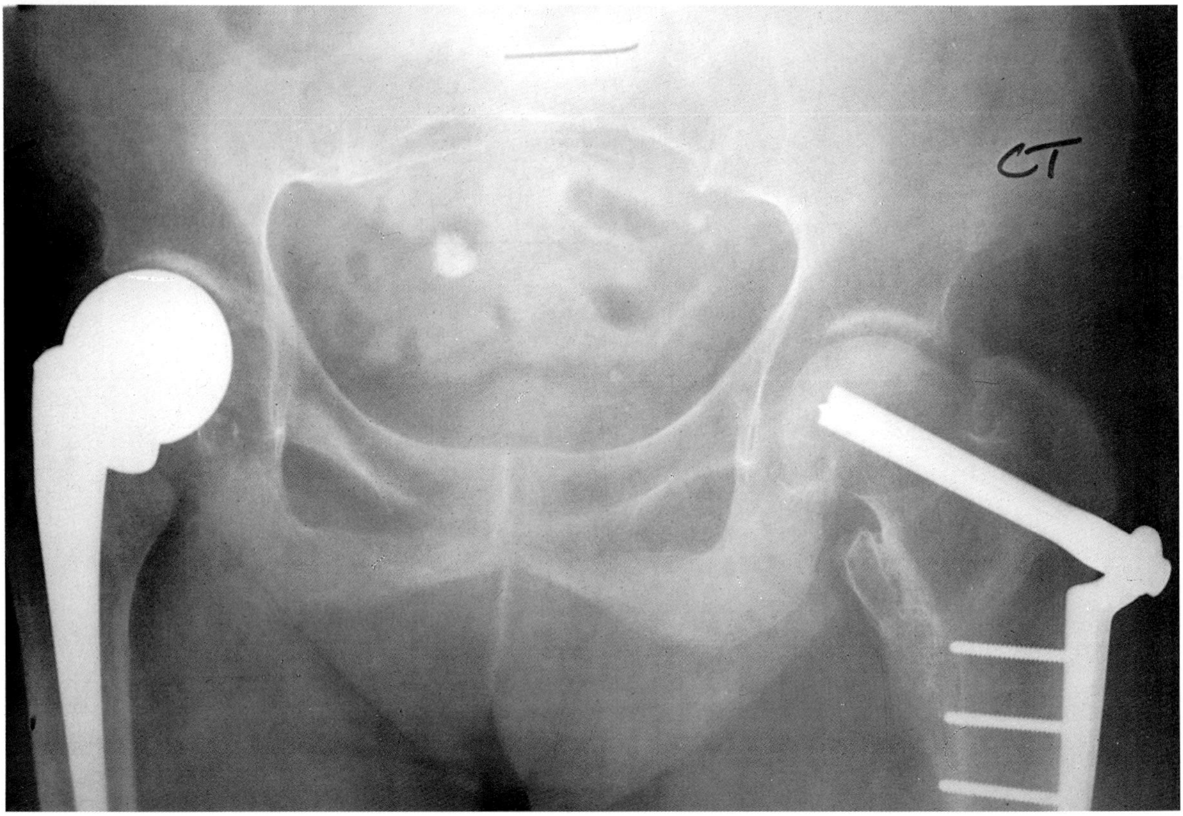

373 Osteomalacia. This elderly lady presented with painful bones, depression and immobility. Note the deformity of the right leg. Diagnosis of osteomalacia was confirmed by finding a raised serum alkaline phosphatase and low serum calcium and inorganic phosphate.

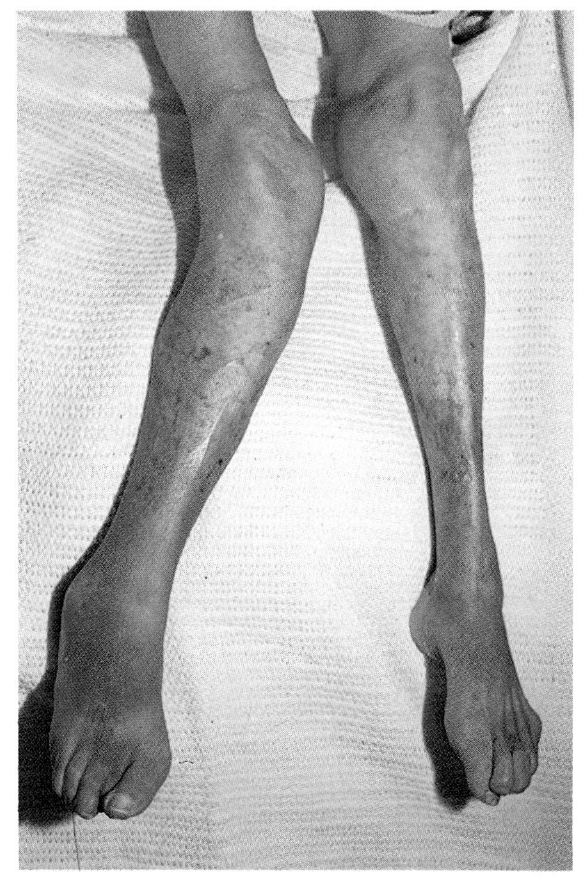

373

374 Osteomalacia. X-ray of the patient in **373** reveals a non-traumatic stress fracture of tibia and fibula. Response to vitamin D therapy was rapid and with physiotherapy she became mobile and independent.

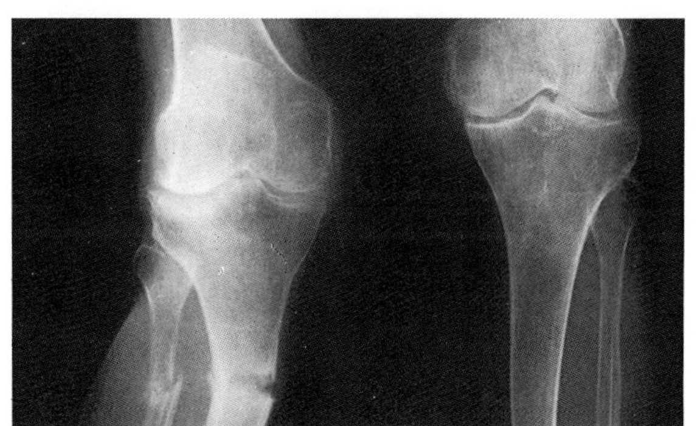

374

375 Osteomalacia. Advanced osteomalacia in an elderly lady who was housebound for several years. Note marked bone translucency, old fracture of the neck of the left femur and Looser 's zone in the right femur.

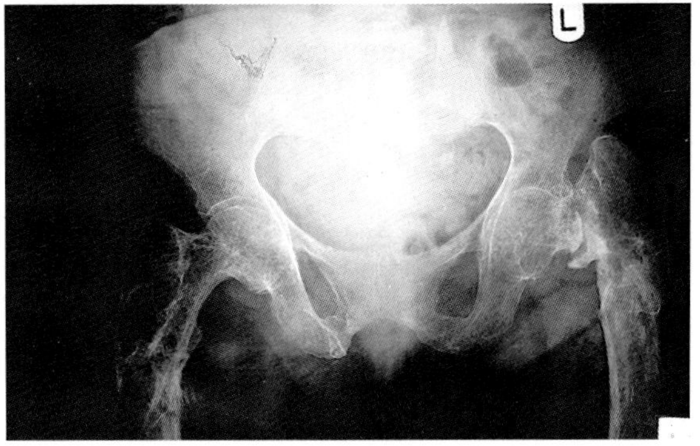

375

376 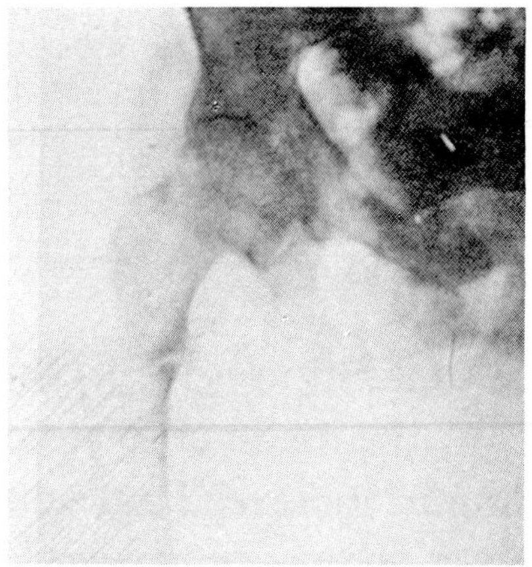

376 Osteomalacia. Looser's zone seen near the lesser trochanter.

377 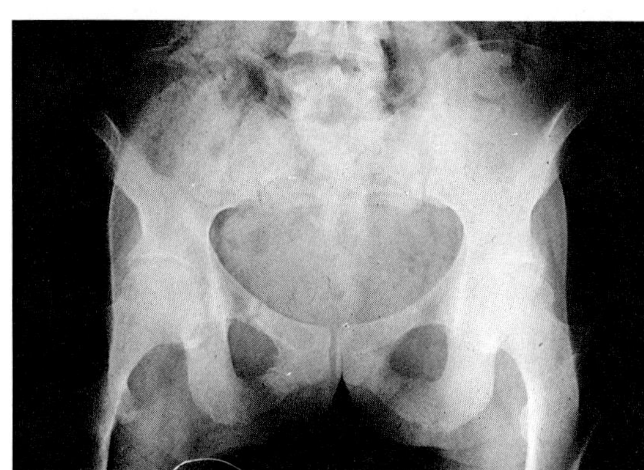

377 Osteomalacia. Looser's zone seen in the right superior pubic ramus.

Osteomalacia
(softening of the bones)

Characterised by defective bone mineralisation with increase in osteoid tissue.

Aetiology
In the elderly the aetiology is multifactorial:

- Vitamin D deficiency
  - Malnutrition – housebound, immobility, lack of sunlight, atmospheric pollution, inadequate diet
  - Malabsorption states and abnormal jejunal mucosa in some elderly
  - Post-gastrectomy
- Abnormal vitamin D metabolism
  - Liver disease
  - Kidney disease
  - Anticonvulsant drugs
- Miscellaneous
  - Malignant tumours
  - Hypophosphatasia

Clinical features
General deterioration in health
Anorexia and weakness
Non-specific aches and pains ('rheumatism')
Bone pains leading to bone tenderness
Proximal myopathy giving rise to waddling gait
Increased incidence of fractures, especially fractures of the neck of the femur
Depression
Immobility
Skeletal deformities

Diagnosis
Biochemistry
Low or normal serum calcium, low serum inorganic phosphate, raised serum alkaline phosphatase and low urinary calcium excretion. It may take up to a year for the alkaline phosphatase to return to normal
Radiography
Reduced bone density with coexistent osteoporosis
Pseudo fractures (Looser's zones) in the cortex of bone are diagnostic
Bone biopsy
Microscopic examination of bony tissue will show excess of unmineralised osteoid tissue greater than 40%
Isotope bone scan
Increased uptake by the bones with focal hot areas
Therapeutic trial with vitamin D
A patient with osteomalacia will respond dramatically with rapid improvement of symptoms

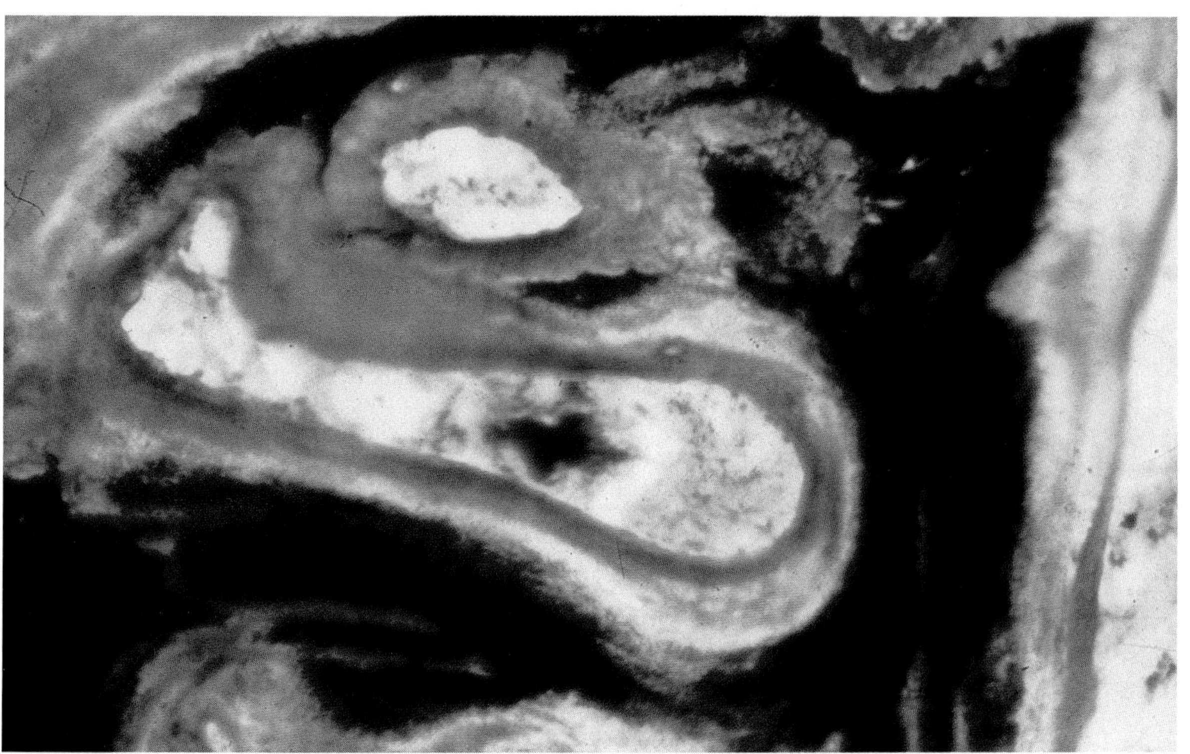

378

378 Osteomalacia. Section of bone reveals the classic picture of osteomalacia. There are wide, uncalcified seams of osteoid tissue (red staining) with decrease in the staining intensity of calcification fronts.

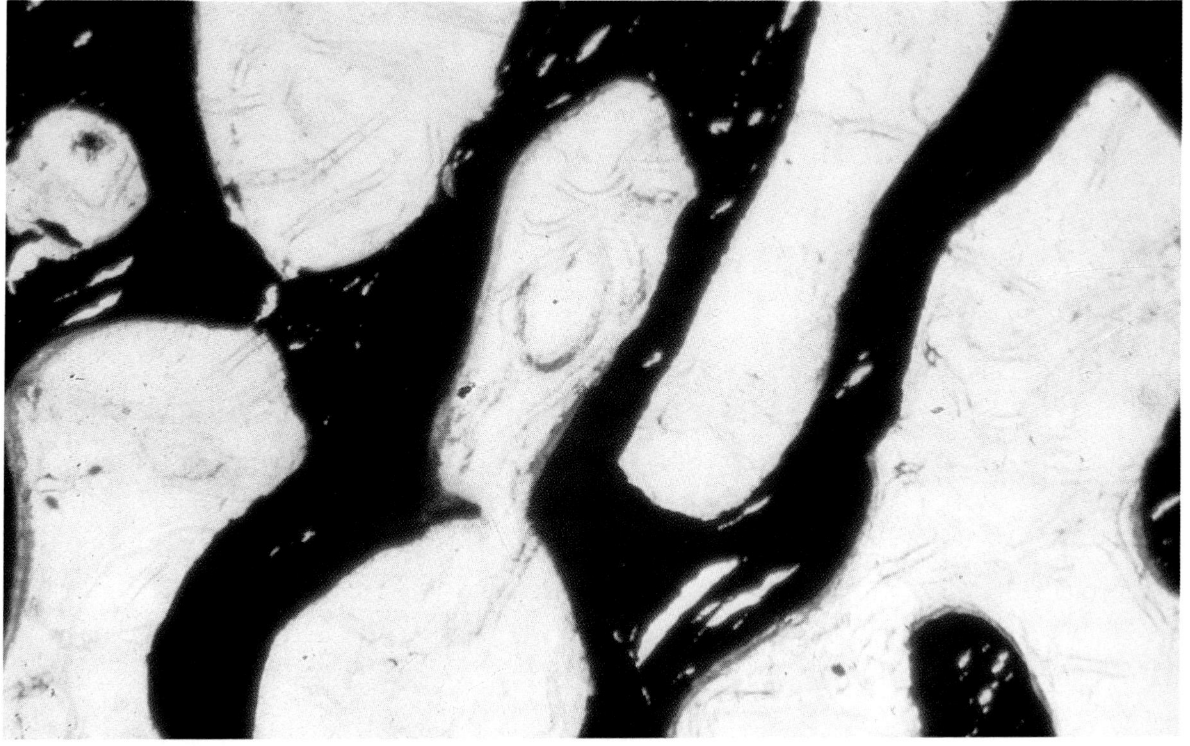

379

379 Normal bone. Section of normal bone shown for comparison with **378**. The calcified tissue stains black and the uncalcified matrix (osteoid) stains red (Von Kossa).

380

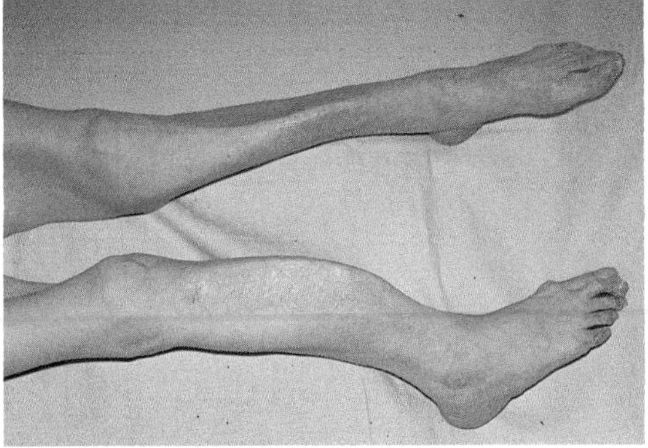

380 Paget's disease. Advanced Paget's disease of the bone showing deformity of the tibiae with bowing and thickening of the bones. This patient also complained of deafness and had cardiac failure.

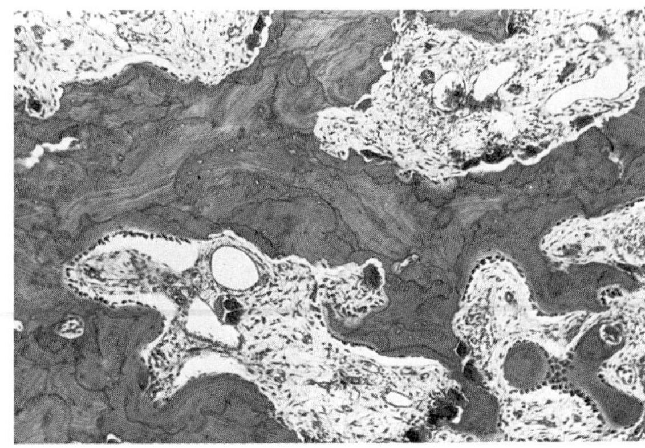

381 Paget's disease. Histology of the bone showing grossly disorganised bony structure. There is rapid bone turnover with increased resorption and accelerated replacement. Note the many osteoblasts along the trabeculae.

382

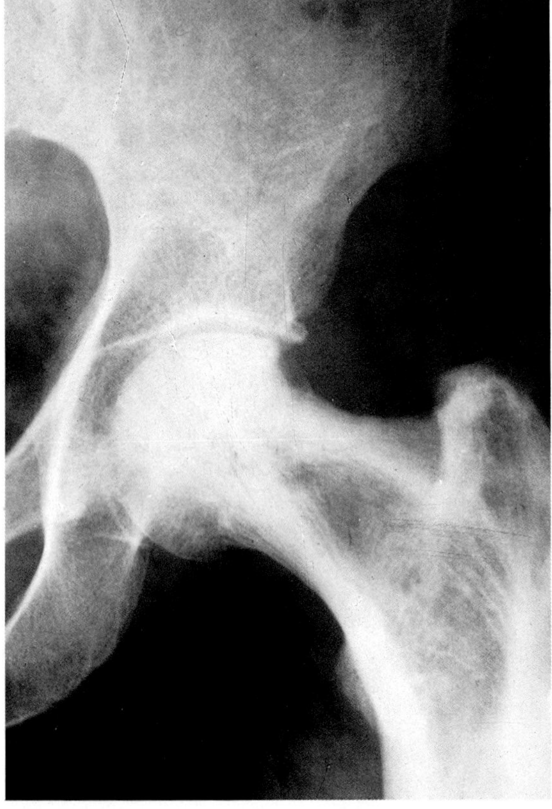

382 Paget's disease. X-ray of left hip showing Paget's disease of the head of the femur.

Paget's disease

Characterised by a combination of excessive bone breakdown and rapid bone replacement, resulting in deformity and increased fragility. Usually the condition is asymptomatic and is only revealed by a routine x-ray or by finding a raised alkaline phosphatase level.

Clinical features
Bone aches and pain mainly in pelvis and legs
Bone deformities – bowing of tibia and enlargement of skull
High-output cardiac failure
Deafness
Visual impairment
Rarely, development of osteogenic sarcoma in the affected bone

Investigations
Serum calcium and phosphate normal
Serum alkaline phosphatase raised
Urinary hydroxyproline raised
X-rays – show lytic areas, zones of increased density, loss of trabecular patterns and deformity
Isotope scan – there is increased uptake by areas involved in the disease

383 Paget's disease. X-ray showing Paget's disease of the femur and pelvis with multiple microfractures on the convex surface.

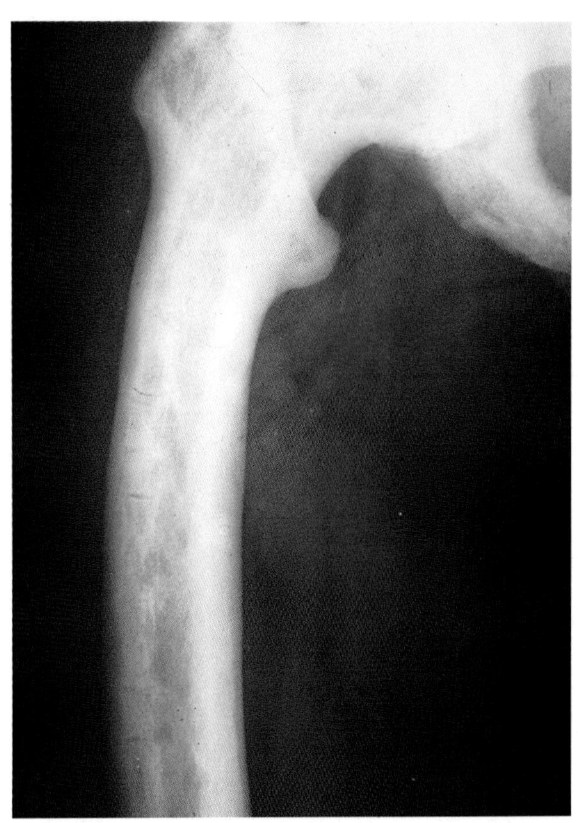

383

384 Paget's disease. Isotope bone scan of skeleton showing the extent of active Paget's disease. The dark areas indicate the patches of Paget's bone.

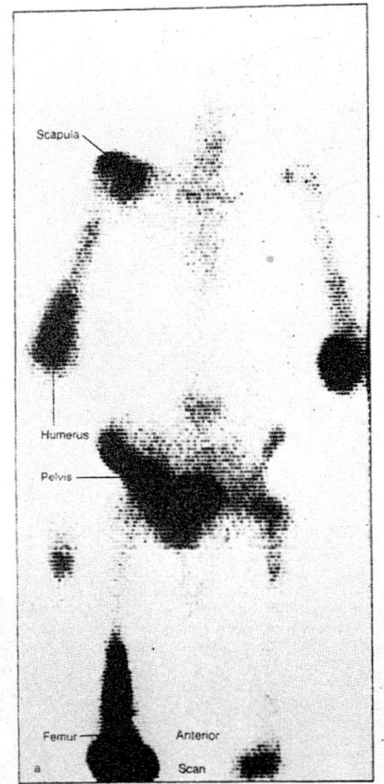

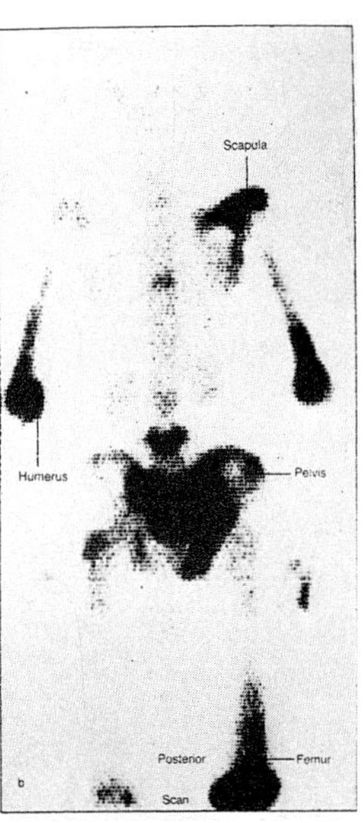

384

385

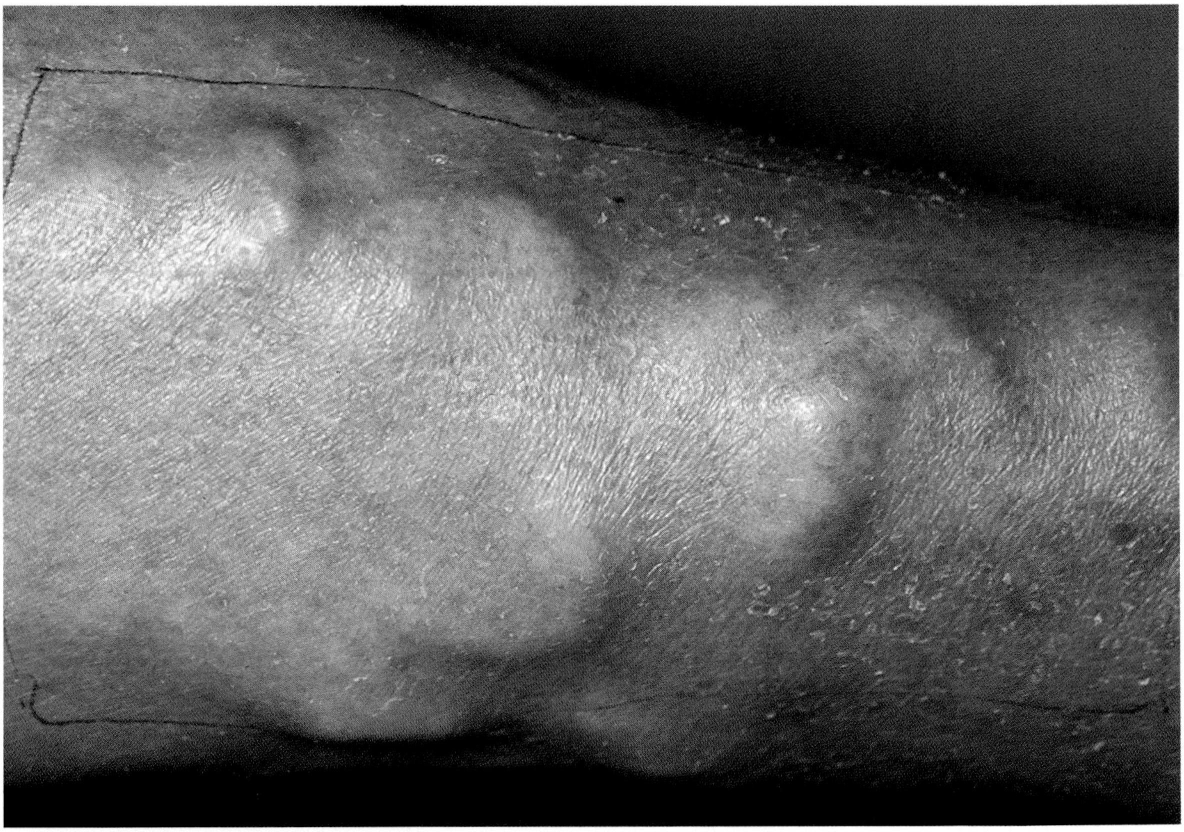

386

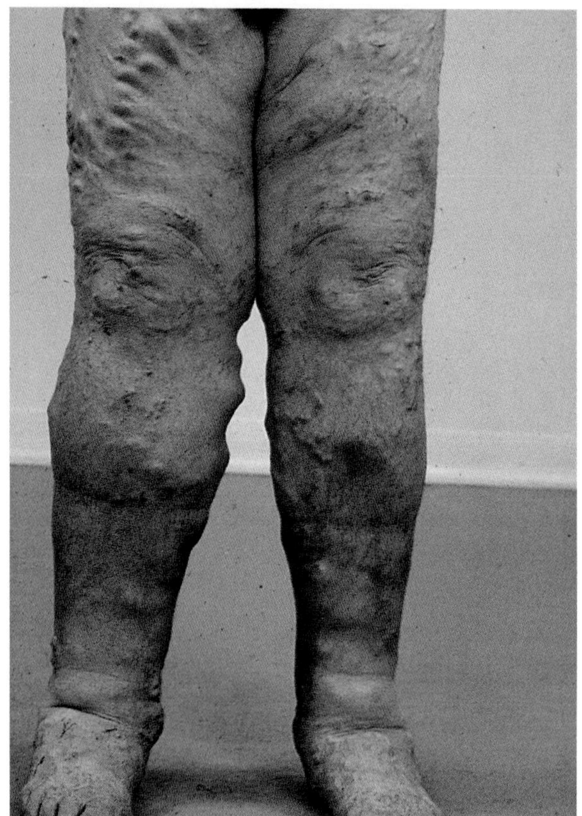

385 Varicose veins. Dilated, tortuous superficial veins with incompetent valves. The greater and lesser saphenous systems are most commonly involved. When varicose veins occur as a result of deep venous obstruction, the patient may go on to develop a post-phlebitic syndrome.

386 Varicose veins. A more severe case with extensive varicosities in both legs.

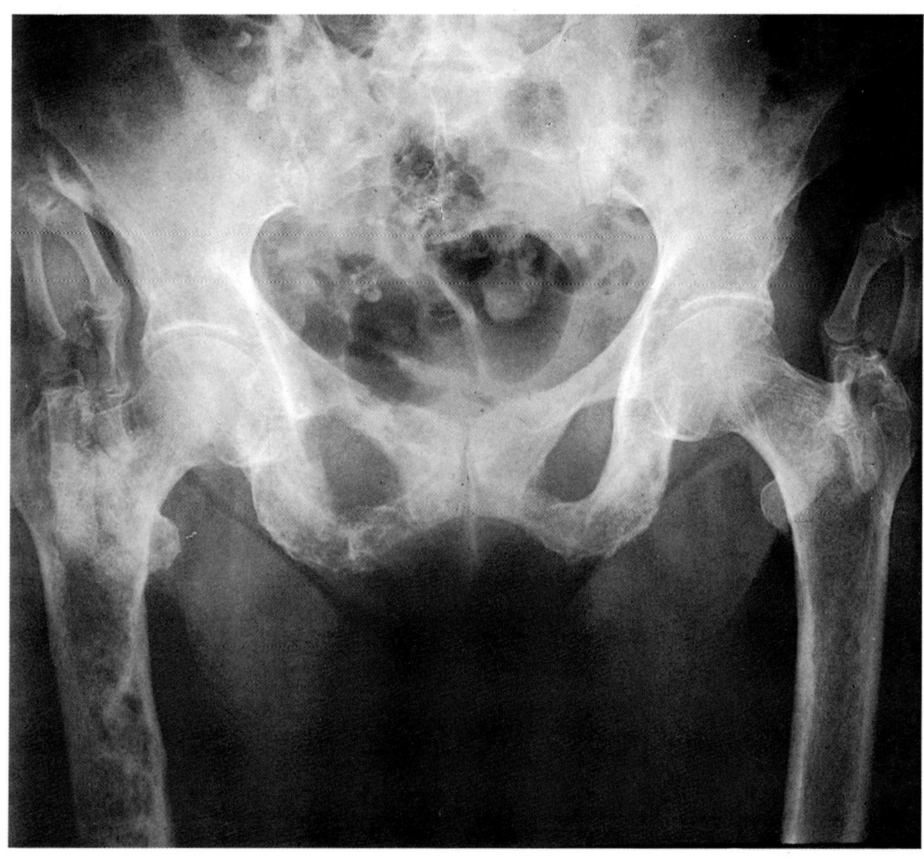

387

387 Bony secondaries. Multiple osteolytic secondary deposits in the pelvis, and right femur, from a primary in the lung.

Deep venous thrombosis

Important aetiological factors:
- Bedrest and immobility
- Postoperative
- Occult cancers, e.g. cancer of the pancreas
- Thrombophlebitis migrans
- Paget–Schrotter's disease – in the arms
- Phlegmasia caerulea dolens
- Obesity
- Lymphomas
- Dehydration
- Congestive cardiac failure

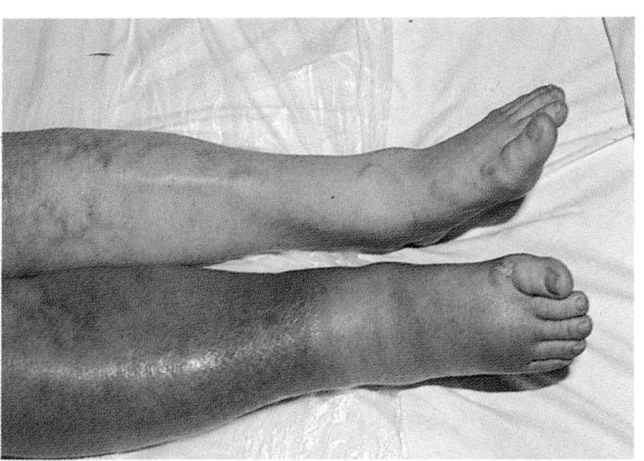

388

388 Deep venous thrombosis (DVT). This elderly and obese lady was admitted with myocardial infarction. After two days of bedrest she developed a massive DVT of the right calf. Note the discoloration and swelling of the leg.

389 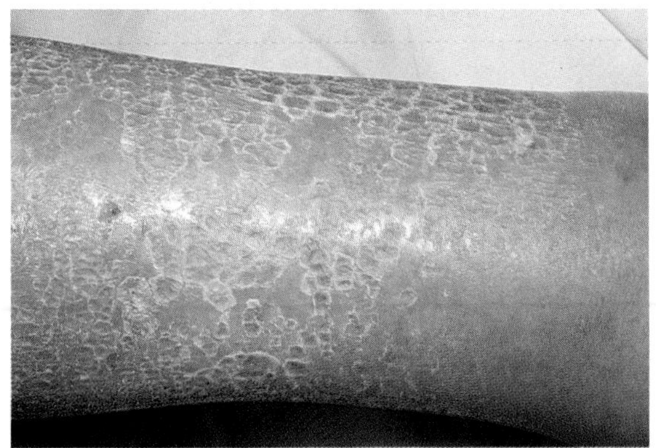

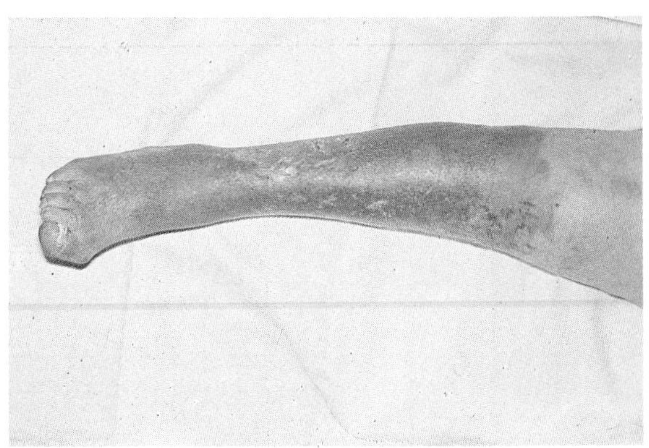 39

389 Post-phlebitic leg. Dry, thin, scaly skin with oedema and pigmentation caused by haemosiderin deposit in subcutaneous tissues.

390 Cellulitis. Considerable soft-tissue inflammation with pain and fever as a result of a minor trauma to the foot.

391 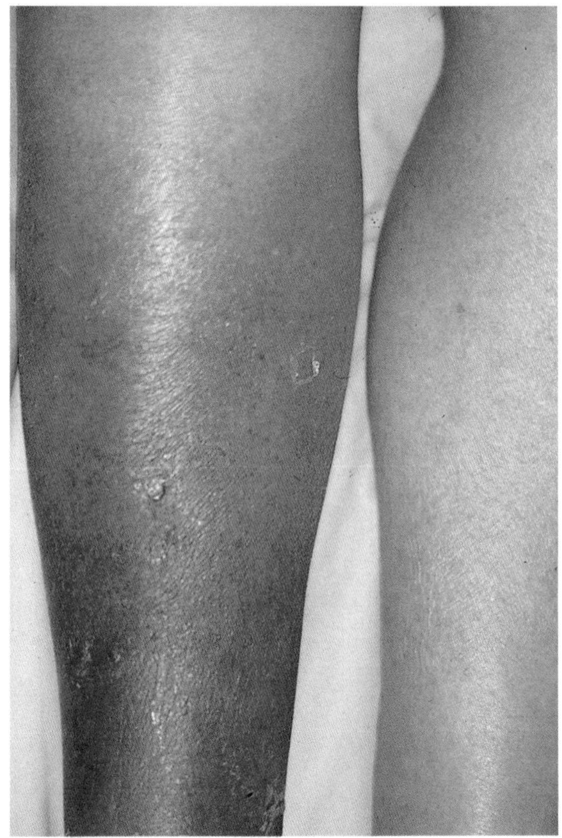

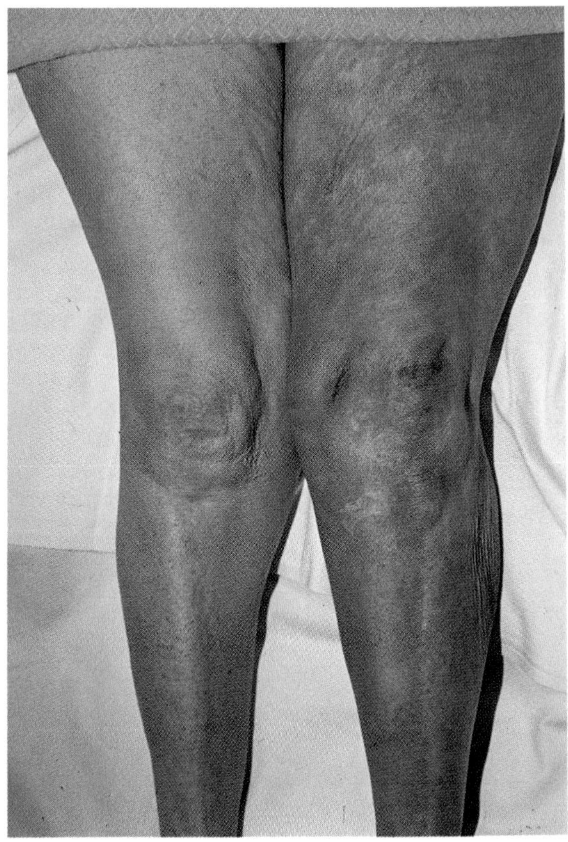 39

391 Cellulitis. A case of cellulitis extending up the calf. This should be differentiated from deep venous thrombosis.

392 Ischaemia of the left leg. Sudden arterial occlusion caused by femoral artery thrombosis. The leg may be saved with early vascular surgery.

393 Acute arterial occlusion. Caused by atheroma in the femoral artery, secondary to an abdominal aneurysm. The tissues of the leg are non-viable and early surgical intervention is required.

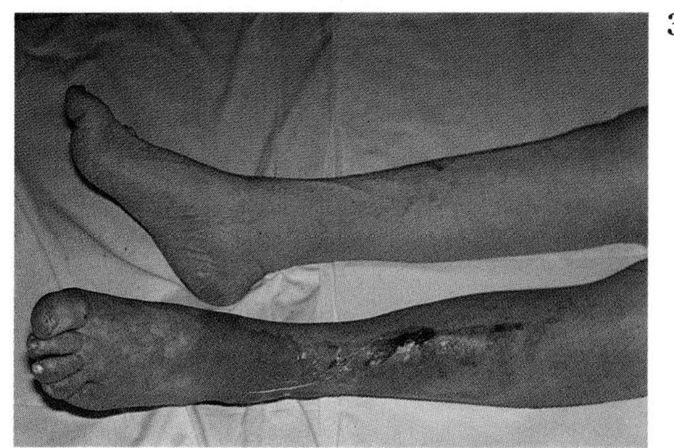

393

Peripheral vascular disease

Aetiology

Atherosclerosis, embolism, diabetic micro-angiopathy, giant-cell arteritis, vasculitis with collagen diseases, Buerger's disease, cold injury, increased blood viscosity, e.g. polycythaemia, dysproteinaemias, beta-blocking drugs

Clinical features

- Asymptomatic in the early stages
- Cold feet, feelings of numbness
- Parasthaesia in the feet
- Intermittent claudication
- Rest pain
- Large blood vessel bruits
- Loss of peripheral pulses
- Cyanosis
- Ischaemic ulcers
- Gangrene
- Non-invasive Doppler methods and arteriography are important investigations, especially if vascular surgery is being considered.

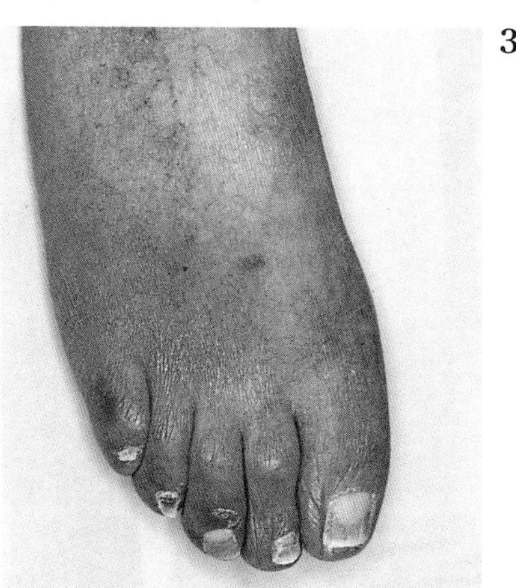

394

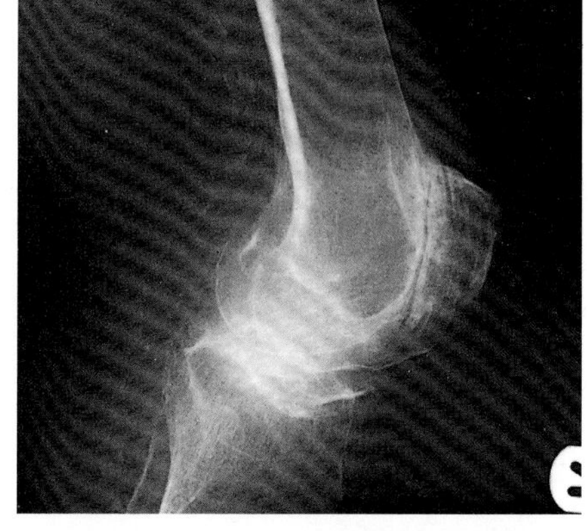

395

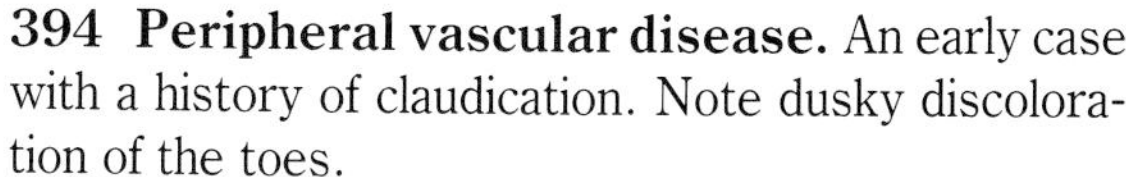

394 Peripheral vascular disease. An early case with a history of claudication. Note dusky discoloration of the toes.

395 Peripheral vascular disease. Plain x-ray showing arterial calcification posterior to the knee – result of widespread artheroma in the arteries of the lower limb.

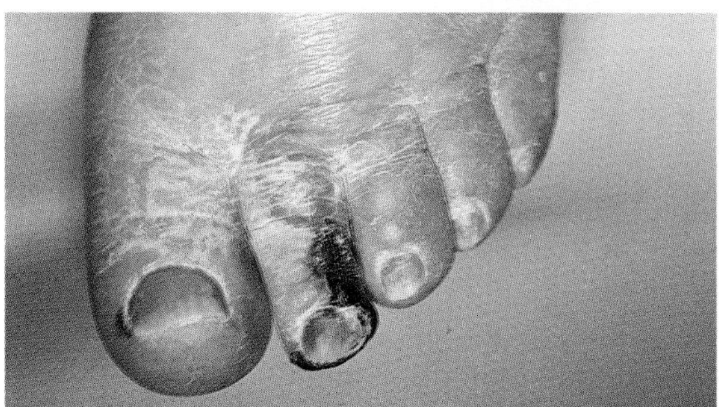

396

396 Peripheral vascular disease. There is ischaemic necrosis of the second toe, with dystrophy of the toenails and the skin is shiny and atrophic. The dorsalis pedis artery is not palpable.

397

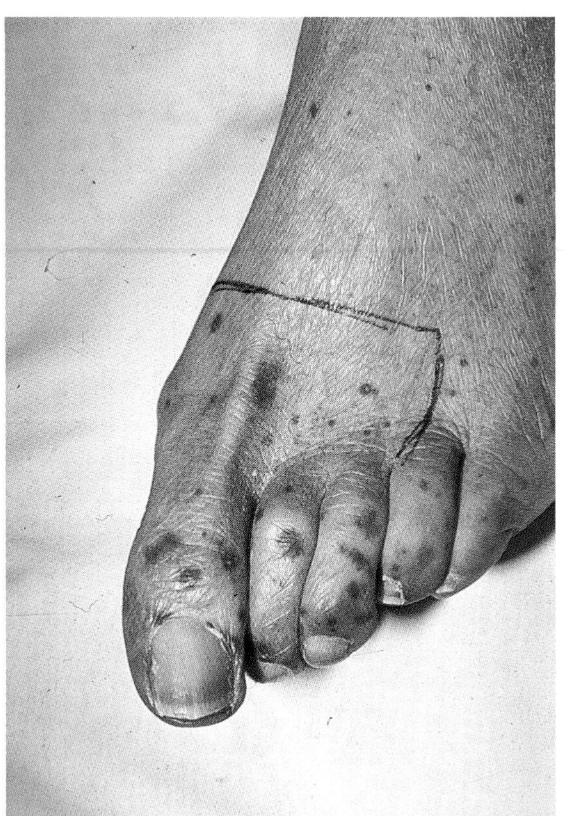

397 Subacute bacterial endocarditis. Showing small embolic infarcts on the toes. The patient had low-grade fever, anaemia and mild cardiac failure. The blood cultures were positive for *Streptococcus viridans*.

Some changes in bacterial endocarditis in the last 20 years in the UK

- More common in elderly now, with 25% of patients over 60 years of age compared with 18% in 1945. Prognosis is usually poor, with mortality of 70%; frequently occurs as a terminal illness.
- *Streptococcus viridans* is still the most common causative organism; less frequently than before, but still over 50%.
- The underlying heart disease is now less often rheumatic mitral disease and is more frequently aortic valve disease of uncertain aetiology.

398

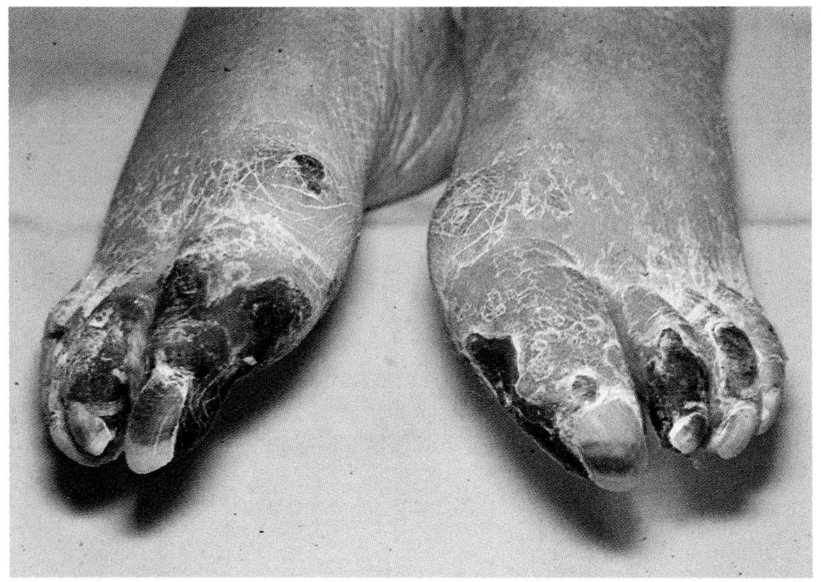

398 Polyarteritis nodosa. Severe vasculitis resulting in ischaemic necrosis of the toes. The patient also had arthralgia, renal involvement and hypertension. Several toes had to be amputated, but postoperatively the patient made a good recovery.

399

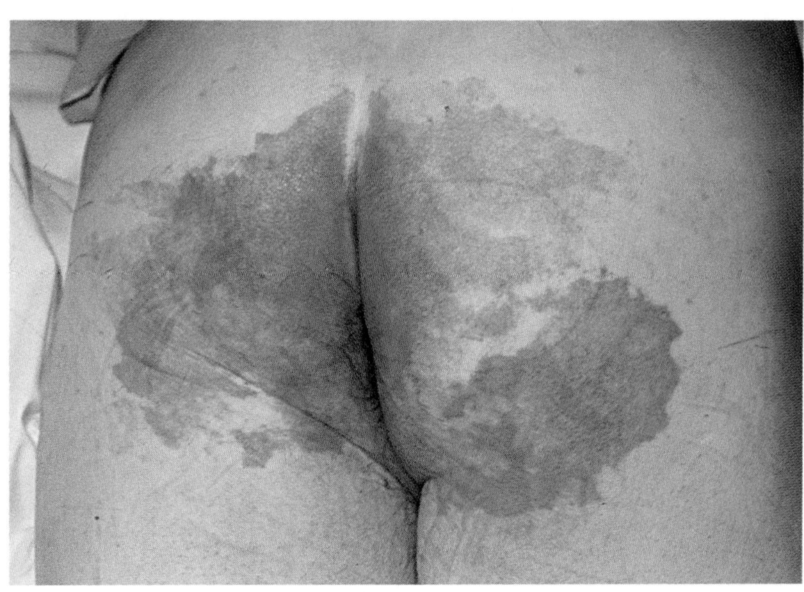

399 Urinary rash. Skin rash caused by urinary incontinence. Untreated, this can predispose to a pressure sore in an immobile patient.

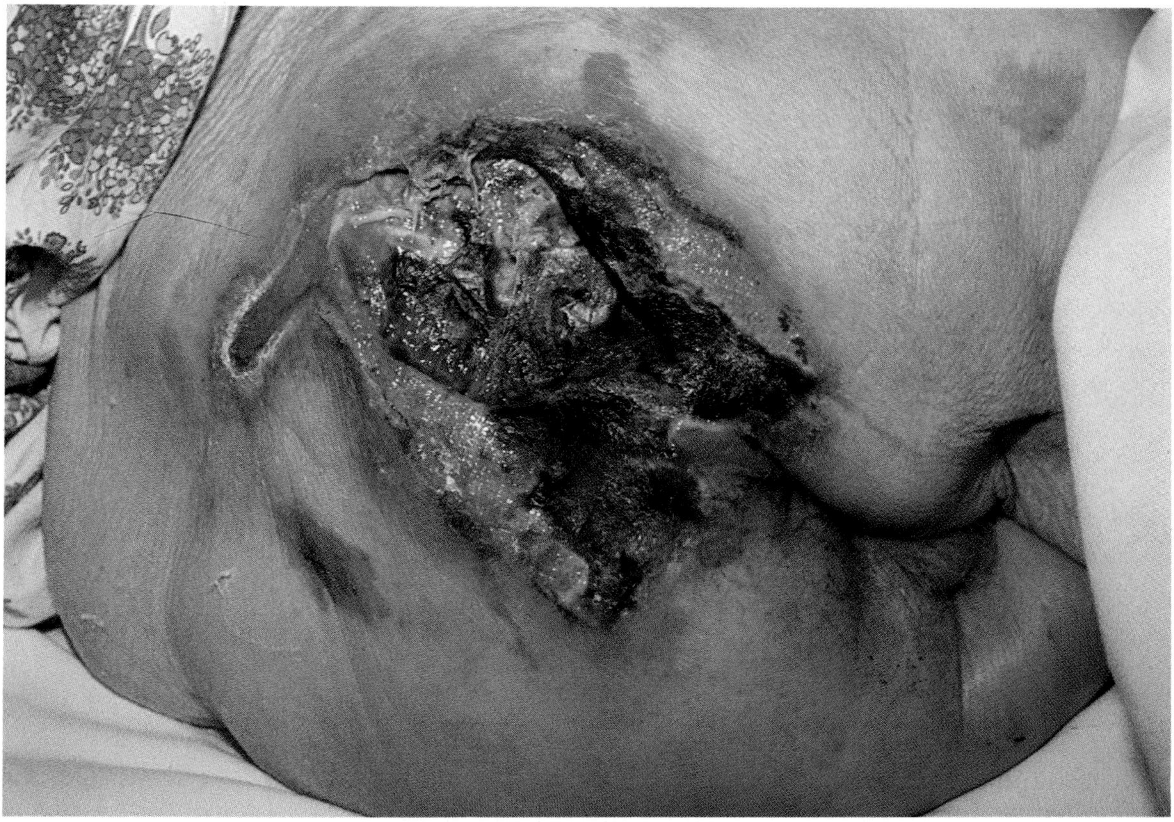

400

400 Pressure sore (decubitus ulcer). A large, deep, necrotic pressure sore over the sacral area. This resulted from immobility, urinary incontinence, dementia, poor nutrition and general debility.

401

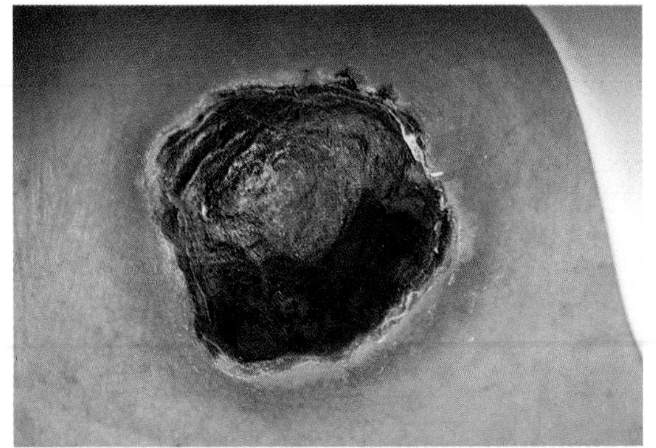

401 Pressure sore over the ischeal tuberosity with dry, black scab.

402

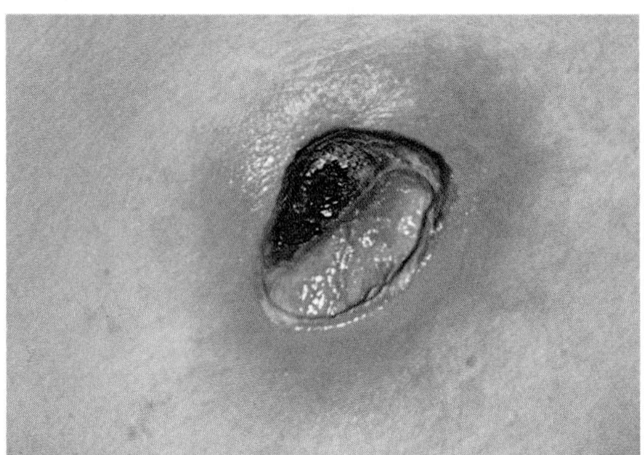

402 Pressure sore that is gradually healing. Note the appearance of new skin around the edges of the sore.

Pressure sores

Two main types:
Superficial – good prognosis if actively treated
Deep-tissue necrosis present

Predisposing factors
Mainly compression and shearing forces, *plus:*

- Poor tissue perfusion
- Immobility and paresis – CVAs, arthritis, fractures
- Poor general health – malnutrition, anaemias, carcinomas
- Hypoxaemia
- Urinary incontinence causing skin maceration

Norton/Exton-Smith's clinical score for patients at risk
Patients scoring over 7 points are considered to be at risk.

General condition	*Mental state*	*Activity*	*Mobility*	*Incontinence*
0 Good	0 Alert	0 Ambulant	0 Full	0 None
1 Fair	1 Confused	1 Walks with help	1 Slightly decreased	1 Occasional
2 Poor	2 Apathetic	2 Chairfast	2 Very decreased	2 Incontinent urine
3 Bad	3 Stuporous	3 Bedfast	3 Immobile	3 Doubly incontinent

403 Pressure sore. A pressure gauge and cushion for monitoring pressure over vulnerable areas in elderly bedfast patients. This device is used to prevent pressure sores.

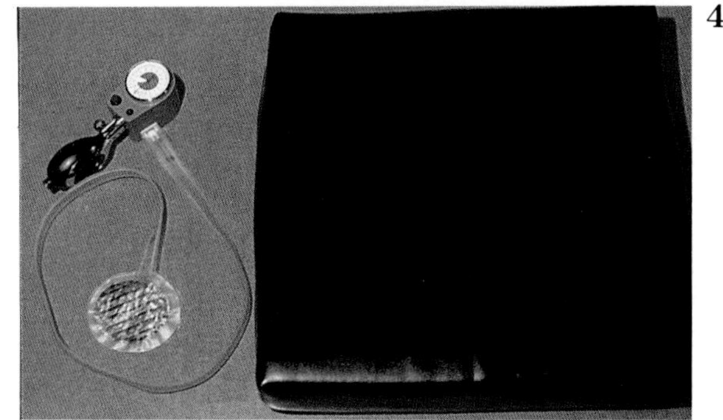

403

404 Oedema of the foot. Mild to moderate oedema of the feet is a common phenomenon in the elderly, especially in those who are immobile. Posture, gravitation and poor venous return contribute to produce such dependent oedema.

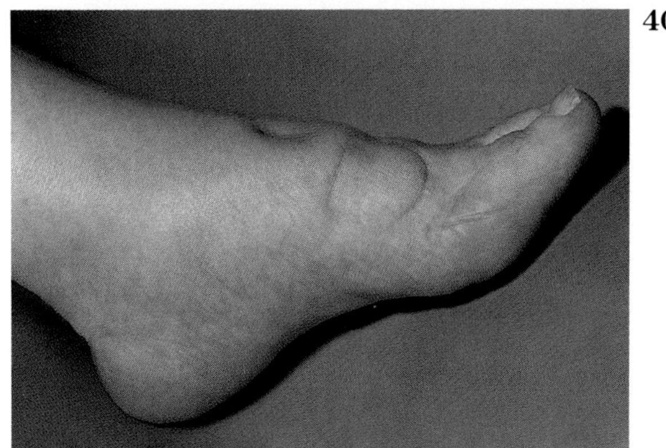

404

405 Ill-fitting footwear. The sore areas on the toes are the result of wearing old, wornout shoes. Such lesions may become infected if there is poor foot hygiene. In the elderly, ill-fitting footwear may cause falls and immobility.

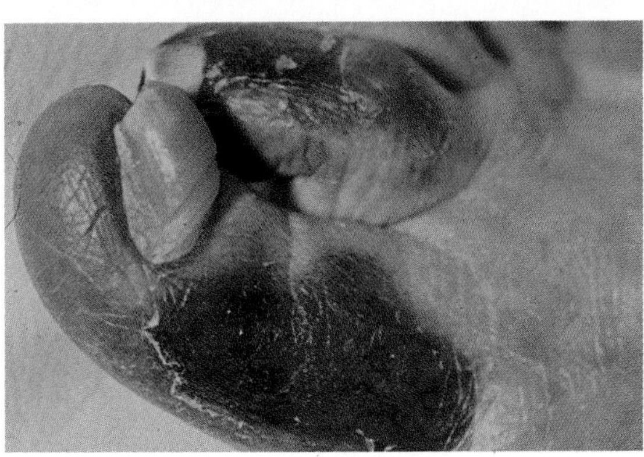

405

Peripheral oedema

- Cardiovascular
  - CCF
  - Venous thrombosis
  - Incompetent venous valves
  - Cellulitis
  - Immobility – gravitational
- Lymphatic obstruction
  - Neoplastic lymph nodes in groin
  - Pelvic tumours
  - Post-cellulitis
- Hepatic failure
- Renal-nephrotic syndrome
- Hypoalbuminaemia
- Drugs
  - Steroids
  - Carbenoxolone
  - NSAIDs
  - Phenylbutazone
  - Oestrogens
  - Fludrocortisone

406

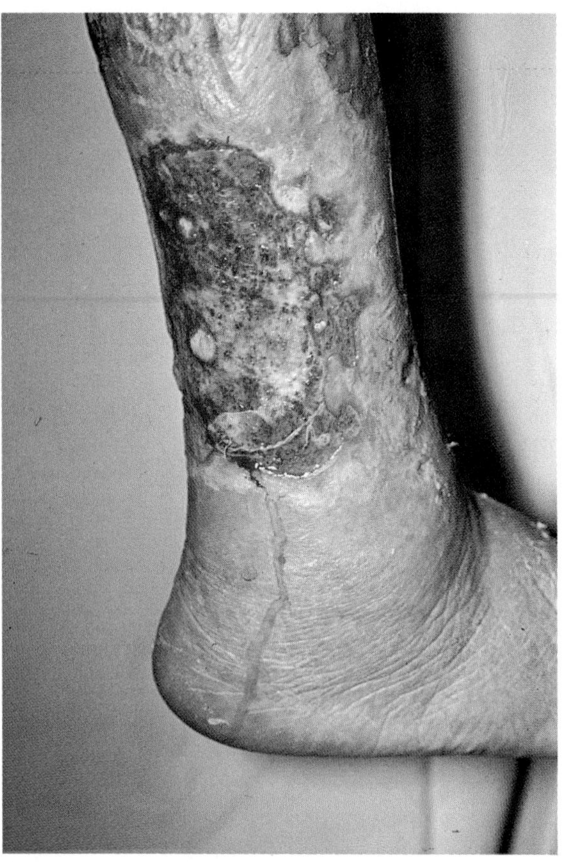

407

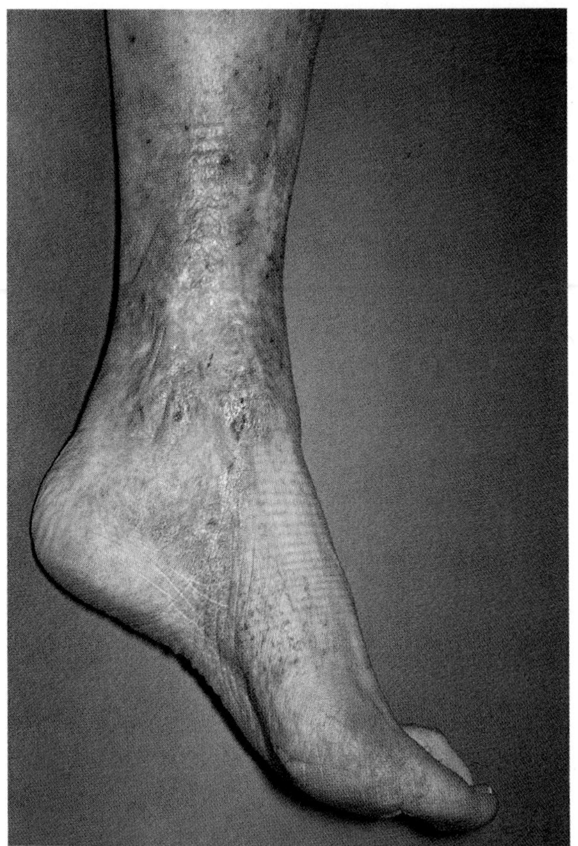

406 Varicose ulcer as a result of post-phlebitic syndrome. Such ulcers are slow to heal and require patient, meticulous nursing care.

407 Healed varicose ulcer. Note the clean healthy skin on the area where there was once a large varicose ulcer. Apart from prolonged nursing care and leg exercises, this patient also required treatment for anaemia.

408

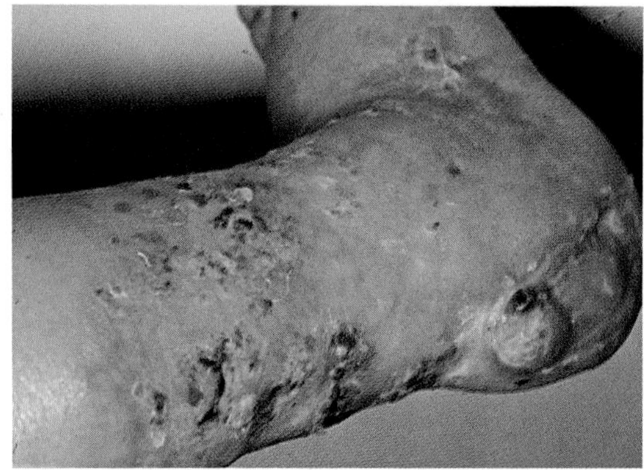

408 Chronic varicose eczema (post-phlebitic syndrome). The foot and ankle are affected. There are varicose ulcers surrounded by weeping, scaly and sticky skin.

Chronic leg ulcers in the elderly

Important aetiological factors:
- Varicose veins and impaired venous drainage
- Peripheral vascular disease, poor foot hygiene, plus trauma
- Pressure sores, especially on heels
- Burns, e.g. erythema ab igne
- Neuropathy
- Ulcerating gouty tophi
- Pemphigus and pemphigoid
- Tumours, e.g. melanoma, basal-cell carcinoma
- Vasculitis, e.g. rheumatoid arthritis
- Dysproteinaemias
- Steroids
- Pyoderma gangrenosum

409

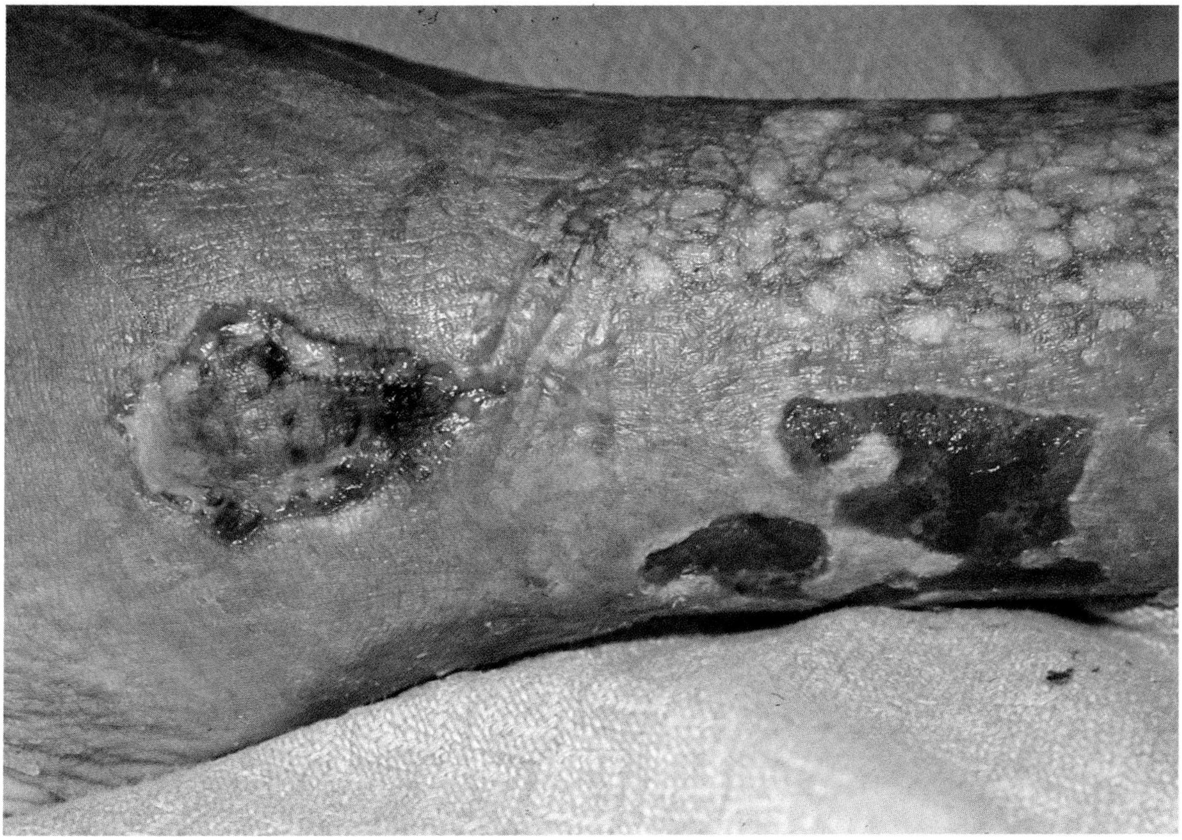

409 Chronic varicose eczema (post-phlebitic syndrome). Note the two clean healing sores on the ankle and an infected sore with considerable slough on the malleolus. The skin is rough and heaped up in places and there is old scar tissue.

410 Varicose eczema. In this case there is considerable roughening of the skin with thickening and hyperpigmentation.

410

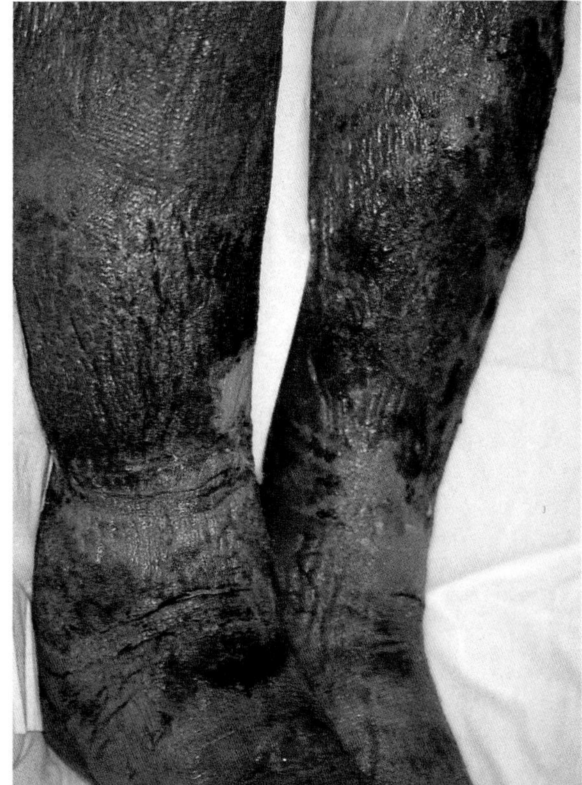

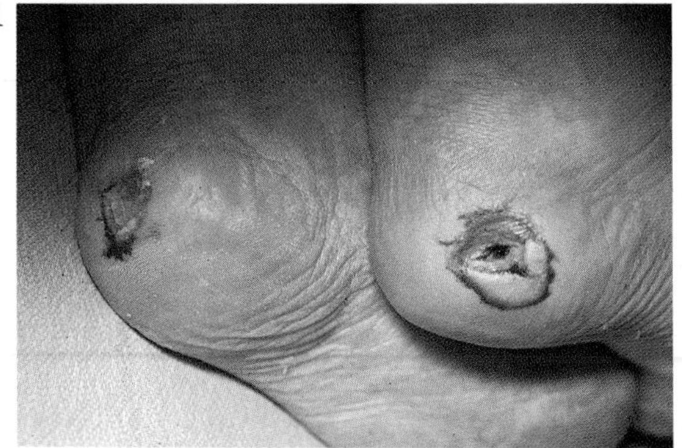

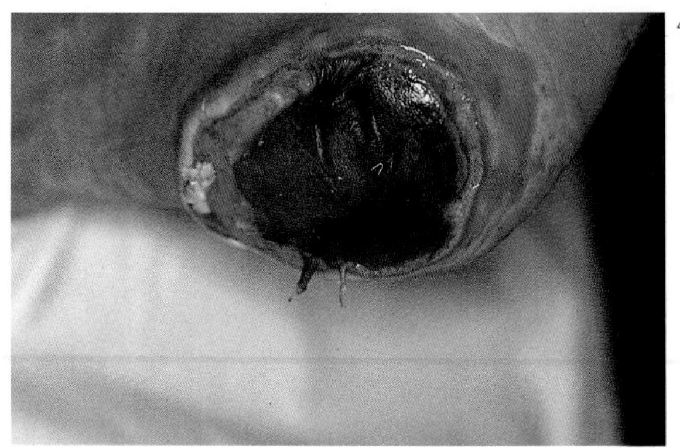

411 and 412 Heel sores. These ulcers are pressure sores. Contributory factors are stasis, arterial insufficiency, obesity and general ill health.

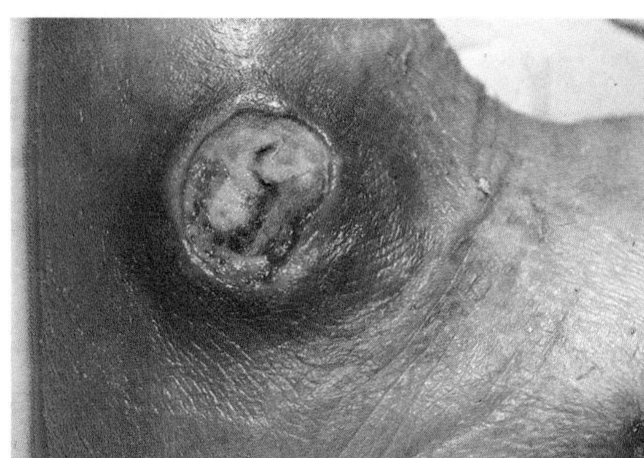

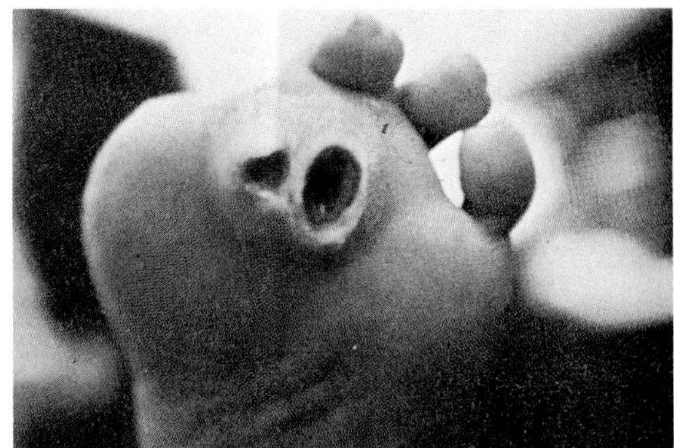

415

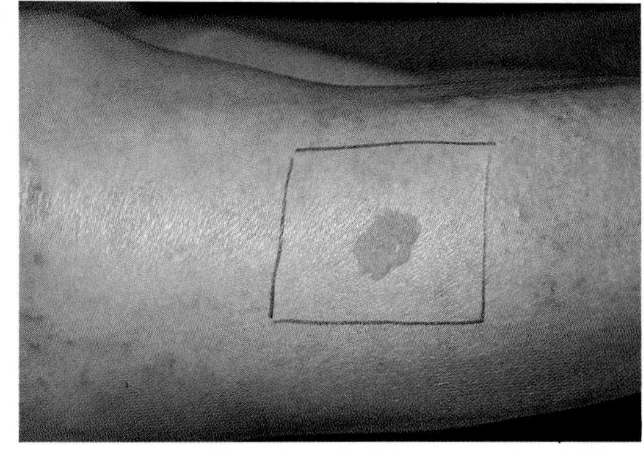

413 Diabetic ulcer on the lateral malleolus of an elderly diabetic. Note the clean edges of the sore. Such lesions are essentially arterial and occur with small-vessel disease.

414 Diabetic ulcers on the sole of the foot. Note the two missing toes which had to be amputated.

415 Xanthoma. Xanthomatous deposit below the knee joint. It consists of lipid accumulating in the tissues in association with large foam cells. This patient presented with a history of ischaemic heart disease.

416 Traumatic bulla. A large blood blister caused by a fall in an elderly lady who was on long-term corticosteroid treatment for chronic asthma.

Problems after a limb amputation

- Phantom limb sensations and pains
- Grief and depression
- Psychosocial problems and loss of occupation
- Negative attitudes to the prosthesis

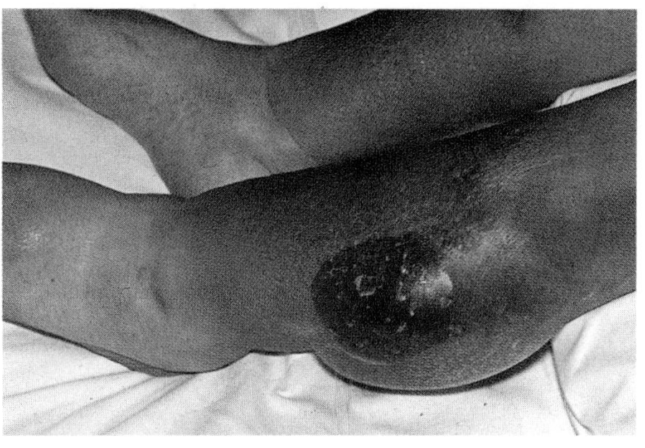

416

417

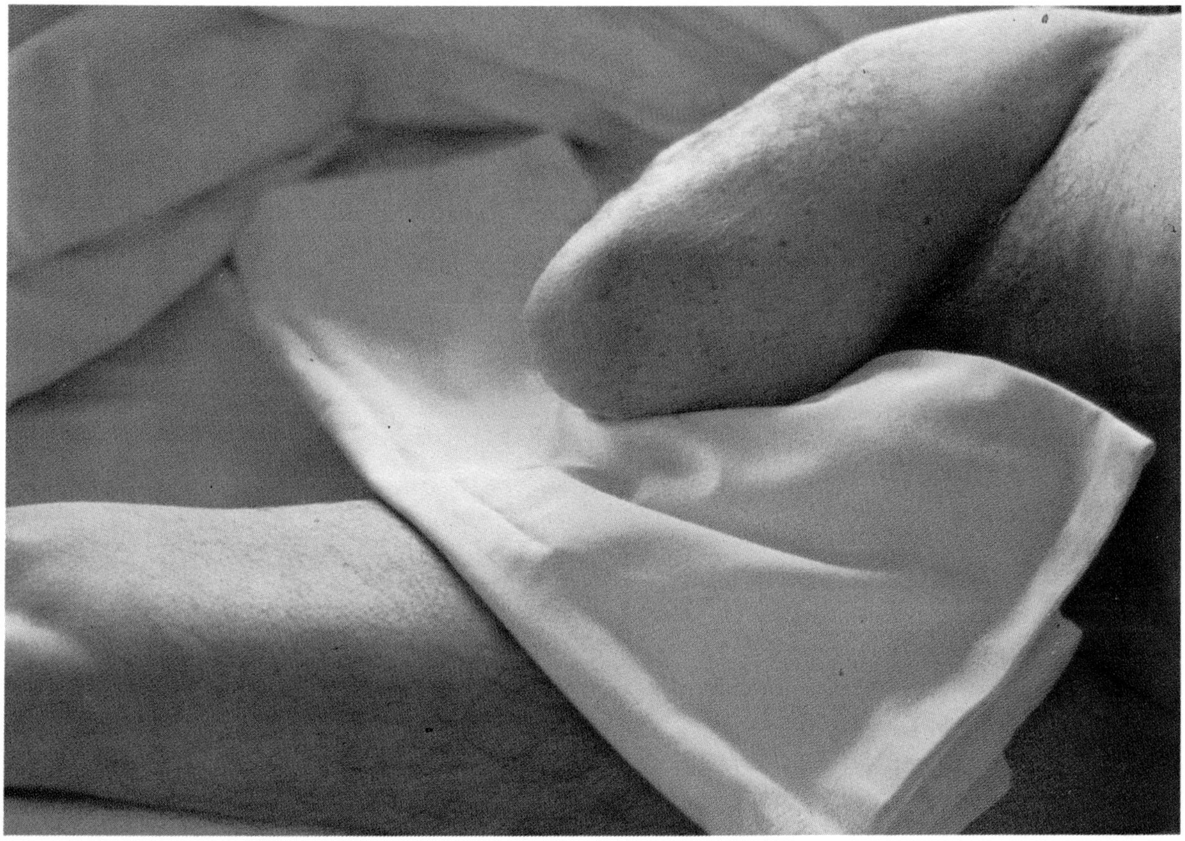

417 Above-knee amputation. This patient had ischaemic necrosis of the right foot. After amputation the patient required prolonged rehabilitation by a multidisciplinary team.

418

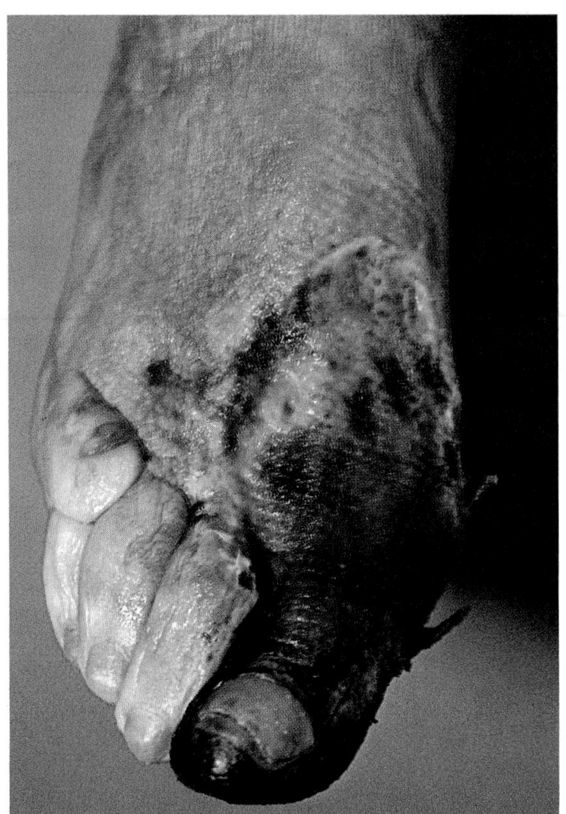

41

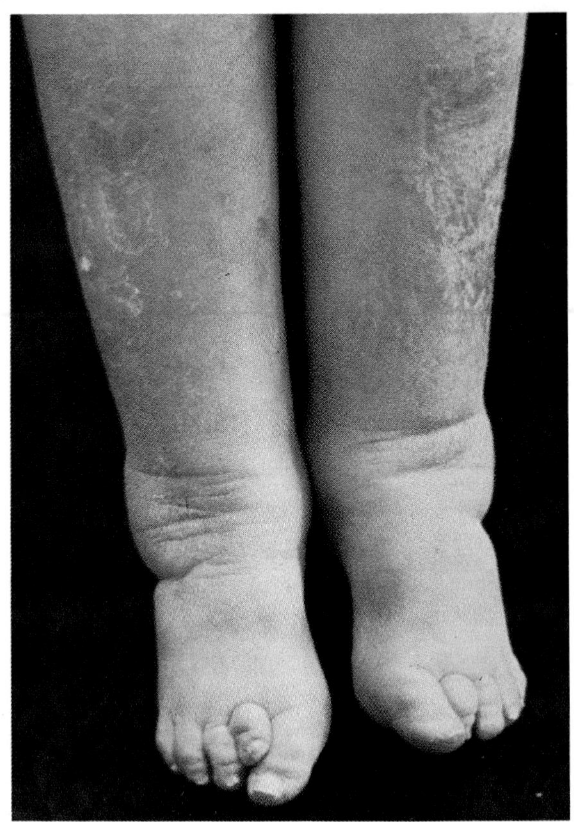

420

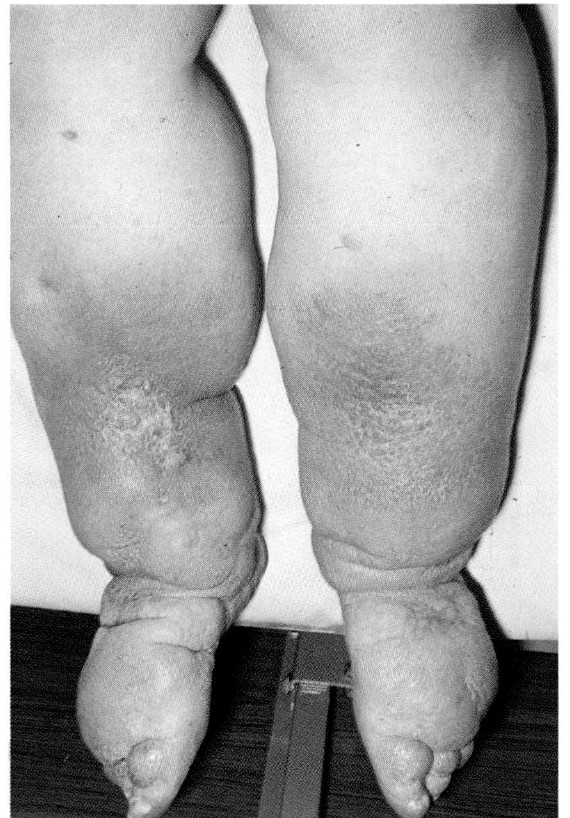

418 Ischaemic necrosis. Result of severe peripheral vascular disease caused by atherosclerosis. This patient required below-knee amputation.

419 Lymphoedema of the legs. Post-thrombotic accumulation of lymph in the extremities. The oedema is non-pitting and resistant to diuretic therapy.

420 Lymphoedema of the legs. An advanced case resulting from a combination of Milroy's disease, stasis, venous insufficiency and chronic congestive cardiac failure.

421 Gout. A classic attack of acute gout affecting the big toe and accompanied by fever and sickness. This elderly patient was obese and had a past history of renal stones.

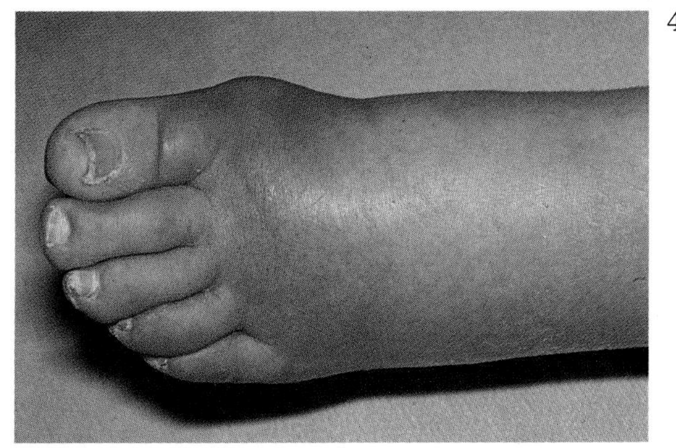
421

422 Gout. Histology of tophus showing deposits of uric acid crystals surrounded by inflammatory infiltration.

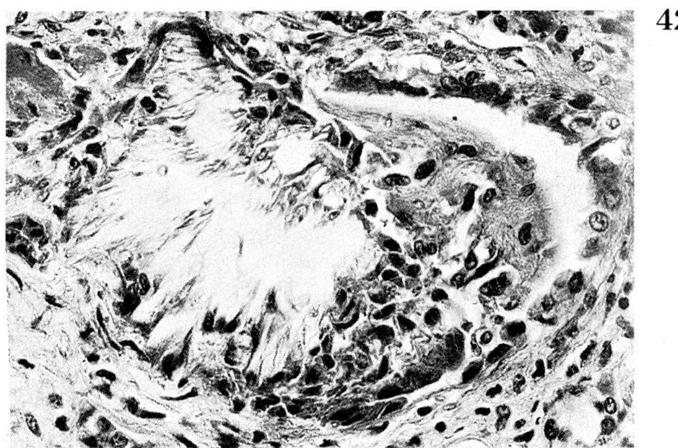
422

423 Multiple foot problems. Feet of an elderly lady showing onychogryphosis, hallux valgus and bunions.

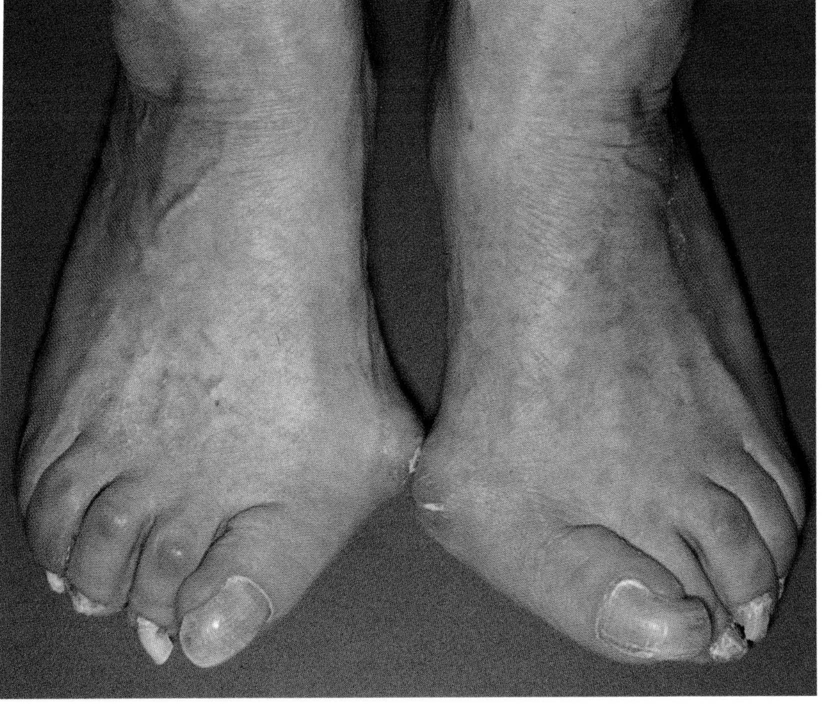
423

424

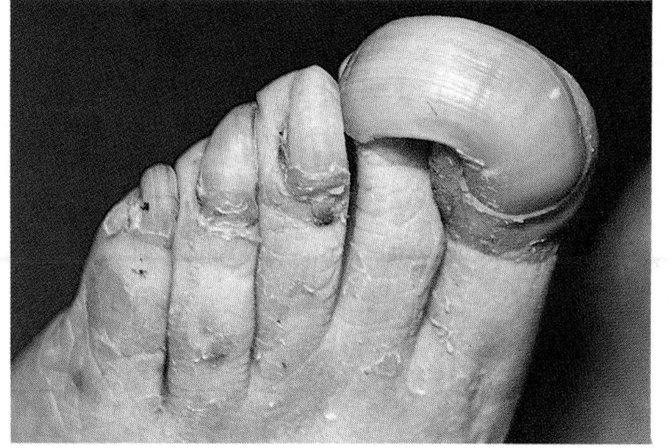

4

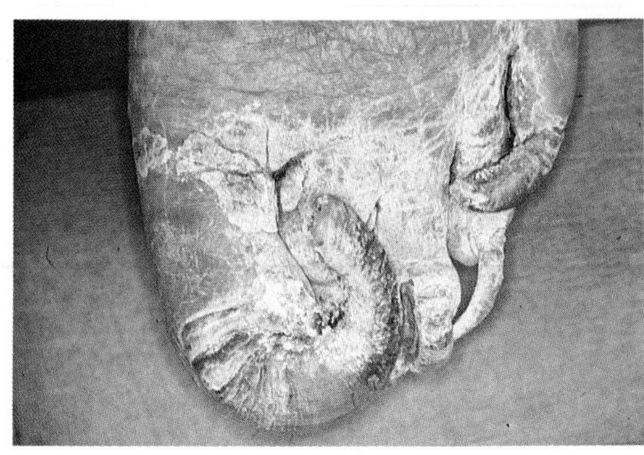

426

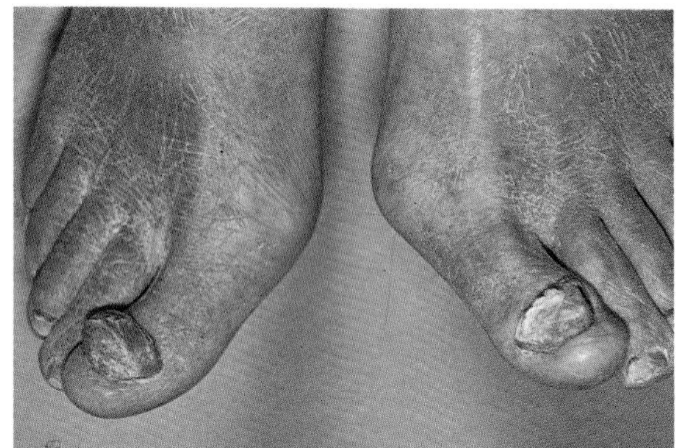

424 and 425 Onychogryphosis. Overgrown, claw-like toenails causing discomfort on walking, immobility and falls. It is usually a sign of extreme neglect and deprivation. Such patients require a thorough geriatric assessment with a full investigation of their social background and living conditions. Expert chiropody will be necessary in these cases.

426 Nail dystrophy. Brittle, rough and deformed toenails in a case of peripheral vascular disease and venous insufficiency. Note bilateral hallux valgus.

427 Bilateral hallux valgus. A common orthopaedic problem in the feet of the elderly. The big toe is abducted so that it lies on top of the other toes. Marked prominence of the first metatarsophalangeal joint occurs with the bony enlargement of the inner side of the first metatarsal head.

427

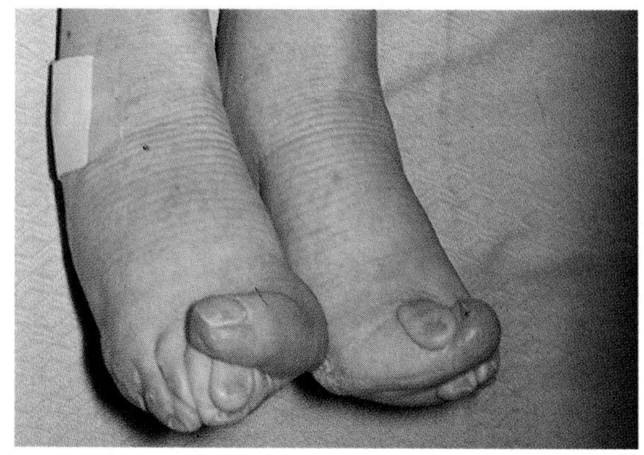

28

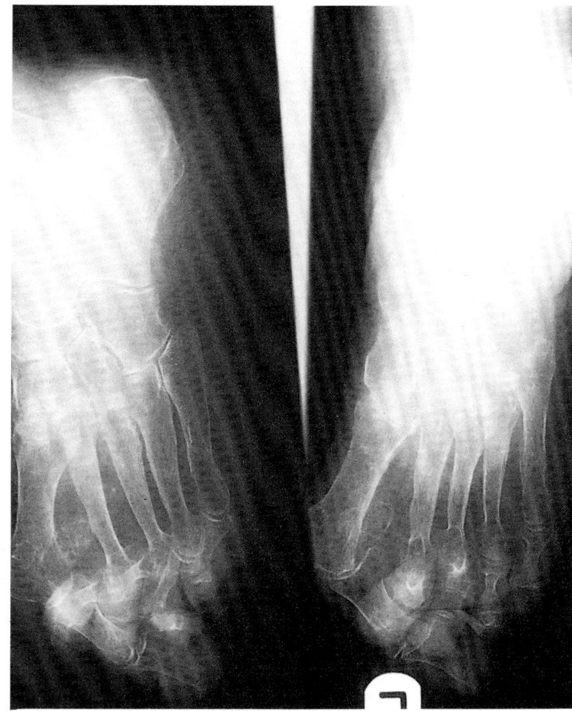

429

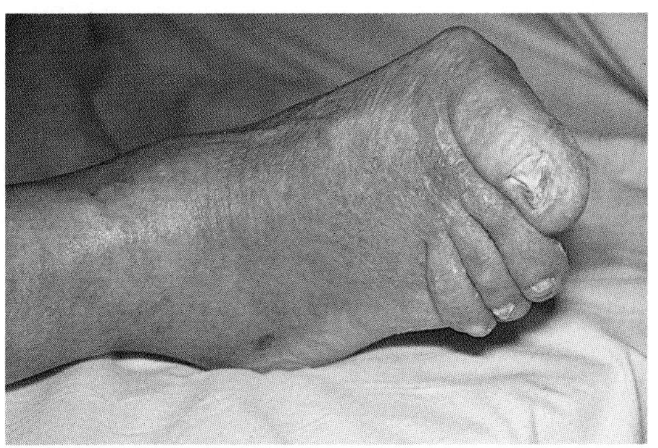

430

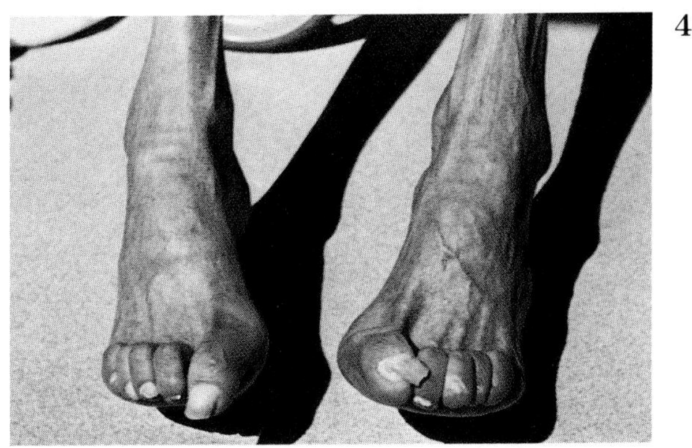

431

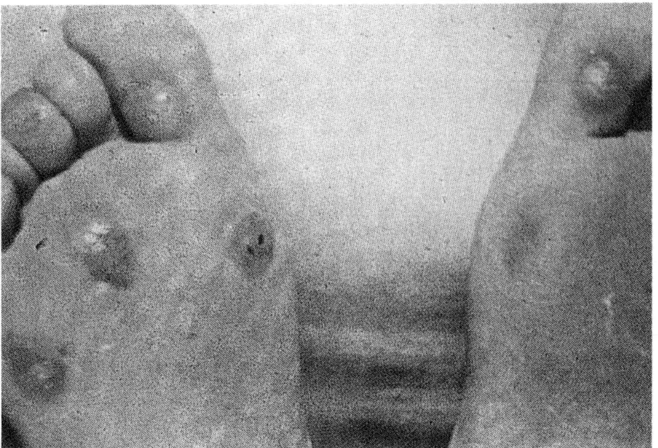

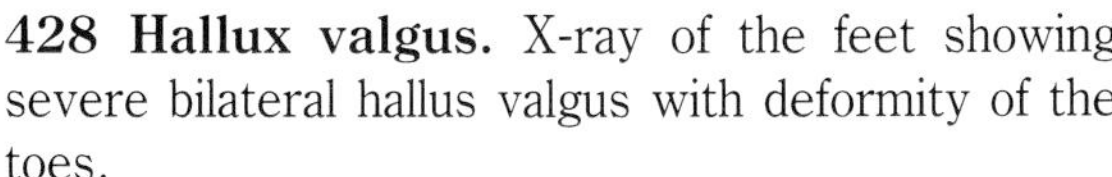

428 Hallux valgus. X-ray of the feet showing severe bilateral hallus valgus with deformity of the toes.

429 Hallux valgus. A bursa (bunion) has formed over the enlarged first metatarsal head. This is painful, interferes with mobility and may ulcerate.

430 Hammer toes. A common problem in the elderly usually caused by prolonged use of ill-fitting footwear.

431 Corns on the soles of the feet, causing pain on walking.

432

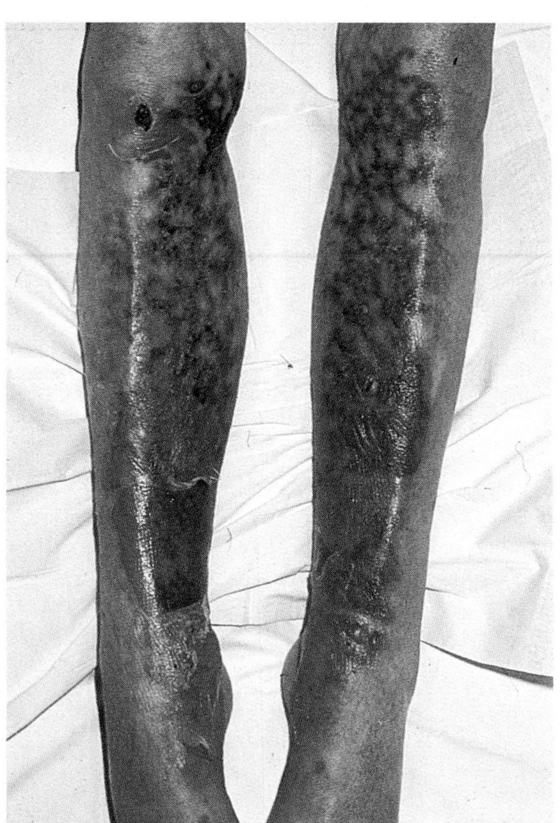

432 Erythema ab igne. The result of sitting too close to a fire. The condition is commonly seen in old people who live in cold houses and have a tendency to sit too near the fire for long periods. Such patients should be investigated for hypothyroidism.

433

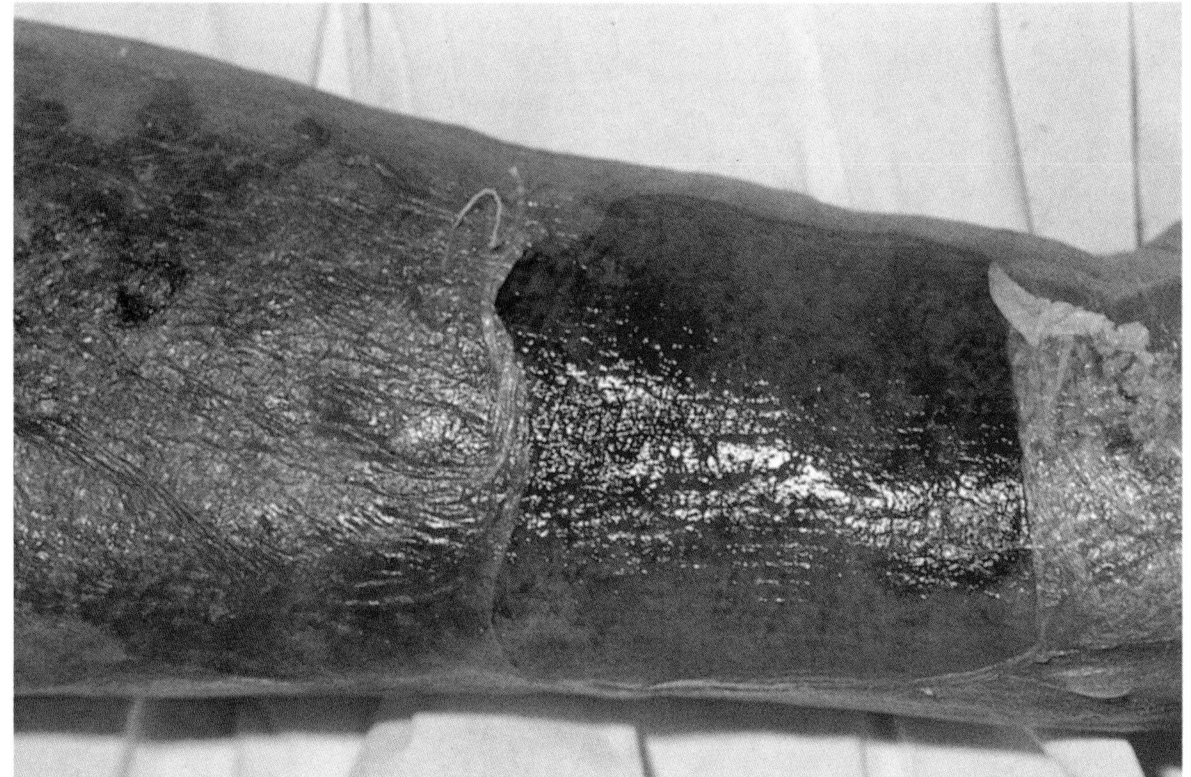

433 Erythema ab igne showing an area of superficial burn.

10 Disorders of the skin

434 Dry skin (asteatosis). Dry, tissue-like, atrophic skin caused by the loss of collagen and associated with advancing age.

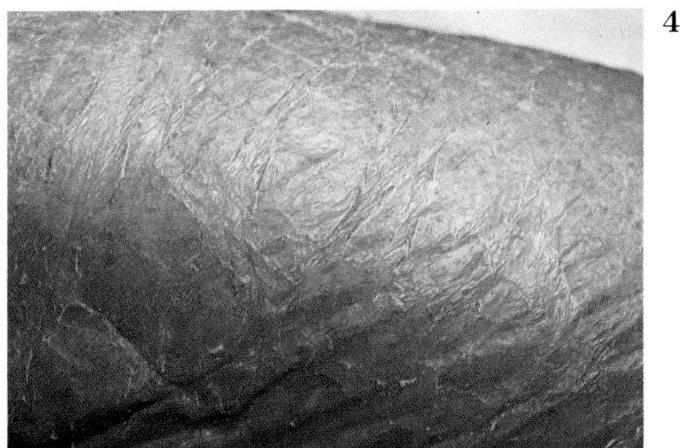
434

435 Loose skin. A sign of ageing exaggerated by weight loss and dehydration.

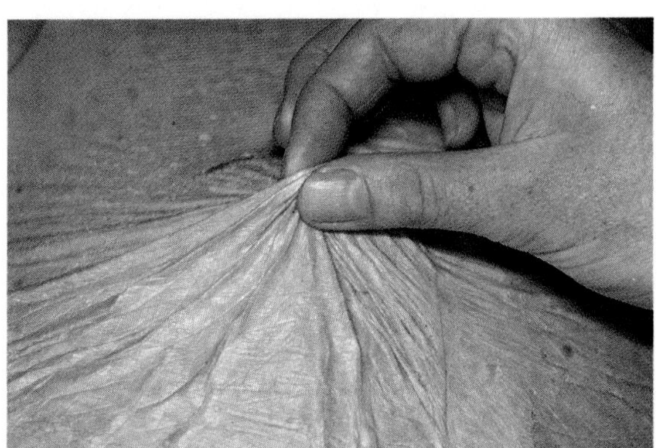
435

436 Dry skin (ichthyosis). Dry skin with cracks in stratum corneum and rhomboidal scales with flaky edges. The histopathologic changes consist of epidermal atrophy and hyperkeratosis. This condition sometimes occurs in association with lymphoma, but in the elderly it is usually chronic and benign.

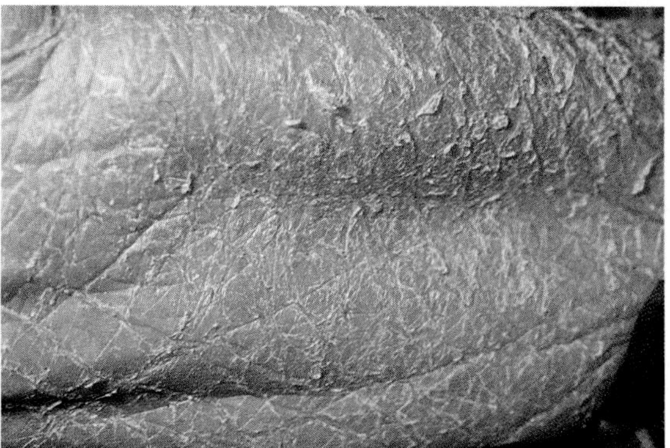
436

437

437 Seborrhoeic dermatitis. This fairly common condition affects the central part of the face, scalp, ears and eyebrows. There may be associated blepharitis. This patient has a dry, scaly scalp with itching. This condition has nothing to do with seborrhoea.

438

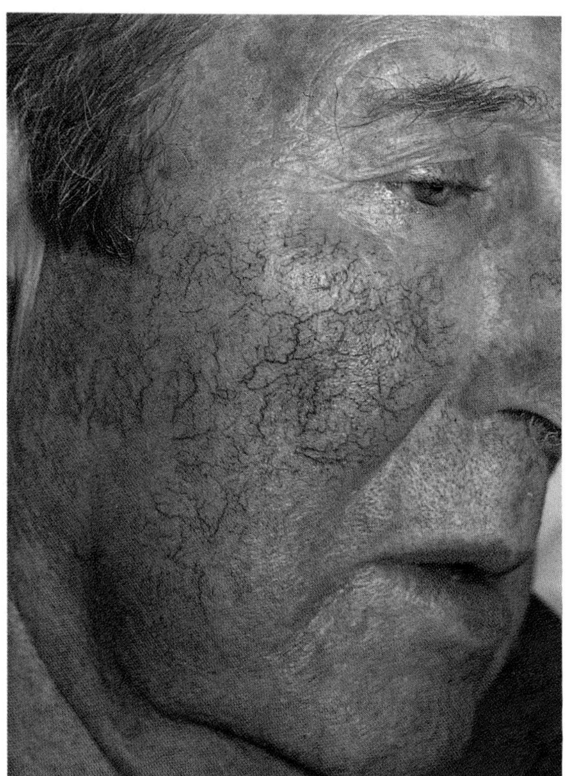

438 Prominent capillary network. Telangiectasia-like vascular pattern on the cheeks of an elderly man. This is a type of benign degenerative change seen more frequently in white-skinned people who are exposed to high-intensity ultraviolet radiation.

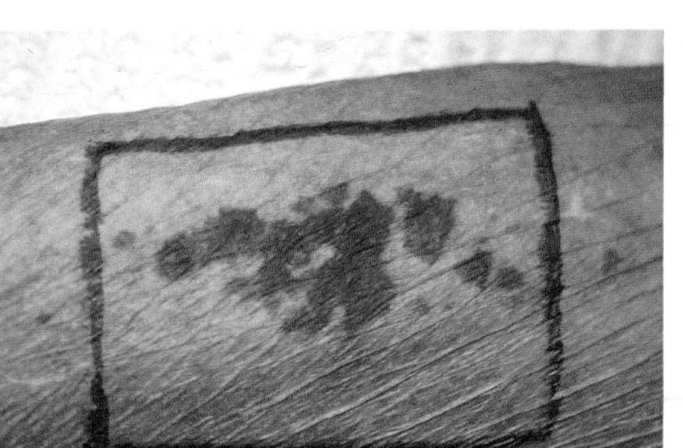

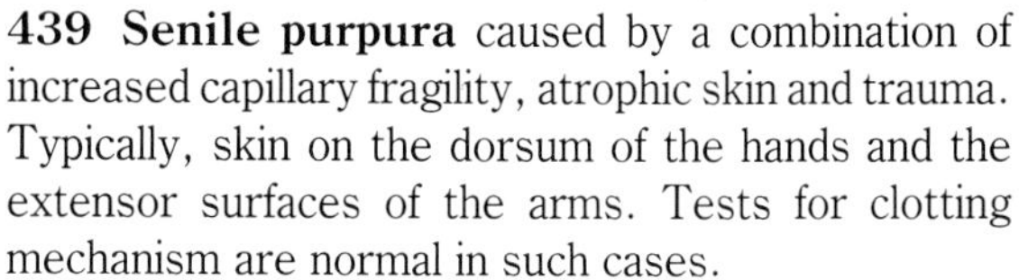

439 Senile purpura caused by a combination of increased capillary fragility, atrophic skin and trauma. Typically, skin on the dorsum of the hands and the extensor surfaces of the arms. Tests for clotting mechanism are normal in such cases.

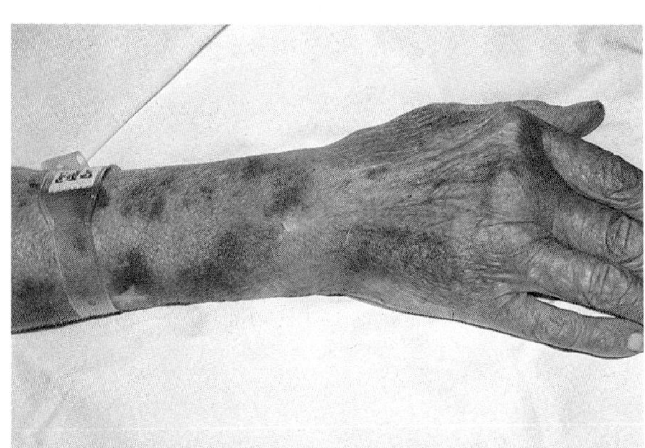

440 Steroid purpura. Large recurrent bruises on the forearm induced by long-term corticosteroid therapy.

441

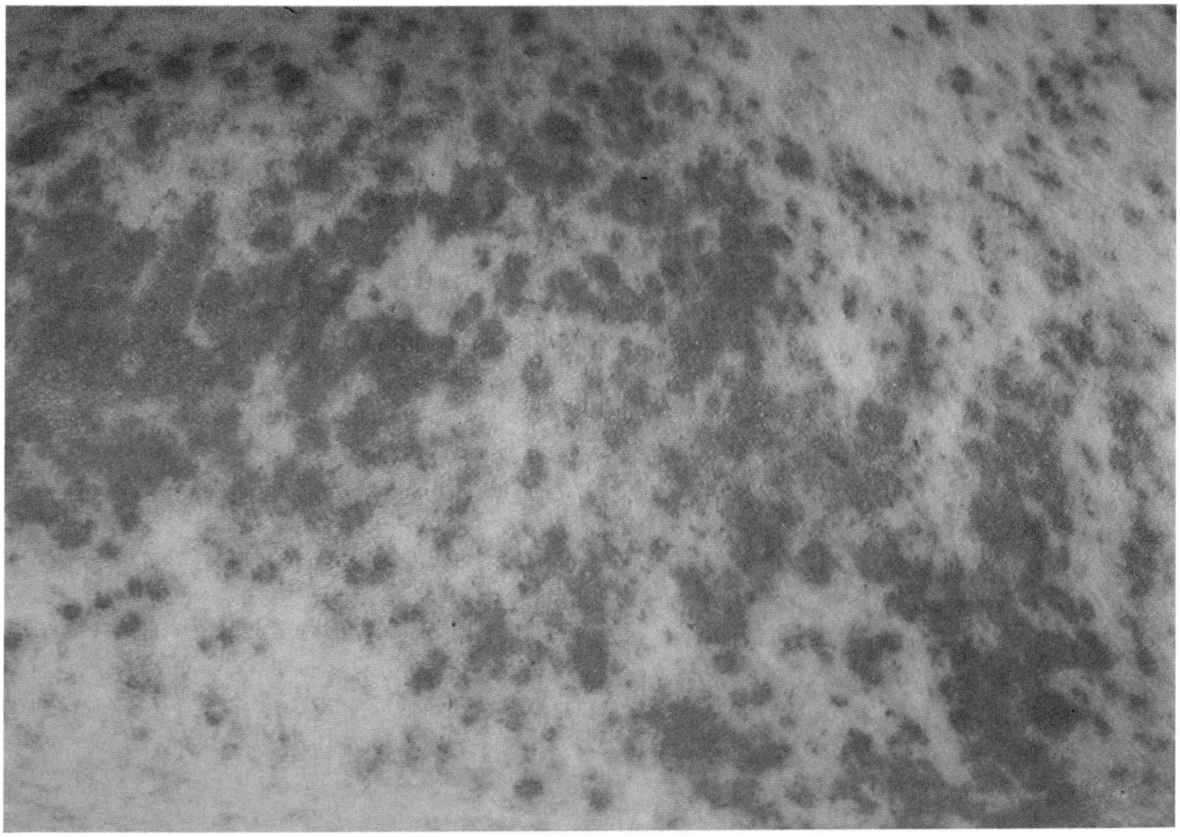

441 Drug-induced purpura. Purpuric rash caused by damage to capillary endothelium induced by penicillin. The platelet count and bleeding time are usually normal.

442

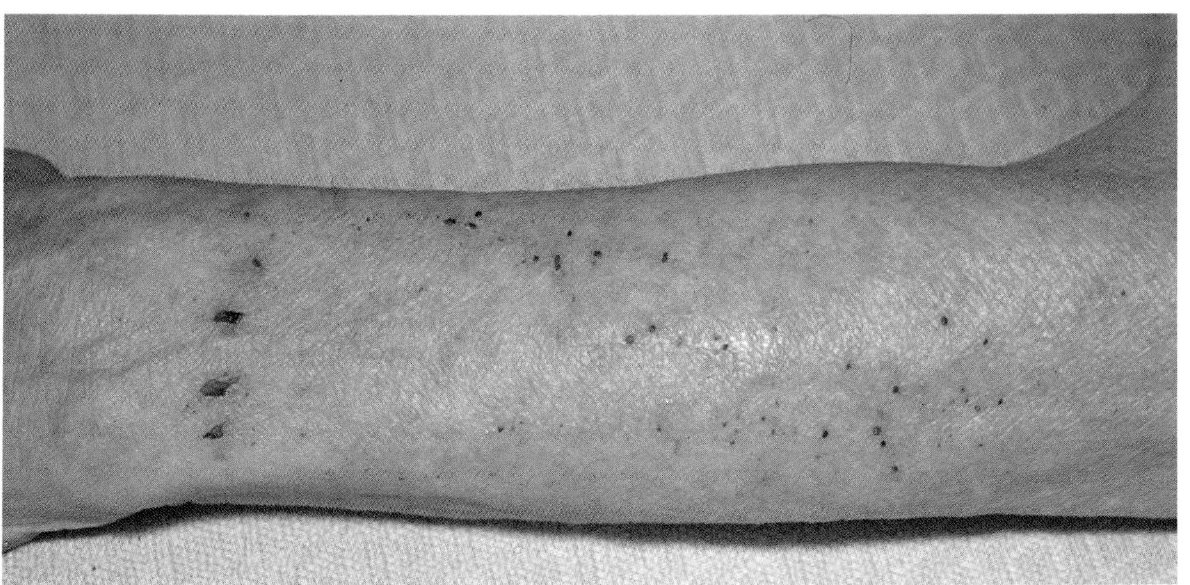

442 Pruritus caused by a combination of iron-deficiency anaemia and dry skin (asteatosis) in an elderly man.

443

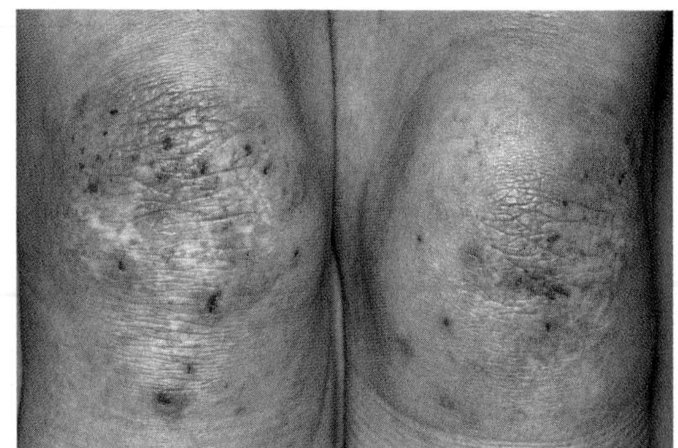

44

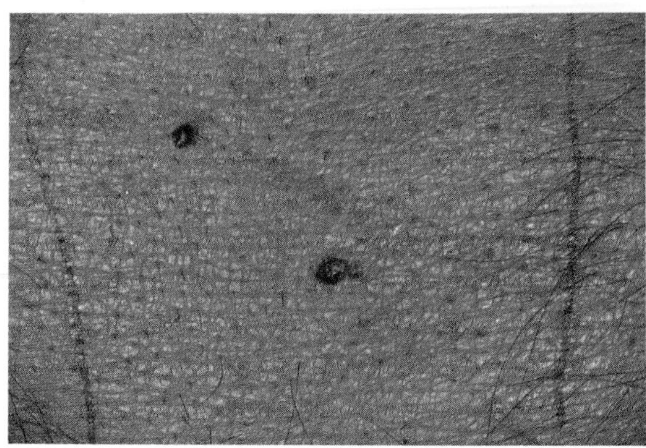

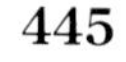

445

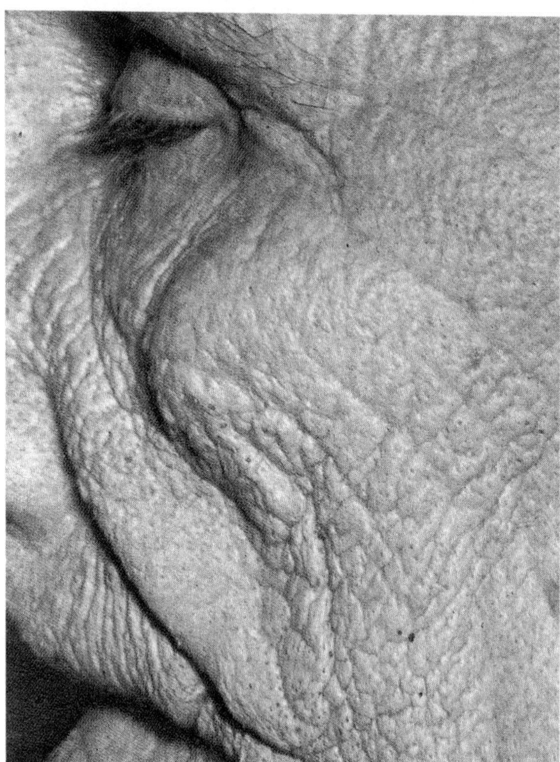

446

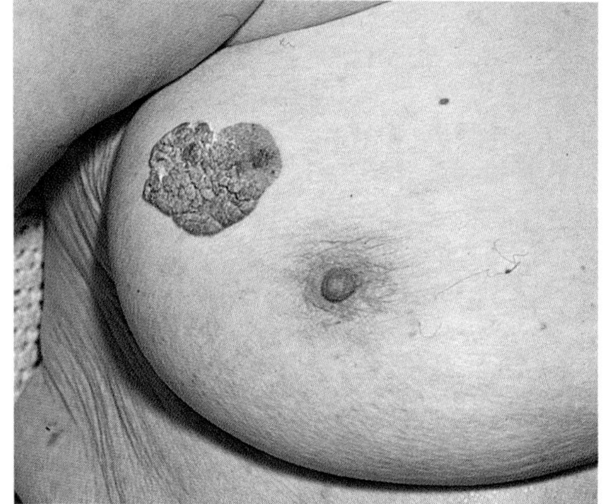

443 Lichen simplex. A frequent cause of chronic pruritus with no obvious aetiology. Sometimes also called 'neurodermatitis'.

444 Senile angiomas (Campbell de Morgan's spots). Small, bright red, raised spots on the skin of the trunk and shoulders. This condition is common in elderly male Caucasians and has no pathological significance.

445 Solar elastotic degenerative change. Excessive wrinkling of the skin caused by changes in dermal collagen. It occurs after lifelong exposure to environmental factors, particularly sunlight.

Pruritus in the elderly

Skin diseases
- Scabies, insect bites, pediculosis
- Eczema
- Lichen planus
- Dermatitis herpetiformis
- Lichen simplex

Systemic causes
- Hepatic, e.g. obstructive jaundice
- Chronic renal failure
- Endocrine, e.g. myxoedema, hyperthyroidism
- Blood diseases, e.g. malignant lymphoma, myeloproliferative disorders, iron deficiency
- Cancer, e.g. lung, stomach, colon
- Drugs, e.g. allergic drug reactions, morphine
- Psychogenic – 'senile pruritus'

446 Seborrhoeic wart (senile wart). Papillomatous, greasy, friable and dark warty lesion. Increasingly common with ageing and appears predominantly on the unexposed Caucasian skin. The growth is benign.

447 Rhinophyma. Thickened erythematous skin of the nose with enlarged follicles, it is a variant of rosacea in which there is persistent eruption with erythema and prominent blood vessels occurring on the forehead and cheeks. Pustules, papules and oedema also occur.

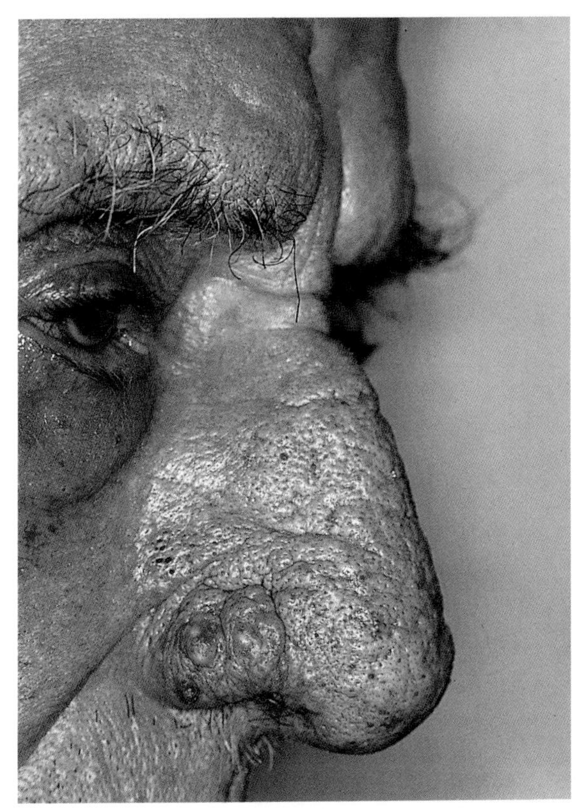

447

448 and 449 Basal cell epithelioma. Most common skin cancer in the white races. Arises from the epidermal or hair follicle cells of the face. The lesion is invasive but metastases are rare. Predisposing factors are mainly actinic radiation and rarely epidermal naevi and xeroderma pigmentosum.

448

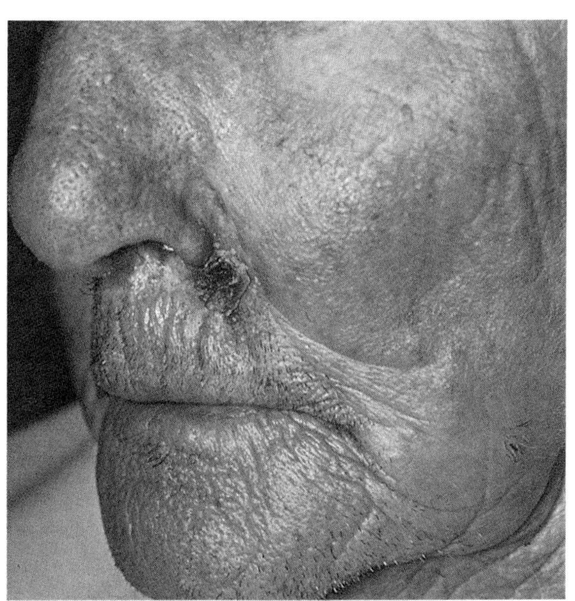

449

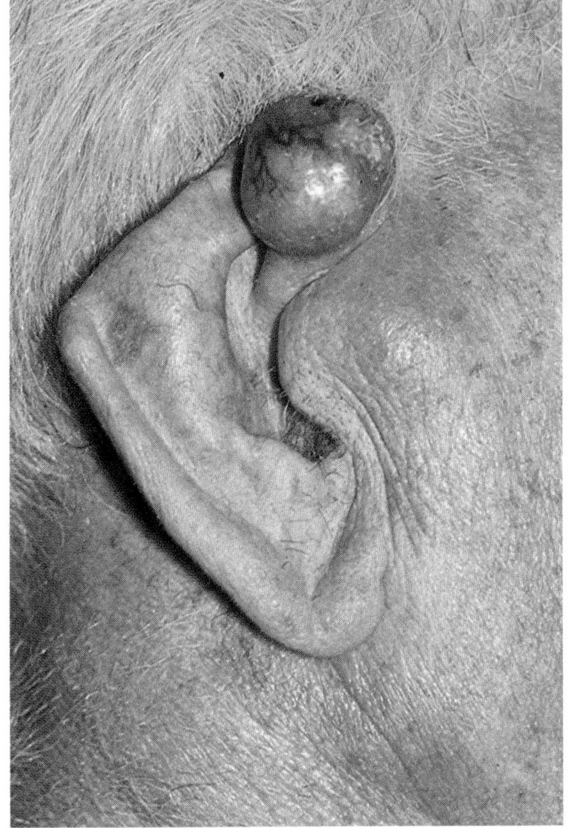

450

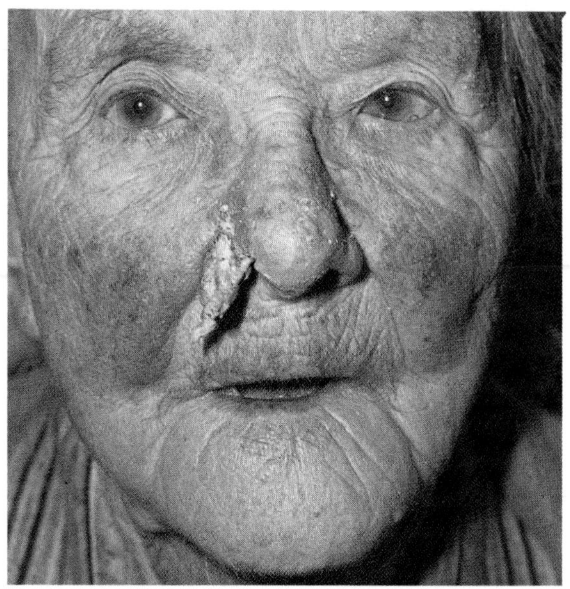

45

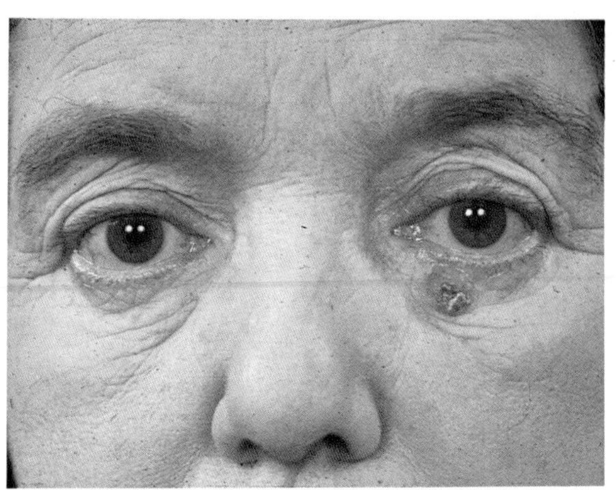

451 Squamous cell carcinoma. In this case the lesion is on the lower eyelid. The more differentiated tumours often have a warty, keratotic crust, while others may be nodular. The edge is poorly defined.

450 Squamous cell epithelioma. This tumour of the epidermis and mucosae arises in premalignant sun-damaged skin. It is locally invasive and likely to metastasise. In this case there is a large mass arising from the nostril.

452

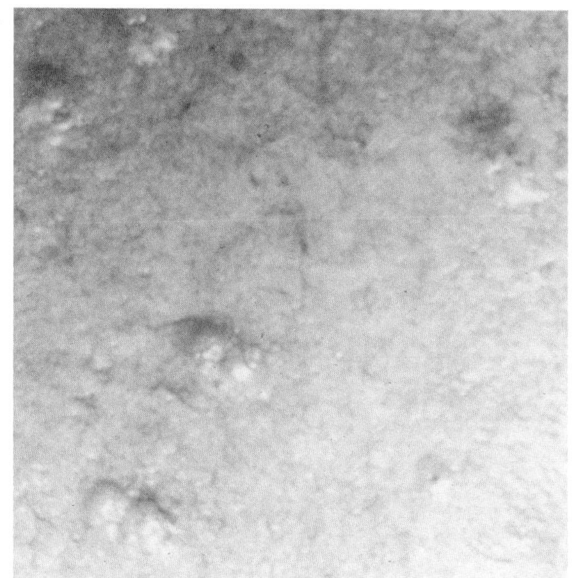

45

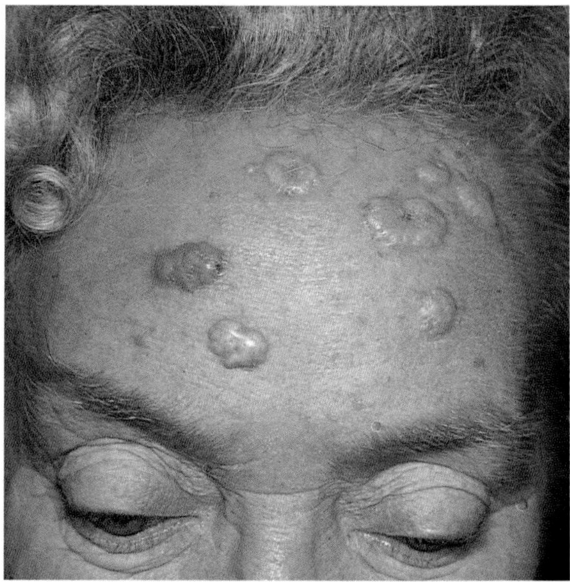

452 Senile sebaceous gland hyperplasia. A benign condition occurring in the elderly and sometimes confused with other skin diseases.

453 Senile sebaceous gland hyperplasia. A more advanced case with prominent lesions on the forehead.

454

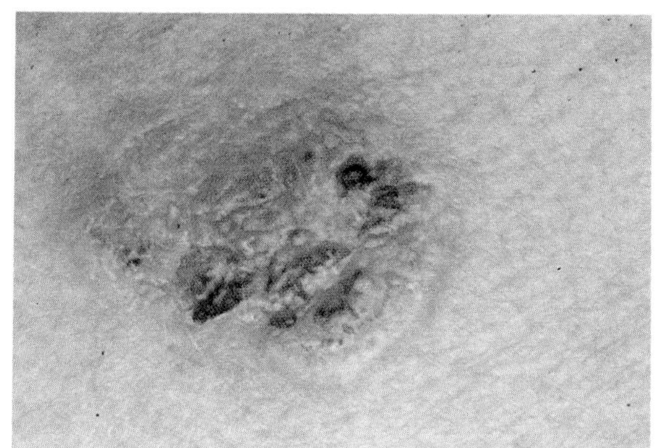

455

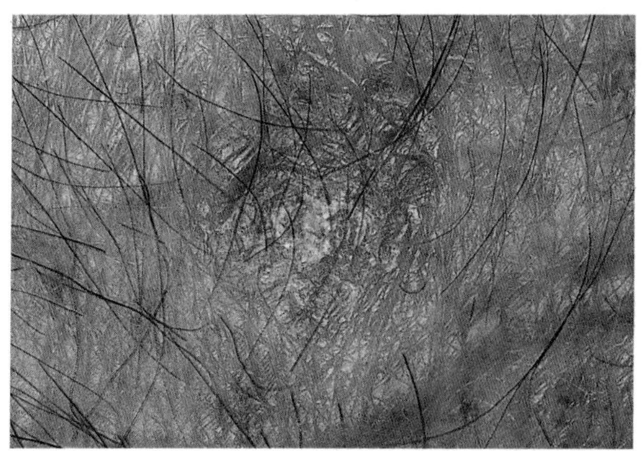

454 and 455 Actinic (solar) keratosis. These lesions occur after long exposure to sunlight and are potentially malignant, with a latent period of usually over 10 years. The most common sites are forehead, cheeks, dorsum of hands and forearms, and in men, ears and bald scalp.

456

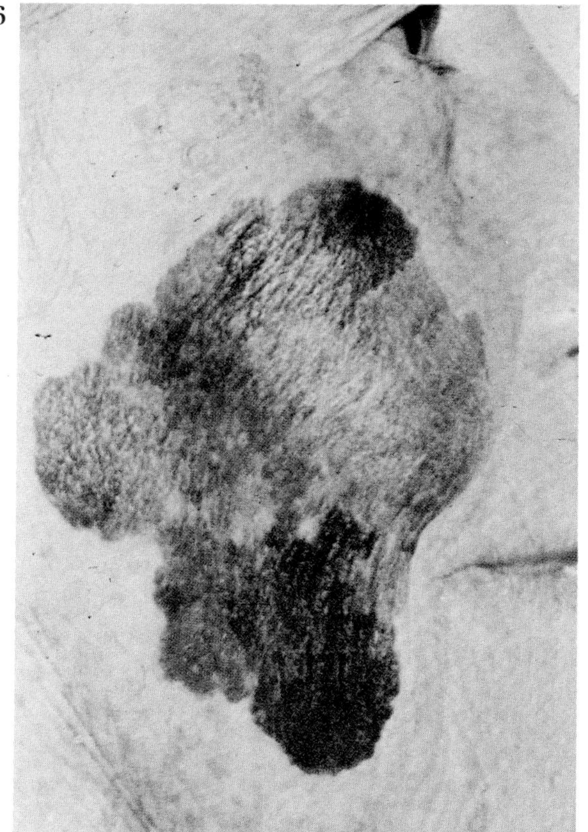

456 Lentigo. Pigmented lesion on the face. Senile lentigo is benign, but lentigo maligna develops into an invasive melanoma in about one-third of cases.

457

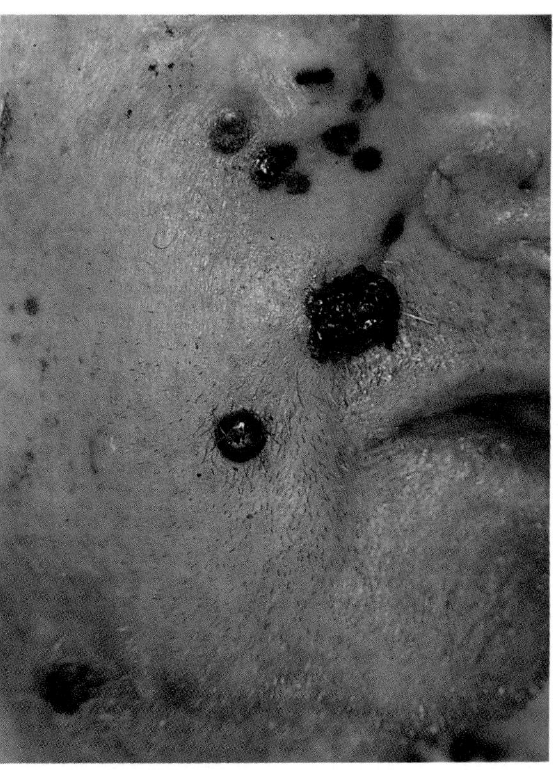

457 Malignant melanoma. A case of metastatic malignant melanoma with secondaries in the lungs and brain.

458

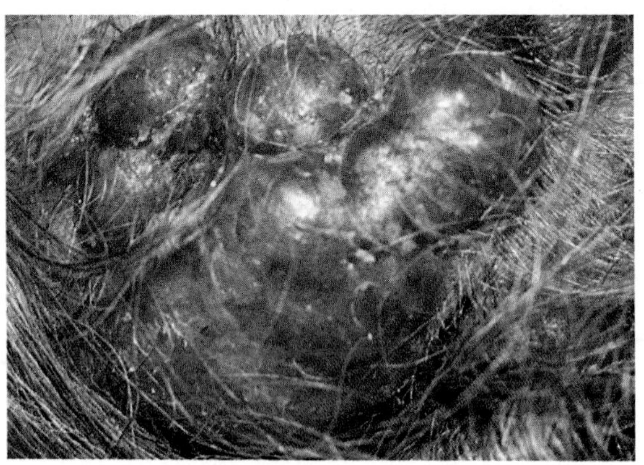

4.

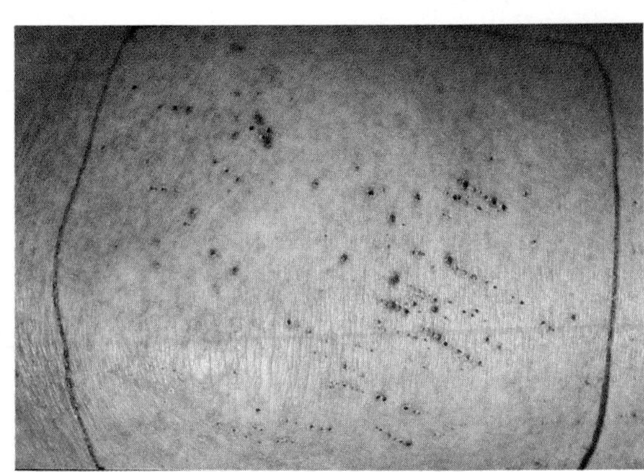

458 Skin secondaries. Cutaneous deposits from internal malignancies are seen occasionally in carcinomatosis. In this case there is a secondary deposit in the scalp from carcinoma of the lung.

459 Scabies. Producing areas of intense pruritus on the lower limbs. This infestation occurs in those elderly people who have poor personal hygiene with self-neglect.

460

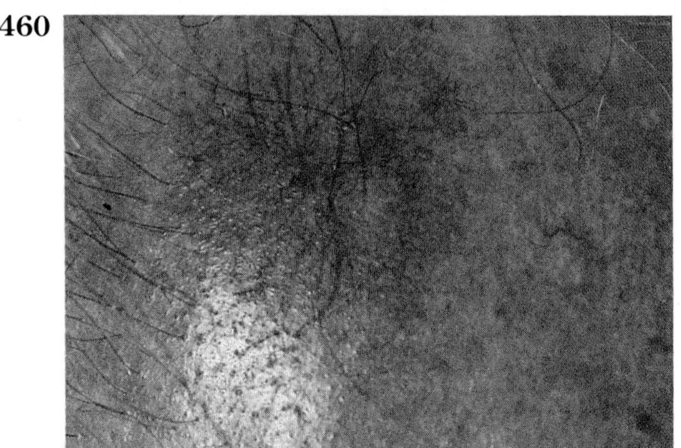

461

46

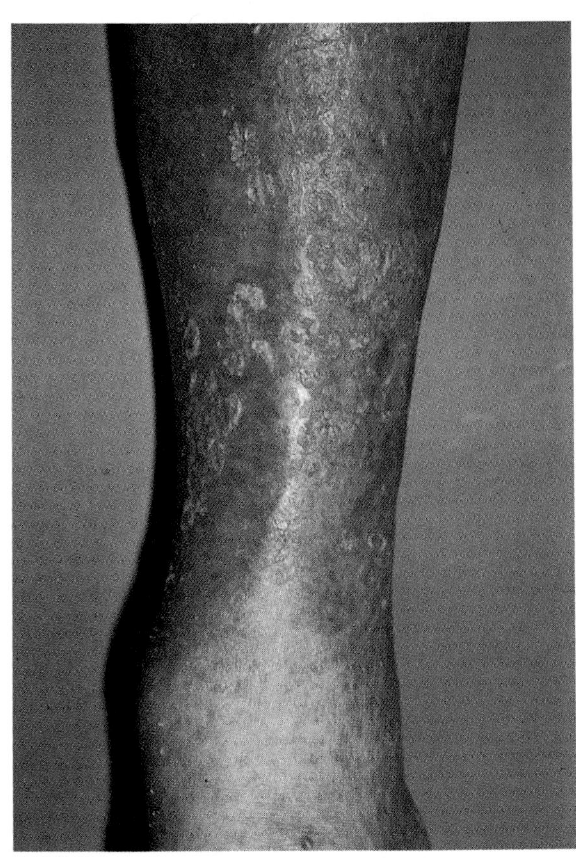

460 and 461 Spider naevus on the forehead of an elderly man who had alcoholic liver cirrhosis.

462 Chronic varicose eczema showing hyperpigmentation around the ankle.

463

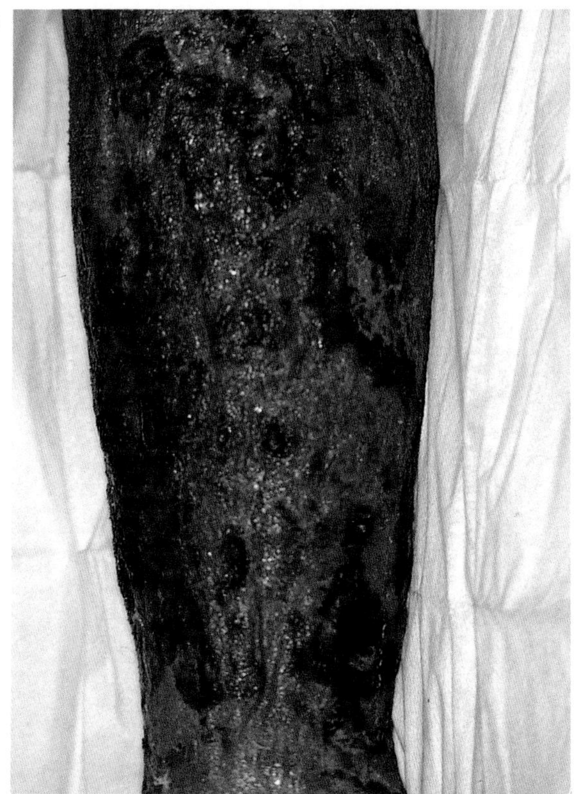

463 Varicose eczema. A case of severe varicose eczema with lipodermatosclerosis and breaks in the skin.

464

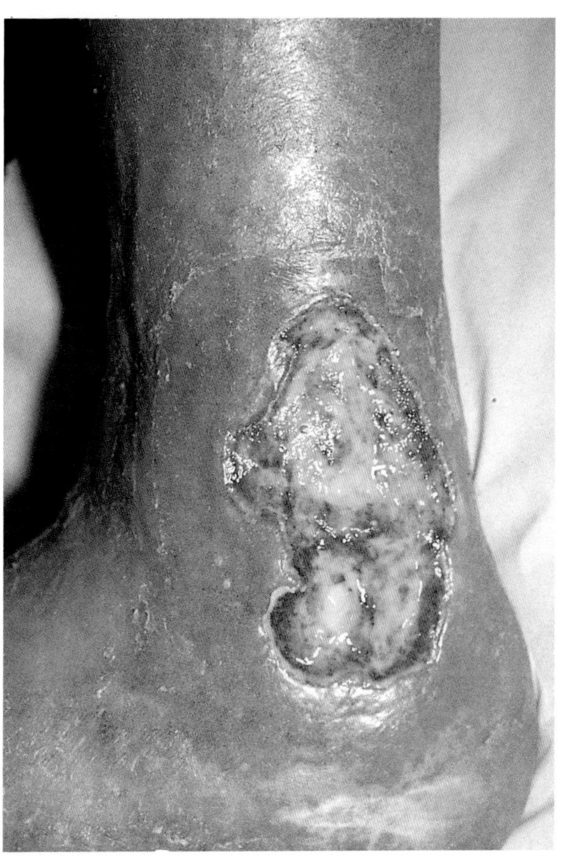

464 Diabetic ulcer. This ulcer occurred in a case of long-standing poorly controlled diabetes mellitus. The patient had underlying arterial disease and also peripheral neuropathy. In the elderly such lesions should be differentiated from the more common venous ulcers.

465

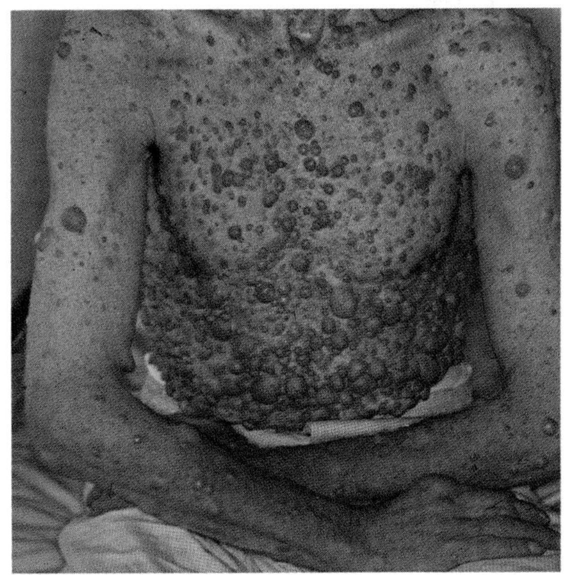

465 Neurofibromatosis (Von Recklinghausen's disease). This congenital disorder begins in childhood and continues into old age. This patient has typical multiple fibromata of different shapes and sizes; there are also pigmented areas in the skin.

466

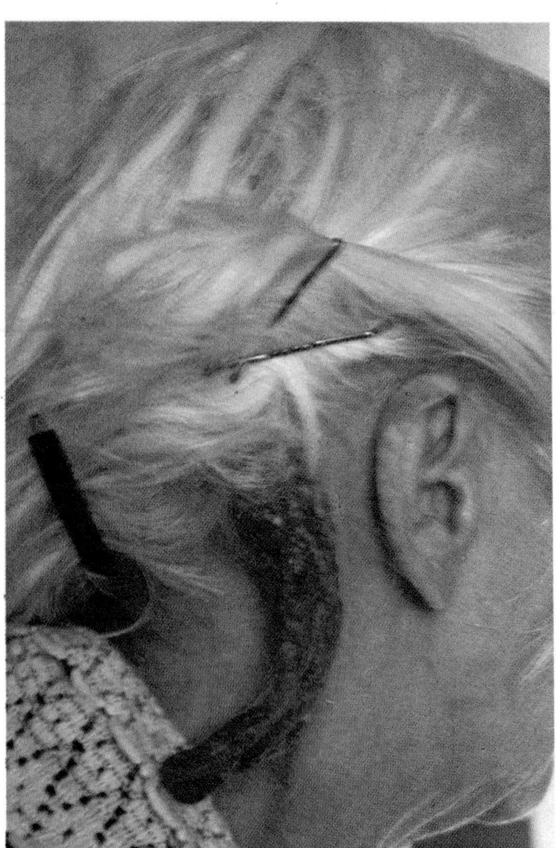

466 Sebaceous horn (large). An oddity sometimes seen in the elderly. It arises from the epidermis and grows slowly. Malignant change occurs rarely in the base of the horn.

4(

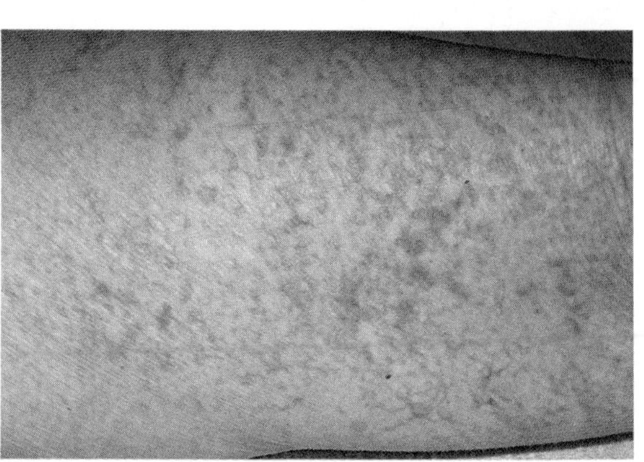

467 Drug rash. Widespread macular rash as a result of taking an antibiotic, which also caused mild pruritis.

46

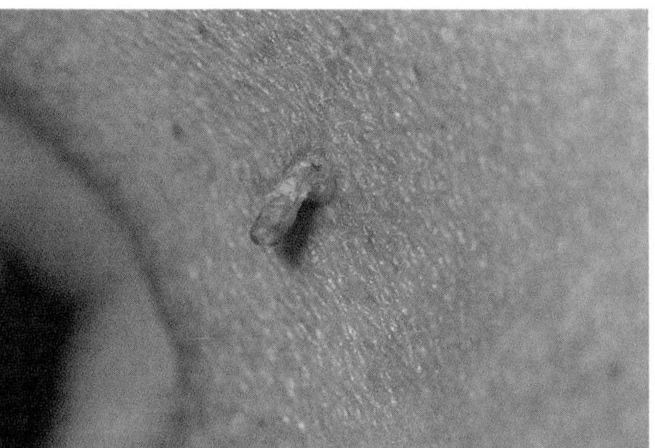

468 Sebaceous horn (small). A much smaller cutaneous horn than in **466**. These lesions usually occur on the face or scalp in elderly persons who are seborrhoeic subjects or who have been exposed to strong sunlight.

469

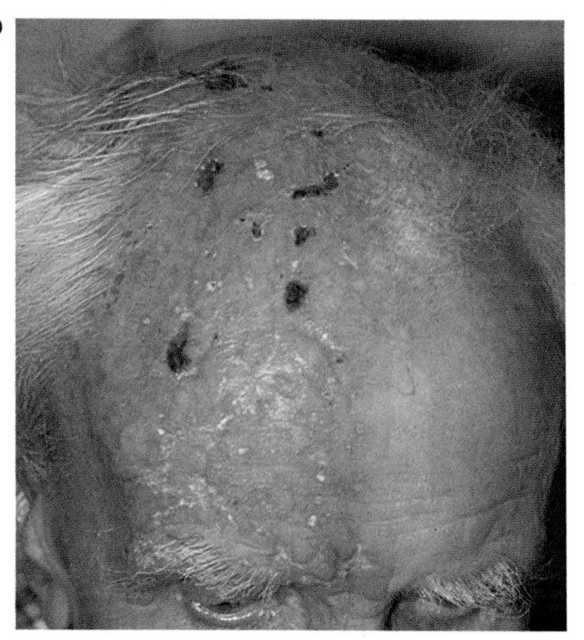

469 Herpes zoster. Frequent cause of painful skin rash in the elderly. In this case, the rash is resolving, but the patient was left with post-herpetic neuralgia.

470 Traumatic bruise. A large bruise on the lateral aspect of the chest wall. This injury was caused by a fall and there is considerable pain due to suffering fractured ribs.

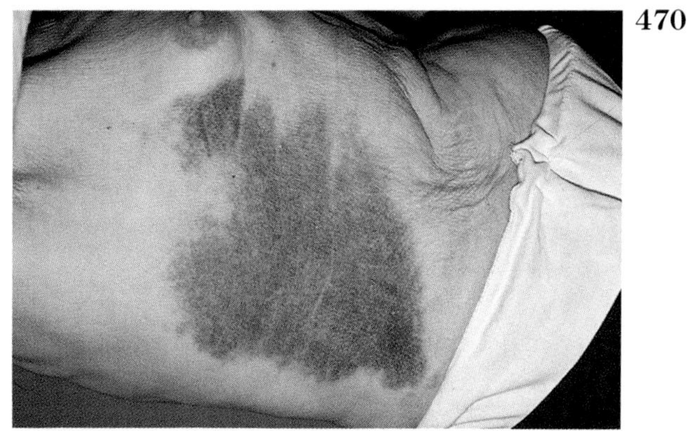
470

471

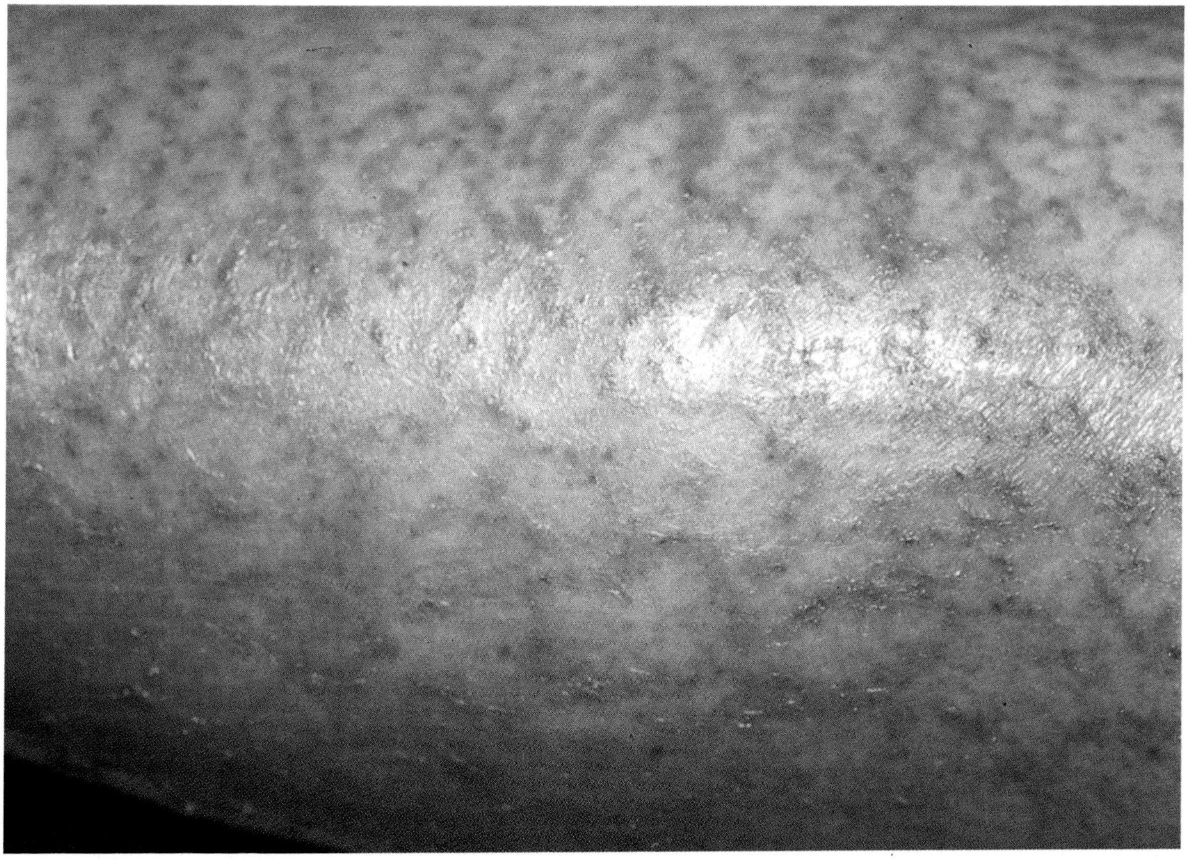

471 Erythema craquele (severe xerosis). Typical reticulation and rhomboidal scaling on the legs, commonly seen in the elderly.

472

473

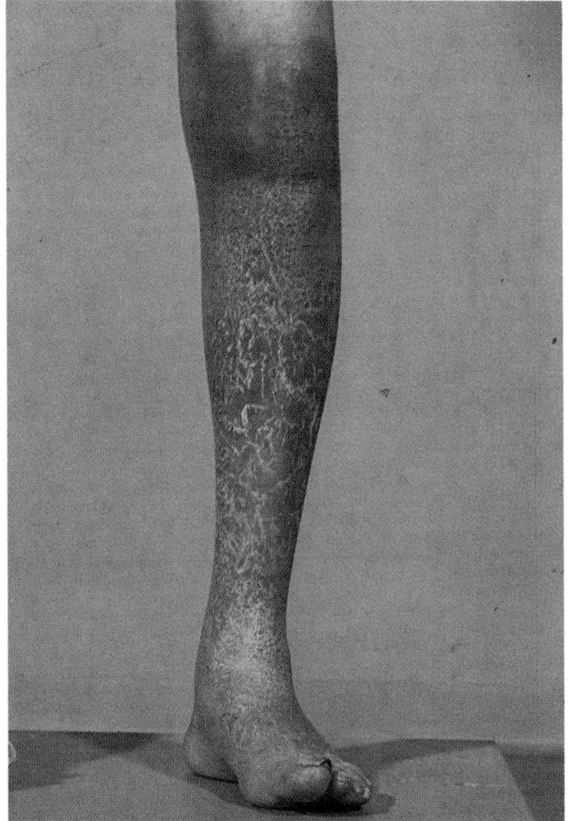

47

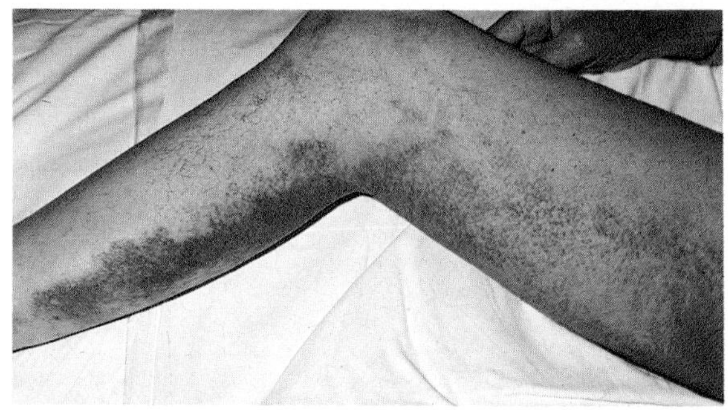

472 Scurvy. Typical 'cork-screw hairs' with perifollicular haemorrhages in an elderly bachelor who had hypovitaminosis-C caused by dietary deficiency.

473 and 474 Scurvy. Sheet haemorrhages in the legs of two other patients with vitamin C deficiency. The patient in **473** was an elderly man who lived alone and had a past history of alcoholism.

Hypovitaminosis-C scurvy

'Bachelor scurvy' sometimes seen in elderly men living alone in poor conditions

Clinical features
Hyperkeratotic papules
Perifollicular haemorrhages
Gum lesions occur only in teeth-bearing jaws
Anaemia
Gastrointestinal tract bleeding
Nasal haemorrhage

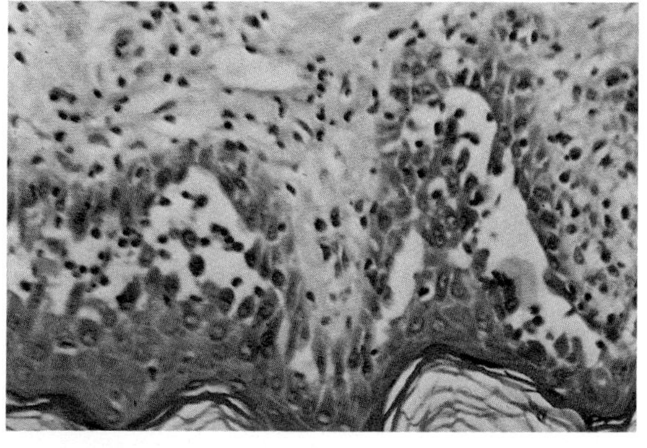

475

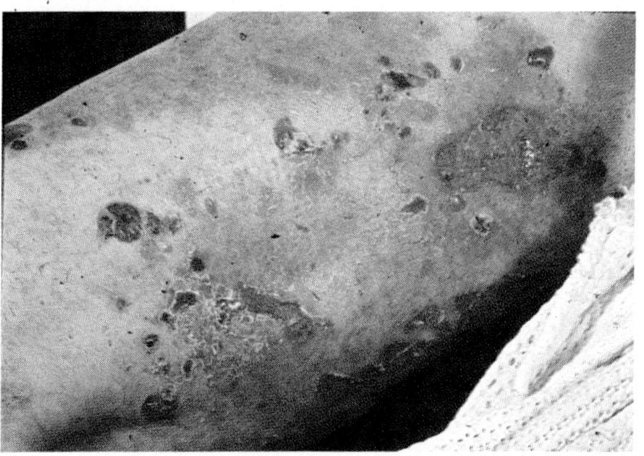

476

475 Pemphigus. Skin histology showing the characteristic of cell splitting within the epidermal layer called acantholysis.

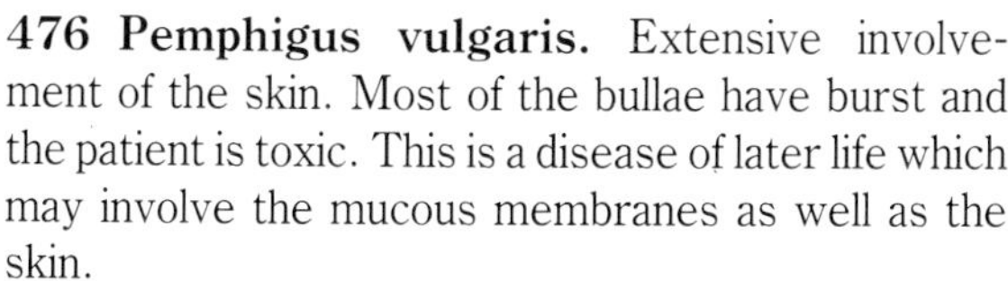

476 Pemphigus vulgaris. Extensive involvement of the skin. Most of the bullae have burst and the patient is toxic. This is a disease of later life which may involve the mucous membranes as well as the skin.

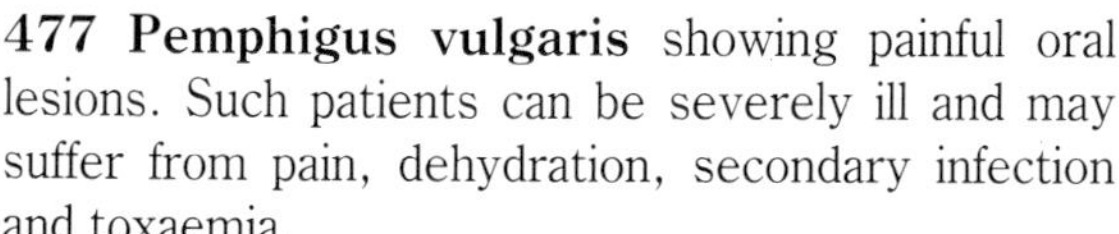

477 Pemphigus vulgaris showing painful oral lesions. Such patients can be severely ill and may suffer from pain, dehydration, secondary infection and toxaemia.

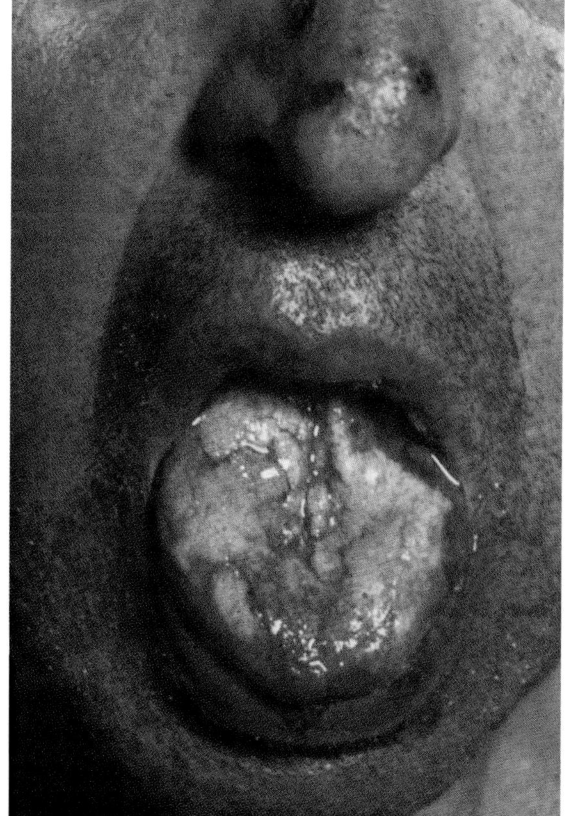

477

Bullous skin lesions (Some frequent causes in the elderly)

Pemphigus vulgaris
Pemphigoid – 80% of cases in over 60-year-olds
Stevens–Johnson syndrome
Drugs, e.g. bromides, iodides, barbiturates, penicillamine

478

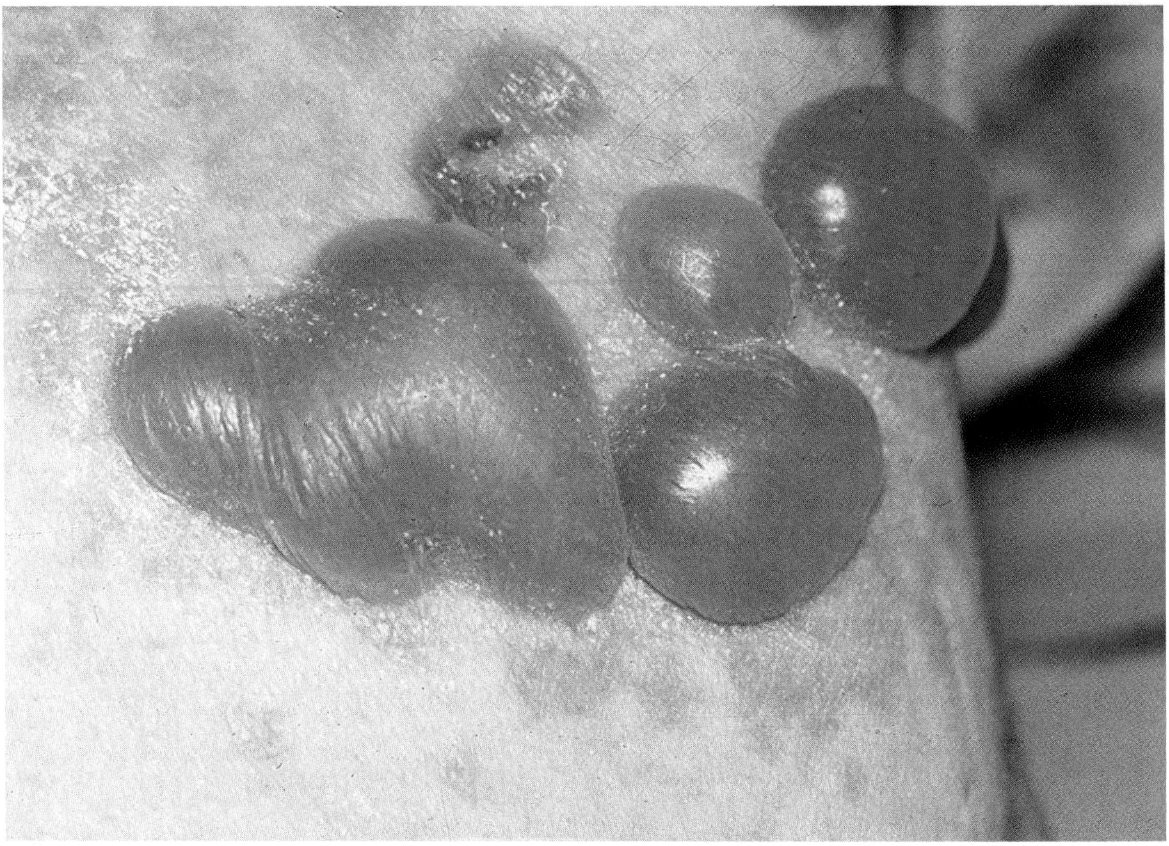

479

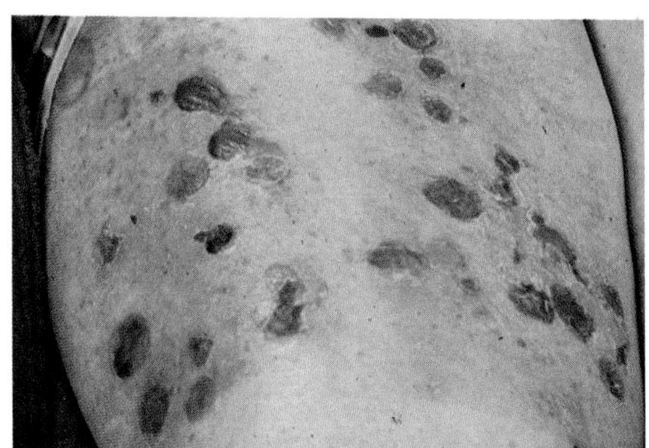

480

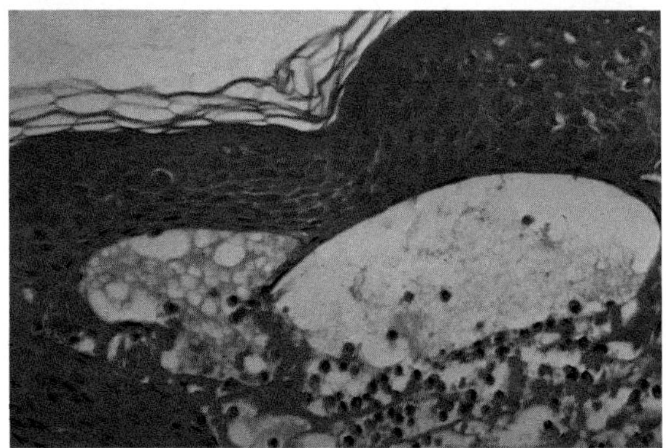

478 Pemphigoid blisters. Tense bullae caused by pemphigoid – a disease of old age in which the mucous membrane is affected less commonly than in pemphigus.

479 Pemphigoid blisters. Here the disease is a few days old and some of the blisters have burst.

480 Pemphigoid. Histology showing that the blister is below the epidermis separating it from the dermis.

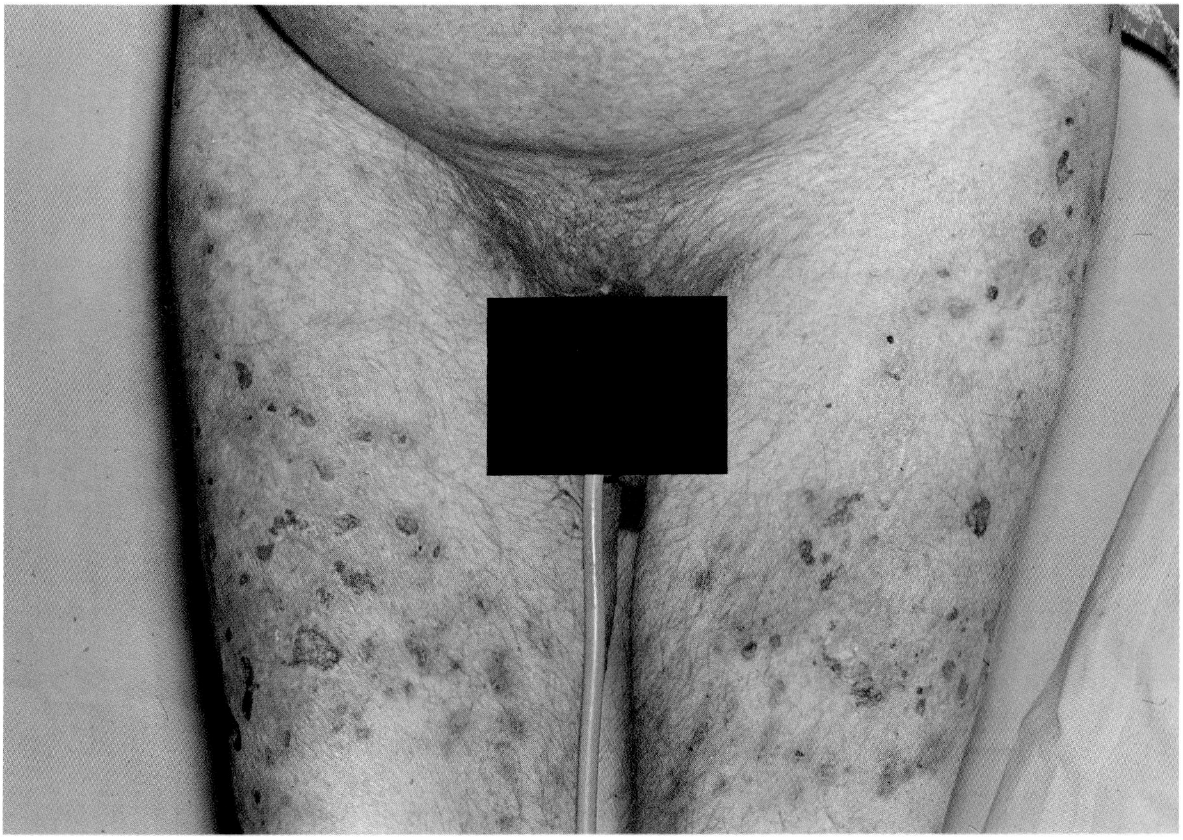

481 **Dermatitis herpetiformis.** Disease of middle and late life causing intense pruritus and associated with gastrointestinal disorder. The blisters tend to occur on the extensor surfaces including the back and the buttocks.

482 **Dermatitis herpetiformis.** Histology specimen showing infiltration by polymorph cells in the dermal papillae.

483 **Psoriasis.** A skin disorder seen frequently in the elderly. It is sometimes accompanied by arthropathy and nail changes.

482

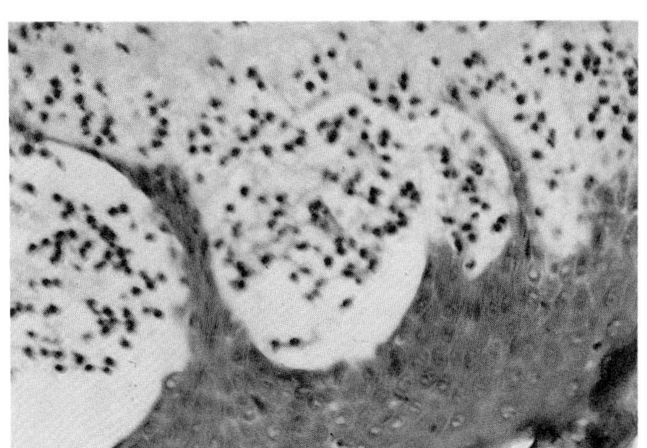

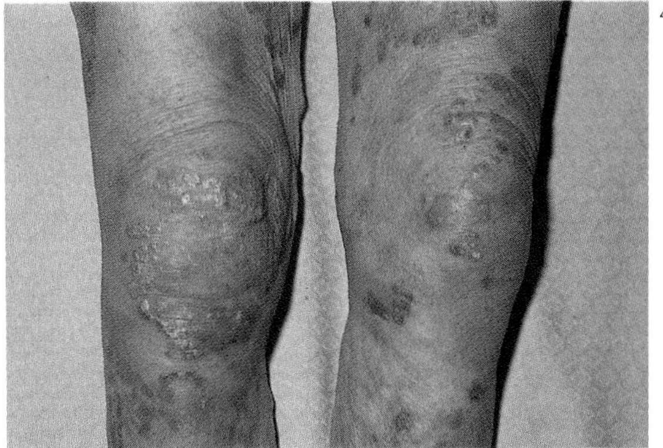

484

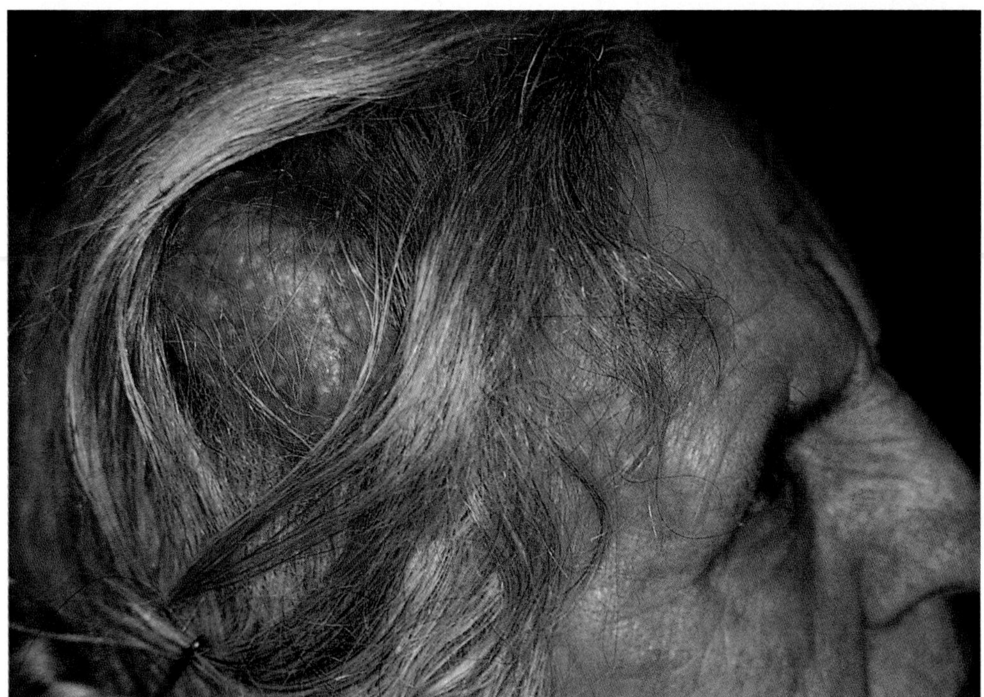

484 Sebaceous cyst. An elderly female with a large sebaceous cyst on the scalp. These cysts are usually symptomless and are also known as epidermoid cysts.

11 Hypothermia in the Elderly

A person is said to be hypothermic when the body temperature is below 35°C (95°F). Hypothermia, which carries high morbidity and mortality rates in the elderly, is a medical emergency and should be treated as such. Between the temperatures of 35°C and 30°C the mortality is 33%. Below 30°C the mortality rises to 70%.

Hypothermia causes about 1% of excess deaths in the winter quarter. About 80,000 of such deaths of people over the age of 65 are related to the cold weather over the year as a whole, with an increase of about 35% in winter. In 1964 it was said that some 20,000 to 100,000 deaths in the elderly each winter in Britain could be attributed to hypothermia. However, the incidence of clinical hypothermia was found to be surprisingly low. This was because, clinically, hypothermia is very difficult to record: it is often silent and leaves no trace at a post-mortem examination. Hypothermia mentioned on death certificates is most likely to be associated with various terminal conditions in the elderly, such as acute exacerbation of chronic bronchitis, bronchopneumonia, strokes and myocardial infarction. Death certificates show that coronary and cerebral thrombosis cause about half of the excess winter deaths; respiratory disease accounts for most of the rest (Bull and Morton, 1978). Also, statistics for 1965–1973 show that the percentage increase was larger in England and Wales than in a number of countries with colder winters, such as Sweden and the United States (United Nations Demographic Year Book, New York, United Nations, 1974).

In a survey carried out by the Royal College of Physicians in 1965 involving 10 British hospitals, it was revealed that over a period of three winter months 0.68% of admissions were the result of accidental hypothermia; 42% of these patients were over 65 years of age. Another study in 1977 revealed that in two London hospitals over a period of three months 3.6% of patients were elderly patients with hypothermia. A national survey carried out in 1973 found that of 1020 elderly people living at home 0.52% were hypothermic.

Pathophysiology

There is an increasing body temperature gradient, from the skin outside to tissues deep within the body — the latter being called the central deep or core temperature. It is this core temperature which is important in terms of body metabolism. The easiest and most reliable method of measuring core temperature is by a low-reading rectal thermometer.

When a person is exposed to cold, the peripheral blood vessels in the skin contract, directing blood away from the periphery and the cold, thus preserving core temperature. The difference between central core and superficial skin temperatures can be thought of as a reflection of the body's thermoregulatory efficiency. There is strong evidence that the body's thermoregulatory efficiency declines with age (Keatinge, 1987).

The impairment of thermoregulatory efficiency in the elderly is usually multifactorial in origin. The main aetiological factors are:

- Physiological fall in body temperature with age.
- Old people are more likely to live in a cold environment.
- Impaired mobility in the elderly.
- Cerebrovascular disease may damage the thermoregulatory centre in the brain.
- Autonomic disturbances in the elderly lead to decreased heat conservation.
- Drugs — for example sedatives, hypnotics, tranquillizers and alcohol.
- Hypothermia is a frequent complication of myxoedema.

There are four main reasons why the elderly are so prone to hypothermia:

- They often live in cold houses to which they have become accustomed.
- They have a reduced sensitivity to cold.
- They therefore respond poorly to cold temperatures; that is, by putting on extra clothes, lighting the fire, etc.
- Those who become hypothermic appear to be incapable of efficient heat conservation by cutaneous vasoconstriction.

Clinical features

Clinical features vary as the body temperature drops. In the early stages there is mild drowsiness, sluggishness of movement and thought, slurring of speech and mild mental confusion. The skin of the patient, including the abdomen and axillae, feels cold. The patient becomes apathetic and may develop restlessness. In the central nervous system, apart from slurring of speech and drowsiness, the patient may have ataxia, increased muscular rigidity, increased neck stiffness and sluggish tendon jerks.

In the cardiovascular system there is bradycardia and the patient may develop various cardiac dysrhythmias. In moderate to severe cases the ECG shows typical features including prolonged PR interval, prolonged QT interval, inversion of the T-wave and appearance of the J-wave.

In the respiratory system there may be hypopnoea and periodic breathing, and bronchopneumonia is usually the terminal feature.

Complications of hypothermia, such as bronchopneumonia and pancreatitis, are often difficult to detect on clinical examination.

Table 2. Main complications of hypothermia

Bronchopneumonia	
Intravascular thrombosis causing	– stroke
	– myocardial occlusion
	– mesenteric occlusion
	– peripheral gangrene
Pancreatitis	
Pressure sores	
Hypoglycaemia may occur, particularly during rewarming	

485

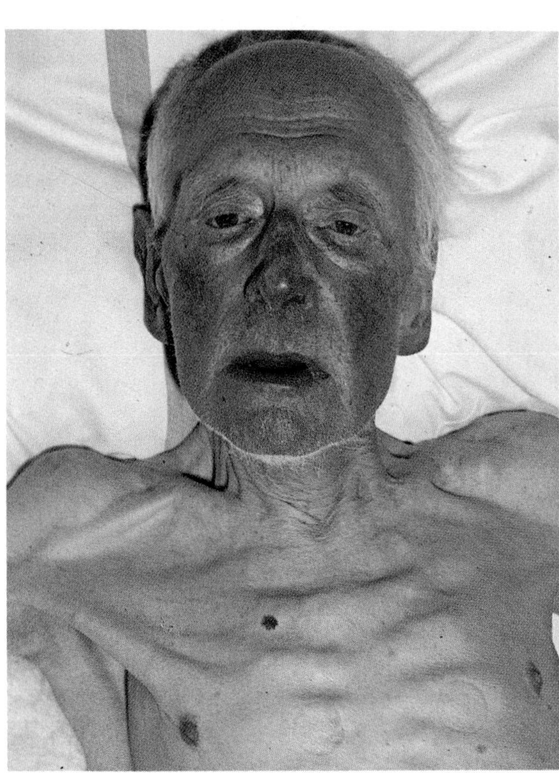

485 Hypothermia. This elderly man lived alone. In spite of being reasonably well-off, he neglected his diet and would not spend any money on domestic heating. He was admitted with bronchopneumonia and hypothermia.

Prevention of hypothermia

Prevention remains the most important aspect of reducing the incidence of hypothermia in the elderly.

The elderly should be educated and warned about the dangers of hypothermia. In the United Kingdom the Health Education Council publishes various booklets and leaflets which explain, in simple language, the methods of preventing, detecting and managing hypothermia; for example, *The Winter Warmth Code, Looking After Yourself in Retirement, Keeping Warm in Winter.* Attention should be directed at housing — especially home insulation and draught-proofing, diet, clothing, supplementary pension, heating allowances, unnecessary drugs, the danger of polypharmacy, and detecting and treating disorders which are associated with hypothermia. Professionals, such as doctors, nurses and health visitors, can help, particularly if there is anxiety about the health of an elderly person. Another source of help in the United Kingdom is the local social services department.

Hypothermia in the elderly is a condition which can be prevented. All efforts should be made to reduce its incidence in old people.

Management

Hypothermia in the elderly is a medical emergency and requires urgent treatment. When confronted with a case of hypothermia outside the hospital, one should:

- Warm the room as much as possible.
- Give warm and nourishing drinks or soups.
- Wrap up the person well.
- Keep the patient in bed or sitting in a comfortable chair.
- Call a doctor or an ambulance.

Do not

- Load heavy blankets onto the person as they trap cold air.
- Use hot-water bottles or electric blankets.
- Encourage movement about the house.
- Give alcohol, because this prompts further heat loss.

In hospital, the treatment is aimed at rewarming the patient at the rate of 0.5–1.0°C per hour while carefully monitoring the blood pressure. This is best achieved by wrapping the patient in blankets. Nursing should be carried out in a room at a temperature of about 25°C. Other measures consist of rehydration, oxygen inhalation if required and antibiotics given prophylactically; occasional intravenous hydrocortisone may be required and, if there is convincing evidence of hypothyroidism, parenteral triiodothyronine should be given.

486 Hypothermia. An elderly lady with accidental hypothermia. She had fallen at home and was unable to get up. She lay on the floor through the night and by next morning her rectal temperature was 29°C.

486

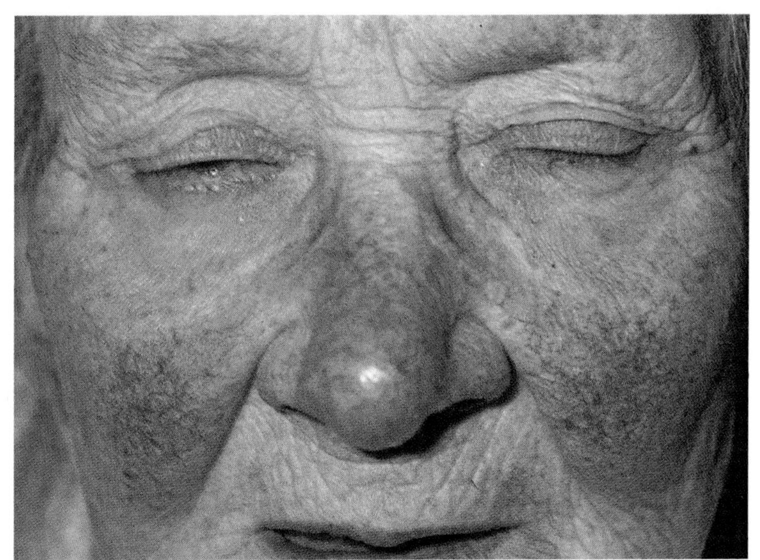

488

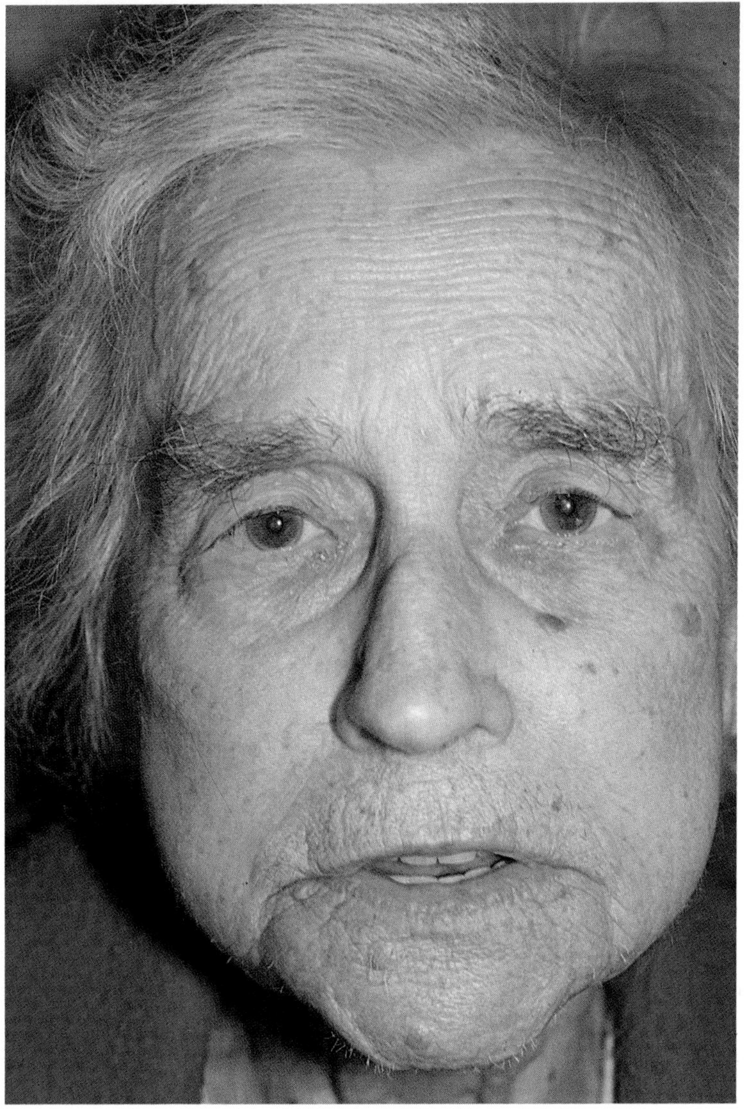

487

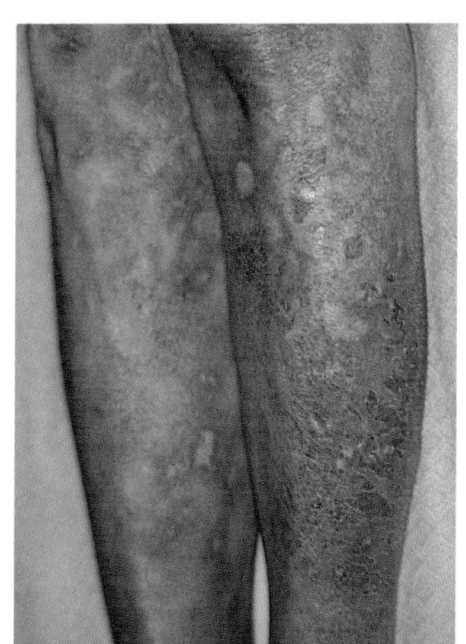

487 Erythema ab agni. This patient presented with pneumonia and hypothermia. She lived in a cold house and spent long periods sitting in front of an electric fire.

488 Anaemia and hypothermia. This lady was admitted twice with hypothermia over a period of six months. She suffered from chronic anaemia and was taking both diuretics and tranquillisers.

489 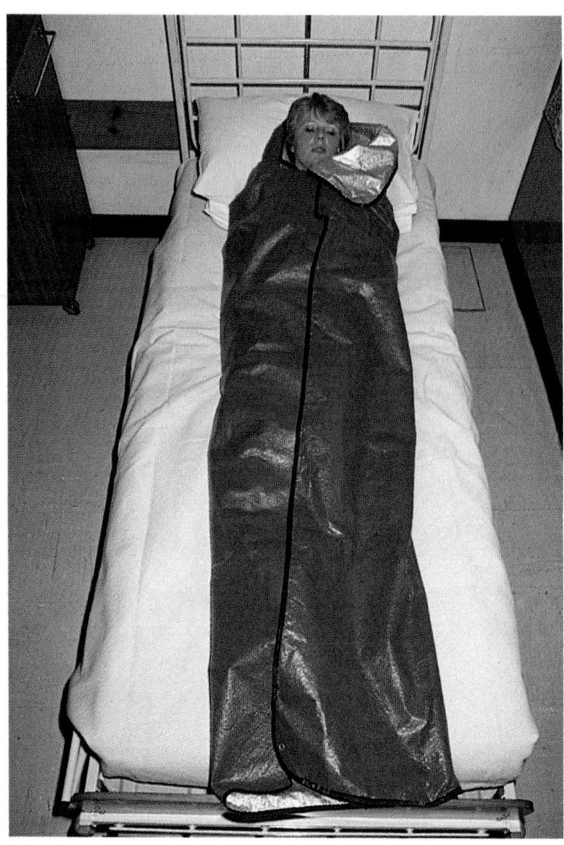

490 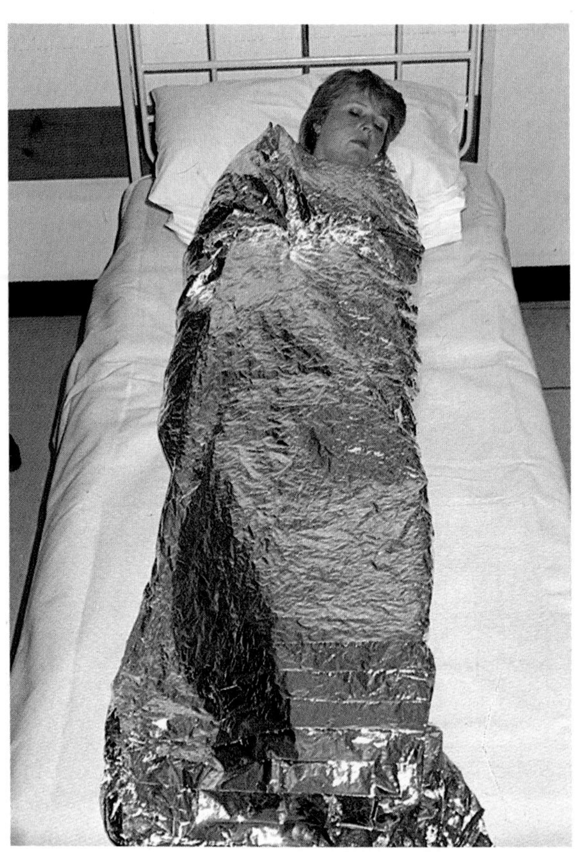

489 Space blanket. This heat-retaining blanket is used as an emergency measure for cases of hypothermia.

490 Foil blanket. This lightweight, heat-preserving foil blanket is a good alternative to a space blanket.

491 

491 Bottle of pills. This bottle of pills was found on an elderly lady who suffered with recurrent falls and came to hospital with hypothermia. She was taking about 10 different drugs. She took these tablets in a most haphazard manner. She was a victim of 'polypharmacy', 'self medication' and iatrogenic illness.

12 Drugs in the Elderly

Adverse drug reactions are common in the elderly and give rise to iatrogenic disease. It is said that up to 10% of hospital admissions in the elderly are due to adverse drug reactions. It is well known that elderly patients are prescribed excessive amounts of drugs and very often there is inadequate supervision of long-term medication.

Poor compliance in the elderly is a difficult problem and also the cause of wasted resources and inadequate clinical response to medical treatment.

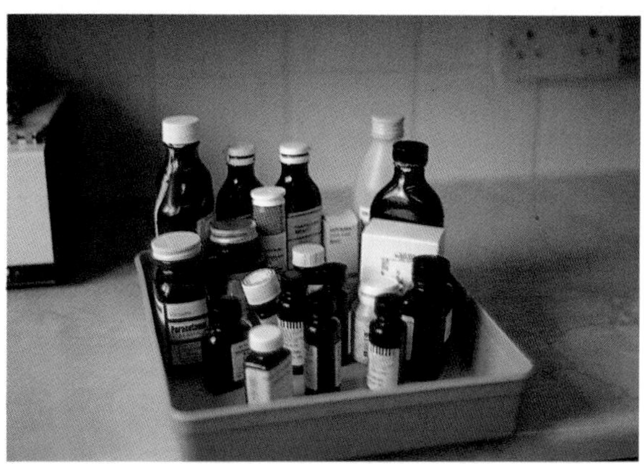 492

492 Polypharmacy. A typical example showing several different drugs being taken by an elderly patient. The patient had no idea about the nature of these drugs and, consequently, the compliance was poor.

Causes of adverse drug reactions in the elderly

Inadequate clinical assessment
Excessive prescribing
Inadequate supervision of long-term medication
Altered pharmacokinetics and pharmacodynamics with advancing age
Poor compliance in the elderly
Usage of new drugs which give rise to unknown adverse effects in old patients

 493

493 Bad labelling. A badly labelled bottle of pills found in an old person's home.

Measures to improve compliance in the elderly

Patient instruction and counselling
Written instructions where necessary
Clear simple labelling on drug containers
Suitable containers for the elderly
Memory aids, e.g. Dossett boxes, calendar packs
Long-term medical supervision
Early discharge letters giving details of drug regimes
Ward pharmacist

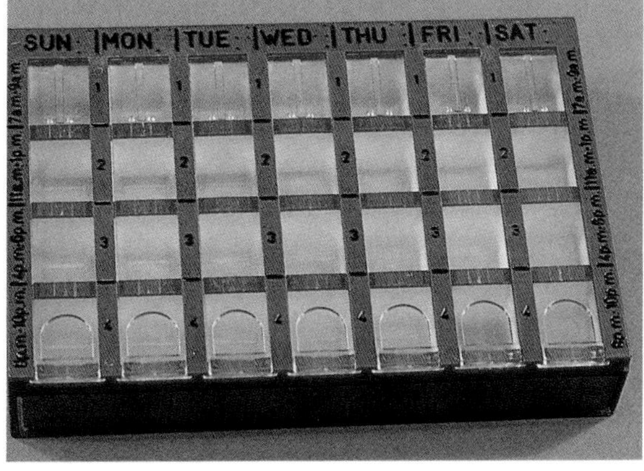 494

494 Dossett box. This dispensing box may help in improving compliance, but it requires a weekly filling and the patient should be able to read the days and times that are printed on the cover.

495

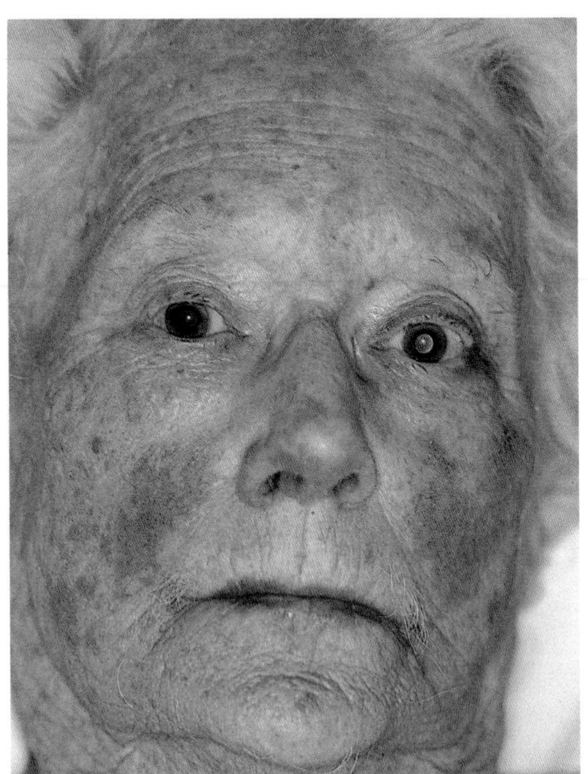

496

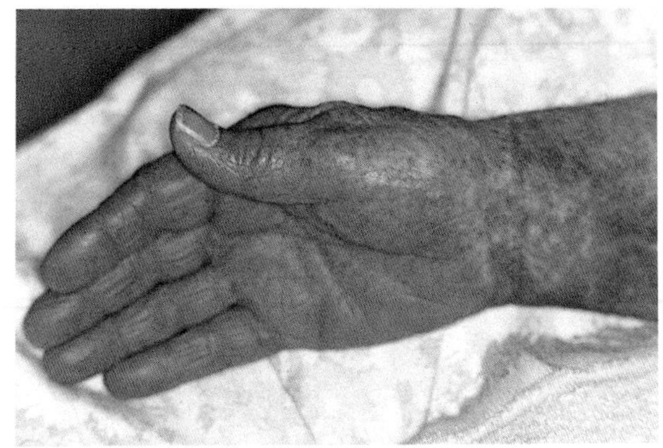

495 and 496 Drug rash. Non-pruritic drug rash caused by an antibiotic.

497

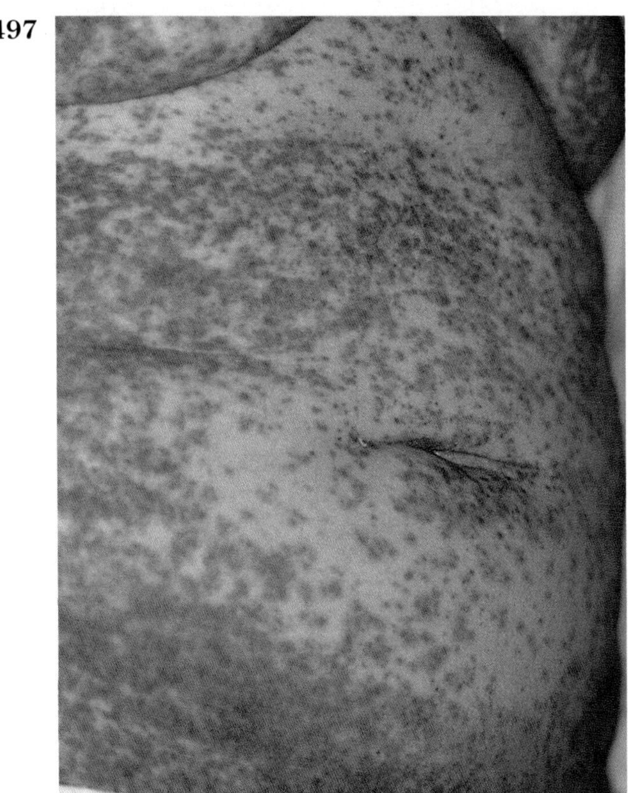

497 Purpura. This extensive purpura was caused by an anti-hypertensive agent (methyldopa).

498 Steroid face. Typical cushingoid face caused by long-term therapy with corticosteroids.

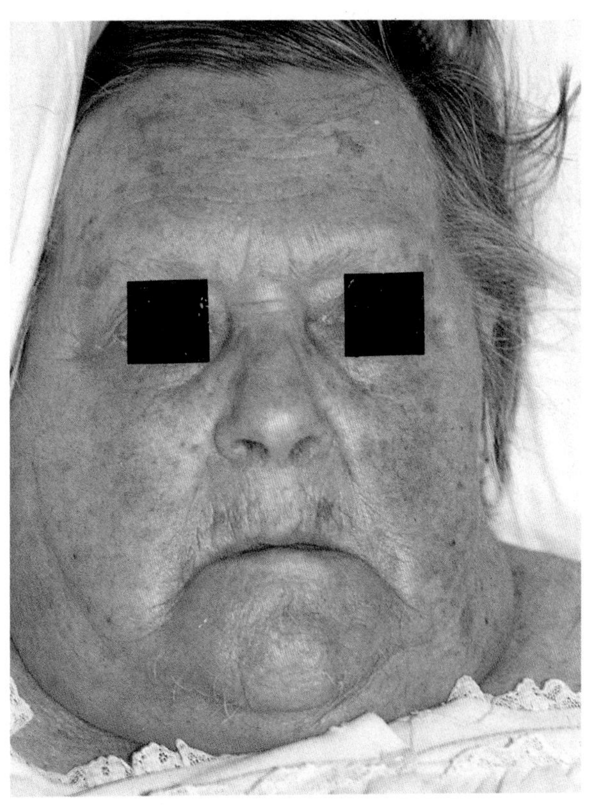

498

499 Parkinsonism. This is a case of drug-induced parkinsonism, mainly akinesia and rigidity caused by a drug belonging to the phenothiazine group.

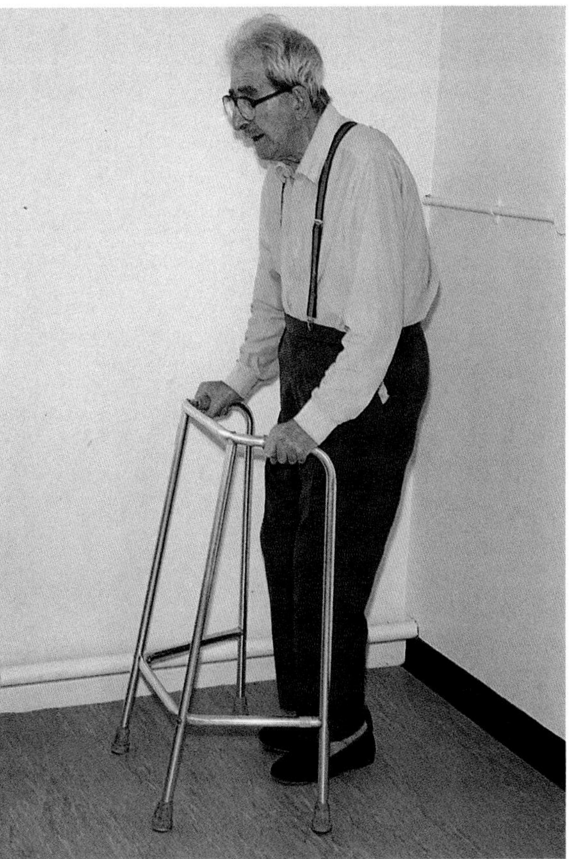

499

13 Abuse of Elderly People*

In recent years doctors, social workers and other health care personnel have become increasingly concerned about the problem of abuse of elderly people in society. The very disabled and the very aged are at risk from being subject to this abuse, often by their carers.

Definition

'The physical, emotional or psychological abuse of an older person by a formal or informal carer. The abuse is repeated and is the violation of a person's human and civil rights by a person or persons who have power over the life of the dependent.' (Mervyn Eastman, *Old Age Abuse,* Age Concern, June 1984.)

Categories of abuse

The different forms of abuse are not necessarily confined to physical injury. In an internal survey carried out by a working party from Bexley Social Services in early 1988, 31 (5%) of the 756 people over the age of 60 studied were found to have been abused. This was at a time when the abuse of elderly people had a low profile. The working party found that the abuse covered eight categories.

Assault
This includes force-feeding, shaking and slapping.

Deprivation of nutrition
Failure to provide a dependant with sufficient food and fluid, either as a punishment, wilful neglect or maybe a spouse suffering from slight 'dementia' – forgetting to feed their partner or give them meals on wheels.

Administration of inappropriate drugs or deprivation of prescribed drugs
Over-sedation to obtain peace and quiet; withholding drugs to bring on a crisis and precipitate admission to hospital.

Emotional and verbal abuse
Intimidation and humiliation; constantly shouting at someone; continually putting them down; swearing at a dependant and causing them distress; emotional blackmail.

Sexual abuse
The incidence is very small, but it is still there; either the carer or other members of the household may be responsible.

Deprivation of help in performing activities of daily living
Failure to provide glasses, hearing aid, appropriate clothing, etc.

Involuntary isolation and confinement
The elderly person is locked in their bedroom and not allowed visitors or friends.

Financial abuse
Withholding money or making dependants sign over their pensions and not spending any of the money on them.

*Reprinted from Sarah Tomlin, *Abuse of Elderly People,* a public information report from The British Geriatrics Society (BGS), May 1989, by kind permission of the BGS.

Table 3. Preventing abuse

Problems	*Solutions*
Dependency on key family member	Share-caring tasks. Draw up a rota
Poor communication	Hearing aid. Help from speech therapist
Sudden change in carer's lifestyle	Consider such disasters before they happen – have planned response ready
Perception of dependency	Counsel to provide more insight
Warnings and 'cries for help', unrecognised by general practitioners and other professionals	Educate to increase awareness
Role reversal	Counsel to provide more insight
Injuries	Educate to increase awareness
Triggering behaviour	Counsel to provide more insight
Apathy/depression	Identify, increase support and treat any underlying illness
Cramped living conditions	Rehouse or adapt present housing
Isolation	Regular visiting by statutory services and volunteers. Encourage other family and friends to become more involved

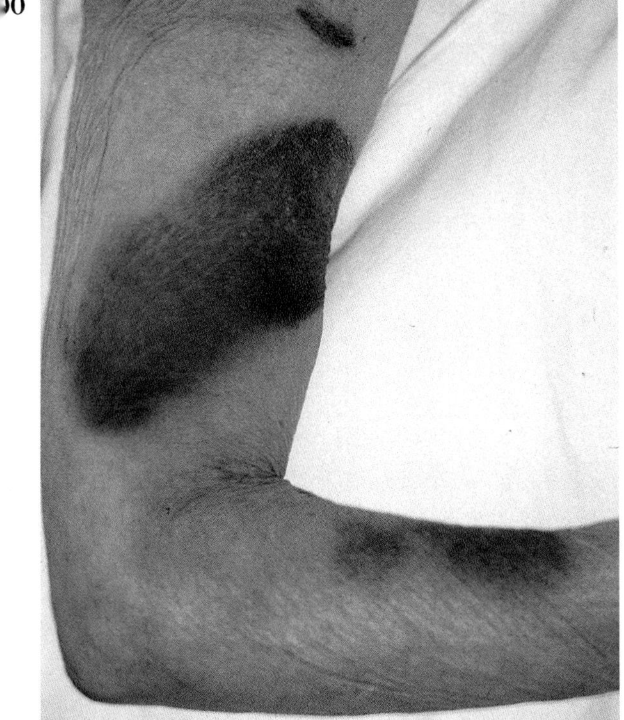

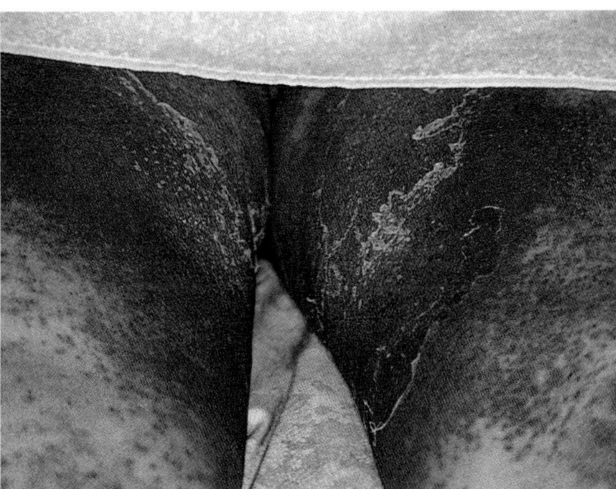

501

500 Elderly abuse. A large bruise on the arm due to rough handling by the carer.

501 Elderly abuse. Severe rash secondary to urinary incontinence in a patient who was being 'nursed' at home by well-meaning, but untrained and inexperienced carers.

British Geriatrics Society: Recommendations on the prevention of abuse of elderly people

1 A greater recognition of the factors leading to the abuse of elderly people within caring situations. The medical profession, both general practitioners and hospital doctors, to play a key role in recognising and acting on these.

2 Further research to clarify the incidence, aetiology and nature of abuse of elderly people within caring situations in the United Kingdom.

3 More financial resources and manpower to be allocated to health services for elderly people, particularly those providing continuing care for elderly people. Also, more money and manpower to be provided to local authorities to provide services for elderly people in the community.

4 Realistic packages of care to be provided in the community by health and social services to provide the intensity of support in the elderly person's home that would create a realistic choice and alternative to residential care.

5 Freedom of choice for elderly people when selecting their own care from a range of viable alternatives.

6 More practical and financial support for the carers of elderly people and acknowledgement and understanding of the stresses of caring.

7 Local authorities and district health authorities to have locally agreed guidelines to be implemented when it is suspected that an elderly person may be the subject of abuse.

8 An intervention order should be introduced that would give elderly people and their carers the right to have their cases examined by local authorities.

9 An independent system of inspection should be established to ensure the standard of care and good practice within residential accommodation, whether provided by district health authority, local authority, voluntary or private sectors.

10 A legally binding contract for residents in hospitals, nursing homes, residential homes, both in the public and private sectors.

11 There should be a greater awareness of the contribution that elderly people make to society.

12 Positive preventative help: regular screening by primary health care team of elderly people and their carers.

List of Useful Addresses

Age Concern, Bernard Sunley House, 60 Pitcairn Road, Mitcham, Surrey CR4 3LL
Tel: (081) 261-9572

Alzheimer's Disease Society, Bank Buildings, Fulham Broadway, London SW6 1EP
Tel: (071) 381-3177

BASE (British Association for Services to the Elderly) 119 Hassell Street, Newcastle under Lyme, Staffordshire ST5 1AX
Tel: (0782) 661033

British Geriatrics Society, 1 St. Andrews Place, Regents Park, London NW1 4LB
Tel: (071) 935-4004

Chest, Heart and Stroke Association, Tavistock House North, Tavistock Square, London WC1H 9JE
Tel: (071) 387-3012

Disabled Living Foundation, 346 Kensington High Street, London W14 8NS
Tel: (071) 289-6111

Help the Aged, 1 Sekforde Street, London EC1R 0BE
Tel: (071) 253-0253

MIND (National Association for Mental Health), 22 Harley Street, London W1N 2ED
Tel: (071) 637-0741

Society of Geriatric Nursing, 20 Cavendish Square, London W1M 0AB
Tel: (071) 409-3333

Bibliography

ALLEN, S.C., FAIRWEATHER, S. and BROCKLEHURST, J.C., *Case Studies in Medicine for the Elderly,* MTP Press, Lancaster, 1987.

ANDERSON, F. and WILLIAMS, B., *Practical Management of the Elderly,* 4th edition, Blackwell Scientific Publications, London, 1983.

BATES, C.P., WHITESIDE, C.G. and TURNER-WARWICK, R., Synchronous cine/pressure/flow/cystourethrography with special reference to stress in urge incontinence, *Brit. J. Urol.,* **42,** 714–23, 1970.

BROCKLEHURST, J.C., *Textbook of Geriatric Medicine and Gerontology,* 3rd edition, Churchill Livingstone, London and New York, 1985.

BROCKLEHURST, J.C. and ALLEN, S.C., *Geriatric Medicine for Students,* 3rd edition, Churchill Livingstone, London and New York, 1987.

BULL, G.M. and MORTON, J., Environment temperature and death rates, *Age and Ageing,* **7,** 210–24, 1978.

KAMAL, A. *Diagnostic Picture Tests in Geriatric Medicine,* Wolfe Medical Publications Ltd, London, 1990.

KEATINGE, W., Winter mortality: Warm housing offers cold comfort, *Geriatric Medicine,* **17**(12), 65–9, 1987.

MACLENNAN, W.J., SHEPHERD, A.N. and STEVENSON, J.H., *The Elderly,* Springer, Berlin, 1984.

MARTIN, A. and GAMBRILL, E., *Geriatrics,* MTP Press, Lancaster, 1986.

PITT, B., *Psychogeriatrics: An Introduction to Psychiatry of Old Age,* Churchill Livingstone, London and New York, 1982.

TOMLIN, S., *Abuse of Elderly People,* A public information report from the British Geriatrics Society, May 1989.

Index